Taking
History
to Heart

Taking

THE POWER OF THE PAST

History

IN BUILDING SOCIAL MOVEMENTS

to Heart

JAMES GREEN

University of Massachusetts Press
Amherst

Copyright © 2000 by James Green
All rights reserved
Printed in the United States of America

ISBN 1-55849-241-0 (cloth); 242-9 (pbk.)
Designed by Jack Harrison
Set in Adobe Berkeley with Adobe Impact display by Keystone Typesetting, Inc.
Printed and bound by Sheridan Books

Library of Congress Cataloging-in-Publication Data
Green, James R., 1944–
Taking history to heart : the power of the past in building social movements / James Green.
    p. cm.
Includes bibliographical references and index.
ISBN 1-55849-241-0 (cloth : alk. paper) —
ISBN 1-55849-242-9 (paper : alk. paper)
1. Social movements—United States—Historiography.   2. Labor movement—United
States—Historiography.   3. Green, James R., 1944–   .   4. Historians—United States—
Biography.   5. Social reformers—United States—Biography.   I. Title.
HN65 .G75 2000
303.48′4′0973—dc21   99-089338

British Library Cataloguing in Publication data are available

This book is published with the support and cooperation of the University of Massachusetts
Boston

To

HENRY HAMPTON

In Memoriam

Contents

Taking
History
to Heart

Spreading the socialist gospel on the Oklahoma frontier: Oscar Ameringer (*fourth from left*), Lulu Ameringer, and their three sons with Socialist Party chairman James Maurer (*left*), ca. 1912. *Archives of Labor and Urban Affairs, Wayne State University.*

Making Movement History

This book is about what I call movement history. It features historical accounts of movements for radical and progressive change in the United States, as well as reports of contemporary struggles for social justice which call up the past for instruction and for inspiration. These narratives emphasize the role of historical consciousness in movement building and in the mysterious processes that create human solidarity. I have tried to show how powerful the past can be in concrete experiences: for example, in the recent experiences of unionized workers who are drawn to history in an urgent search for a usable past that will help them broaden and strengthen the labor movement.

Besides these narratives of people making movement history, *Taking History to Heart* offers reflections on the work of doing movement history—the work of discovering it and recording it, reading and writing it, learning it from activists, and teaching it to workers. I tell a bit of my own story here, thinking back on my efforts to find a voice for telling movement stories in public—a voice I could use to reach movement activists and a wider audience of concerned citizens. I recount experiences of trying to break down the walls that separate people from their past and that divide those who study the past from those who have lived it. The public history projects I describe usually centered on moments in the past when people struggled to build movements for social justice. These projects were experiments in trying to make movement history come alive in certain communities and to make it relevant to ongoing efforts to organize for social change. So, this book also includes some description of those movement building efforts. In writing about some of the social movements of my own time, I recall what I learned from engaging in them, and what I tried to contribute to them as a historian. I have tried to knit these threads into one narrative fabric in order to show how doing movement history involved being a participant and an observer, an activist and a scholar.

Movement history is a term that could be used to describe all kinds of writing about social protest. Although it is not recognized as an academic field, historians, sociologists, and political scientists have produced countless research studies of social movements. I make frequent references to this vast literature, but I employ the concept of movement history in far more particular way—as the body of work produced by scholars and activists passionately engaged in the study of social protest for moral and political reasons as well as intellectual ones. I place my own work in the context of the critical writing produced since the 1960s by historians who identified with the social movements of that era, especially the civil rights movement, as well as with oppositional struggles that came before and after, such as the women's movement.

We share with other practitioners of our craft an obligation to tell the truth about the past, but at the same time we have criticized the canon of objectivity that once reigned in our profession, pitting partisanship against scholarship. Indeed, much of our work was initially dismissed as being too ideological, too subjective to be considered "real history." Radical historians of my generation helped create a kind of crisis within the American historical profession about its claims to objectivity and neutrality.[1] Since the 1960s our critique has opened up far more tolerance within the history profession for those seeking different pathways to the truth. And our scholarship, now reaching a maturation point, has made a contribution to a fuller understanding of the American past. It has done so by exposing the motives of the rich and powerful and the consequences of choices they made in the name of progress. It has also offered a fuller, richer picture of our past by giving voice to oppressed people and oppositional cultures, by recalling alternative visions of the past and the protest movements that created them. History teachers may now offer students texts that accurately present the contributions of the black freedom movement and the women's liberation movement in our own times and in past times. Some recent surveys help students to appreciate the neglected contributions of the labor movement, for example, in the excellent *Who Built America?* books and videos, which explain how workers helped "democratize America."[2]

Movement historians have gained credibility in their profession by correcting an imbalance in U.S. history that was created by an overwhelming emphasis on elites as makers of history. Readers can now see clearly how collective protest by oppressed groups has influenced politics and shaped social policy in several critical periods.[3] Indeed, as Alan Dawley writes in *Struggles for Justice:* "Because of a long tradition of democratic struggles beginning in the Revolution and running through the labor and populist revolts of the late nineteenth century, popular forces had more influence on the state than anywhere else in the world."[4] It is easier now to understand how popular movements for social justice humanized U.S. society by attacking its worst brutalities and by forcing our citizens to confront troublesome problems created by class, race, and gender injustice, and by xenophobia and homophobia. As Eric Foner demonstrates, these movement-inspired struggles have redefined ideas about American freedom.[5]

But movement history is not entirely the work of professional scholars. Movement historians have reached out to others who have their own compelling stories to tell, and have collaborated in the presentation of those stories. At its best, this kind of oral history involves a dialogue about the past, conversations in shared spaces, public and private. It is a process different from one undertaken by a solitary researcher. This kind of history-telling produces what Alessandro Portelli calls a "plural authorship" in which the interviewer and the subject may recognize their differences but still agree to speak across the experiential line that divides them.[6]

And so, the term movement history is not used here simply to define subjects of study. It is meant to incorporate various sorts of historically conscious work by movement activists, the trained and the untrained, the observers as well as the observed; it is meant to encapsulate the kind of work we do together as teachers and students, writers and readers, speakers and listeners, leaders and supporters. Most of the history in this book evolved out of conversations and collaborations with people in political motion, folks struggling to revive defeated social movements and to enliven new ones.

So, my development as a movement historian owes much to the relationships I have formed with people different from myself: with elderly veterans of the 1930s social movements, with feminist sisters who are historians of their own movement, with working class students in my university, with African American activists and intellectuals in Boston, and with white labor union officials, including those who had many reasons for distrusting a radical professor trying to stir up their past and cause trouble with their members. Making such alliances naturally required crossing certain borders of age, class, race, gender, and professional status. Transgressing these lines sometimes created conflicts, tensions, and wounded feelings. But these border crossings, though confusing and ego bruising, created the relationships that have made doing movement history worthwhile.

My own journey has taken me to a place where I can work as a critical intellectual within a movement context. Many social critics have separated themselves from popular politics—maintaining a critical distance from social causes. There is a different intellectual tradition that I admire, one of engagement. Social critics in this tradition participate in what Michael Walzer calls "local insurgencies," trying "to connect the small event to a larger vision," while, at the same time, "holding the protagonists to their own idealism." Unless critical intellectuals engage in social struggles, they risk indulging in obscure discourse that has "no echo outside the academy since the critics have no material ties to people, parties and movements outside." But, Walzer adds, to be engaged as a social critic means to risk being captured by the movements one supports. Activist intellectuals need to be "critical of power structures that inhibit popular participation in political life (including the power structures of popular parties and movements)." We need to work at "a certain difficult distance" from our movements, says Walzer, but still keep faith with the hopes of popular struggle, outlasting the defeats while, at the same time, sustaining "a form of criticism internal to, relevant to, and loyal to democratic politics."[7] These are good words of advice for those of us who have chosen to join with social movements as active participants and as critical intellectuals.

Thinking back to my youth, it is not easy to see why I became an activist or why I dedicated my life's work to popular movements for progressive and radical change in the United States. The history books I devoured as a kid lionized heroic figures like Daniel Boone and Andrew Jackson, and pitied others, like Osceola, war chief of the Seminoles, and Crazy Horse of the Sioux. I did not read any books about the leading figures in movement history—about Sojourner Truth or Frederick Douglass, Susan B. Anthony or Eugene V. Debs, or about those martyred for the cause of social justice.

I was not a "red-diaper" baby like many of my cohorts raised in the households of radicals. I was the child of religious parents from small-town America who taught me to be thankful for my blessings and to be respectful of my superiors—lessons they learned as children in the Depression. Midwestern Catholicism shaped their moral world, and mine. Everything I knew about Communism came from the telegenic Bishop Fulton J. Sheen, whose one liners amused us while his jeremiads about the Russians scared us silly. I knew nothing of social movements. The hysterically conservative *Chicago Tribune* that arrived on our door step each morning was for reading comic strips and baseball scores, not for finding out about the civil rights movement or labor unions—which its editors loathed. I grew up in the rock-ribbed Republican country of northern Illinois where the only thing I heard about the labor movement was from my boss, who told me that a union organizer had been beaten up for trying to cause trouble with his Mexican "hands" (with whom I worked on his huge nursery farm during the summers).

Unlike my employer, who resided in the pretty village settled by conservative Scots Presbyterians, my family lived on the other side of the Fox River with the Italian and German families. We moved to this little factory town, where we remodeled and expanded a tiny company house against the advice of my father's school superintendent, who said that all of the other teachers lived in the town on the hill above the river, not in Carpentersville, the factory town named for the entrepreneur who founded the Star Manufacturing Company and built the house we made our home.

My parents seemed comfortable with our hardworking, blue-collar neighbors, and so were my sisters, my brother, and I. We attended mass and parochial school at the little stucco mission church, St. Catherine of Siena, built for the

Italians employed at the "bolt works" where a smelter belched flames and a stamping press hammered away all day—producing the indelible sights and sounds of my childhood on the Fox River. We worshiped with Italian families and were taught by the Sisters of Mercy to embrace our fellow parishioners. My Protestant playmates didn't like "mackerel snappers," especially dark-skinned italians, but we were raised differently.

Though my father's job as a teacher made us middle class, his salary was working class, and so were his house, his neighborhood, and his church. He had worked in a candy plant and a paint factory while he earned his master's degree on the G.I. Bill, and then, in the summers, he earned extra money as a milkman and a bricklayer. The Chicago-based Irishmen who got him a temporary union card to lay brick provided many hilarious summertime stories, always told with warmth and affection, as were the descriptions of the Italian stonemasons who sang while they worked restoring churches with the less skillful Irish "brickies."

My dad loved those summer jobs far more than teaching because he had inherited an avocation for building and fixing things from my grandfather who owned and operated his own machine shop in Oshkosh, Wisconsin. My grandpa Green figured out how to fix Ford Model T's before anyone else in the city and took his knack west in 1909 for a stint in Montana, where he worked as a blacksmith, mechanic, and chauffeur for copper king Marcus Daly, the Irish immigrant who "did not care for any man but an Irishman and . . . did not give a job to anyone else." My grandfather was not an Irishman, but he was a cracker-jack mechanic. When he returned from Butte, Frank Green married a young garment worker employed by the Oshkosh "B'Gosh" overalls factory. At the time, my grandmother Mary Hein served as recording secretary of her union local. When she was very old, and when I told her I was studying the labor movement, Grandma told me a story about the thrill of her youth: serving as a delegate to her national union convention in Detroit.

As a boy I used to visit F. W. Green's workshop, which buzzed with lathes and grinders, glowed from the fire of a blacksmith's forge, and smelled of machine oil and cigars—an unforgettable place. I thought my grandpa could make any-thing from steel. My mother's father also impressed me. A quiet widower born on a cattle farm near Wauseka, Wisconsin, he chanced to leave the livestock business for work as a railroad switchman. Eventually, my grandpa DiVall be-came "master" of the giant Milwaukee Road rail yards outside Chicago. Steeped in railroad lore, he told me stories and sang me songs about the haughty engi-neers and rambling gandy dancers, and took me to railroad bars to drink Coke in a whiskey shot glass. Sitting with him atop his tower in the Bensenville yards, I watched wide-eyed as he sent box cars with mysterious cargoes all over the United States. He was the equal of any self-made millionaire in my eyes.

Literate but not educated, skilled but not refined, my grandparents exuded a sense of pride in themselves as people with a craft. From them I learned that folks who worked with their hands for a living and wore work clothes were just as good, even better, than anybody else. My father thinks that growing up this way made me the historian I am today. I suppose our family and community histories do give us a feel for the past and may even invite us to place ourselves within that past. My grandparents were born in rural Wisconsin and raised in places called Freedom and Black Earth, small towns I used to think of romantically as seedbeds of midwestern democracy and progressivism. When I went back to Wisconsin for the 1968 Democratic primary to campaign for Eugene McCarthy and against Lyndon Johnson and his Vietnam War policies, I watched television with my grandfather as the president announced his surprise decision to retire. Grandpa was as delighted as I was.

However, I wasn't raised in the midwestern progressive traditions of my ancestral Wisconsin. My parents didn't discuss politics at the table, though they admired FDR, their generation's father figure, and they voted for our "intelligent governor," Adlai Stevenson, even when he ran for president against the likable Ike, another father figure. By 1960 I was old enough to share their enthusiasm for the handsome John F. Kennedy, but we identified more with his Catholicism than his liberalism. I wasn't reared with a passion to engage in radical movements, and I wasn't schooled to write movement history, which simply didn't exist in our textbooks.

My first inkling that protest movements existed came in 1960 from reading Arthur Schlesinger's *Politics of Upheaval,* published just before the author became President Kennedy's special assistant.[8] The radicals of the 1930s were no more than minor figures in "The Age of Roosevelt," and not to be taken too seriously. Schlesinger's history carried a message: great men made history. For my parents' generation it was FDR, for mine it would be JFK. Inspired by Kennedy and then moved by his death, I volunteered to work on Capitol Hill, spending two summers in Washington as an intern for the liberal senator from Illinois, Paul H. Douglas, a socialist intellectual turned politician. In the second summer term, 1966, I got up the nerve to question the senator's support for the Vietnam War. As I became disillusioned with Kennedy liberalism, with leaders like Douglas, and with historians like Schlesinger who served the court in the days of Camelot, I found new heroes in Daniel and Philip Berrigan, the antiwar priests, and in one of my college professors at Northwestern—Robert Wiebe, who stopped business as usual one day and opened his social history seminar to a discussion of the Vietnam War.

I began graduate studies in 1966 at Yale University. I was committed to traditional political history, intrigued by the outcomes of "critical elections," but soon I joined others of my generation in a search for America's radical past. My interest in movement history flowered in 1967 at about the time that I became actively engaged with the student and antiwar movements. My journey into the radical past began that year with a trip to New Orleans where I found the remarkable memoir of a Louisiana radical—a poet and a dreamer named

Covington Hall who had left a typed manuscript about his amazing experiences, "Labor Struggles of the Deep South."[9] Through this apostate son of the Confederacy, I learned about the amazing Industrial Workers of the World, who lit the fires of protest in the coldest corners of capitalist America.

Soon, my search took me to a less alluring place—the seemingly endless ιιᴀᴄⅼᴏ οf Ωᴋlɑhᴏmᴏ ᴄity on the trail of Oscar Ameringer the pioneer socialist and humorist of the Southwest. When I met Oscar's seventy-two-year-old widow, Freda, she was still operating the same noisy presses that once produced their radical weekly *The American Guardian*. Oscar Ameringer was an apostle of commonplace socialism who learned how to reach a popular audience with a class-conscious moralism, with criticisms that appealed to workers and to rural and small-town people who were trying to save a threatened way of life. Ameringer's marvelous autobiography, *If You Don't Weaken*, told the story of a socialist troubadour coming upon another America in rack-rented Oklahoma. There he encountered poor whites exploited by landlords and other parasites—pioneers disillusioned with the dream of frontier democracy. Oscar offered the Okie story as an American tragedy. After they fought to make their dream come true by creating a grassroots socialist movement, these people, like the Joads, were "tractored out" and pushed out onto Route 66 in their tin lizzies until they ended up in California "ragged, hungry, and shivering."[10]

Ameringer wrote humorous articles and pamphlets for the movement, like his famous people's history, *The Life and Deeds of Uncle Sam*, and his storytelling ability (the art of *fabulieren* he acquired in Bavarian beer halls) made him a favorite at the big summer encampments the socialists organized in the Southwest. A lifetime of telling stories this way earned him his "supreme position in the American labor movement as a man of laughter, wit, and satire," according to Carl Sandburg, who compared Oscar to the greatest of our critical humorists, Mark Twain, and to his popular populist contemporary, Oklahoma's own Will Rogers. What a pleasure it was to follow Oscar Ameringer's journey as a radical activist and intellectual.[11]

Going this way soon led to intellectual encounters with other historians who had taken a similar route in earlier times. They were public intellectuals who had been influenced by populism, progressivism, feminism, and socialism, and they told stories about social struggles, stories with a moral about human possibilities asserted in the face of long odds. Unlike the scholars who pursued the quest for objectivity, the progressive historians brought passion and partisanship to their scholarship.[12]

Mary Ritter Beard was one of the historians who believed history could contribute to the cause of human rights. For her, this meant mainly "writing and promoting the history of women's rights," to which she brought "enthusiasm and a sense of political mission."[13] Like other progressives, Beard "realized that views held about the past generally had consequences for the present."

History mattered to these public intellectuals not because the past determined the present, but because, in Warren Susman's words, "the way one thought about the past had consequences for the way one acted in the present."[14]

When Mary Beard wrote her short history of workers' struggles seventy years ago, she remarked: "For a long time this wide-spread labor movement was almost entirely ignored by everybody save those who took part in it or were in sympathy with it." Members of the professional classes thought about it "only in times of crisis," like World War I, when the war effort depended on labor, which was suddenly "watched with awe, tense and constant, like a mighty power." It was, she thought, "a significant comment on American intellectuals that it was not until 1918 that there was any authoritative or exhaustive history of the American labor movement." Even then, it was not undertaken by historians but rather by economists "who could not after all entirely ignore labor in studying industry."[15]

These writings pay homage to progressive historians of Mary Beard's generation, and to other public intellectuals like her spouse Charles Beard, the great historian of class conflict, who, in his presentations to British workers, "denounced the heartless scholars who had removed themselves from the plight of the people."[16] These chapters were composed in light of a tradition that included the progressive historians of the Beards' generation and populist intellectuals who followed, such as my own graduate school mentor, C. Vann Woodward, who wrote the book on movement history that most inspired me as a student—the biography of Tom Watson, an "agrarian rebel" whose failure to create an interracial people's party ended in tragedy. Woodward wrote the book during the Depression when another interracial movement of poor people seemed necessary. "It was no dead past I was trying to bring to life," he recalled, "but one very much alive and full of meaning."[17]

When I arrived at Yale in 1966 to study with Woodward, I met several students who had volunteered to fight segregation in the South and who were eager to study with the author of *The Strange Career of Jim Crow,* the book Martin Luther King called "the historical bible of the civil rights movement." They shared their experiences as we immersed ourselves in Woodward's writing about the New South and its myth of reconciliation—a myth his books were meant to subvert. It was a reconciliation that subordinated black people to white supremacy and subjected many white people to grinding poverty. Though he reacted strongly against late 1960s student radicalism and black nationalism, Woodward supported our generation's excursions into movement history; he even encouraged us to read an older Marxist literature blacklisted by the history profession.[18]

It was a time for discovering W.E.B. Du Bois and his unique contributions to U.S. history, for reading the new paperback edition of *Black Reconstruction,* the epic story of "the part which black folk played in the attempt to reconstruct democracy America."[19] It was also a time for reading the unrecognized writings of Philip Foner, the prolific Marxist labor historian whose book on the Industrial Workers of the World helped send me off on my first exploration of movement history—a study of the Brotherhood of Timber Workers, an interracial union that appeared mysteriously deep in the piney woods of Louisiana, in the heart of Jim Crow's territory.[20]

While we learned from these historians, we joined in the New Left criticism of Old Left writers for whom the class struggle explained almost everything. We were far more attracted to the unorthodox Marxism of E. P. Thompson and C. L. R. James, who understood class struggle and class consciousness in much more subtle ways and who wrote with literary grace about the cultures of common people—about Haitian slaves and English artisans taking history into their own hands. From these mentors our generation of social historians gained the energy and direction needed to write history from the bottom up, as an alternative to elitist, top-down political history, which explained opposition movements as conspiracies. We believe social conflict was endemic in our economy and that social protest reflected real injustices, not paranoid fantasies.[21]

But many of us had to agree with our guru Herbert Gutman when he said in 1981 that the new social history remained much too fragmentary; that it was inaccessible to the very kinds of people it chose as subjects of study.[22] Seeking a wider audience for the kind of movement history that inspired me, I returned to that older tradition of narrative writing represented by the Beards, by Vann Woodward, and by Edward Thompson, who wrote "with continual human reference, affirming certain values over others," trying, as one admirer said, "to make his readers active valuing agents" as they thought about history and politics.[23] Though Thompson's literary talents could not be duplicated, his way of telling movement stories could be emulated. His writing about dissenting sects and oppositional cultures in England was informed by the new social history but not weighed down by its conceptual terms and its analytical frameworks.

"We are heirs to a grand story telling tradition," Jacquelyn Dowd Hall declared, writing of her own debt to historians inspired by the women's movement. "Our method consists of downright perverse willingness to sit for months in the archives, learning from strangers." Why do we do it? We are doing it, she says, "for imagined readers who stretch far beyond the academy; for our ancestors; for our children; and for the women's movement that makes our work possible and necessary." But, Hall suggests, we are not doing it just to reach our audiences, and we are not doing it just to save the lives of our historical subjects. We are also doing it for ourselves, because, she writes, we are telling these stories "to save our lives."[24]

As Hall explained more recently: "We bring to our writing the unfinished business of our own lives and times; moreover, the experience of travelling so long in the country of research *becomes* our past, for our stories grow from a process of remembering and forgetting our encounters with the relics, fragments, whispers of an always already-recollected past." Thus, we live the history we have learned, as well as "the history we have experienced and inherited, passed down through groups with which we identify."[25]

Many of us first became excited about movement history by listening to the stories of old activists for whom "remembering was a conscious political act." It is possible for us to retell their stories, and even our own, in a dramatic way, in literary forms that can be, as Hall suggests, as "life-affirming as the novel."[26] This does not mean however that we must simply invent a dramatic narrative structure to impose on a random sequence of events. We live our lives as stories with a beginning, a middle, and an end. Storytelling need not be imposed on the structure of life; it can flow naturally out of the course of life because stories are lived and told.[27]

There are intellectuals who "deconstruct" our stories to show that these stories have more to do with our own language and values than they do with what really happened in history. The criticism of texts that governs much academic discourse these days does not "ground itself in history, in community, in politics" according to William Cronon. It does not ask readers to care about what really happened. But historians implicitly believe "that a good story makes us care about its subject." This is the power of historical narrative. "When a narrator honestly makes an audience care about what happens in a story," writes Cronon, "the story expresses ties between the past and present in a way that lends deeper meaning to both."[28]

Many historians today worry that "specialized, 'self-absorbed' scholarship" has "eroded traditions of good writing and good storytelling." They feel that by turning inward to talk to one another, they have lost contact with other audiences with whom historians used to talk. Remarkably, writes the editor of the *Journal of American History,* "this feeling of isolation from popular audiences is coming at a time when there is great popular interest in history."[29] Movement history offers one medium for telling the dramatic and often tragic stories that move people, for writing narratives that ask readers to care about what happened to people in struggle, people ignored or treated with condescension by other historians.

Every good story contains something, "openly or covertly, something useful, some kind of counsel," wrote Walter Benjamin in 1936. It "is less an answer to a question, than a proposal concerning the continuation of the story that is just unfolding." To offer this kind of counsel to others, he said, "one would first have to be able to tell the story."[30] And then one would have find someone to tell the story to.

After discovering powerful movement stories in my own research and that of many others, I began experimenting with ways of telling them in public. In a series of newspaper "opinion editorials" and book review essays I attempted to bring the insights of movement history to bear on current political issues and social problems.[31] Besides newspapers and magazines there were other outlets for movement stories: protest rallies and strike meetings; television and radio interviews in which reporters asked for "historical perspective"; museum exhibits and holiday festivals; public library lectures and public television film documentaries; historical commemorations and worker reunions; and even projects connected with public monuments that allowed for the inscription or depiction of movement history in lasting forms.

Most of my time and energy was devoted to sharing movement stories with union activists, usually when we met in educational programs but sometimes in less formal settings. This book reflects on some of those experiences in which workers often seemed to find inspiration in movement stories of past struggles that reaffirmed their own values and commitments. It also describes how sometimes they found more, how they found some of the counsel they needed to think about solving the problems of today and tomorrow. It reports on how these workers gained an understanding of how tough choices were made in the past, how history was shaped by human intervention, how certain decisions explained what happened to the movement, what went right—and wrong. Historical narratives can do more than redeem the memory of past struggles; they can help people think of themselves as historical figures with crucial moral and political choices to make, like those who came before them. For activists in besieged unions, movement history creates an opportunity to consider moral questions, political problems, and strategic proposals in the light of history, as part of the labor movement's continuously unfolding story.

Labor education immediately challenged me to connect historical knowledge with questions derived from the experience of people in struggle. Trade union students constantly posed problems, challenging me to share what I knew in useful ways. Even in the most discouraging days, when unions were hurting and when their leaders were acting badly, "trying to be for labor" when it was "flat on its back" was not so difficult because my students shared with me a sense of urgency about rebuilding and changing the labor movement.[32] The hundreds of labor activists who studied movement history with me helped sustain my desire to become a movement intellectual, to work as someone engaged with workers in struggle—not only as a supporter but as an educator and writer.

Little did I imagine ten years ago—in the depths of my fight with the state's top labor official—that many of these students, and many other allies, would lead large union locals in Massachusetts, as well as the state Federation of Labor, and hold high positions in Washington at the newly reformed AFL-CIO. Nor did I imagine that my critical history of the labor movement, published in 1980, would seem so in tune with the ideas of new AFL-CIO leaders who replaced the old guard in 1995. The emergence of a New Voice labor leadership in Washington has created some new opportunities for dialogue between intellectuals and movement activists; and for labor historians it has created a new will to overcome what Leon Fink calls the "powers of historical pessimism" that remain occupational hazards for professors of history.[33]

The case for good movement history cannot rest simply on telling the story of past oppressions and oppositional movements. The narrative strategies employed in movement history are intended make the audience care about people in struggle, but if we, the historians, seek only to defend our forebears and rescue them from obscurity, we risk being dismissed for simply offering elegies to lost causes. So, besides telling certain movement stories, we are obliged to explain why movements fail, often tragically. As the influential movement historian Howard Zinn wrote in 1970, we seek to "recapture those few moments in the past which show the possibility of a better way of life," but we need to do more than celebrate examples of "morally desirable action." Radical historians have "to show how good social movements can go wrong, how leaders can betray their followers, how rebels can become bureaucrats, how ideas can become frozen."[34]

In seeking to demonstrate how people make their own history, we may find ourselves dreaming that oppressed people live only to make history. Movement history provides glimpses of human beings at exceptional moments when they engage in collective struggle—hardly the normal course of human affairs—moments when "ordinary people did extraordinary things." The movements we discover, describe, and interpret rarely lasted for long. They were often suppressed, sometimes with stunning violence, but sometimes they were also betrayed by their own leaders, or merged into less participatory, more hierarchical organizations. Their demands were often impractical, confused, or easily co-opted by opportunistic politicians. And oftentimes, their militants simply became tired and discouraged.

The movement intellectual Richard Flacks, an early leader of the student left, emphasizes the difference between "making history and making life." The heroic model of history espoused by the left often ignores this truth: "Movements are rooted in commitment to daily life, in efforts by people to overcome threats to their accustomed collective life or to claim rights they believe they are entitled to." Those who participate in these efforts "are therefore disposed to return to their lives once such a return is possible as a result of movement gains."[35]

Indeed, the new social movements of our time thus appear less like crusades to change the world led by revolutionaries in more romantic times, and more like struggles to save the world, to defend precious values and traditions, and to preserve the gains it has taken generations of struggle to achieve. Therefore, the stories we have to tell are not all uplifting ones. Many are stories of pain and loss, which may be told as tragedies or offered as redemptive narratives, like Barbara Kingsolver's moving account of the women warriors in the desperate 1983 Arizona copper miners' strike. Even in these painful accounts of defeat, inspiring stories of courage and creativity emerge—stories about struggles for community survival rooted in old forms of mutality. People engaged in defending themselves sometimes begin to feel they are part of something larger—some kind of collective movement for social and economic justice. In these struggles a sense of self-respect and mutual admiration often appears as people in motion experience in new ways the joys of human solidarity.[36]

There is a role for historians in this desperate era, a role we can play in recovering lost memories and recalling forgotten places in movement history, a role in recording silenced voices and retelling tragic stories. "A sense of history has become a condition of our survival," says the multitalented writer and critic John Berger. "A striking feature of our time," he observes, "is that its sense of history is now most intense not in the universities, but in popular movements of survival and struggle." It leads him to issue this challenge: "The most urgent task today for those intellectuals who might have once been traditional intellectuals is to invoke the historical experience of the ruled, to underwrite their self-respect, and to proffer—not to display—intellectual confidence."[37]

Thanks to a recent survey of popular historical consciousness by Roy Rosenzweig and David Thelen, we know how much people care about history, and how much they rely upon their own interpretations of the past to affirm their own identities and to confirm the endurance of their families. We also know how they use history creatively to make sense of the present and to shape the future. But these personal narratives rarely connect with the story of progressive social change, except in the case of African Americans who remain very conscious of how their freedom movement altered history. Few white Americans interviewed in the survey analyzed by Rosenzweig and Thelen "offered narratives about ordinary people acting to change the world." They told depressingly consistent stories of moral decay and political hypocrisy which left them without much sense of hope. Unlike African Americans, they did not push beyond their personal, familial sense of the past to gain an understanding how groups altered the course of history. In the late 1990s Americans of European descent lacked a comparable sense of how collective struggles created progress and how people can "make a difference in the world."[38]

Of course, the civil rights movement exists within living memory, whereas the social and political struggles that empowered generations of white immigrant workers have passed into history. Still, it must be said that historians of the black freedom struggle have been able to perpetuate that memory and transform it into a usable past for millions of young Americans born since the 1960s. Just as the civil rights movement gave birth to other radical movements that followed, the historians of that movement provided a model for what others of us have attempted to do in preserving the memory and interpreting the history of other struggles. Much of what follows in this book has been influenced by the civil rights movement and its historians—activist scholars like Vincent Harding and documentary filmmakers like the late Henry Hampton, whose work exudes the sense of hope that can be derived from an awareness of what the civil rights activists accomplished.[39]

Much of my work as a movement historian has been addressed to white working people who lack this hopeful sense of what past struggles mean for the present and the future. My challenge is to learn from people like Harding and Hampton how to tell compelling stories in public that confront the widespread popular mistrust of history presented by professionals.

My experience as a teacher and writer enhances my confidence that many other people can gain hope from the history of popular movements, even from accounts that reveal their failures and shortcomings. But the challenge of movement history goes beyond invoking the experience of the "ruled." It requires much more than strengthening individual and group identities that help "underwrite self respect"—to use John Berger's words. The power of history in "popular movements for survival" is obvious, but its importance in creating visionary movements for social change has been neglected in this hopeless era— a time when intellectuals pronounce "the end of history" as a process that can lead to a new human community in which the ruled are at last able to achieve self-rule.[40]

It is tempting to agree with Berger that questions about who rules and who profits are no longer compelling. In a world where poor people are preoccupied with questions of survival it is easy to forget that in the past people like them have asked and answered questions about how to create a new world in which millions of human beings no longer struggled simply to survive. Movement history is one way to help people regain some sense of the better communities people imagined and attempted to create in the past. It is one way of moving beyond the natural focus on personal identity and family history about which most Americans seem to care very deeply, according to *The Presence of the Past: The Popular Uses of History in American Life*. As one author of the study writes: "Recognizing how the civil rights movement broke the fetters of a stable racist order or how the CIO challenged management rights can inspire people to work for social change in the present." Indeed, as Roy Rosenzweig suggests, it may not be possible to build movements for progressive change unless people can imagine "a set of past and present connections to groups of people who aren't kin or ancestors" and unless they can recall the alternative visions and "imagined communities" the movements of the past offer up to us.[41]

Many of the stories told in this book are tales of defensive struggles waged by the ruled against the rulers—struggles that often ended in defeat and disappointment. In these accounts of people in struggle we can find heroic examples of personal courage and transformation, of communal solidarity and political imagination. We can also see people "experimenting with new democratic forms" in the ways they did through the farmer and worker insurgences a century ago when self-respecting citizens acted together to survive and to imagine a better world. In the chapters of this book that concern our recent past we can find some of the same ingredients. Out of the local "cultures of solidarity" created in the survival struggles of the late twentieth century will come the experiences and insights people will need to create larger, wider movements for social justice in the next century.[42]

These stories from our own time tell us that history has not come to an end point with what conservatives like to think of as the triumph of free market forces and the "universalization of Western liberal democracy as the final form of government."[43] During the past two centuries progressive and radical movements have continued to challenge the laws of the marketplace and to question the meaning of a democracy manipulated by elites. These movements have continued to expand and enrich the idea of democracy and the meaning of freedom. In the next century new movements of this kind will be called upon to do so again.

The plan of the book is the following. Part 1 offers three chapters about the practical work of doing movement history—and how it evolved through a series of experiences that begin in 1967 and extended into the early 1980s. Chapter 1 is a personal account of discovering movement history as a student while at the same time engaging with the student and antiwar movements of the late 1960s. It focuses on my involvement with the journal *Radical America*, founded in 1967 to explore the history and politics of American radicalism. Discovering and exploring movement history with the "Radical Americans" offered a direct connection with an activist audience it was impossible to reach through my work as a university history teacher. The *RA* collective was militantly committed to debating the ideological issues of the 1970s raised by neo-Marxists and feminists, by neopopulists and black nationalists, among others. The journal offered an intense political education without the dogmatic indoctrination demanded by other leftist groups of the time. *Radical America* also allowed me to learn from other historians and activists how to write history for a highly politicized audience.

Chapter 2 describes an outreach effort inspired by my experiences in Britain with the History Workshop movement, an exciting collective effort to "bring the boundaries of history closer to people's lives" and to make history a democratic activity. It reviews our efforts to organize History Workshop events in Massachusetts as a way of sharing the richness of written social history with audiences of workers and union activists who lived that history. These projects offered our little band of historians a chance to cross boundaries, to mobilize memories, to present history in community settings—to see if our kind of "people's history" would engage a popular audience and even provide an opportunity to "share the authority" for historical interpretation.[44]

Chapter 3 concerns our effort to build a community at my university in which to practice a "pedagogy of hope," so that working people could "begin to get history into their own hands," as the Brazilian popular educator Paulo Freire had put it.[45] Learning to teach movement history to workers depended, of course, on creating a free space in which I could learn from them and they could learn from me. This chapter describes the political and cultural struggle of a history teacher reaching out to union members whose leaders remained dubious about university education and deeply suspicious about the sixties radicals who were trying to provide a new kind of worker education. It also accounts for the ways in which labor education helped some worker activists gain the historical awareness and critical consciousness they needed to reflect on their own practice and to learn from their experiences and those of others.

All three chapters in Part 1 explore the difficulties of working as a university-based professor while engaging in radical movement politics. At first, it seemed that academic life would not allow a person to be an activist or even a scholar who addressed activist concerns. The movement intellectuals I admired from the progressive era—historians like the Beards and socialists like Oscar Ameringer and Covington Hall—were deeply connected to the social struggles of their time. But during the twentieth century the possibility of a permanent connection between intellectuals and democratic movements dimmed as education itself became more formal and intellectuals became professional academics far removed from plebian society. A decade ago, Russell Jacoby noticed the vastly diminished role of public intellectuals and bemoaned the tendency of university-based scholars to become disengaged, overwhelmed by the "tides of professionalism."[46] Part 1 describes my efforts to escape this world in order to produce history for activists and community-based groups, but it also reflects on my rather unusual experience as a adult educator in an urban public university where it has been possible to work as a movement intellectual with one foot in the political world and another in the academic world—at least in a special corner of that world affected by the democratic impulses the reform movements of the sixties and seventies generated.

Part 2 features chapters on various efforts, my own and others', to reclaim movement history for the public. Popular historical consciousness in the United States has been influenced by countless messages delivered through the official custodians of the national memory and through historians who write the governing narratives about our past. In response, protest movements, and their historians, often recover countermemories that challenge official versions of historical truth. Some of these efforts to tell movement stories in public are described in the following chapters; they may be read as attempts to subvert what John Keane calls the "tyranny of the present"—a present devoid of political possibility. They promote instead "a democratic remembrance of things past."[47]

Chapter 4 reports on the efforts organized by the Massachusetts History Workshop to engage trade unionists in recalling and sharing memories of earlier moments of solidarity in Boston's labor history, the subject of my first efforts in the field of public history.[48] The chapter focuses on a tension-filled attempt to commemorate the May Days of 1886, a centennial that aroused a lot of suspicion among some union officials and won the support of others who, dismayed over labor's loss of heart, wanted to recall earlier traditions of struggle, even though they were associated with radicalism in the union movement's past.

Chapters 5 and 6 were motivated by the study of labor history sites suitable for marking as nationally significant by the federal government. While writing an introduction to a labor-history theme study for the National Historical Landmarks Program, I discovered the difficulty of recognizing places of significance to workers. For example, the program criteria excluded cemeteries and graveyard monuments and emphasized structures with architectural integrity. Few structures of integrity remain to remind us of the economic and civic lives experienced by unionized workers, those birds of passage who passed through the fields, mining camps, the factory towns, and city slums without leaving a trace. Eventually, their wandering ended when they died and were buried in graves on bleak hillsides or in crowded city cemeteries, their graves marked humbly, if at all, their remains unburdened by granite stones with grandiloquent epitaphs.

The National Park Service survey of potential labor history landmarks stimulated the writing of these two chapters as studies of how worker history is forgotten and remembered and how places of memory are involved in that curious process.[49]

Chapter 5 focuses on the memory of one tragic event, the 1886 bombing and riot in Chicago's Haymarket Square which electrified so many labor radicals and was actively recalled for a long time in the United States and in other nations. It reviews the dramatic story of the trial and execution of the anarchists held responsible for the bombing and revisits their monument in Chicago's Waldheim Cemetery, which became a world-reknowned site of memory, a place to enact rituals of commemoration. How was the memory of the Haymarket martyrs preserved for a half century in the face of official contempt? And then, after the living memory died, along with its radical custodians, why was it revived in our own time? What was the role of movement activists and historians in the process of remembering and forgetting?

Chapter 6 concerns other forgotten places of memory in the South, places where movement people struggled and suffered in their efforts to contest oppression. Southern history captivated me as a student, and its often bloody mysteries kept a hold on me, pulling me back again to explore two phenomena: how storytelling traditions in the South kept certain oppositional memories alive and how movement activists and historians released silenced voices and uncovered hidden places in efforts to expose another side—an underside—of southern history.

Chapter 7 describes and evaluates efforts to tell movement stories through the medium of documentary films in which movement people could be seen and heard telling their own stories. It reflects on collaborations with a number of filmmakers, especially Henry Hampton, whose documentary classic about the civil rights era, *Eyes on the Prize,* showed that movement storytelling could reach a vast public, and could raise the most profound questions about democracy. The chapter concentrates on the production of a seven-part documentary film series on *The Great Depression* for public television, produced by Hampton's Blackside, Inc., where I learned some lessons about dramatic, visual storytelling—lessons from filmmakers with whom I collaborated in creating stories of struggle and survival from the 1930s, including the saga of the era's greatest social movement, the CIO. I hope these reflections help to explain why movement history owes such a debt to Henry Hampton, and why this book is dedicated to his memory.

The chapters in Part 3 explore what people in struggle have learned from the history of their own experience and from the history of movement people who came before them. They argue that seeing history with movement eyes makes a difference in how oppressed people understand their own situation and in how other people in society perceive the nature of oppression and the importance of struggles to overcome it.

Chapter 8 reviews the struggle against racial segregation in Boston and examines the stakes involved in how that struggle is recalled and interpreted. It criticizes the prize-winning book *Common Ground* by J. Anthony Lukas for leaving out the history of the civil rights movement and for drawing misleading lessons about the consequences of the traumatic fight to desegregate the city's public schools. Instead of seeing "the busing" as a horrible mistake made by an elitist judge, as an unfair burden put upon working-class whites, this essay offers a different reading of recent Boston history, one seen with movement eyes by an observer who was also a participant in the political conflicts over busing as well as in the new social movements that emerged from those conflicts.

Chapter 9 is an account of movement history in the making, set in a very different locale—the Appalachian coal mining region where the United Mine Workers engaged in a desperate strike against the Pittston Coal Group in 1989. It is a contemporary story of movement building—a case study of how movement activists learned from their history and tried to apply its lessons. In waging an "Appalachian Intifada" against an anti-union corporation, the miners and their allies frequently invoked memories of CIO insurgents from the 1930s and civil rights activists from the 1960s—often to make a case for defying unjust laws and anti-union judges in a massive civil disobedience campaign. The Pittston strike offers a glimpse of how working people learned from their own experience and from movement history; it also shows how they responded to their leaders' call to create a people's movement against corporate greed, how they drew upon older traditions of militancy and solidarity, and how they inspired other union activists all over the country.

Chapters 8 and 9 offer contrasting cases. In the latter an old social movement form is revived during a militant mine union strike involving traditional workplace issues and exuding a lost language of class struggle. In the former a

Rainbow Coalition is created out what have been called the "new social move-ments"—struggles to protest the oppression of specific groups and communities whose participants share a strong sense of cultural identity. Progressive intellec-tuals have been engaged in passionate debate about whether or not "identity politics" negates any sort of unified progressive politics in a conservative age.

My choice as an activist is to work with those seeking to build a multicultural social movement of workers, a movement for radical change, but I don't think our mission will be subverted by other progressives organized around single issues or around cultural affinities. Indeed, a truly diverse movement for social change can only be created in our time by people who share a deep sense of mutual respect. It would also require some kind of democratic power sharing among constituent groups that has been missing in many protest organizations and coalitions. The task of creating the first really diverse movement for social justice in American history lies ahead of us in the next century.

In the present, however, our new movement building efforts must be based on lessons derived from the new and the old forms of struggle and from the different intellectual approaches taken by students of the old and the new. Sociologists of the new social movements are fascinated by the psychological and cultural processes that produce collective identities. Unlike traditional Marxist scholars, they do not see political opposition emerging out of predeter-mined processes (like "capital accumulation") or rational calculations of group interest that might once have produced class-based parties or worker move-ments. According to social movement scholar William Gamson, the new theo-rists are more interested in the ways collective identities form (through the use of language and ritual, for example) than they are in the reasons protest groups adopt certain organizational structures, strategies, and ideas. For example, ac-tivists in the Puerto Rican radical movement now look back and "inveigh against the Leninist type of party structure" they adopted after embracing Marx-ist and nationalist ideologies. This old way of doing things, writes Andres Torres, meant that the Puerto Rican movement ignored what today might be called "the politics of identity."[50]

My approach to movement history remains concerned with the old problem-atics of class and nation that have preoccupied radicals for the past century. I do not believe classes or nations will disappear in the next century or that new identity-based social movements will be exempt from the tensions created by class and national identity. Still, these new movements and their interpreters have taught us much about the way collective opposition is created and sus-tained. Indeed, this new knowledge of movements is often more revealing than what we have inherited from the old Marxist tradition, which relied on class consciousness or its absence to explain insurgency and left us knowing not much at all about the process of movement building.

The new social history of workers shows us that powerful group identities exist within the working class, loyalties that have often been ignored or suppressed by labor and radical movements. These affinities should not be understood simply as obstacles to unity, as wedges that divided working-class people and prevented them from attaining a true consciousness of their common lot. Another view emerges from new studies of working-class difference, a more complex picture of worker consciousness in which collective identities based on race and gender, religious and national loyalty, ethnicity and sexuality coexisted and even complemented strong class loyalties. These investigations also show how community-based organizing has mobilized workers' power and heightened an awareness of class that transcended local group loyalties.[51]

The final chapter "On Becoming a Movement Again" argues that even an old, and until recently, moribund, social movement—organized labor—can be broadened and strengthened if different cultural identities are seen as important in negotiating new forms of class solidarity. For example, the "social movement unionism" emerging around the world in recent years is rooted in these identities, and in popular struggles for sovereignty, as well as in expressions of worker solidarity. These new social movements of workers in Poland and South Africa, in the Philippines and Brazil, may seem outlandish to workers in the most economically advanced nation in the world. But these movements are being studied carefully by labor activists in the United States who see in them the ability to transcend some of the enduring tensions that have fractured our own union movement—the separation of workplace from community struggles, for example, the tension between participatory democracy and organizational stability, and the conflict between economic self-interest and an altruistic sense of social justice and the common good.[52]

These examples of social movement unionism abroad are still relatively unknown to many union members, however. What is much more familiar is the social learning they have experienced since the 1970s during the long crisis which devastated industrial communities and destroyed labor unions across the nation. The final chapter of this book shows how, in the jaws of defeat, working people found new ways to fight back, to create new coalitions based on old values of community welfare and human solidarity.

These struggles for community survival also involved a look further back into earlier phases of movement history. The power of the past has been evoked in cultural expressions like the popular proletarian art of Ralph Fasanella, in the labor lore unearthed by Archie Green, in Moe Foner's union-backed Bread and Roses Cultural Heritage Project, in the labor folk song revival led by Pete Seeger and, more recently, in the "Ghost of Tom Joad" that appeared to Bruce Springsteen and in the apparitions of Mother Jones and Joe Hill recorded by radical troubadour Utah Phillips and the young musician Ani DiFranco on their compact discs "The Past Didn't Go Anywhere" and "Fellow Workers."

Chapter 10 describes the historical component to this learning process. "On Becoming a Movement Again" examines this search for a usable past by labor organizers and rank-and-file workers seeking to rebuild old worker organizations and to create new ones during the 1990s. They have consciously examined the early movement-building phases in labor history and the more recent experiences of 1960s social movements. Revisiting the past in the current climate of crisis, they have created innovative approaches to organizing and mobilizing workers.

For example, the Justice for Janitors campaign described in the last chapter, employed old-fashioned movement tactics like civil disobedience to unionize low-wage service workers, mostly immigrants and people of color. Stephen Lerner, who initially headed this effort for the Service Employees International Union, deliberately drew upon the lessons of movement history. "As we seek to revive the labor movement," he declared, "we should take history to heart." Rather than being less confrontational, he argued, labor activists should become "more vocal, aggressive, militant and creative in fighting for workers' rights" because, he concluded, every great "non-violent movement in the twentieth century" has been built around direct action and civil disobedience.[53]

Seeing the past with movement eyes has helped thousands of labor and community activists envision a revived form of social movement unionism that welcomes broad alliances, that embraces cultural diversity, that fosters international solidarity, and that displays tactical creativity. We need a labor movement that practices as well as preaches democracy, that extends it and defends it—one that can help restore a belief in the possibility of a society based on economic and social justice for all. The intelligence and imagination, the courage and tenacity required to build such a movement may be summoned in part from the stories we tell from the past. These qualities may also be discovered in the movement building stories being played out in these times.

Thus *Taking History to Heart* concludes with examples of how powerful the past can be in building the progressive movements of the present and the future. Ongoing struggles for social justice are seen as extensions of older stories still unfolding. In their telling, these stories can become part of popular effort to shape a different future from the one global capital has in store for us, a future in which new crusades for equality, democracy, and social justice appear as extensions of nearly forgotten stories kept alive within movement culture by activists and historians working together.

Part One

PRACTICING MOVEMENT HISTORY

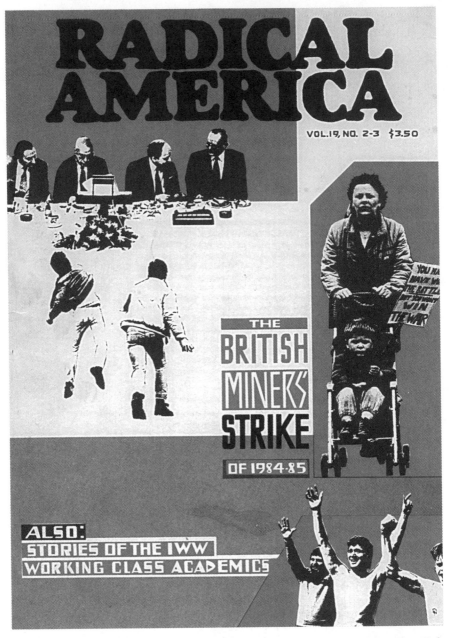

Probing workers' struggles: cover of *Radical America*, 1985. Cover design by Nick Thorkelson. *Courtesy* Radical America.

CHAPTER 1

Discovering Movement History
with the "Radical Americans"

History is a form within which we fight, and many have fought before us.
Nor are we alone when we fight there. For the past is not dead, inert,
confining; it carries signs and evidences also of creative resources which
can sustain the present and prefigure possibility.

EDWARD THOMPSON, "The Politics of Theory"

In 1968 FBI director J. Edgar Hoover warned union members to be aware of
"fanatic, anarchist revolutionaries" from the Students for a Democratic Society
who would try to infiltrate their organizations. These subversives believed
"unions should be destroyed, along with Government, the military, private
industry and law enforcement." They left behind them "a bitter wake of arson,
vandalism, bombing, and destruction."[1] This was the official characterization of
what SDS leaders called a summer "work-in" during which students would seek
blue-collar jobs.

The SDS turn to the working class attracted my attention, but not just because it provoked Hoover. I wondered if such an outreach by a few hundred
young radicals could link up the student movement with worker struggles, the
kind of thing that happened briefly in the intoxicating French May Days of
1968. My curiosity led me to the SDS convention in 1969. It took place in the
crumbling Chicago Coliseum where a debate over black nationalism degenerated into a weird opera as platoons of delegates chanted slogans at each other. I
recall peering through a damp haze at the speakers' dais where national SDS
leader Mike Klonsky defended black nationalism (embodied by the Black Panther Party), though I could hardly hear him through the din. When Jared Israel
of the Progressive Labor Party faction spoke, taking a "hard class line" against
black nationalism, a political chorus chanted "racist, racist, racist." In the process of breaking up, SDS seemed an unlikely means of connecting student
radicals with labor union activists.[2]

I returned to my historical work at Yale University, still looking for points of
engagement with the Movement. I had attended antiwar demonstrations in
New York City with my friends, but the New Left exerted little influence at Yale.

When students occupied Columbia University, the Yalies remained calm. Along with a few other activist students, I looked forward to studying with the radical historian Staughton Lynd, who was on leave doing antiwar work. The history department voted to deny Lynd tenure, ostensibly for academic reasons. Like Lynd, we thought the decision reflected political animus. The department chairman said that Lynd's protest against the U.S. war effort in Vietnam was "too strident" because it had included a trip to Hanoi. To protest against the history department decision, some of us turned the sherry-sipping Charles M. Andrews Society of history grad students into a democratic organization.[3] But our intervention in Lynd's case was fruitless. We were sobered by the price he paid for acting on his convictions and by the difficulty we would all face in combining movement politics with historical endeavors. That spring of 1968 Staughton Lynd warned radicals not to allow the university to become the "emotional center" of our lives and to keep "one foot solidly off campus" so we could alternate intellectual work with Movement work.[4]

Roads Not Taken

I had come to graduate school in 1966 intending to study political history and believing that the new quantitative studies of voting behavior would correct the elitist bias in the old political history and help explain how the public really behaved in the political world. For my first seminar with the famous southern historian C. Vann Woodward, I wrote a paper about how the Civil War was played out over and over again in midwestern presidential elections. This was difficult work. I toiled over endless computer printouts and tried to make sense of pointless statistical regressions—all to determine what motivated voters in the critical elections of the 1890s. Fellow students indulged my interest in voting behavior, but my research bored them.

Tired of quantitative history and baffled by statistical analysis, I envied the more exciting topics Woodward's students had chosen to study about Reconstruction and its aftermath. Paul Worthman was digging up impressive evidence about white and black workers in the Birmingham coal-steel district. He was also encouraging me to explore labor history and badgering me to read "this amazing book," *The Making of the English Working Class* by E. P. Thompson, which helped inspire a generation of student radicals to become social historians. Bruce Palmer, a white civil rights volunteer in the South, was probing the ideology of the populist movement. John Blassingame was reconstructing the extraordinary black community of New Orleans during and after the Civil War. Barbara Fields was beginning her work on emancipated slaves in Maryland. Morgan Kousser, who tried to help me crunch election numbers, was showing how disfranchisement worked. Tom Holt was illuminating the leadership qualities of black officeholders in the reconstructed states. Larry Powell was breaking new ground in researching the Yankee carpetbaggers. And my roommate

Bob Engs was studying the education of freedmen at Hampton Institute, near his hometown. They all seemed to be exploring the roads not taken in southern history, those pregnant moments filled with political possibility. I yearned to join them on this kind of expedition.

Seeking a way out of election analysis, I searched for a more engaging research topic. In the process I recalled an intriguing lecture I had heard in an undergraduate course on southern history about "rustic radicalism" in the Louisiana piney woods. Professor Grady McWhiney, a charming raconteur from Baton Rouge, told us about an amazing strike of black and white timber workers in 1911 that stirred up the region and helped Socialist Eugene V. Debs carry Winn Parish in the 1912 election, with the vote of Huey Long's daddy.[5] This strange episode, so out of character with the idea of a solid South, seemed like a hot topic, and a chance to go to New Orleans.

Woodward encouraged me to go forward, to go to Louisiana to do the work, to explain how a strike of redneck lumberjacks and black sawmill hands turned into an interracial union movement that allied with the Industrial Workers of the World. Finding the memoirs of the IWW poet Covington Hall in the Tulane library took me to the Wobblies and their culture I had known through the songs of IWW martyr Joe Hill. Reading about Wobblies in the southern piney woods conjured up ghosts of a labor movement worlds apart from the one presided over by AFL-CIO chief George Meany, who supported U.S. Cold War policy in Vietnam and elsewhere and who loathed the antiwar movement. Meany abhorred the direct action tactics that typified the Wobblies and the New Left. He opposed the March on Washington for Jobs and Justice in 1963 because he believed street demonstrations were a disreputable tactic. His desire to make unions respectable was so intense that he once bragged, "I never went on a strike in my life, never ran a strike, never ordered anyone on strike, never had anything to do with a picket line."[6]

In this political context those of us who chose to study labor history from the bottom up wanted to recall the reasons why the workers' movement arose, why it became so militant at times, and why it was so violently repressed. Our motives were expressed in the words of the protagonist in Wallace Stegner's 1971 novel *Angle of Repose,* a retired and disabled historian of the American West familiar with Wobblies and the bloody mine wars that raged in the Rockies. Stegner, who had written a wonderful novel based on the life of the legendary troubador Joe Hill, has his character reflect on how the power of unions in the 1960s dimmed an awareness of what they had fought against. By reconstructing the life of his grandmother in western mining camps, the narrator is reminded of how intimidated the miners were and "of how rotten a string tied their lives together." Telling their stories—the stories I was discovering in Oklahoma mining towns—might provoke incredulity in modern readers, but they demonstrated, says Stegner's historian, "our need for a sense of history: our need to know what real injustice looked like."[7]

A Kind of Crisis

During the late 1960s New Left historians aggressively challenged the history profession's claims to neutrality and objectivity, and debated leading scholars who presumed to define what was "real history." We helped create a kind of crisis in the history profession that erupted dramatically at the 1969 meeting of the American Historical Association. I can still hear, at a packed session, one of our leading lights, Jesse Lemisch, intense but impishly funny, giving his passionate critique of Cold War historians and their phony "neutrality."[8] When he finished, there were clenched fists and shouts of "right on." The civility that reigned in our gentlemanly profession was being blown apart. Ten times the usual number of historians packed the business meeting, enthralled by a floor fight over a resolution condemning U.S. intervention in Vietnam. Besides this passionate debate, the Association experienced its first contested presidential election when Staughton Lynd, backed by the "radical caucus," challenged the officially anointed nominee, R. R. Palmer. Eugene Genovese, the Marxist historian of slavery who had attacked Staughton Lynd's "moralistic" approach to movement history, took the floor and escalated the debate. The antiwar activists should be "put down, put down hard and put down once and for all," he shouted. There was pushing and shoving to get to the microphone, and a few professorial punches were thrown.[9]

These wild goings-on among ordinarily stiff professors highlighted a growing crisis of authority provoked by official lying about the war in Vietnam. "Brazen mendacity by the federal government," wrote Peter Novick, "produced a concomitant increase in skepticism about 'official truth,' and, for some, about truth of any kind—not least the academic." Historians like Arthur Schlesinger Jr., who had ascended to high places, were among "the best and brightest" who justified the war. Now they were accused of being deceitful. Official lying by people "with impeccable scholarly credentials" furthered skepticism about the objectivity of liberal scholarship—the subject of withering critique by Noam Chomsky.[10]

Radical historians not only criticized the profession's pretensions to objectivity. We also objected to the veneer of genteel civility that covered up serious issues. We mounted a generational protest against the gentlemen's club that governed the profession. As the young historians of *Radical America* wrote, this club not only barred women, it exuded an "upper class tone carried over from the days when history was written principally by wealthy men of leisure" who produced "dry monographs and patriotic textbooks" written to reinforce "comfortable notions about the status quo."[11]

The Yale history department was that kind of "gentlemen's clubhouse." When I arrived, the famous faculty included no women or people of color. In the first year one of the women graduate students I knew dropped out, and the other suffered a nervous breakdown. One of the two African American students in the department spent as much time as he could in another city working at a community service agency in the black community. There was only one student in my cohort with ethnic working-class roots. At a sherry party for new graduate students this native of Paterson, New Jersey, met the official historian of Yale, George Wilson Pierson, who asked the student to explain his national origins.

Those of us excited by radical troublemaking in the professional association returned quietly to Yale, passing through its medieval gates and disappearing like monks into the dark corners of the immense library with its faux gargoyles. But even the downbeat New Haven campus would be roused by the Movement in the violent spring of 1970 when the murder trial of seven Black Panthers, including Party leaders Bobby Seale and Ericka Huggins, created a few weeks of high tension and political excitement.

On 14 April 1970 a courtroom scuffle broke out when court officers intercepted a note passed from one Panther official to another. When the judge sentenced the two black militants to six months in jail for contempt, the campus erupted in protest. Students turned many classes over to discussion of the impending trial. A Panther Defense Committee appeared to organize a mass demo on May Day. At a packed rally of 4,500 a week later in the whale-shaped Yale hockey rink, Reverend William Sloan Coffin, a leading opponent of the U.S. war in Vietnam, called for civil disobedience on the courthouse steps. Then one of the Panthers who had been arrested for contempt stole the march and had the crowd shouting "strike! strike! strike!" That night nine of the twelve residential colleges voted to do just that and to open their doors to protestors who would pour into New Haven for a May Day rally on the city green.[12] The graduate schools also voted to strike and I was elected to the overall student strike steering committee.

The Yalies packed up their stereos and headed home in their sports cars until they could return to safely take their exams. New Haven police mobilized and the National Guard stood at alert, fearful that a race riot could erupt on May 1. Student strikers even went out into white working-class neighborhoods to explain that the Panthers were framed and why the big May Day rally constituted no threat of violence. I remember ringing doorbells of the small homes in blue-collar West Haven and engaging housewives in rather interesting conversations about the trial of Bobby Seale. Yale's sophisticated president, Kingman Brewster, issued a sensational statement saying that he doubted a black revolutionary could get a fair trial in the present climate. Then he welcomed nonviolent protestors to the university, thus removing Yale itself as a target for the protest. Brewster incurred the wrath of Vice President Spiro T. Agnew, who tried to rouse the blue-blooded alumni against this class traitor. It all made great copy for Gary Trudeau's "Doonesberry" comic strips in the *Yale Daily News*.

Then, on April 30, the day before the big rally, President Nixon announced the invasion of Cambodia, a massive escalation of the war in Southeast Asia. The tense feelings aroused by the Panther trial suddenly reached a fever pitch.

The media predicted mayhem and bloodshed on May Day. But this doomsday forecast was wrong because students and faculty, radicals and liberals, organized to keep things nonviolent. The Black Panthers offered adroit leadership to the campus strike committee while they went into the "most explosive sections of the city" and kept things cool, "advised gangs of out-of-towners to take the shit out on their own time," and taught the student movement "that well-timed restraint is a great test of political sophistication."[13]

On a bright May Day our anxiety was relieved by listening to Allen Ginsburg recite his poems in a dining hall, by watching Jerry Rubin and Abbie Hoffman perform from the sanctuary of the staid Congregational church on the New Haven green, and by seeing the Yippies cavort in ritualized charges toward the police. Like other campus crowds that protested the Cambodian invasion, the thousands who joined a few Yale students and faculty exhibited what Maurice Isserman called "a kind of good-natured, redemptive millenialism"—a belief that the American people shared a desire for peace.[14] That night, as crowds gathered after a curfew, the National Guard moved in and tear-gassed the campus while the police beat up a few demonstrators.[15] But the May Day rally had been a success, mainly because the Panthers had, in the words of Francine DuPlessix Gray, demonstrated "the high political talent" to call a mass rally, win national publicity for their "political prisoners," and make the rights of Bobby Seale and the other Black Panthers "a cause to which a great university could rally."[16]

The call for a national moratorium to protest the war was followed by the stunning news of the students slain by National Guard troops at Kent State. These events, and then the shootings at Jackson State, created a sense of urgency among those of us organizing the Yale strike. We wanted to take advantage of the campus's May Day opening to pressure the university to take more responsibility in the New Haven community. The student strike committee demanded that Yale open a day care center for employees, stop construction of a social science center, and establish adult education courses for the community instead. We wanted the university to provide unemployment compensation for its workers and expand, rather than deplete, the city's housing stock. The Yale workers' union endorsed these points and some were later included in the demands on Yale made by seven Black and Puerto Rican neighborhood groups.[17] These protests were the first attempts to make this institution of vast wealth and power accountable to its workers and its neighbors in New Haven, a struggle that escalated in the 1980s and continues today.

An Uncomfortable Place

Leaving New Haven in the summer of 1970, I put the sixties behind me in more ways than one. I left with a lingering sense of euphoria created by the Movement coming together on one campus during those May Days. I encountered an entirely different mood on the campus where I began my first teaching job. When I arrived at Brandeis University, a small liberal arts school established by the Jewish American community in Waltham, Massachusetts, FBI agents were questioning faculty about radical students accused of committing a bank robbery in Brighton in which a police officer was killed. Among those wanted by the police were two Brandeis students, Susan Saxe and Katherine Ann Power. They were on the run—deep in the radical underground.

The Brandeis campus had been highly politicized in the 1960s when Angela Davis studied with Herbert Marcuse, but in 1970 it was an uncomfortable place to be a radical. Many faculty were deeply committed to the state of Israel and its war against Palestinian "terrorists." They were angry at the student left on campus and the faculty who nurtured it. I had been hired, I suppose, because of my Yale credentials, and because some of the activist graduate students wanted someone to teach social history. I still looked like a graduate student and could be seen at student meetings, where I felt more comfortable than I did with my senior colleagues who, in some cases, minced no words in putting down student radicals and New Left historians. One of the senior profs in my department was John P. Roche, a social democratic Cold Warrior who had worked as one of the White House intellectuals justifying U.S. intervention in Vietnam. When I met him, he said to me: "I suppose you think I was a whore for Lyndon Johnson."

During my first year as a university history instructor, I wrote an article for a New Left magazine about the dilemma of radical historians in the universities. I remained involved in the Radical Historians Caucus, trying to win support for resolutions to democratize the professional associations and to end the Vietnam War, but it seemed doubtful that these groups could defend radical teachers in jeopardy—activists like Staughton Lynd who, after being fired by Roosevelt University in 1969, became a "teacher in the Movement" setting up a "free school" in Chicago based on his experience with freedom schools in the civil rights movement.[18]

It also seemed unlikely that radical activities in the professions could link up with movement work in the real world. What would become of those radicals who remained in the academy? Would they be lost to the Movement after they swallowed what Lynd called the "bait of tenure"? Would they become the prisoners of abstract Marxist theory like the French professors of the left who, we joked, thought they were "building socialism book by book."[19] Or would they reject activism, like Professor Eugene Genovese, who insisted that "being a good historian" was "full-time work." Those of us who worried about being activists and scholars were the subjects of Genovese's scorn—those of us who, "never having been able to reconcile the warring tendencies within them, proclaim their neurotic indecision as a political principle and demand that everyone else adhere to it."[20]

Was it possible to be a movement historian in the university without becoming a neurotic? Could a scholar and teacher avoid the isolation and alienation of academic work and still connect with the independent activities the Movement generated? The prospects did not seem very favorable. Staughton Lynd not only lost his job. He was blacklisted. There was a Ph.D. glut and, ergo, a "job crisis." Those of us who won the coveted jobs weren't too sure we could keep them. As a first-year assistant professor, I was told by my department chairman that E. P. Thompson, my intellectual hero, did not write "real history." A year later the head told me that the department would not offer me a contract extension through my tenure-decision year. Writing movement history wasn't making for a successful academic career. The students rallied to support my struggle for a contract extension, the department split over the issue, and I was allowed to stay for three more years, but there would be no tenure bait for me to swallow.

These discouraging developments made me doubt that radical movement history would ever be accepted as "real history" by my professional colleagues. But my worries were allayed somewhat by senior historians outside my own department. Though he was an outspoken critic of student radicals, black power militants, and the New Left causes I espoused, Vann Woodward remained supportive of my work and endorsed my fight for a contract renewal. Melvyn Dubofsky, an accomplished labor historian, praised my early research on the Wobblies in the piney woods and cited it in his definitive history of the IWW, a book he wrote with objectivity but also with "sympathy and compassion for an old cause that still exists."[21] He also surprised me with an offer that seemed premature: a nomination to succeed him as visiting lecturer in labor history at the University of Warwick's Centre for the Study of Social History, then headed by E. P. Thompson.

As he did for so many others, Herbert Gutman took a visceral interest in my work and shared the joy of my discoveries. When I presented my first academic paper at the Negro History Association meetings in Birmingham, Alabama, he asked me up to his room where we went over my essay on the Brotherhood of Timber Workers line by line. He then amazed me by suggesting I send it to the state-of-the-art social history journal *Past & Present,* care of Eric Hobsbawm, the great British labor and social historian. Herb Gutman made me feel I was part of a crusade to remove workers from the narrow boxes in which they had been placed by historians who believed wage earners and their struggles were isolated from the rest of society and that in the South black and white workers were totally alienated from each other. Our mission was like that of the superb radical journal *Southern Exposure,* whose editors published labor history in the same vein. The periodical examined, in Gutman's words, how "several generations of Southern workers have confronted their oppression" and used their cultural resources to create "social and political movements" that helped to sustain "an egalitarian and democratic vision of the South."[22]

At a difficult time this kind of scholarly verification and friendly affirmation made it seem as though there might still be a place for a movement historian in a university. But in the early 1970s the most important support for my work came from outside the academy—from the movement activists who published the periodical *Radical America*. Paul Buhle and other graduate students at the University of Wisconsin founded *RA* in 1967 as "An SDS Journal of American Radicalism." It was a youthful effort to recover "hidden histories of resistance" and to uncover the social sources of radicalism in factory conditions and community life." When Buhle and fellow Madison editor Jim O'Brien moved the journal to Somerville, near Boston, they asked me to join the editorial collective in an effort to broaden "the format" and, in Buhle's words, "to make the mag more popular and more widely circulated." This was a fascinating prospect because *RA*'s move from Madison represented a symbolic break with the journal's roots in the student movement. It would now be "largely concerned with the history, development, and prospects of the American working class."

I met Paul and Mari Jo Buhle when I went to Madison in 1968 to talk with them about our mutual interest in the history of the old socialist movement. Paul and I shared a fascination with the Industrial Workers of the World, dismissed by most labor historians as marginal and romantic. To us, the Wobblies showed how direct action and solidarity could extend participatory democracy to the workplace and how even workers at the bottom of the workforce (like blacks and women in the 1960s) could be mobilized. The Wobs might even appeal to our own rebellious generation of industrial workers addicted to "youth culture." If "the IWW evoked romanticism," Buhle recalled, "we hoped to make the most of it."[23]

From the very beginning *Radical America* reflected the countercultural impulses in the New Left, opening itself to feminism, surrealism, anarchism, and to the kind of humor expressed in the underground newspapers of the day.[24] *RA* published a whole issue of comics (which sold thirty thousand copies) edited by Gilbert Shelton, "a history graduate school dropout with a proud anarchism." The juxtaposition of scholarly history articles with various expressions of youth counterculture may seem odd in retrospect, but, for a while, Buhle recalled, it caused no surprise. "We were all part of the same Movement."[25]

RA editors passionately rejected "the slogan-ridden Marxism-Leninism" of the factions who competed for SDS's legacy. In the spring of 1970 they bemoaned the breakup of SDS and the reversion to what one writer called the dead "frozen language of the bureaucratic left."[26] They concluded that "the student movement collapsed because it was too far removed from ordinary working men and women." In one way or another, the editors asserted, "Blue-collar America had to be an essential part of the movement's future constituency." Labor historian David Montgomery followed with a similar appeal in 1970 published as an *RA* pamphlet; it carried added weight, coming, as it did, from an experienced union militant who had suffered for his radical sympathies. Montgomery had worked in factories during the 1950s as a Communist and a militant member of the United Electrical Workers Union, which had been purged from the CIO in 1949 for refusing to support Cold War policies at home and abroad.[27] Montgomery's historical work helped young radical historians see "labor" not just as an ossified bureaucracy headed by hostile white men, but "as a *movement*" that could not be understood "simply by the study of union institutions."[28]

In order to assess contemporary workers' struggles *RA* editors drew upon critical Marxist theory developed by the European New Left, especially by the Italian revolutionaries who saw in the "hot autumn" of 1969 a genuinely autonomous workers' movement at odds with the corporations, the Communist Party, the big unions, and the social democratic state. They also reached back to ideas of C. L. R. James, the great West Indian writer and revolutionary strategist, who was, as Buhle recalled, "our greatest influence" in the late 1960s.[29]

James wrote insightfully on many subjects—on Hegel and Marx, on West Indian cricket and Pan-Africanism, on Herman Melville and Toussaint L'Ouverture, commander of the Haitian revolution. Born in Trinidad, James lived in Britain during the 1930s, where he joined the Trotskyist movement and helped form the Pan-African nationalist movement. He came to the United States in 1938 and emerged as a leader of opposition groups within the Trotskyist Workers Party. Until his deportation from the United States in 1953, he wrote essays and books calling for a return to Marxist fundamentals. "The Moscow tradition" ruined Marxism, he said in a later interview. Marxism had been perverted by Stalinism and cynically undone in modern Communist nations where, he argued, state capitalism ruled the workers. Alienation afflicted workers in the Soviet Union and Eastern Europe just as it did in the United States and Western Europe, declared James and his comrades in *Facing Reality*.[30]

James's "respect for ordinary people, his conviction that society's rank and file are about to remake the world, gave ordinary activities . . . a place in the masses' centuries' long march toward freedom," as one perceptive writer put it. Instead of lecturing workers on correct political lines, movement intellectuals should make their views known "as a contribution to that democratic interchange and confrontation of opinion" that would be the "very life blood of a socialist society." What a contrast to the rhetorical vanguardism of the new Marxist-Leninist parties-in-formation whose cadre of former student radicals defined the "correct line" on almost everything.[31]

A Shadow Alternative

James's ideas helped *RA* writers discover the hidden power workers exercised in society. It took a "big gulp of persuasion to swallow whole" James's belief that socialism advanced inexorably, stage by stage, "as a shadow alternative under capitalism," Paul Berman remarked. But even if it was hard to see the signs James saw of the "invading socialist society," his work contributed a great deal to those who believed industrial society could be transformed from within. At a time when many former student radicals looked to Third World revolutionaries for inspiration, James told us to look deep into our own society to find the seeds of liberation.[32]

Applying James's ideas to labor history, George Rawick wrote an important essay on "working class self-activity" showing how the workers' movement helped save the United States from fascism in the 1930s by forming the CIO and strengthening democratic politics. Laborers took their own initiative during the Great Depression because craft unions ignored unskilled proletarians in basic industry. These "workers had to look to their own resources and to whatever aid they could receive from radical organizations," said Rawick. When unions responded to this "self-activity," officials usually tried to restrain rank-and-file militancy, for example in the sit-down strikes of the 1930s. Thus, the radical potential of working-class self-activity remained unfulfilled.[33]

Rawick's essay was followed by others in *RA* aimed at "destroying the myths held by the Movement about the working class."[34] New Left theorists had argued that blue-collar workers had simply been "bought off" by consumerism and that they, like their leaders, had been co-opted by "corporate liberalism," a term coined by historians who wrote for *Studies on the Left,* a journal that ceased publication in 1967.[35] *Radical America* editors criticized the co-optation theorists for pessimistically reading back into the past the discouraging mood of the sixties about the prospects for a revived workers' movement.[36] Radical Americans saw the potential for a new movement in various forms of rank-and-file militancy in the past, the sit-down strikes, for example, but they also saw some potential in the present as well—in the wildcat strikes in the coal fields and auto plants. Blue-collar youth were rebelling against authority on the shop floor while some of those in uniform were protesting the war in Vietnam.

"As the present grew worse, especially in terms of Left political initiatives, the working-class past grew more lustrous and fascinating," Paul Buhle remembered. For the radical history graduate student of the time, this past posed an exciting intellectual challenge: to search beneath the surface of trade union conservatism to discover hidden sources of opposition to capitalism's regime.[37] Buhle took Marxism seriously but refused to be trapped in a discourse about the sterile dogmas. Instead of returning religiously to old texts, the "Radical Americans" proposed a Marxism that valued culture, not as "superstructure," but as the basis for other forms of radicalism like black nationalism, feminism, and the anti-authoritarianism of a youthful counterculture. Buhle later said that *RA* writers tried to open up the "darkened rooms" where Marxists debated so as to ventilate those chambers with "the fresh air that contemporary movements breathed into the left."[38]

A Complicated View of the Lower Classes

RA's search for oppositional veins in labor history coincided with a strong impulse to understand black history and women's history. The civil rights movement provided a model. "Blacks have shown the role history plays in defining a social movement," wrote the authors of a sixty-page essay connecting women's history to the current concerns of the feminist movement. According to Mari Jo Buhle, Ann D. Gordon, and Nancy Schrom, women were "returning to historical questions in search of their collective identity and for an analysis of their condition." This article, published in 1971, was highly influential and widely reprinted and set an agenda for *RA*'s future work promoting a "feminism informed by history."[39]

In the same year, *RA* published another influential historical essay: Hal Baron's tour de force on the "political economy of racism" in which he explored the threat black workers posed to smoothly functioning capitalist order and emphasized the unfulfilled "potential of black-oriented working-class political leadership."[40] Like the authors of the essay on women's history, Baron adopted a class-conscious approach to movement history without neglecting the enormous divisions within the working class. In both essays, history helped women and blacks to "define the *specificity* of their oppression."[41] While Marxist-Leninist sects explained these oppressions with old-fashioned class analysis, *RA* editors published historical studies of conflicts within the working class along lines of race and gender.[42] As a result, the journal played a part in "one of the intellectual advances of our time," according to Paul Berman, "the revolution in American social history," which provided "an infinitely more detailed, complicated view of the American lower classes."[43]

A Household Industry

I joined the *Radical America* editorial collective a year after its move to Boston, actually to Somerville, where we met for most of the 1970s. The student movement phase of our lives had ended but we hoped our generation of radicals would play a new role in the real world. We hoped to write about history and politics for movement activists and for intellectuals who taught working-class students. We often heard from activists, students, and teachers who used our articles (and the pamphlets produced by the New England Free Press) in college courses, study groups, organizing campaigns, and various educational activities. The journal attracted a small but loyal readership from these radicals who kept movement culture alive in political groups of community organizers and factory colonizers, radical professional caucuses, cooperative printing and publishing shops, women's consciousness-raising groups, prisoner outreach activities, defense committees, antiwar protest organizations, and even alternative institutions.

Feeling isolated and frustrated in my university department, I found this supportive setting one in which to practice movement history. It would become my movement school—an island of movement culture to inhabit, a place apart from my departmentalized university place. It was a different kind of place altogether, one of those, Edward Thompson said, that "socialist intellectuals must occupy, some territory that is their own . . . where no one works for grades or for tenure but for the transformation of society." In these places there would be "fierce" criticism and self-criticism but there would also be "mutual help" and the exchange of "theoretical and practical knowledge."[44]

Thompson offered us a model of someone who wrote history with grace and power but not for "the academic public." He wrote his great book, *The Making of the English Working Class*, thinking about the left and about the audience he had first encountered as an adult education tutor "in evening classes of working people, trade unionists, teachers and so on."[45] Thompson's writing about plebeian life offered workers "a new past to live from," wrote Marcus Rediker, a different "social memory" that allowed readers to think "forward to a new set of possibilities."[46]

Of course, Thompson did not simply record and retell stories about people making their own history when he wrote his master narrative of the early English working class. He also posed moral questions about the past, questions derived from radical politics, humanist values, and socialist theories. Yet, he subjected abstract Marxist theory to withering criticism and refused to ignore "the disasters of real socialist theory" as reflected in repressive socialist states. So, he understood history as more than a reading of past experience, more than a telling of heroic stories. The historian needed to interrogate past experience, to engage it with informed questions honed by theoretical inquiry.[47]

Though my intellectual heroes, Thompson and Staughton Lynd, left the academy to work as movement historians and social critics, I remained in the university, but tried, as Lynd suggested, to keep one leg outside. As a young historian with an academic job and salaried "gig," I encountered my share of prejudice from Movement activists who scorned scholarly work. Against the residual anti-intellectualism of the New Left cadre, *Radical America* "upheld the idea [of] serious thought and hard brain work" and cultivated historical and theoretic writing and thinking among activists outside the academy.[48] It also compelled those of us who were history professors to learn how to write for activists. Besides learning new writing and editing skills, we needed to acquire some production skills. Except for the final printing, each issue of the magazine was manufactured entirely by our volunteer collective: we needed to create a cooperative mode of production, to divide all tasks of writing, editing, corresponding, and layout on some equitable basis. Like other comrades who published radical journals in those days, we created a "household industry."[49]

I joined the editorial group a little while after Linda Gordon came on board. She was also teaching history in a university and was drawn to a collective committed to "more popular kinds of work."[50] Though we were the only editors with academic jobs as historians, most of the others were as immersed as we were in movement history. Paul Buhle was about to depart the collective and leave a legacy of open-minded inquiry that would guide our explorations of movement history in the 1970s. Shortly after I arrived, we were joined by Margery Davies, who was writing her Ph.D. thesis at Brandeis on the feminization of clerical work. Frank Brodhead, researching a Ph.D. dissertation on British history at Princeton, worked as a staff member for the radical group RESIST and contributed a vast range of historical knowledge to our work. Jim Kaplan, a tenant organizer, expressed a strong point of view about the libertarian lessons to be drawn from workers' history about race and class. Allen Hunter, an SDS leader at Madison, taught high school social studies and read an amazing range of critical theory he could apply to our discussions. After taking her leave of the Harvard history department, and skewering its members in the *Harvard Crimson,* Ann Withorn continued to practice as a human service worker while she pursued a different intellectual course: a historical study of how radical movements like the Farm Workers' union provided social services to the poor.

The editor who helped me the most was Jim O'Brien. He had completed a dissertation at Wisconsin on the origins of the American New Left and continued to write about the U.S. Left throughout the seventies with more knowledge and insight than anyone else. Jim drew me into the work of the New England area chapter of the Radical Historians Caucus which included non-academic conferences on radical history in 1972 and 1973, a newsletter (which he still helps to edit), and two bibliographies on working-class history published by the New England Free Press, where he worked for many years as an all-around printer and editor, first in the South End and then in Somerville's Union Square.[51] Like many others I benefited from his superb editorial skills, his sharp historical judgments, and his realistic political assessments. Jim O'Brien kept us from taking ourselves, and our ideas, too seriously. He wrote in the kind of satirical tradition lost to most New Left intellectuals. From his tongue-in-cheek review of the Bible as an academic history book in an early *RA* number to his 1982 classic, "North American History from the Standpoint of the Beaver," Jim kept us laughing while we were talking and thinking.[52] In 1973 he teamed up with another Wisconsin alum, the artist Nick Thorkelson, to produce a cartoon history of the United States for *RA* that sold twenty thousand copies here, and then was translated into Italian. Five years later they offered readers cartoon theory in their "Marxist analysis of baseball."[53]

A Period of Discovery

As soon as I joined the *RA* collective in August of 1972, comrades asked me to make a contribution to movement history: to review the labor history of the 1930s for a special issue on worker militancy in the Great Depression.[54] I jumped at the chance to contribute to an issue that would include an article by Staughton Lynd on the "possibilities of radicalism" in the early thirties. This study emerged from his oral history work with militants who, as young steel workers, had risen up against the AFL union bureaucrats.[55]

The other article accepted for the issue was written by two students who had been active in the Movement at Harvard. Their experience of discovering movement history in a remote corner of America represented a particularly exciting encounter between young historians and the heroes of causes lost but not forgotten. At the Radical Historians Caucus workshop on oral history in 1972, Dale Rosen and Ted Rosengarten told us about their research on the Communist-led Alabama Sharecroppers Union of the 1930s and their discovery of a union activist named Ned Cobb.[56] They had been "combing through Talapoosa County court records and local newspapers" and had acquired a "white man's version" of the Union's early days. Ready to leave with this research in hand—that is, "the written account of what had happened"—they learned that the "villain" of the story was still living in the county. On a cold day in January 1969 they went out to meet him. After they shook hands, the old man said he was always happy to see his people. He meant movement people—the young northern whites in blue shirts who had worked on voter registration drives and marched in Selma and Montgomery. Cobb was not surprised to see them; it was a moment his own movement experience told him to expect. The young historians began by asking Cobb why had he joined the union back in 1932. He began, telling one story and then another and then another for eight hours. This story Rosengarten soon fashioned into the powerful book *All God's Dangers*.[57] It was the most compelling of the many "oppositional narratives" that appeared in the 1970s.[58]

A Mini-Movement of Historians

Working with the *Radical America* and with the Radical Historians Caucus in 1972 allowed me to join a mini-movement of radical historians to recover lost fragments of an alternative history that we could then share with others, especially with activists. But we also wanted to reach a growing academic audience of students and faculty open to the new history. Some of our mentors, Herbert Gutman and David Montgomery, Eric Foner and Alice Kessler-Harris, for example, had emerged as leading scholars of American history. Their success encouraged us as did the continuing influence of the brilliant British social historians Christopher Hill, Eric Hobsbawm, and E. P. Thompson, who still wrote in the Marxist tradition and published in the journal *Past & Present,* now considered at the cutting edge of historical scholarship.

For a few days in 1973 at Rutgers University during the Anglo-American Conference on Social History, all of us came together to discuss and celebrate our work. Herb Gutman presided over the ensuing intellectual carnival like a gleeful ringmaster, nodding his approval of this paper and that, grabbing us novices by the arm to introduce us to the British writers we admired so much. I arrived at the conference when Edward Thompson held the floor. It was the first time I had seen him in action—a dramatic-looking white-haired figure, he reminded me of the English actor Peter O'Toole. He stood in the midst of the vast crowd turning around slowly as he spoke, almost as if playing to a London audience, at a theater in the round. He spoke dramatically of customs English poor people kept in common and used to protect themselves and their culture against the gentry and the crown. In the lunchroom, Thompson held court, embracing the attention of younger historians who had been excited by his work and his example. For me there would never be another conference such as this.

Of course there was plenty of debate. Even Thompson faced some sharp queries about the women missing from his *Making of the English Working Class*. The dean of British Marxist historians, Eric Hobsbawm, took aim at New Left historians for allowing ideology to control their study of history. Lean and gaunt, peering through black-rimmed glasses, the don of socialist historians appeared owlish on the platform but he spoke with a kind of casualness cultivated in frequenting jazz clubs and plebeian pubs. Hobsbawm used Staughton Lynd's *Radical America* article as an example of what was wrong with studies that focused on "what might have been." The discovery of working-class resistance was exciting, Hobsbawm granted, but he wondered if the new movement historians harbored fantastic notions about what had been possible in past time.[59] I found Hobsbawm's objections a bit academic especially in light of the excellent contribution Staughton and Alice Lynd had made that year by publishing their collection of "personal histories by rank and file organizers." Their book showed in case after eloquent case how local militants had fought to keep the labor movement from being centralized and bureaucratized.[60]

I commented on a paper by David Montgomery in which he emphasized the militancy and solidarity of skilled craft workers in their struggles during the 1910s. Emboldened by my experience in weekly *Radical America* arguments about history and politics, I criticized the paper for being too positive about the AFL's craft unions.[61] When I met Montgomery before our session I was nervous, but he put me at ease and joked about the tone of my remarks. He spoke to me, not as someone who had criticized his work, but as a comrade and fellow worker in the movement history shop.

Montgomery readily agreed to contribute to a *Radical America* symposium I organized on the popular book *Strike!* by Jeremy Brecher, a radical historian who shared our New Left antipathy to bureaucracy and our fascination with the creativity and spontaneity that characterized the mass struggles of working people. Montgomery reminded us that while bonds of mutuality among workers could be the basis of resistance, it took deliberate action by strong leaders to move beyond opposition to a struggle for control. "Very small and very courageous minorities," frequently led by conscious leftists, often made the difference in the outcome of these struggles. Defiance of authority was not enough to build a workers' movement, Montgomery argued. Rank-and-file insurgencies needed to find leaders to further their struggle, to make it more conscious and deliberate.[62]

Throughout the mid-seventies *RA* published articles about various kinds of oppositional activity among workers from the past and the present. Some of them delighted "in the discovery of militant tactics per se"—the kind of thing Montgomery cautioned against. The best of them examined the mutual relationships workers formed on the job and showed how they became the basis of more conscious and deliberate actions. For example, Mike Davis's sharply written article, "The Stop Watch and the Wooden Shoe," about IWW resistance to scientific management, and Dorothy Fennell's superb participant-observer report on life "beneath the surface" of official labor relations in an electrical manufacturing plant.[63] Writers like these revealed, as Casey Blake later observed, that our working-class history was "far richer, far more turbulent, and far more complex than anyone would have imagined from its treatment at the hands of earlier historians, even those on the left."[64]

A Debate about Race, Gender, and Class

Of course, race relations added profoundly to the complexity of working-class history and politics. In 1974 we published an article by Noel Ignatiev, who argued that racism governed white workers' "class" consciousness. He based this argument on his experience as a steel mill worker and on his historical study of white racism, which, he argued, explained the popular acceptance of "capitalist rule."[65] Some *RA* editors looked for a more complicated explanation. But those of us who were involved in community-based organizations in the Boston area could readily see that there was no hope for unified movement building because of the rigid segregation of life in Boston and the particularly obnoxious forms of racism that prevailed in the city's neighborhoods and institutions, private and public.

When the federal court issued its order desegregating the Boston public schools, everyone waited tensely for the city to explode, and it did. When the buses started rolling in the fall of 1974, mobs of whites attacked black school children on their way to and from school, and all people of color feared for their safety. In defense of their neighborhood schools, local people supported organized white resistance groups whose leaders often encouraged racial hostilities. For weeks Boston seemed to teeter on the brink of race war.

Radical America people joined in antiracist work that included organizing for a massive "defend the children" demonstration and house sitting with a black family under attack by white gangs in Dorchester.[66] We also decided to publish an editorial about why movement people everywhere needed to support court-ordered desegregation, even though it seemed, to many leftists, like a throwback to the "liberal" civil rights efforts of the sixties that had been strongly criticized by black power advocates and white "revolutionaries." Indeed, to some radicals who now led communist groups, the Boston busing order seemed to be a "plot" to divide the working class. A few liberals and self-styled populists were saying that the violence in Boston was based as much, if not more, on class resentment as on race hatred.[67]

The editorial Allen Hunter and I wrote for *RA* took a different view. Because Boston neighborhoods suffered from unemployment, poor housing, and inadequate schools, it had been tempting "for liberal journalists and leftist groups alike to explain away white working-class racism as a product of 'lower-class frustration.'" These critics of busing romanticized "the ethnic pride and community solidarity of neighborhoods like South Boston" and de-emphasized the racism that arose in defense of "community schools."[68] They also ignored "a determined civil rights drive" Boston blacks had begun decades earlier. School desegregation was, we argued, an extension of movement history, not a product of manipulation by a few elites. Even though the busing plan provoked conflict, it deserved the support of all activists interested in building a progressive working-class movement of whites and blacks. It seemed obvious to us that there was no way to go around racial conflict to forge working-class unity, as some left groups proposed. Travelers on the road to solidarity needed to confront the dragons of racism; there was no safe passage around them. "The only hope for working-class unity in Boston," we wrote, "lies in a direct assault on segregation in all its forms and in an organized defense against the racist attacks which segregation fosters."[69]

At the same time, *RA* probed the problem of racism in the past and present, and it explored women's history more deeply, as part of an effort to bring feminist insights to movement politics. When I joined the collective, only two women served as editors, but during the mid-seventies more women came on board until we were what Linda Gordon called a "sexually equal group."[70] The editors looked more critically at the journal's emphasis on "the working class." In the early seventies many writers seemed devoted to a kind of "workerism"—a romance with the shop floor militants who stood up to the bosses. These writers had offered fascinating subjective accounts of alienation and resistance on the job, often highlighting the role of informally organized work groups as foci of resistance.[71] But they failed to explore the cultural character of white male work groups; they also ignored the misogyny of floor life, which turned male worker solidarity against women.[72]

Marxists had not provided a "good definition of what class is for women," wrote the editors of a special issue on women's labor in 1973. For women, they argued, class was an experience to be "understood not just in the shop but also at home, in bed, and in movie theaters."[73] Subsequently, feminist authors did write articles about contemporary working-class life that examined the politics of housework and cultural activities like watching daytime television, organizing parties to sell plastic food containers (Tupperware), and enjoying family camping trips. They also explained how working-class women used various free spaces like beauty parlors, battered women's shelters, and self-help groups for their own purposes.[74]

Taking Leave and Taking Stock

I took a leave from *RA* in 1975 to spend a year in Britain where I made contact with many socialists involved in community-based working-class history projects, in workers' education, and in shop floor politics. This was a time when the powerful British unions were making their last stand against capital and the state. Before leaving the United States I introduced a special issue of the journal on U.S. labor in the 1940s—the most comprehensive effort the journal made to explore working-class life and labor politics in a critical period. It also attempted—without fully succeeding—to incorporate a sensitivity to race and gender issues in working-class life. "American Labor in the 1940's" was a vintage *RA* production with lots of photos and wartime art, including an evocative painting of Boston Navy Yard by Calvin Burnett, an African American artist who worked there. The issue highlighted the numerous wildcat strikes by defense plant workers during World War II who rebelled against frozen wages, extended work days, and lethal conditions. These spontaneous rank-and-file actions—which verified *RA*'s search for worker resistance at "the point of production"—took on a larger political meaning in the accounts we published. The wildcats challenged organized labor's "no strike pledge" and the government's phony slogan that all Americans made "equal sacrifices" on the home front. The walkouts unsheathed the only weapon the rank and file could use against the submission required by big labor, industrial capital, and the wartime garrison state.[75]

Stan Weir's wonderful memoir of the 1946 general strike in Oakland, California, exuded the same spirit. It began when truck drivers and streetcar operators walked off the job to support striking department store saleswomen. "The city filled with workers," recalled Weir, who had been a merchant seaman during the war. After milling about downtown for several hours, they then "organized themselves" to shut down all stores except pharmacies and food markets. For twenty-four hours a carnival spirit prevailed. The strikers allowed bars to remain open but prohibited the sale of hard liquor. Bartenders put their jukeboxes on the sidewalks and played tunes free of charge. The number one hit song, "Pistol Packin' Mama, Lay That Pistol Down," echoed off the buildings as couples danced in the streets. "The participants were making history, knew it, and were having fun," Weir wrote in a way that celebrated one of those moments in people's history *Radical America* had always searched to find.[76]

But the euphoria didn't last. After workers closed down the city for another day and prevented access by anyone without a "passport" (a union card), the Oakland general strike ended without any concessions to the women retail clerks. This debacle was a small example of the larger failure of the workers' movement to break through the state-dominated industrial relations system that had contained workplace struggles—the same system that had forced the new industrial unions to become more centralized, less democratic, and more concerned with limited economic gains, developments illustrated in the articles by Nelson Lichtenstein and Ronald Schatz on CIO unions in the defense industries.[77]

The special issue on labor in the 1940s represented a high point of *RA*'s efforts to uncover hidden sources of resistance in the workplace and to explore how labor officials combined with the state to limit the potential growth of a labor movement controlled by the rank and file. The issue also revealed the shortcomings of our efforts. It did not fully explore how women and people of color were excluded from the very informal work groups of white men that led the wildcat strikes, including a few "hate strikes" against African Americans. It did not explain why most defense workers labored under wartime constraints and hardships without protest, why most of them seemed content with highly centralized unions that "delivered the goods." It did not explore the downside of wartime strikes which made John L. Lewis, a popular figure in the 1930s, a public enemy during World War II when he ordered union coal miners to launch illegal walkouts. Finally, our consistent criticism of Communist Party conduct during the war years (when its leaders supported the no-strike pledge and favored overtime work) stopped short of fully evaluating the negative consequences of the CIO purge of leftists in 1949–50 which deprived the movement of its best organizers and most active opponents of racism, sexism, and Cold War militarism.[78]

Comradely critics within the collective and outside of it pointed out these shortcomings, and we accepted their criticisms, hoping our future efforts in labor movement history would become even more comprehensive. We were actually aware by 1975 that the rank-and-file rebellions of previous years were not going to coalesce into a new kind of radical movement, and we knew that our emphasis on shop-floor spontaneity missed important political questions: questions about gender, culture, sexuality, and race relations that absorbed the collective's attention in the late 1970s. In this vein *RA* published two important articles on shop floor struggles written from female perspectives, Mary Bularzik's historical study of sexual harassment and Susan Porter Benson's essay on the "clerking sisterhood" among department store saleswomen.[79]

RA's hopeful search for hidden expressions of working-class rebellion gave way to a far less romantic exploration of unions as they actually existed. The New Left dream of an "extra union" movement of rank-and-file workers and community activists—a new IWW—faded as we focused more on the struggles for democracy and autonomy within existing unions.

I returned from England eager to explore these struggles and report on them for *RA*. I solicited two articles about contemporary wildcat strikes by former student radicals who had become shop floor activists in two large production plants owned by General Motors and General Electric. I was now one of the few *Radical America* editors who maintained contact with independent radicals struggling within their plants and unions.[80] They reported on a growing sense of frustration among union members faced with an onslaught by corporate employers and a timid response by entrenched union leaders.

In the fall of 1977 this tension exploded on a national level during the coal miners' strike that soon became a highly-charged test of whether rank-and-file workers could beat back the concessions their union officers seemed willing to make to aggressive employers. In the winter of 1978 I traveled to the storm center of the miners' resistance in West Virginia with *RA* editor Frank Brodhead to report on a strike that had become a rank-and-file movement against corporate greed. It was an eye-opening experience. Southern West Virginia was wildcat country and we went there in the midst of a nationwide outlaw strike. The United Mine Workers of America faced hostile coal operators with an honest but inept leadership in disarray, unable to satisfy either the truculent employers or the militant members. UMWA officials accepted many "take-aways" the industry demanded, but when they put the contract out for a vote, the rank and file rejected the concessions. Union miners then launched a virtual insurrection against their own leaders, who called for an end to the strike. President Jimmy Carter issued a back-to-work order, only to see the miners defy it.[81]

Traveling in West Virginia during the hard winter of 1978, we could see the mood of defiance written on the glum faces of picketers. Like other radicals, we saw in grassroots militancy the energy for a new democratic labor movement. The miners' resistance seemed to augur a new era of class struggle. But their willpower and solidarity did not strengthen other unions facing a determined assault by corporate America. Several years earlier, *RA* associate Stan Weir, an experienced union militant, had written that while rank-and-file groups had rejected many of the sweetheart deals their union representatives negotiated, and had even used massive wildcat strikes as part of their protest, they had not been able to coordinate their activities on a regional or national level or to mobilize a new kind of workers' power to replace institutionalized collective bargaining. By the late 1970s the new democratic labor movement Weir envisioned had not emerged. There was still formidable resistance to "alternative ideas from the rank and file."[82]

Most of the *RA* editors supported my continuing efforts to write about workers' history and politics, but movement politics were now concerned far more with cultural issues than workplace problems. Some of the editors simply objected to articles focused on white male miners and factory workers. They wanted to turn the journal's attention to different subjects—to issues of gender, race, sexuality, and cultural identity, and to the new concerns raised by international liberation struggles in the postindustrial world.

I learned a great deal from the other editors about "the new social move-

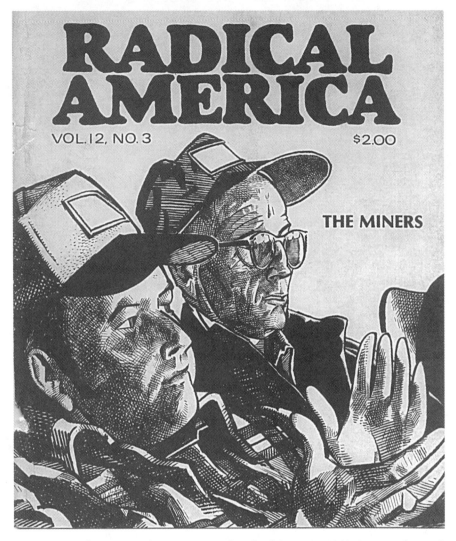

Depicting coal miners' militancy: cover of *Radical America,* 1978. Drawing by Nick Thorkelson based on author's photograph of a Miner's Right to Strike rally in Beckley, West Virginia, 20 March 1978. *Courtesy of the artist.*

ments" of the time, and from writers who contributed incisive reports from the field to *RA*'s "From the Movement" section. It was obvious by 1979 that cultural issues concerning "the family, sex, religion, crime, abortion, homosexuality" raised far more popular anxiety than economic issues, and that the New Right had seized the initiative on these issues. Moreover, as Linda Gordon and Allen Hunter pointed out, feminism had become the far right's main target. The New

Left that once raised the banner of cultural liberation was long gone, and now radicals, outside the women's movement, could muster no serious response to the New Right. Those Marxists who saw issues of family and sexuality in hard class terms had completely missed the boat, as far as we were concerned.[83]

As a movement historian who focused on workers' struggles, it also appeared to me that women's history reflected movement needs much more than labor history, because feminist historians seemed so closely connected to women's struggles. Labor historians had failed to make this kind of connection with union activists, and our historical work had still not provided a "critical, political edge" to the debates about change within the labor movement. I envied sister historians like Linda Gordon whose historical work seemed to have clear implications for movement strategy. Indeed, her own book on birth control, published at a time when abortion was a crucial issue for the women's movement, made an impact, reached a wide audience, and aroused a hysterically negative response from a few male historians.[84]

In 1980 I took leave from the collective, but continued to write articles about race, class, and culture. In 1983 I edited a *Radical America* "Reader" entitled *Workers' Struggles, Past & Present,* which served as a retrospective on more than a decade of creative historical and political discussion about U.S. workers, their points of conflict, and their experiences of solidarity. That discussion offered activists a better understanding of what had gone wrong with the labor movement and what could be seen, in retrospect, as neglected opportunities and unrecognized possibilities.

My experience as a member of the *Radical America* collective made me a movement historian. The journal provided a political community and a free space for critical debate and comradely cooperation. It served as a communications center that connected us with hundreds of activists in the United States and around the world engaged in movement work during the 1970s. It operated as a school for learning about all kinds of liberation politics created by oppressed people and for studying how those people created their own protest movements and visions of a just society.

RA's largest readership came from New Leftists who had made the long march through graduate school and were then teaching in a variety of educational settings from public high schools to elite universities. Writing movement history for this audience and for a small group of activists in workplace and community struggles required translating historical scholarship and some political theory into plain language with pointed analysis. Some articles we published failed to meet the challenge. They were written voluntarily and often in great haste by activists and intellectuals busy with other pressing matters. Rereading some of my old *RA* articles is not always a pleasant experience. But it was the kind of practice required of someone who wanted to do history for movement people. This kind of experience was unavailable to me in the academic world, which demanded an entirely different kind of writing.

Radical America gave me the intellectual and political confidence to under-take a popular survey of labor history in the twentieth century, a project for which I was academically unprepared. *The World of the Worker,* published in 1980, reflected *Radical America's* approach to working-class history, with its strengths and its weaknesses. Unlike other labor history texts, the book made an effort to focus on workers themselves in their shops, communities, and families, as well as on their organizations and their leaders. The interpretation was based on the notion best expressed by David Montgomery that a "mutual-ism" developed in workers' "daily struggle for control of the circumstances of their lives." It appeared in their "values, loyalties and thoughts" as well as their everyday actions. It was reflected in struggles for control that moved from "the spontaneous to the deliberate as workers consciously and jointly decide what they want and how to get it." No socialist movement could emerge within the working class unless it was rooted in these working and living habits.[85]

The book gained a greater readership than I expected, not only among stu-dents of labor history, a growing field in the 1980s, but also among union educators and their students who believed in the need for a strong, radical labor movement, who trusted the instincts of rank-and-file members but were disillu-sioned and disgusted with the union officialdom that ruled the house of labor. This audience appreciated the "consciousness-raising solutions" one critic said I presented to complex problems. The book, like my articles in *RA,* was not as easy to read as it should have been, and therefore was not accessible enough to a wider audience. The writing was burdened by attempts to combine compelling narratives of labor's most dramatic stories with convincing analyses of what went wrong with the movement in crucial periods.[86]

The book addressed questions about racism, sexism, trade union authoritari-anism, and anti-Communism that had been neglected in previous surveys. This too was a legacy of *RA's* insistence on embracing a complicated view of working-class life with all its contradictions. It was part of our effort to give labor history that "critical edge" it often seemed to lack. But *The World of the Worker* de-pended too much on blaming the misleaders of labor—the union bureaucrats and labor fakirs—for everything that went wrong. Its emphasis on the sup-pressed potential of a militant rank and file—so much a part of union politics in the 1970s—was not balanced with an explanation of why union members often accepted business unionism or why they abandoned the social unionism radical and progressive leaders advocated.

The extremely rich body of labor history scholarship produced in the last twenty years offers a vastly more intricate understanding of working-class life, union politics, and movement building. It is also an understanding shaped by two decades of assault on working people and their organizations and by a rebirth of a social movement impulse within labor's ranks. I hope to convey some of this in rewriting *The World of the Worker.*

Indeed, it is clearer now than it was then that our society needs a strong, inclusive labor movement controlled by the rank and file, a movement that can learn from a critical understanding of its past, one that can value those moments of solidarity *RA* celebrated without neglecting the ways in which the labor movement limited its own appeal to a minority of working people. *Radical America*'s approach to workers' struggles reflected the intellectual and political concerns of the late 1960s and 1970s, a time when we emphasized and sometimes exaggerated the potential of working people as agents of social change—a time when we hoped that a new autonomous workers' movement would replace the old moribund organizations whose leaders no longer aspired to change society.

Our expectations have changed and so have the possibilities for change within the existing labor movement. The problems of future movement building posed in the rest of this book consider existing labor organizations as important arenas in which these problems will be solved. But true to my *Radical America* roots, I also expect more new movements for workers' power and social justice to emerge outside the house of labor. What I learned from *RA* and what others learned is that these emergent movements will provide much of the energy and creativity workers will need to gain some control over the future.

Publicizing people's history: Massachusetts History Workshop brochure, 1984. Drawing by Nick Thorkelson. *Courtesy of the artist.*

CHAPTER 2

"Bringing the Boundaries of History Closer to People's Lives". The Massachusetts History Workshop

In 1976, while I was in Britain, E. J. Hobsbawm invited me to present a paper at his social history seminar in Birkbeck College, University of London. A few years earlier he had helped me publish my first attempt at movement history in a British journal. He still held an interest in what he called my "redneck radicals," the "social bandits" I discovered in the old Indian territory of Oklahoma who robbed banks like socialist Robin Hoods, like the "primitive rebels" Hobsbawm had studied.[1] I decided to speak about New Left labor historians whom Hobsbawm had criticized and to defend Staughton Lynd's brand of "guerilla history," in which working-class activists remembered how labor unions became bureaucratized and imagined what they might have become.[2]

After the seminar, we adjourned to a pub near the British Museum where I met Hobsbawm's students. The most friendly was a woman named Anna Davin, who was working with him on a dissertation about London's children. Anna was familiar with *Radical America* from her earlier student days at Warwick University where she studied with Edward Thompson. She greeted me warmly as comrades in the movement did in those days and immediately told me about the History Workshop group in which she was an active participant.

Later, Anna took me on a memorable walking tour of people's history sites in old London and told me about her efforts to aid local residents in recovering their past. We shared our sense of excitement about the new social history being written about working people in the United Kingdom and the United States. I confessed my frustration that radical historians in the United States were isolated in history departments far removed from the working people we wanted to reach and from the protest movements we supported.[3] Anna insisted that it didn't have to be that way, that the boundary around academic history could be stretched, that we could breach the wall scholars erected between the past

51

and the present. No one ever excited me about doing people's history the way Anna Davin did.

Ruskin and Oxford

Anna introduced me to the History Workshop's founder Raphael Samuel, a pioneer in social history who was history tutor at Ruskin College, a school for workers in Oxford. During the 1950s when he was called Ralph, Samuel had been "simultaneously the pariah and heart-and-soul of the Oxford political scene," according to his college mate Stuart Hall. Steeped in the culture of the British Communist Party, inherited from his talented mother, Ralph found his world blown apart by the Soviet suppression of the Hungarian workers' revolt in 1956. Intellectually and emotionally convulsed, he was rescued from a prolonged breakdown by Christopher Hill, the great socialist historian at Oxford University, who recommended Samuel for a position as tutor to the trade unionists at Ruskin College. Samuel commuted from London, where he pursued his passionate love affair with the East End—its history, politics, and popular culture.[4]

While at Ruskin, he became known as an eccentric but inspiring teacher who identified with the seasoned trade unionists living uncomfortably in Oxford and striving to express themselves intellectually. In 1966 Samuel joined his students in creating the History Workshop "as an attack on the examination system, and the humiliations it imposed on adult students." Instead of demanding a mastery of great books, he asked students to read the original historical sources and to become real historians instead of passive readers. This "alternative educational practice" was intended "to encourage Ruskin students—working men and women drawn from the labour . . . movement—to engage in research, and to construct their own history." Samuel argued that "adult students, far from being educationally underprivileged—the working definition adopted by the college authorities—were peculiarly well placed to write about many facets of industrial and working-class history." He helped worker students use their experience as a basis for new learning. He shared their preoccupation with "movements of popular resistance" and urged them to write their own historical accounts.[5] This was just the kind of work that radical historians in the US aspired to do, but except for Staughton Lynd, few of us were connected with union workers or with places like Ruskin College.

When I expressed my fascination with all this, Anna and Raph arranged meetings for me with other activist intellectuals and worker historians in the History Workshop group. As I soon discovered, they were making what Hall called an "astonishing intervention in the redefinition, the deprofessionalization and the rewriting of social history."[6] They were succeeding in democratizing historical practice in ways radical historians had only begun to do in the United States. These British socialist and feminist historians had overcome their isolation in universities and had resisted the pressures of their profession. They had created a popular history movement through which they shared radical history with working people in countless venues from Aberdeen to Kentish Town and from Manchester to Colchester, where, according to a report, "East Anglians, including teachers, adult students, sixth formers and trade unionists, formed the bulk of the workshop." People came from "far afield" to enjoy "book stalls, friendly stewards, free accommodations with sympathetic local people," and "an atmosphere of smooth and unhurried organization which allowed those attending to concentrate on the prime purpose of the weekend—the exchange of ideas and enthusiasms about work on the history of East Anglia."[7]

One of the most memorable experiences of my time in England came in Raph Samuel's basement kitchen. He lived in the old artisan-immigrant district of London called Spitalfields where I joined a small group planning the East London History Workshop while Raph made garlic soup on an ancient stove. These plans led to a workshop at the Hoxton Music Hall in East London to be key-noted by a local Labour MP who would discuss the area's unique labor movement. According to the program, the Workshop would end with "a late night hour of *your* East London songs, and an evening of 1930s dancing."[8]

Before returning to the United States, I participated in the 1976 workshop on the history of workers' education at Raph Samuel's Ruskin College. It was one of "those great, crowded, celebratory festivals of learning, with people of all sorts— Ruskin students, history undergraduates, eminent professors, amateur enthusiasts, committed researchers, and socialists of all kinds with a passion for history, pursing and quarrying a rich variety of themes . . ." in what Stuart Hall recalled as "an atmosphere of absolute egalitarianism which Raphael, the Great Leveller, rigorously imposed."[9]

The 1976 History Workshop in Oxford not only perked my interest in teaching movement history to workers; it convinced me that the history workshop method might be applied in the United States. Though we lacked a Ruskin College, we did not lack the will or the desire to break down the academic boundaries around social history. Some of us had become deeply engaged in oral history and other community-based projects. We had not organized a British-style History Workshop movement, but we had our movement historians, like Lynd doing guerilla history in Gary, and our worker historians, like Scott Molloy, a Providence bus driver and a founder of the Rhode Island Labor History forum.

Those of us lucky to get university jobs in the 1970s often felt marooned in stuffy history departments, but if the "Oxbridge" radicals of our generation could escape the British ivory towers for venues like the Hoxton Music Hall, then maybe we could do so as well. The class gulf between academics and workers actually seemed wider in Britain than in the United States, where many of us taught working-class people at community colleges and public universities. Furthermore, many activists of our generation who had left the academy shared our passion for "people's history" and our desire to make it public. They could be our allies in "deprofessionalizing" social history and sharing it with our fellow citizens.

Oral history projects were the medium we used to begin individual and group dialogues with working people. These experiences enabled us to expand the dialogue in less private settings, to experiment with a movement-inspired version of public history that oral historian Ron Grele defined as an effort "to help members of the public do their own history and aid them in understanding their role in shaping and interpreting."[10]

Lynn

With these motives in mind I approached two activist historians who lived in my Cambridgeport neighborhood. They were both studying history at Boston University in the early years of John Silber's reactionary regime. Susan Reverby had been active in the Coalition of Labor Union Women and Health PAC, and was researching the history of nurses. I met Martin Blatt in the parking lot of a Somerville supermarket for one of the United Farm Workers' boycotts. He was studying the life of the nineteenth-century abolitionist and free-love anarchist Ezra Heywood, whose politics resembled his own. They liked what they heard about people's history in Britain and together we formed the Massachusetts History Workshop in 1978.

I proposed organizing a workshop in Lynn, Massachusetts, to bring the city's remaining shoe workers together with social historians, including those we knew who were studying the city and its remarkable tradition of working-class solidarity and union democracy. As one of these historians, Paul Faler, wrote in a special "Lynn Voices" feature in *Radical America,* the city's shoe workers had often been openly "hostile to capitalism," displaying the "radicalism for which the craft of shoe making is notorious." Faler agreed to participate in a Lynn workshop hoping we could find out more about how "traditions and ideas are transmitted from one generation of working people to the next."[11]

An embodiment of Lynn tradition was poet Vincent Ferrini, who was well known in local radical circles. Vincent had graduated high school and followed his immigrant anarchist father into the shoe factories while receiving his real education in the Lynn Public Library. During World War II Ferrini worked in General Electric's Lynn River Works, supported the Left-led union there, the UE, and wrote poems praised by Mike Gold in the Communist *Daily Worker.* I once heard him recite his lament for Lynn, which captured the romantic memory of workers' power in the time before the factories closed. His poem "The City" spoke to the experience of many Massachusetts cities stunned by the shock of deindustrialization. Once the "shoe hub of the world" where "160 factories hummed," the city became a "graveyard of factories—Monumental tombstones accusing with broken eyes." "And we shoeworkers," Ferrini wrote:

Idly mushroom in union halls arguing.
Skeptical of the future, we talk of the past:
Of crowded union meetings,
The honest speeches inspiring guts to sacrifice,
The monster demonstrations and unbreakable strikes.

But when the unions refused to make concessions to the shoe bosses, the bosses took their factories out of state, leaving the thousands of Lynners stranded, "huddled in tenements" in the "shadows of dead factories."[12]

Working in a deindustrialized state like Massachusetts, we in the workshop needed to explore this past without being utterly discouraged by the present state of affairs, because, as William Carlos Williams, another factory-town poet, once wrote, the past might be "our greatest well of inspiration, our greatest hope of freedom (since the future is totally blank if not black.)"[13] After writing so eloquently of Lynn's early democratic traditions, Paul Faler called the city's situation "bleak and ominous." Nonetheless, he declared, working people remained proud of their city, perhaps because they realized "their labor created it," and because they retained an old notion of labor's creative potential.[14]

The Lynn Workshop idea became a reality because Marty Blatt was already working there, employed by the Essex Institute to help mount an exhibit funded by the National Endowment for the Humanities called "Life and Times in Shoe City: The Shoe Workers of Lynn." The Institute was located in Salem, some social distance, though only a few miles, from working-class Lynn. The curator of the exhibit was happy to see our proposal to gather workers together in the "Shoe City" with the support of the Essex Institute. Marty was already working in the community with boundless energy and enthusiasm, collecting oral histories and artifacts. He was making contact with various elderly, religious, and union groups and was able to reach retired shoe workers through the union office, rest homes, housing projects, and various social settings. Jennie Stanckiewicz, the business agent for the shoeworkers union, suggested we describe the event as a reunion and party in order to appeal to the retired shoe workers. We wisely took her advice but we wondered how, in such a festive setting, to feature the historians who had written so well about Lynn's democratic traditions.

Besides Paul Faler we knew other social historians who had studied Lynn's workers, including Mary Blewett and Alan Dawley, as well as historians of twentieth-century Lynn workers—John Cumbler, Ronald Schatz, and Libby Zimmerman.[15] They all agreed to participate. Our modest goal was to put these historians in contact with the retired workers of "Shoe City." Rather than presenting papers, the historians agreed to initiate and lead discussions based on their work, and thus draw out the shoe workers' stories and memories. Jeremy Brecher, the activist historian, had organized a similar project with Brass Work-

Gathering historians for the first History Workshop, Lynn, 1979. *Left to right:* Alan Dawley, Martha Coons, Mary Blewett, Marty Blatt, Susan Reverby, Libby Zimmerman, Paul Faler, John Cumbler, Jeremy Brecher. Photograph by the author.

ers in Connecticut, and his presence aided in fostering the kind of dialogue we sought.

The first history workshop was a great success. Seventy former shoe workers attended the event at the Hibernian Hall in West Lynn, near GE's giant River Works, where a walkout had begun the previous day. A few of the strikers attended and discussed their issues, as did a few historians and community activists. But the retired shoe workers were the center of attention. Some of the stitchers and cutters had not seen each other since they had been together "at the bench" in the waning days of Lynn's "shoe game." The event worked above all because it was a genuine reunion and party for the elders, who spoke individually and with great power and eloquence about union democracy in their shops. A few of the male elders took too much time to talk, as they probably had done many times before at union meetings. Ralph Pirone told us about radical shoemakers in his native Italy. And he spoke dramatically about one of his countrymen who learned the shoe trade in Massachusetts only to endure a terrible ordeal that struck him "like a bolt of lightning"—the execution of Sacco and Vanzetti. Pirone told us that Nicola Sacco had once worked as a first-rate trimmer in Milford, Massachusetts, where no one believed "Nick" was guilty of the murder for which he and Bartolomeo Vanzetti were executed in 1927.

Our reunion format encouraged speech-making by women as well as by men.

Two of the best speakers were women CIO militants who testified to their movement beliefs. Mae Young, blind and frail, spoke with a clear memory about a shoe strike in 1903 when the local merchants and grocers opened a soup kitchen for the strikers. Margaret DeLacey remembered carrying on Mae Young's work in the hard years of the Depression—organizing "a very democratic union" of shoe workers in Lynn. But we had also promoted dialogue and fuller participation by placing a historian at each table to raise questions for small group discussion; this format drew many contributions from the women who attended and fondly recalled their days together in the shops.[16]

The first history workshop affirmed our hunch that working people would welcome public celebration and open discussion of their history, even when, as in Lynn, the past was haunted by the specter of industrial decline and urban decay. We learned that historians studying a community like Lynn could engage in dialogue with people who lived there. We could narrow the gap between the observers and the observed. We could "bring the boundaries of history closer to people's lives"—in the words of the British History Workshop.[17] The experience enhanced our confidence about engaging in public history, even in communities we contacted as outsiders.

Lawrence

The second history workshop, with Lawrence textile workers, revealed the difficulties of engaging in people's history. The idea of doing a workshop there in "immigrant city" had been stimulated by Ralph Fasanella, the proletarian painter who had worked in the city during the 1950s depicting the life of workers in the vast woolen mills. When Phyllis Ewen and I interviewed him for *Radical America* near his rooming house in Boston's North End, Fasanella told us that Lawrence workers were breaking the silence about their past and about the great Bread and Roses strike of 1912 when thousands of immigrants from thirty different nations followed the lead of young women who stormed out of the woolen mills to protest a pay cut. They electrified the nation with their mass strike, which to mainstream labor leader Sam Gompers seemed more like a revolution than a walkout.[18]

Returning to the area in the late seventies to display his work, Fasanella exerted his street-smart, wisecracking presence and expressed his class-conscious view of labor history in a series of public and private encounters. In 1980 the painter addressed a group of Lawrence union members, including some who had actually marched on the picket line as teenagers. As Fasanella showed slides of his paintings, "the buzz of conversation grew louder and louder" as "People talked about what their parents did in the strike, the dinner table conversation in their homes, the places where important events took place during the strike." As union reporter Tom Herriman observed of this history-

Interviewing Ralph Fasanella about his Lawrence paintings, Boston, 1980. *Photograph courtesy of Phyllis Ewen.*

through-art event: "For most of the people in the room, the strike had been a central, shaping event in their lives, and it was the first time they had ever publicly discussed their feelings about it."[19]

We were interested in organizing a workshop in Lawrence because we thought we might be able to further this public discussion of the past. The event could recall multinational expressions of solidarity and militancy at a time when unions were confronted with the challenge of organizing immigrant workers. Marty Blatt, Susan Reverby, and I were encouraged by support we received from the state humanities foundation and from historians working in Lawrence, notably Sarah Nordgren, Larry Gross, and Paul Hudon, employed at the nearby American Textile Museum. We would not organize the event alone, but rather with the help of others involved in the city, especially the historian Susan Porter Benson, who was teaching social history to workers in Lawrence through another humanities foundation grant made to the Amalgamated Clothing Workers Union. She agreed to be our organizer on the scene and to enlist the aid of Ertha Dengler, who headed the Immigrant City Archives.

As we began to plan the workshop, I received a call from Moe Foner, a gifted leader of 1199, the militant hospital workers union in New York. He had been talking to Ralph Fasanella and Bill Cahn, the left-wing journalist and author of a popular book on Lawrence and the strike, and they cooked up a plan for a commemorative Bread and Roses pageant in Lawrence during the spring of 1980. Foner was very impressed by an article Paul Cowan wrote in the *Village Voice* about the suppressed memory of the strike. Cowan described an interview with the daughter of a teenaged striker named Camella Teoli, a mill girl who testified before Congress in 1912 about being scalped in a cotton-twisting machine. The daughter, who insisted on using an assumed name, knew nothing of her mother's "political past" and when Cowan gave her Camella's testimony to read, she said: "Now I have a past. Now my son has a history he can be proud of."[20]

I was very impressed with Moe Foner when we met on one of his pageant planning trips. The Bread and Roses Cultural Heritage Project he developed for Local 1199 represented the best effort anyone had made to share workers history and culture with union members. Foner knew how to work with community leaders who, in Lawrence, had grown up with the same fear of the past that haunted Camella Teoli.[21] Foner had discovered—perhaps from Cowan and Fasanella—that some of these people were now ready to restore the memory of the 1912 strike as an expression of immigrant unity rather than as a horrible conflict led by godless outside agitators which was the official memory of the 1912 and 1919 strikes.

Ingatius R. J. Piscatello, a lawyer descended from immigrant mill workers, had become head of the Lawrence Historical Society, and he knew why old timers were afraid to talk about the 1912 strike. He hoped to commemorate the great conflict without blaming the children for the "sins of the fathers," who had ordered the police to attack striking immigrants and their children. Piscatello and Foner found an ally in Mayor Lawrence LeFebre, who also had worked in the mills. The mayor hoped the commemoration of a multinational strike would win more support from the Latin and Asian immigrants now flooding into the city. The Bread and Roses pageant on 25 April 1980 accomplished what Moe Foner had imagined. It was a community mobilization of memory about class struggle and social solidarity. A street was named after Camella Teoli, a day was set aside to commemorate the strike, and a painting of a strike scene by Ralph Fasanella was hung in the visitor's center of a new state heritage park.[22]

Though impressed by what Foner and Piscatello accomplished in Lawrence, we had decided not to get involved in their pageant, which was intended to celebrate the unity and solidarity of 1912, not to explore the social history of mill worker communities, which was the workshop's main concern. Instead of fixing our gaze on the big strike and its legendary leaders, we wanted to reprise the Lynn event and invite retired textile workers to share their memories of life and work in the mills, even if they did not want to recall the events of 1912 and 1919, and even if they did not want to talk about unions. We asked David Montgomery to lead off the workshop because we knew he would be comfortable in an audience of workers and because he could raise questions about social and cultural history, as well as labor history.[23]

The day of the workshop was bleak and so was the turnout, but we filled four long tables and listened expectantly as Montgomery called for testimonies. We were a little taken aback when a little man stood up and began to give us a speech. It was Angelo Rocco, the immigrant who had arrived in Lawrence in 1908 and three years later had become secretary of "una branch italiana" of the Industrial Workers of the World. When the great strike broke out in February of 1912, it was he, Angelo, who sent the telegram to Joe Ettor, the IWW organizer in Brooklyn, asking for help. Standing barely five feet tall, he offered personal memory as history. All he needed was a soap box. He was a great raconteur, a wily immigrant lawyer who had been drummed out of his profession by city elites. He spoke with his hands as well as his raspy voice, telling a story about solidarity that appealed to all of us as it had to Studs Terkel—an immigrant, proletarian version of the American Dream.[24] It was a thrill to be taken back on a personal journey through the events that led to the Bread and Roses strike. However, as Sue Benson warned us, Rocco was infamous for exaggerating his own role, and neglecting the role of immigrant women who were the subjects of study by Ardis Cameron, another historian who attended the workshop that day.[25]

After hearing Rocco's romantic ode to Bread and Roses, we were unprepared for the cynicism and defeatism expressed by other workers. As textile union business agent Daniel Downey told the workshop: "I imagine most of you have come to listen to the old timers. We'd like to forget about it, to be honest," he said of Lawrence's labor history. "How beautiful it is to sweetly forget the club-bings of 1912, the jailings of 1919, and the clubbings again of 1931."[26] We didn't know how to respond to Downey as he shared with us the agony of remember-ing and the power of forgetting a discouraging past.

After the workshop we adjourned to the American Textile History Museum for a sobering evaluation. One of our advisors, Mary Blewett, criticized our inability to elicit testimony from the women in the room and our passivity in the presence of organizer types like Rocco and Downey, who took their time to testify without encouraging any dialogue. She also faulted us for not planning to make a long-term investment, as she had done in her oral history work with textile mill people.[27]

There were other shortcomings. We had heard about the many ethnic ten-sions that plagued Lawrence, in the past and the present, but we had not been prepared to address the meaning of this tradition that conflicted with the Bread and Roses solidarity myth. We were also silent when some speakers shared bitter memories born of defeat. One of them asked us what historians had to offer in response, and our answers were pretty lame. In the evaluation session, one historian who participated thought we should have explained why even bitter memories needed to be recorded. Tom Leary suggested that in the future we might distribute a few blatantly offensive quotes about labor from textbooks or business publications to show why workers' memories were important to the

Recalling the Bread and Roses strike: Angelo Rocco at the Lawrence History Workshop. *Photograph courtesy of Phyllis Ewen.*

public and especially to young people. Leary also thought we should have included local residents in planning the event and in preparing the booklet to commemorate the event. Still, he doubted that we could have repeated the participatory aspects of the workshops in Britain where he thought working people were more class conscious and where unions encouraged more historical consciousness.[28]

We left the evaluation meeting questioning the wisdom of organizing one-time events in industrial cities. We had not been good enough social historians to prepare for the awkward discussions of ethnic conflicts or for the depressing memories of defeat we encountered. We were painfully aware of what oral historian Michael Frisch later observed at a celebration of militant 1930s strikes: that older participants recalled, not days of glory, but the "bad old days" of conflict, before unions had become institutionalized with no-strike contracts and grievance procedures. Instead of focusing our workshop on sharing social history and recording evidence about social life in Lawrence, we might have focused the discussion more on contrasting and evaluating divergent memories of the past and their meaning for the present.[29]

Afterward, our group felt somewhat less chagrined. The event received favorable coverage in the city newspaper as a continuation of the effort to record Lawrence's silenced voices.[30] When we listened to tapes recorded during the event, we found some interesting recollections of life in Lawrence that Martha Coons later wove together with photos into an attractive booklet that was requested by several dozen retired textile workers. Our effort contributed in a small way to the public reclamation of the 1912 strike memory, later reflected in the Bread and Roses Festival that began on Labor Day in 1984. We returned to the city and took part in the festival three years after it started. The History Workshop prepared a slide show on child labor to present at the event. One of our members, Patricia Sherman, created a moving script based on the testimonies of children and the comments of photographer Lewis Hine, who took many pictures for the Committee on Child Labor. The narration of the show was provided by the president of the state teachers association, a woman who had been a teacher in a nearby Massachusetts mill town.

By then, the Bread and Roses Festival had taken off. In 1987 nearly twenty thousand people descended on the city's Merrimack River waterfront and common to celebrate the strike, to sample ethnic food and music, and to recreate in street theater the dramatic return of the strikers' children to the city in 1912. City Hall and the business community now embraced the festival, as did unions trying to organize the new immigrant workers who flooded into the city. It was, wrote the *Boston Globe* reporter, summarizing a speech by the president of the Massachusetts AFL-CIO, a commemoration of a strike that still had "meaning for a city in which thousands of immigrants, according to union organizers, still face discrimination and poor working conditions."[31]

There were many signs in the later 1980s that the lost labor traditions, symbolized by the Bread and Roses strike, were being recognized and mourned, and that movement culture was being rediscovered and celebrated. Ralph Fasanella's canvas (1977) depicting the Bread and Roses strike became a surprisingly popular poster, an icon of the labor-folk revival. It graced the cover of a new edition of William Cahn's book on Lawrence introduced by the president of the Amalgamated Clothing Workers, whose local officers supported our workshop.[32] Obviously, this folk renaissance appealed to unions, not only ones with radical traditions like Moe Foner's 1199, but also to worker organizations struggling to survive and to revive their activist traditions.

Brighton

After the Lawrence workshop I traveled to the national gathering of History Workshoppers in Brighton, England, to share news of our work and to compare notes on the progress of people's history here and there. The British movement that seemed so joyful and unified at Ruskin College in 1976 now seemed troubled. Our counterparts in Britain had fallen out over the politics of social history and the accomplishments of people's history.

Sharp confrontations had characterized the previous year's workshop in Oxford. The prophet of radical social history, Edward Thompson, attacked theoretical Marxists for ignoring cultural traditions and historical peculiarities and for focusing instead on the structural determinants of historical change. These "structuralists" seemed to deny the role of human agency. In response, the cultural theorist Stuart Hall criticized Thompson and his followers, the "culturalists" who seemed to believe that socialism could simply be "rediscovered" through what Hall called "recuperative historical reflection." For example, the workshop's notion of "people's history" celebrated oppositional cultures but ignored hard political questions about ideology and consciousness. It was "as if, simply to tell the story of past oppressions and struggles" would reveal "the promise of socialism, already there, fully constituted, ready to 'speak out.'" Against this "simple populism" Hall defended the need for theory abstracted from human experience.[33]

At the 1980 workshop in Brighton I was a confused American pragmatist caught in a very European intellectual quagmire. I stood with Thompson and social history against the theoretical Marxists who ignored the creative potential of working people. But I was also involved in a debate with populist intellectuals in the United States who rejected the entire Left tradition of approaching people's history through the study of class conflict and class consciousness. Populist historians like Lawrence Goodwyn complained that the socialist approach imposed theory on history and ignored the indigenous cultural traditions and experiences essential to lively opposition movements. Class consciousness was "the grandest abstraction of them all," Goodwyn wrote in a review of my book on the socialist movement in the Southwest. I protested, insisting that evidence of class consciousness emerged from evidence of lived experience. I also argued that populist historians were not being honest about their own use of theory in studying movement culture. Their notions of democracy and culture were obviously derived from political theory as well as from social history.[34] History only answered the questions we put to it.

At the Brighton Workshop I discussed these problems with Raphael Samuel, who believed that theory could help shape intelligent questions about the past, questions that would be reshaped by what we discovered from the past.[35] "Tell the American comrades to create their own kind of people's history." That was Samuel's message to me in Brighton. He thought we might even escape some of the ideological disputes that seemed to preoccupy our British comrades.

I spoke with other people's history advocates in Brighton who complained that debates over history and theory had in fact distracted the History Workshop movement from its public mission.[36] One of them was Ken Worpole of the British Federation of Worker Writers. He had charged that the *History Workshop Journal* was too preoccupied with "end products and the "correct socialist consciousness of the final texts." He feared that the Workshop might become a "textual movement" rather than a popular movement promoting community-

based, worker-written history. In his defense of the "local people's history movement" in Britain, Worpole quoted Antonio Gramsci, the brilliant Italian Marxist
who had been imprisoned by the Fascists. Gramsci, who emphasized the role of
"organic intellectuals" in popular struggles against authority, issued this warning to other socialist intellectuals who wanted to push popular consciousness
beyond "common sense." Avoid being locked in a "specialized culture" for
restricted groups, he wrote from prison, and never forget to "remain in contract
with the 'people'" in order to find in this contact the problems "to be studied
and solved."[37]

Boston

I returned to Boston from the Brighton gathering eager to make more contact
with working people, to push further with the History Workshop belief that
workers could participate in researching, writing, and interpreting history. Encouraging reports arrived from around the United States. Herbert Gutman had
received a $400,000 grant from the National Endowment for the Humanities to
assemble a new social history of work in America and to elicit the opinions of
workers in shaping the project.[38] Movement-inspired oral history had reached
into the lives of many working people who now shared their stories, as African
American union activist Lillian Roberts did with our workshop colleague Susan
Reverby.[39] The Southern Oral History Program at Chapel Hill, directed by Jacquelyn Dowd Hall, had undertaken a large project to reinterpret industrialization in the Southern Piedmont by using the testimonies of textile workers.[40] In
Boston a union carpenter named Mark Erlich who was active in radical politics
had interviewed his fellow workers for an exciting book project, an effort that
would become a new model of how to do history with and for union workers.[41]
The ambitious Oral History of the American Left Project directed by Paul Buhle
had seen its efforts reflected on the movie screen in Warren Beatty's Hollywood
film *Reds* about John Reed and Louise Bryant, the American radicals caught up
in the romance of the Bolshevik Revolution. The film made artistic use of
radical elders as witnesses and suggested "a public fascination with the living
voices of the radical past greater than historians themselves anticipated."[42]

   The movement historians collected oral testimony not simply as raw evidence of experience but also as a record of how people told their stories and
made their own historical interpretations. In some cases, workers' views of the
past seemed more convincing than those offered by scholars.[43] This exciting use
of oral history was epitomized in the work of Jeremy Brecher and his colleagues,
who organized a group of local residents to explore the experience of immigrant
workers in the brass industry of Connecticut's Naugatuck Valley. The Brass
Workers History Project produced a superb oral history book in 1982 and
planned a video about the workers of Waterbury for public television.[44] In
making this long-term investment in a community history project Brecher and

his colleagues had fulfilled what I thought was the History Workshop's most important mission: involving workers and community members "in the interpretive process." Local people not only told about their personal lives and "what they had observed or experienced," they accepted the invitation to participate in the process of interpretation.[45]

Encouraged by this flowering of people's history, our workshop developed plans for a third project. We wanted to work closer to home so that we could collaborate with working people in a longer-term interpretive project. We also hoped to participate in an emerging public discourse about work initiated, in part, by the popular oral historian Studs Terkel in his best seller *Working*. Still, it was a surprise to read a *Boston Globe* editorial asking: "Why isn't that story of work the major component of our history?" The writer referred to the British History Workshop's local oral history productions in which working people spoke about their work, but the writer also cited the failings of workplace oral history, which often recorded simple anecdotes. The editorial ended by calling for wider public discussion that would help Bostonians understand "the social, political, and economic implications of the work we do."[46]

Here was a challenge we were ready to meet. We would do it by opening the door on the hidden world of office work in Boston. That door had already been put ajar by the unique organizing efforts of Nine to Five, the Organization of Women Office Workers, founded in the city during the early 1970s, and by active union campaigns at Brandeis, Harvard, and Boston University. During these efforts office employees spoke out about their experiences as working women.[47] We met with some of the young organizers involved in these organizing drives to see how oral history might be used to support their efforts. At the very least, it would reveal something about the world of office work in the past, and how it was experienced by a "silent generation" of women.

Did the absence of unionism among women office workers imply acceptance of the patriarchal power structures imposed on them? We wanted to use oral history to look for evidence of informal work groups and female support networks among an earlier generation of women workers. By examining the hidden history of office workplaces, we expected to learn more about women's work culture and office workers' consciousness. My own thinking was greatly influenced by what I learned about clerical workers and about informal work groups from *Radical America* writers, as well as from Jeremy Brecher, Susan Reverby, and others in the Work Relations Study Group, and from Jacquelyn Hall and her students in the Southern Oral History Program at the University of North Carolina, who, by learning to listen, uncovered all kinds of unexpected behavior in the seemingly pacific world of the cotton textile-mill worker.[48]

This time workers would be involved from start to finish in planning the workshop and in writing the booklet; and women's voices would be heard loud and clear because women workers would be the focus of our efforts to make movement history public. The workshop received a grant from the state humanities foundation for the clerical workers history project. We hired one of the union activists, Carol Yourman, to direct the project and she transformed a sketchy idea into an exciting consciousness-raising process. Under her leadership a dozen women who worked or had worked in offices undertook an oral history project, interviewing thirty older clerical workers. This interaction in turn contributed to the success of the workshop, which aimed at bringing together both generations to engage in a dialogue about the past. In this case, oral history became a vehicle for gathering information and for organizing. It could also lead to consciousness-raising through a collective mobilization of memory.[49]

The workshop itself took place during National Secretaries Week in April of 1982 and attracted over two hundred women and a few men. They heard presentations by historians of clerical work as well as by union organizers and clerical workers, active and retired. The workshop took place at the University of Massachusetts—Boston's College of Public and Community Service, where an exhibit of photos and documents about clerical workers was also mounted. It succeeded in promoting a dialogue between two different generations of women workers, a process that highlighted the impact of the women's liberation movement on the consciousness of younger office workers.

The morning session set the tone for the day with historians of women's work, Margery Davies and Susan Reverby, and two retired office workers, an African American named Margaret Willis and an Irish American named Eleanor Coughlin, who recalled "the hideous regimentation" of offices in the 1940s and 1950s. It wasn't quite so bad now, she said, but the wage discrimination remained, she added in words that became a *Boston Herald* headline the next day: "We're still the lowest part of the totem pole." She also explained how contact with younger women interested in history convinced her that she, as a worker, had something significant to say. We were off to a fine start.

The opening session energized the room and helped to focus the small group dialogue, carefully planned so that younger women and older women participated in each discussion. We found what had been missing in the Lawrence History Workshop. The only complaint we heard at noontime was about the food; it was supplied by a countercultural group, Food Not Bombs, and the retired women whispered about the "health food" having "no taste."

The afternoon session focused on the ambiguous legacy of trade unions in the history of office work. Sharon Hartman Strom offered a brief historical account of how organized labor disrespected and distrusted "the girls in the office." But she also highlighted the courageous work of Florence Luscomb, a heroic figure on the Boston Left, a suffragist and socialist who headed the Office and Professional Workers union before it was expelled from the CIO in 1949 for being "Communist dominated." Partially blind and stricken with Alzheimer's disease, Luscomb could not leave the nursing home she entered after living for many years in a communal house she had shared with young activists in Cambridge.. But her historic role was recalled by her successor, Ann Prosten, who explained how the office workers who staffed the CIO unions played a tremendous role in organizing the new unions. The afternoon group discussion moved from the shortcomings of unions to a discussion of the new breakthroughs female organizers had made at Boston University where they had forced the authoritarian president John Silber to recognize their union.

The Lynn and Lawrence workshops produced popular commemorative booklets, but ended without any further collaboration between historians and workers. We wanted to use the clerical workers' project to promote joint work between historians, workers, and union activists. Organizers invited participants to sign up if they were interested in working together on a history of Boston office workers. Over thirty people volunteered and in the months that followed, they met to discuss how a group of workers could research, interpret, and write its own history. Eventually committees formed for research and historical interpretation, as well as for graphics and production. Writing history by committee was often problematic, especially on a voluntary basis, but at the end of a one-and-a-half-year process, a collective product did emerge.

The production of the booklet involved nearly one hundred people (including those who offered or conducted oral history interviews). *They Can't Run the Office Without Us* was published in January 1985 with over fifty illustrations and title borrowed from the 1982 workshop, which itself challenged the myth of clerical workers as caregivers, marginal to the production process.

The writing group wanted to make the book accessible to office workers by making sure they recognized their own voices. Thus the oral history testimony collected by union activists became the basis of the narrative for *They Can't Run the Office Without Us*. The writers also imparted their own varied voices to the narrative and interpretation. Like the Southern Oral History Program's magnificent collaboration interpreting the cotton mill workers' world, this project involved an "accountability to different voices." In both projects a feminist perspective helped in the listening process. The historians learned to hear each collaborator's voice and in doing so attuned themselves to hear the different voices of the workers they interviewed.[50] In the end, I joined Patricia Reeve, another historian with academic training, in drafting the final version of three of the six chapters. After earning a master's degree Pat had become Boston director of Nine to Five, The Organization of Women Office Workers, and she knew how to help us make sure that our text released the authentic voices of the workers we had interviewed and the ones who spoke to us from the past.

The booklet received some encouraging notice, including a favorable review in the *Boston Globe*'s "Living with Work" column. The Yale University clerical and technical workers' union used the book for its shop steward training classes shortly after completing a successful strike. The project contributed to the literature already produced by worker writers, some of it published by Single-jack Press in California and by a remarkable Pennsylvania periodical, *The Mill*

Hunk Herald. Like the History Workshop groups, local publishers in Britain, and the "Dig Where You Stand" groups in Sweden, our group sought not only to record workers' oral testimony and edit it for publication, but also to encourage workers to write their own history. The clerical workers' history project gave the women workers a chance to see themselves as narrators and writers. Like Stan Weir's Singlejack Books series, produced by worker-writers, *They Can't Run the Office Without Us* tried to make work a public issue by "publishing writings about life-on-the-job by people who live it."[51]

Workshop Methods in Massachusetts

Massachusetts History Workshop created community settings in which to share the rich past that movement historians had discovered, a past that remained locked between the pages of monographs. In some of these settings local people offered their memories as well as their interpretations of the past. At our workshop in Lynn elderly shoe workers struck a harmonious chord of memory. In Lawrence we discovered a divided memory. Some participants bitterly recalled their defeats, while Angelo Rocco celebrated the mythical aspects of the 1912 strike.

The Lawrence Workshop failed to probe the complexity of working-class memory. If we failed as "progressive historians . . . helping natives discover their history," it wasn't because we insisted on "cleansing history" of its complications. Nor was it because we recorded the "wrong" stories—as Paul Cowan did when he assumed that Camella Teoli remained silent about her experiences in the 1912 strike. Oral history is full of misremembered stories. Ardis Cameron, author of the superb study of immigrant women in the Lawrence strike, has addressed this criticism of recuperative history. She points out that people often tell "wrong" stories as a way of "righting" the wrongs in other stories told by their enemies. In these story sharing encounters, people like Angelo Rocco may express what oral historian Sandro Portelli calls "the truths of the heart."[52]

None of our projects compared with the sustained community involvement and community impact of the Brass Workers History Project in neighboring Connecticut, and none of them helped build a permanent institution for preservation and commemoration like the labor history societies in Illinois, Rhode Island, New York, and other states. But Massachusetts History Workshop projects did extend the boundaries of social history out of the academy and into local communities; they also allowed us—the activist historians—to enrich our own experience by working in collaborative community settings.

We shared our experience with other activist historians in Britain and other parts of the United States and reported on our work to colleagues at meetings of professional historians. Popular history projects became the subject of more attention at the meetings of the democratized Organization of American Historians; they fit in best at the meetings of the Oral History Association, especially the marvelous 1988 conference organized by Ron Grele in Baltimore, and at the sessions sponsored by the National Council on Public History, which devoted a whole issue of its journal to our collective work.[53]

Public history originated in the academy as a field of study and a way of preparing historians and archivists to serve various institutions. Thus, it differed fundamentally from a people's history rooted in the protest movements of the sixties, which aimed to democratize the teaching and writing of history. While the field of public history became more professionalized in the 1980s, it remained open to the possibility that public-spirited historians could redefine their roles and encourage "members of the public at large to become their own historians."[54]

By the mid-1980s radical historians assembled an impressive collection of reports on politicized public history projects. In their anthology *Presenting the Past,* Susan Benson, Steve Brier, and Roy Rosenzweig took a hard look at our popular experiments, criticizing their celebratory populist character and arguing for the infusion of more critical perspectives and interpretations. Still in all, they concluded with a measure of enthusiasm. "Even in their current form, people's history projects can be a potent force for sustaining a vision of social change," and could even encourage the development of ongoing social movements, "not merely by celebrating the past" and drawing lessons from it. People's history, rightly done, could also show how present institutions and relationships are not timeless structures but are rather the products of "human agency" and deliberate choices. It could reveal how working people make lives for themselves at home and at work and it could even encourage participants to think about how people might again take history into their own hands.[55]

These were the goals of the Massachusetts History Workshop's projects. At best, participants felt empowered, even inspired, by our reunions, celebrations, and forums. At least, they offered rare opportunities for fellow citizens to engage in egalitarian discussions about moments of solidarity and about movements for justice and equality usually missing from public discourse. On some of those occasions, we learned, the old movement stories told in public gave counsel to participants engaged in creating new movements for social change.

Our workshop efforts with women organizing in Boston offices clearly indicated that working people's history could be an ingredient in movement building, as it was on a much grander scale in other parts of the world. During the early 1980s, I participated in two meetings that made this plain. One gathering to support Solidarnsoc in Poland revealed how the intellectuals reinterpreted national history for the workers' movement. At another meeting I heard the head of the black textile workers' union in South Africa tell us that educating his members about people's history was a top priority in the struggle to create a democratic labor movement.[56]

What would it take for more leaders of our own AFL-CIO unions to recognize the importance of historical consciousness? And what could movement historians do to make the case? The answer seemed to lie in creating the popular forms of workers' education like the one I saw at Oxford in Ruskin College. There, within a university unionized workers could reflect on their own experiences, while they learned collectively from each other and from a shared exploration of the past.

THE
LABOR
STUDIES
PROGRAM

Celebrating a Decade
of Worker Education

The
College of
Public &
Community
Service

UMass/Boston

Making the university accessible to trade unionists: Labor Studies Program brochure for a tenth anniversary dinner, 1989. *Clockwise from top:* union students, Bill Fletcher Jr., Labor Studies students, Patricia Reeve, Cheryl Gooding. *Photographs © Randy H. Goodman '90.*

CHAPTER **3**

Learning to Teach Movement History to Workers

The year I spent in Britain discovering the History Workshop also started me thinking about teaching movement history and sharing it with workers in a college setting like the one I had seen in Ruskin. In 1975 and 1976 I had a chance to lecture in American labor history at the Centre for the Study of Social History at Warwick University in Coventry, Britain's bombed-out motor city. The Centre had first been directed by E. P. Thompson, who invited David Montgomery to be the first American lecturer in 1969. That was when students occupied the administration building and discovered documents exposing the influence of car industry executives in university affairs. By the time I arrived in Warwick, Thompson had left the Centre, and the sit-in of 1969 was folklore. The new director, Royden Harrison, was an avuncular socialist of the old school who created a relaxed atmosphere in an old farmhouse filled with zealous social historians. I taught labor history to a seminar of master's degree students. Some of them were local working-class people who had joined radical groups and worked in the industrial Midlands, where unions had gained enormous shop-floor power in the postwar years.

One of the Warwick students introduced me to a teacher in the venerable Workers Education Association, which provided instruction in union halls. As a result, I was invited to teach a session on U.S. unions for the shop stewards at the big Massey-Ferguson farm equipment plant near Coventry. My first experience in workers ed was challenging because it was not easy to explain to militant British shop stewards why U.S. union leaders seemed so conservative, and often so far removed from their members. An evening in a well-appointed workingmen's club topped off my first attempt at labor education; it introduced me to middle-aged union men far more interested in what I had to say about labor history than any of my university students had ever been.

Being Inspired

Curious about this world where workers met intellectuals, I attended the marvelous History Workshop of 1976 at Ruskin College, mentioned in the previous chapter—a conference devoted entirely to the history of workers education. I learned about worker students and their interaction with radical teachers, and was encouraged to read about Charles Beard, the American progressive historian who founded Ruskin College at Oxford in 1899, and about Mary Ritter Beard, the pioneering historian who taught courses for the Women's Trade Union League. I read about R. H. Tawney, perhaps the most influential socialist intellectual in twentieth-century Britain, who "found himself" through workers education and then became its enthusiastic prophet while writing history inspired by that movement. I also read about A. J. Muste, the radical pacifist whose critical teaching at Brookwood Labor College angered the AFL hierarchy in the 1920s; about Claude Williams, the messianic radical who formed Commonwealth College in Arkansas; and about Myles Horton, who created the Highlander Folk School in Tennessee, which served as a training ground for the new CIO unions in the Depression years and later for the civil rights movement.[1]

Workers education offered a way of learning to teach movement history to workers and a way of engaging with them in movement building. Myles Horton reflected on how educators made this connection in the 1930s. "We had a movement at one time in the CIO," he recalled. "We worked together. There was a social movement that was not just unions organizing for wages and better working conditions and security. It was people organizing to do things in their community, taking political action, learning about the world. . . . Education was part of that; it was a kind of spark that kept those things ignited."[2]

We lacked a vibrant workers education movement like the one I observed in Britain and we missed flash points of worker-student unity that appeared in France during May of '68 and in Italy during the "autunno caldo" of 1969. But in the past, American intellectuals had successfully engaged workers in the process of building radical and progressive movements.

A Rocky Road

My own engagement with movement politics led me down a road traveled by many New Left radicals, a road we hoped would lead to a revived, radicalized labor movement. This was a kind of toll road, manned by gatekeepers from powerful organizations with conservative leaders. It was a rocky road to run, one strewn with anti-intellectual boulders strategically placed by the founder of the American Federation of Labor, Samuel Gompers, during his war to protect the union members from the radical intellectuals, even though many of these dreamers were workers themselves. Gompers's hostility to the "fool friends of

Sparking social movements through education: Myles Horton (*right*) with union leaders at Highlander Folk School, 1949. *Courtesy State Historical Society of Wisconsin, photograph Whi x3 43721.*

labor" was written into history by Selig Perlman, who told the story as one of a continuous struggle of "organic labor" against the "dominance of intellectuals." During the 1930s, when the left reemerged in the movement, a political challenge would again be posed in "the classic terms of the intellectual problem."[3] This defense of pure-and-simple unionism by the "practical men" prepared the ground for the purge of the left during the Cold War years when workers with radical or progressive ideas were forced out of the movement. At the high tide of popular anti-intellectualism in 1954, the progressive historian Merle Curti explained that some intellectuals had become disillusioned with trade unions, while those who "stuck with the movement either ceased being intellectuals," in a critical sense, or learned to accept and respect the movement's "tough fabric of custom."[4] When the popular anti-intellectualism of the fifties receded, it remained strong in the House of Labor.

The hostility of AFL-CIO leadership to radicals seemed to be shared to some degree by many rank-and-file members who harbored their suspicion of outsiders, like former student radicals. We were constantly reminded of one notorious incident: hard-hatted construction workers beating up on long-haired, antiwar demonstrators in New York City.[5]

Nonetheless, in the late 1970s possibilities opened up for former student radicals to participate in workplace and community struggles and to engage working people in educational activities. Perhaps an early enthusiasm for participatory democracy helped prepare former New Leftists for popular education work. In any case, it was not surprising to learn in 1988 that far more of our veterans of '68 engaged in "social and trade union work" than their European cohorts.[6]

When I began to engage workers and their unions in Boston, I hit a wall of suspicion. It was one thing to write labor movement history with a sharply critical view of union bureaucrats and frozen ideas, as I did for *Radical America*'s leftist audience; it was quite another matter writing radical history for the actually existing movement. When my first two books on labor history began to reach this audience, some trade unionists reacted negatively. These books would have been ignored by union leaders if I had remained an academic historian. But I was also a movement activist in regular contact with their members, including some determined insurgents. Therefore, my interpretation of labor history attracted some very tough readers who did not like what they saw. They would put me to the test: Would I persist and earn some credibility as a labor intellectual despite their opposition?

Persistence depended on finding allies. My natural allies came from the ranks of younger activists in Boston who shared my political background and values— a cadre of brilliant labor and community organizers (some of them former student radicals, and many others from less privileged backgrounds). They often posed questions about the past derived from their own political practice, and they supported my work as a historian. Allies also came from unexpected places, like the last Catholic labor school in the United States, an institution created after World War II to counter leftist influence in the labor movement. The two Jesuits who ran the church's Labor Guild were intellectuals and students of history (and were quietly independent of the AFL-CIO chiefs); they sold my books to students in their evening labor school and asked me to lecture there.

Most gratifying was the support offered by some Boston trade unionists whose fighting instincts had been aroused by employers' assaults. They were frustrated by a skittish union officialdom. Far from being anti-intellectual, these union loyalists hungered for discussions about history and values, and for serious debates about the issues (though many took the conservative side on the issues we raised.) Far from being complacent, they worried passionately about the fate of organized labor and wanted to look back to the past—to find out what had once made their movement strong.

I relied on their support to create a space within our state university for an independent labor education program where union activists could be recognized as thinkers as well as activists, where they could reflect on learned experience, positive and negative, and where they could study movement history, warts and all. In this free space we could learn from each other.

Breaking Out

Inspired by comrades in the British workers education and History Workshop movements, I returned from the England in 1976 determined to break out of my isolation as an assistant professor of history in an elite university by working on the farm workers boycotts and helping our librarians organize a union affiliated with Nine to Five, the women office workers organization. And as previously noted, my work with *Radical America* involved reporting on contemporary rank-and-file struggles and taking up Eric Foner's challenge to write a survey of twentieth-century workers history that would bring the insights of the new social and labor history to a wider audience.[7] I also accepted a promising invitation to lecture on local labor history at the Boston Public Library. In Massachusetts, where all politics is local, it seemed that Boston's labor history provided a promising subject for an initial experiment in doing public history.

The lectures resulted in a book written for a public audience, and addressed questions about trade union conservatism and labor radicalism.[8] The public lectures and the book led to the first opportunities to do worker education at the Boston Community School founded by radical entrepreneur extraordinaire, Michael Ansara, and at the Catholic Labor Guild run by the last two Jesuit "labor priests" in America.

Finding a Free Space to Teach

These opportunities all arose in the last year of my "terminal contract" as an assistant professor of history at Brandeis, and in the depths of the academic "job crisis." Planning to stay in Boston where I had become deeply engaged in movement politics and public history, I considered leaving the academy. But then, more mysterious forces created a temporary teaching job in UMass-Boston's experimental adult education college. My new colleagues wanted someone to teach and write history and remain engaged in community and labor struggles! The college faculty and library staff were fighting for a union contract and there were lots of sixties radicals involved in this campaign and a variety of social causes in Boston's boiling cauldron of movement politics. The action, it seemed, never ended at my new school in the old Boston Gas Building. This experimental college wasn't well appointed or well respected by other academics, but for me it was just the place for doing movement history in public.

In 1966 the University of Massachusetts opened a campus in Boston despite strong opposition from various educational and financial elites. The College of

Public and Community Service (CPCS) opened in 1973 as a result of a demand for public higher education to fulfill its urban mission. UMass Boston's Chancellor Frank Broderick, a biographer of W.E.B. Du Bois, thought the faculty's zeal to "provide disadvantaged students with the best in higher education" had tended to isolate the new campus from "large parts of the urban community."[9] Creating CPCS was part of an effort to open the university to a wider range of city dwellers.

The college grew from a few hundred students to nearly one thousand in the early 1980s. The adult students came mainly from the ranks of human and legal service workers, community agency staff and organizers, then later police officers, advocates for the elderly, and union activists. The student body has consisted of over 60 percent females and about 30 percent people of color, a high percentage for a New England college. The college emphasized equity in access and educational opportunity, stressed community service and activism for its faculty, and attempted to blend career education and liberal education— to provide a new kind of access to the university for working-class adults in front-line human service and neighborhood agencies. The faculty offered these workers opportunities to gain new competence in their fields and to become more reflective practitioners and more effective advocates for change.[10]

The curriculum was designed to evaluate student competence in career areas like human services, paralegal work, community planning, and in intellectual areas like political economy, history and culture, the self and society. I joined an interdisciplinary general education faculty organized to infuse liberal education and critical thinking into career-oriented studies. We did not emphasize acquiring knowledge for its own sake, the goal of traditional liberal arts education.[11] We hoped our students would also gain the competence to think critically and "to employ knowledge effectively."[12]

The college's philosophy drew upon Dewey's progressive ideas about the value of experiential learning and the need for egalitarian educational opportunities in a democratic society. CPCS encouraged faculty to evaluate experiential learning and to certify the competence students had gained through performing various social and occupational roles. No credit was given for experience, however.[13] Students were asked to work through a process of assessment and reflection and then demonstrate that their experience met criteria for competence the faculty had developed in various areas—ranging from professional skills like assessing client needs to intellectual skills like legal reasoning. So, instead of the exclusively course-based, graded college curriculum that many of our students had found oppressive in high school and in other college settings, the college developed an alternative curriculum for adults, emphasizing learning as an ongoing process that began before and continued after particular academic courses. Instead of competing for grades, students aimed to meet the same criteria and standards in a kind of contract learning situation; when they came up short, they continued to work with faculty to achieve competence.[14]

All of this put us at odds with those traditionalists in the faculty and the administration who wanted UMass-Boston to be a "Harvard for the poor." In a time when "excellence" was measured only by competitive success, we insisted on certifying competence measured by a person's ability to perform public and community service effectively without sacrificing a critical and an ethical view of one's work. In an era when the experimental programs in higher education began to dissolve, the college provided alternative education for poor and working people, people who would not otherwise have become college students.

The college attracted a faculty and staff of activist-educators who also wrote about the ethics and delivery of human service work, about women's studies, about the politics of community control and the tactics of community organizers, about shelter poverty, about the use of popular music in protest movements, about racism in Boston's schools. It included radicals with diverse political backgrounds, professors like Paul Rosenkrantz, our *consigliere*, a social psychologist who had been a Communist Party activist in the maritime union and in the South. Besides these faculty trained in traditional graduate programs, the College hired practitioners to teach a variety of courses, including Kip Tiernan, the founder of Rosie's Place, the first shelter for roofless women in Boston; Frank Manning, a socialist with a 1930s union background, who became the state's leading advocate for the elderly; Nelson Merced, the first Puerto Rican to serve in the Massachusetts legislature; and Gus Newport, the former mayor of Berkeley. One semester I saw the name "Moses" next to an algebra course. Someone said it was Bob Moses's course. "Do you mean the Bob Moses of the civil rights movement?" I asked incredulously. Indeed, the Robert Moses who had played a now legendary role in the Mississippi freedom struggle had come to teach math at our school.

The college provided support for bridging the gap between citizenship and scholarship created by academic professionalism. It also gave me a chance to overcome the "complacent disconnectedness" of academic teaching and writing described by another radical historian, Mike Merrill, in a fascinating report on his first venture into workers education at about the same time. The union workers he taught were intent on learning the "how" as well as the "what"—a trying experience, he found, for an intellectual not trained to make the connections between knowledge and action that these students wanted. Mike's "sobering experience" of teaching in union halls made him even more doubtful that this kind of teaching and learning could take place in schools, unless, he speculated, "the schools could be made working-class institutions," unless the professors also became organizers, and unless scholarship itself could "be made into a popular activity" like the British History Workshop.[15]

Before I could settle in at the college, there was a battle to fight with older faculty who opposed hiring another sixties radical, but thanks to Ann Withorn, my *Radical America* comrade, and to support from outside my department, I won a tenure-track position on the faculty. I could continue experimenting with how to do workers education and how to present movement history to movement people.

At first, I taught a course on how social movements shaped U.S. history using Howard Zinn's *People's History of the United States,* published in 1980, and asked Howard to take time out of his battles with Boston University czar John Silber in order to talk to our students. But I also wanted to teach about the history of work. Rather than begin by teaching labor history, which seemed too narrow a focus for the wide range of students who enrolled in my courses, I borrowed a leaf from Herb Gutman's book and taught about work and work relations over a broad sweep of history, from the decline of feudalism and the rise of industry, emphasizing the cultural as well as the class struggle over the terms of employment and the measures of work. Students read Maurice Dobb on the breakup of feudalism, E. P. Thompson on exploitation, and E. J. Hobsbawm on machine breaking, Eugene Genovese on slavery, Nancy Cott on "the bonds of womanhood," Tom Dublin on the Lowell factory system and its "mill girls," Paul Faler and Alan Dawley on the shoemakers' resistance to the industrial revolution, W.E.B. Du Bois on Reconstruction, Eric Foner on the meaning of freedom for emancipated slaves, and Herb Gutman on immigrants and the shock of industrialization. Using David Montgomery's superb essays on workers' control struggles together with Harry Braverman's revealing book on the degradation of labor in the twentieth century, students learned how concerted activity and trade union militancy arose out of the capitalist drive to control all aspects of work as well as the behaviors of the people who performed it.

One year a seminar of extraordinary students met this extraordinary literature and created a peak experience for me as a seminar leader. The Thursday night gang, which always continued the seminar at Richard's Pub, included Jim O'Halloran, a garrulous man and head of the printer's chapel at the *Boston Herald* who would decide to do a thesis on Dorothy Day and the Catholic worker movement; Mike Bonislawski, a machinist at the GE River Works in Lynn who went on to do Ph.D. work in labor history on the anti-Communist movement that split his local union; Jeff Crosby, another machinist in the same plant, who headed the slate that brought the left back to office in the same Lynn local; Elizabeth Connor, a dedicated socialist who had helped "colonize" Baltimore's Sparrows Point steel plant; Michael McDevitt, an officer of the AMTRAK workers union who became a union-side lawyer; Wally Soper, a troublemaker with a sense of humor who became a union organizer and activist for Jobs with Justice; Janice Fine, a brilliant community organizer, who went on to MIT—of all places—to write a doctoral thesis on new union organizing strategies; and Tim Costello, a Teamster militant and writing partner of radical historian Jeremy Brecher—"Cosmic" Tim, who seemed to have trucked everywhere and read everything. What a group of students, and what a privilege it was to be in the same seminar room with them for a whole year as we traveled down the exciting roads charted by the best social historians.

Since the college's curriculum was highly flexible and not entirely course based, other exciting opportunities arose. Drawing upon the experience of the trade union students at the Ruskin History Workshop, I offered a "doing history" activity for those who wanted to gain competence in researching and writing the history of their own communities, workplaces, and social struggles. Engaging in these learning activities convinced me that the working people in our college needed and wanted to "get their history into their own hands," to use the words of Brazilian educator Paulo Freire.[16]

The British History Workshop approach sought to engage "the imaginations of trade unionists in adult education by getting them to explore their own occupations." Our adult students often found the study of their own occupations a good place to start because it provided more entry points related to their own experiences. Through these specific entry points, they could gain a greater feeling of mastery over a historical problem and learn to think more confidently about addressing broader questions in labor and social history.[17] When our students focused on specific topics, like an industry, a union, a community, or a strike, they could act like historians in their own right and begin to demystify historical scholarship.

Worker-students at our college produced histories of their own occupations, like the impact of Taylorism on postal workers, and wrote fascinating reflections on their own work as organizers of Mississippi pulp wood workers, Maine paper workers, and Miami building-trades workers. From these starting points, they began to study how social movements emerged from workplaces and communities to challenge the forces of capital and the state that now seemed so triumphant. It was easy for our working-class students, who had been pummeled by these forces, to adopt a pessimistic view of the past that "the more things change, the more they remain the same." It was a revelation for them to discover the rich vein of oppositional history uncovered by the new social and labor historians.[18]

Opening the University to Union Workers

At the same time, other movement historians were reaching out to unionized workers. Herbert Gutman, Steve Brier, Susan Porter Benson, Alice Kessler-Harris, Mike Merrill, Dorothy Sue Cobble, and David Bensman all shared my desire to create spaces in universities, places where we could teach movement history to workers. We also shared an interest in reviving labor education as a medium through which intellectuals could participate in movement building.

During the 1970s and 1980s we tried to connect with a labor movement facing the terrible onslaught described in the previous chapter, and as movement educators and activists, we tried, as Myles Horton reflected, to "anticipate a social movement." You try to "do things in advance that prepare for a larger movement," he explained many years later. "If you've guessed right," he wrote in his autobiography, "then you'll be on the inside of a movement helping with the mobilization and strategies, instead of on the outside jumping on the bandwagon and never being an important part of it." Horton and people at Highlander guessed right about the civil rights movement in the 1950s, and, as a result, their school was built into the movement as it gathered momentum.[19]

In my third year at CPCS, a new dean arrived. Murray Frank came from the college in New York established for union members by District Council 37 of the American Federation of State, County and Municipal Employees. Murray encouraged my efforts to create a labor studies degree program. One student, Darleen Gondola Bonislawski, bolstered my hope that union workers wanted and needed such a program. Darleen was one of the most remarkable of many working-class women who found their way to the college. Raised in a North Cambridge housing project, she worked in the cafeteria in the Harvard Business School, where she inherited union leadership from her feisty mother and nourished her class resentments as she served lunches to the future kings of the Fortune 500. Darleen showed a passionate interest in my labor history course and in our popular history book about Boston's workers, and in 1980 she became the first student to major in our new Labor Studies Program, which drew upon the curriculum already created to train paralegal workers.

The college's curriculum offered several advantages to working-class adult learners. It created possibilities for students to negotiate with evaluators over prior learning and therefore reduced the students' deference to the arbitrary authority some professors exercised in a graded curriculum. It provided valuable flexibility for working students by freeing them from the demand that all credits be earned in the classroom. It encouraged students to present prior learning for evaluation toward their degree requirements and provided an introductory self-assessment course that increased the self-confidence of many students enormously. Our self-assessment workshop helped students to explore their work lives and cultural backgrounds. They were encouraged to make presentations on various workplace and union problems based on earlier learning experiences.

This workshop also raised questions about cultural awareness among diverse groups of workers separated by race and gender, skill and trade, and so forth. The evaluation work and life experience for credit presented some philosophical and pedagogical problems, such as the difficulty of testing academic knowledge in a succinct competency statement based on specific criteria. Since the rest of the curriculum was also divided into specific statements of learning outcomes, we risked cutting students off from the open-ended inquiry into the arts and humanities often denied working-class people. Besides, experiential education created the danger that learning would remained grounded in "prior learning" and fail to move students to "new learning." Genuine education comes about through experience, but as Dewey pointed out, not all experiences are "genuinely or equally educative."[20] Indeed, some experiences may lead to miseducation and inhibit the possibility of having richer learning experiences in the future. One of the most difficult challenges for educators who value experience lies in helping students examine the information they have received and the opinions they have formed about "others" and to open the way for new learning about other peoples' experience.

In confronting this challenge the college created some of the best learning experiences we offered. In the initial "assessment" workshop, students from different unions and industries and cultural backgrounds could learn about each others' experience, begin to understand and respect differences, and explore common ground. It even provided an opportunity for improving cultural awareness among workers who were separated in many other respects.

Like the graduates of the AFL-CIO-Antioch bachelor's degree program, our labor studies students usually rated interaction with the other unionists as the most valuable aspect of their educational experience.[21] Excited by the wealth of experience students brought to the college, we attempted to emulate the movement approach to adult education pioneered by Myles Horton at Highlander, where, he recalled, "we took people who were already doing something in their own community, in their unions. They would talk about their problems and how they dealt with them and exchange ideas. It was peer learning; they would learn from each other. Then we'd learn from history and other things, but . . . it wasn't subject oriented; it was problem oriented."[22]

During the past eighteen years ninety-four trade unionists earned their bachelor of arts degrees in labor studies from the University of Massachusetts-Boston because they were willing and able to balance the demands of life, work, and learning, and because they were willing and able to take advantage of the alternative curriculum our college offered students—a curriculum that offered workers meaningful access to higher education.[23] Despite serious cutbacks at the university and despite the decline of labor studies in other state universities, our little program survived and expanded as a result of modest support from the college and critical support from local unions.[24]

Our success in attracting trade union members and helping them complete a labor studies degree required more than offering an alternative, adult-oriented curriculum; it also depended upon offering tuition assistance. Throughout the sixties and seventies the University of Massachusetts at Boston offered low-cost education for working-class people, but with the fiscal crisis of the eighties and cuts in legislative support, tuition and fees were raised to cover costs, thus excluding many of those whom the campus was supposed to serve. Fortunately, the tuition-waiver program offered to many government employees kept the door opened. Our college extended waivers to other groups of workers. Each semester for the past dozen years, ten to fifteen union members belonging to six union locals have received tuition credits—usually the equivalent of 50 to 80 percent of overall costs—generated by their own unions through an agreement with our college. In return for tuition assistance to their union members, officers and staff of several local unions provide instruction and internship opportunities to the program. At first, many of our students were officers, staffers, and radical activists who had dropped out of college and wanted to complete their degrees, but then, because of the tuition support, more rank-and-file members started to enroll, especially from public-sector unions.

Finding Friends, Encountering Enemies

Although individual trade unionists found their way to our program, it was a difficult challenge to convince local trade union leaders that their members could benefit from the kind of college education we offered. Outside of a few public sector union leaders, these officials were not college educated and they simply did not conceive of the university as a place to send their members for education. Many of them encouraged people in the ranks to participate in noncredit labor extension courses to learn the nuts and bolts of bargaining and grievance handling. But they thought college education was for managerial and professional people. If workers went to college, it meant they would leave the ranks to "better themselves." Worse, they might return to the local with their educational credentials and with new ideas about challenging the incumbent leaders. It seemed pointless, therefore, to request official AFL-CIO backing for our program. The answer was a foregone conclusion.

In any case, the program was intended to be independent of union influence, a free space in which union members could engage in critical education, and if they chose, hone criticisms of their own leaders and organizations. As a result, my own standing with the AFL-CIO became more and more problematic during the early years when the program was taking shape. I teamed up with an obstreperous group of union insurgents who held lively conferences in our college on "Putting the Movement Back in the Labor Movement." Some of these militants had been elected to offices in local unions and all of them had been active in struggles to defend unions against hostile employees. The activists who emerged in Boston-area unions during the eighties were extraordinary people. Experienced, tactically talented, and deeply committed, they were determined to reform and rebuild the labor movement. I chose to support their efforts, even though this meant antagonizing powerful union officials.

In 1981 I wrote for the *Globe* on the illegal air traffic controllers' strike in that year. "Where's Labor's Solidarity?"—later reprinted in the dissident magazine *Labor Notes*—asked why other unions did not support the PATCO strikers and provided answers from labor history that explained why the right to strike was lost. The editorial also argued that unjust laws had to be defied in order for the movement to meet the crisis.[25] This initial effort to make labor history public criticized labor law and the unions' capitulation to it and was not well received by AFL-CIO officials.

Following the busting of the air traffic controllers' strike, labor relations in Massachusetts became far more contentious. And by the mid-1980s even old-fashioned business unions felt the tremors of insurgency as younger activists called for change.[26] Struggles against plant closings and concession demands generated surprising militancy among unions, even in Boston, where extreme moderation had reigned since the traumatic defeat of the police strike in 1919.

In the early eighties radical reformers took over the locals of several service-sector unions with largely female and minority membership, locals once ruled by corrupt officials. Two young working-class guys from South Boston were elected to head the union of support staff at Boston City Hospital with the help of some feisty radicals and disfranchised workers of color. Another socialist, Celia Wcislo, who worked in the same hospital, teamed up with hospital organizer Nancy Mills to win election to the largest service workers local in the state, Local 285, of the Service Employees International Union. They immediately helped recruit their members to our program through an agreement with the college to provide pro bono instructors in return for reduced tuition for their members. Furthermore, Local 285 offered us a solid base of support in a large union with progressive leaders who were willing to encourage their members to study in our education program.

The most exciting and controversial figure on the Boston labor scene was Domenic Bozzotto, an Italian American bartender who had been active in the civil rights movement before becoming the president of the Hotel and Restaurant Workers Union Local 26. He took control away from the front-of-the-house bartenders and waitresses and fought for the back-of-the-house workers, mostly immigrants and people of color. The local quickly plunged into a series of mass mobilizations of its multinational membership, which made us feel like the IWW had risen from the dead. Domenic exuded charisma. He made people believe in the power of rank-and-file workers, and he could mobilize them to win real victories. He also could be a devilish prankster who, it was alleged, threatened to let loose rats in Boston hotels to win wage hikes for the maids toiling at the back of the house. A tactical genius, he willingly allied with radicals of all stripes, confident that he could outsmart and outmaneuver them all.

When I first asked Bozzotto if I could recruit his local's members to our labor education program, he seemed friendly, showing none of the discomfort many union guys felt with academics. I participated in the local's "never surrender" campaigns and shared a cell with some of its members when a bunch of us went to jail after being arrested for sitting in at the bus station during the Greyhound strike. Soon afterward, I asked Bozzotto if he wanted to co-teach a course on organizing. He seemed doubtful at first but then agreed to do so in return for tuition credits for his members. Our association provided further evidence that my work as a labor educator was a threat to the AFL-CIO leadership, because

Bozzotto was leading groups of insurgent union activists who criticized that leadership for failing to meet the crisis of the 1980s and for refusing to mobilize their own troops to do the solidarity work unions needed.

The insurgents formed the Massachusetts Labor Support Project, which quickly became an instant mobilization agency—"dial-a-mob" is what activist Rand Wilson called it. A few younger activists from old-line unions like the Ironworkers and the Sign Painters took the risk of getting involved with this left-led coalition movement, attracted by the need to do solidarity work for striking workers at TWA, Greyhound, Hormel, Eastern Airlines, and International Paper at Jay, Maine. Rand Wilson then became the director of a Boston chapter of Jobs with Justice, formed by a coalition of unions determined to seek community allies in an effort to recreate the social unionism of the 1930s. Steve Early, an organizer for the Communications Workers and an experienced labor journalist, played an important role as a strategist and as a critic of AFL-CIO officials who remained committed to the old forms of business unionism created in the years of prosperity when corporations and trade unions could bargain in relative peace. These leaders did not like being told that business unionism no longer met the needs of a labor movement in crisis and they didn't like seeing me quoted to that effect in the *Boston Sunday Globe Magazine*.[27]

What made the situation tricky for these officials was that other labor leaders, including some from established unions, had become increasingly militant in their effort to fight back against management attacks. During the Greyhound strike the stolid building trades, now led by a firebrand named Tommy Evers, filled Copley Square nine thousand strong and battled mounted police to shut down the bus station on the day before Thanksgiving, the busiest travel day of the year.

Evers was a very strong-willed leader raised in Charlestown, a tough Boston neighborhood where he was apprenticed as an Ironworker. In 1972 his local had been sued to force the entry of black workers into the apprenticeship program. As a local union leader during and after "the busing," Evers defended his local. When he became state leader of the building trades he tried to revive a movement lulled to sleep by its monopoly over government work. He even supported others who wanted to fight, including militant interracial unions of hotel workers and school bus drivers. After a life-threatening heart attack, he also reached out to the left and considered hiring radicals to organize non-union construction workers of color.

Evers also participated when the Labor Support Project organized a militant May Day demonstration against Harvard University's investment in Shell Oil. The United Mine Workers' ambitious Shell boycott attracted a lot of union support for the event, causing concern at the AFL-CIO headquarters, which opposed these activities. A smaller group of labor activists also participated in a rally and occupation of a Boston coin shop selling the South African Krugerrand, where Evers made a stirring speech, much to the chagrin of other AFL-

CIO officials. As we walked the picket line, I talked to him about enrolling in our Labor Studies Program (which he did for a term) and about the idea of organizing a big commemorative event on the next May Day, the centennial of the great eight-hour general strike led by the building trades in 1886. This commemorative event, described in the next chapter, created serious problems for the president of the state AFL CIO, Arthur Osborn, who was deeply sus-picious of my work as an educator and historian.

For example, he objected to an op-ed piece for the *Boston Globe* I wrote in 1986 about a surprising strike that erupted at the General Electric River Works in Lynn. That March nine thousand workers walked out to protest the suspen-sion of a shop steward and the company's sabotage of the grievance procedure.[28] I wanted to help the strike leader, Local 201's business agent Ron Malloy, who was a student in our Labor Studies Program. He had just led a progressive slate to victory over the entrenched anti-Communist leadership that had ruled the union since the days in the fifties when the International Union of Electrical Workers (IUE) displaced the left-wing United Electrical Workers (UE). The IUE's anti-Communist leaders fought four bitter battles to keep the original CIO union from regaining power in Local 201.[29] My editorial for the *Globe* infuriated the old-guard powers in the IUE district office because I suggested that its war against the UE had reduced union strength at G.E. The influential IUE district chief had complained bitterly that I had branded his organization "a company union." His suspicions grew when I presented a slide show history lecture to the shop stewards at Local 201 that included a frank discussion of the war between the UE and the IUE, and then invited David Montgomery, a UE veteran, to the union hall in Lynn to speak about that "living history."

About this time, state AFL-CIO leader Arthur Osborn gave a speech to the administrators of public colleges and the two dozen trade unionists whom he had placed as trustees on their boards. He advocated for labor studies, but not the "negative" kind of labor history that pointed up the alleged shortcomings of unions and their elected leaders. Marty Blatt of the History Workshop heard the speech and was sure Osborn was targeting our kind of movement history.

Breaking the Ice

But in 1988 more encouraging signs appeared. The desperate strike that year by International Paper workers in the small company town of Jay, Maine, gener-ated inspiring community support and regional backing. The strikers made an attempt through the town meeting to limit IP's use of strikebreakers, a major problem for unions and labor law in the eighties; this reminded me of Herb Gutman's work on how nineteenth-century communities responded to "the invasion of the village green" by industrialists—the theme of a Labor Day edi-torial I wrote on how the past resurfaced in contemporary strikes.[30] During a support demonstration for the Jay workers I met a paper worker on a picket line who had read the editorial.[31] He asked me to come up and speak at the regular Wednesday night meetings held in the high school gym where, one night, so many people had crowded in to hear Jesse Jackson speak that they had to applaud—as they did long and hard—with their hands raised above their heads.

Jesse Jackson's 1988 presidential campaign generated palpable support from white workers, the so-called "Bubba" vote the Democrats had lost to the GOP in the Reagan years. I wrote an editorial about Jackson's campaign arguing that a new populism had emerged that could make a class-conscious appeal while still emphasizing racism, the Achilles' heel of earlier populist movements. Although most unions backed native son Governor Michael Dukakis, key union activists worked for Jackson, and several won seats as his delegates to the Democratic convention. The *Globe* editorial on Jackson's "class act" elicited some positive responses from mainstream union guys who recognized Jesse's powerful appeal to their members—a sign that movement politics, inspired by the civil rights movement, had begun to penetrate a few corners of the House of Labor.[32]

That summer employers launched a major attack on the backbone of organized labor in the Commonwealth—the unionized building trades. The non-union contractors organized a well-financed referendum campaign to strike down the state's prevailing wage law that helped ensure that publicly financed jobs would be done by union labor. Once again, a struggle erupted over a life-or-death matter for unions because the building trades unions depended largely on public work. These unions had been committed to conservative business practices and had excluded women and minorities, though for a variety of reasons the percentage of females and workers of color in their apprenticeships had grown in the mid-eighties. Led by new progressive state leaders, the building trades mobilized their entire constituency for the first time in a hundred years; they linked up with other unions and social movements through an overall AFL- CIO effort headed by Arthur Osborn, who proved an effective leader and coalition builder.

As vice president of our faculty staff union at UMass-Boston, I noticed how isolated we were as members of the National Education Association. Though we had elected progressive presidents to head the Massachusetts Teachers Association, we remained an island of professionals in a turbulent sea of drowning blue-collar unions. I wrote about the campaign for a teachers union newspaper that reached over sixty thousand public school teachers throughout the state.[33] Trade union officials appreciated the gesture because our teachers association was politically potent though often at odds with the AFL-CIO and its affiliate, the rival American Federation of Teachers. In 1988 my association stood with the rest of the labor movement.

The unions began the campaign to save the prevailing wage law way behind in the public opinion polls, but the mobilization, using new movement-building tactics, turned the tide. The anti-union measure went down to defeat by a good margin.[34] Jubilant over the victory and the favorable public attention labor received, Arthur Osborn reached out, thanked me, and when I asked, he agreed to speak in public at a forum we organized for the Labor Studies Program on how the movement won this one. The continuing crisis of the movement created a context in which we could cooperate and learn from each other.

Forging a Link

The coalition-building that began in 1988 made it easier for us to gain union support for our program. By now dozens of graduates were working in local unions and offering us their support. It took a few years to demonstrate that while many of our students did hope that a college degree would allow them to move to another place in their work lives, they did not want to leave the labor movement.

Two-thirds of all who graduated before 1990 had remained in the labor movement, often in leadership positions. Some needed and wanted the diploma to advance their careers in labor-related vocations, but most seemed drawn to higher education for reasons of personal growth and political commitment—to empower themselves as advocates and leaders for the movement. The program recreated the link "between worker and education and progressive social action" forged by the clothing workers unions and later by the radical teachers at Brookwood Labor College and Highlander Folk School.[35] Our college was a transition house for radicals who had plunged into the unions in the seventies and now needed some time to pause and reflect after being active in their unions during the bitter battles of the 1980s; they needed the free space to think and reflect and to meet people outside their locals and job sites.[36] Many of these students remained active as insurgents criticizing undemocratic and ineffective leaders in their unions, while others had taken on leadership roles in the locals and were pushing to create change at a higher level. Other students were rank-and-file members and local officials who remained union loyalists. Our program welcomed both groups. Despite our critics' belief that we were simply training union radicals, we decided our efforts must remain unbiased and open to all, a requirement of public education. Though most of us who taught had been critics of the union establishment, we did not want to make the program itself part of a "counter-movement" of the left against incumbent labor officials.[37] This was the role assumed by the radical labor schools of the 1930s whose founders rejected public universities as a base for worker education and made their independent schools into oppositional institutions. We chose a different path and attempted to create a space for critical worker education within a university, though this intention did not protect us from the criticism that we were engaged in ideological indoctrination.

By the end of the 1980s, however, even some of our former critics began to acknowledge that we had opened up meaningful access to the state university to union workers who were, in the words of one national union president, largely

Engaging in labor studies with union workers: Estelle Thompson leading a class of CIO activists at Highlander Folk School, 1947. *Courtesy State Historical Society of Wisconsin, photograph Whi x3 43725.*

"ignored and underserved."[38] Our students and graduates were our ambassadors and even our missionaries to union organizations whose leaders remained suspicious, if not hostile, to our efforts.

By the end of the 1980s our students and graduates included the presidents of two large public employees unions, the business representative for Boston city workers, the president of the State Building Trades Council and of the large electrical workers local in Boston, as well as the vice president of the utility workers and the head of the big industrial union at General Electric in Lynn. They brought an end to the days when our program could be marginalized and red baited. Their experience also showed that our students graduated and continued their work in the labor movement.

The program even began to win some favorable attention from the State AFL-CIO after a talented iron worker named Bobby Haynes became secretary treasurer. Educated at UMass Boston, he was not especially threatened by intellectuals. He ardently defended the AFL-CIO against its radical critics, but he also believed the labor movement had to change and made no secret of his discontent with national union officials. Haynes thought unions needed allies in the universities, in the communities, and in other institutions. As a leader of the 1988 fight to save the prevailing wage law, he concluded that the labor movement could no longer go it alone. Bobby was committed to building up labor education within the University of Massachusetts, even if it meant taking on some of those who criticized our program. In fact, he drafted a state law placing a union representative on the boards of public institutions of higher learning. When he became a trustee of the university labor educators gained an important ally.

From the beginning the program attracted more women as students than was usually the case in traditional union training efforts. Our early ties to public employee unions with female officials helped start us on the road to leadership development for women activists. Our progress accelerated when Cheryl Gooding volunteered to assist me in developing the program while she worked as the representative of our new faculty staff union. When she became associate director she put her experience to good use. She had graduated from our college while working at Greater Boston Legal Services, where she organized a union of paralegals. Cheyl expanded the agreements we had made with union locals so that students would receive reduced tuition. As a result, we recruited an even larger number of women and more workers of color.

Some students entered the program through the Women's Institute for Leadership Development (WILD), which Cheryl helped to organize with other labor educators. WILD organizers even managed to win the tentative support of the State Federation of Labor for their efforts to train women union members for leadership roles. Women workers responded warmly to the WILD summer institutes, just as they had in the early 1900s to the Women's Trade Union League school in Chicago, attended by Fannia Cohn who later led the effective education programs of the International Ladies Garment Workers Union designed to give workers "the mental and moral equipment" they needed "to serve the labor movement" and "be useful to their class."[39] The account of WILD's effort at coalition building and leadership training written by Cheryl and her successor, Patricia Reeve, is a good example of how the new labor education movement of the 1980s reached union members with new approaches and challenged old barriers to participation.[40] As a result of these efforts, our Labor Studies Program became more diverse, so that by 1992, 60 percent of the students were women and 24 percent workers of color. But beyond inclusion, beyond providing leadership training for women, we needed to offer new learning about issues of diversity, the hardest issues to address in a movement dominated by white males who often held traditional ideas about race, gender, and sexual preference.

In Boston, which remained one of the nation's most segregated cities in terms of housing and labor markets, a critical workers education program needed to examine the hardest issue of all: racism. Our program was fortunate enough to be assisted in this effort by Bill Fletcher who taught as a field instructor. He had been raised in New York by parents who belonged to unions. His father had refused to turn against unionism even though his local was "mobbed up." Fletcher brought his family traditions to Harvard where he joined other students in fighting for a black studies program headed by the socialist Ewart Guinier, a program the university was undermining. He took a job as a welder in the General Dynamics shipyard where several socialists and union reformers were active, and then in 1980 became an organizer for the Boston Jobs Coalition, where he worked on the front lines of the tense fight for affirmative-action hiring in the predominantly white, male construction industry. Bill remained active in these struggles even after he joined a remarkable group of paralegals at Greater Boston Legal Services whose union, District 65, had begun to organize other service workers. He became an organizer for the child care and human service local of District 65 at the time it merged with the United Auto Workers.

I worked with Bill Fletcher in various movement activities, including Mel King's 1983 mayoral campaign, and when I edited a collection of *Radical America* labor history articles that same year, he read my introduction and said he wanted to talk about the commonalities in our approaches to problems of race and class in movement building. Our conversations convinced me that our union students needed to learn from Bill. He agreed to teach courses on black workers history and workplace discrimination.

We shared a passion for doing movement history and cooked up a plan to present it in multicultural format. Through Bill's contacts, we reached Bernadette Devlin McAliskey in Northern Ireland and invited her to a forum we called "Green and Black" held in March of 1986. The idea was to show the connections and parallels between the black freedom movement and the Irish Catholic civil rights movement. Bernadette enthralled a packed house at our college, describing the influence of our civil rights movement on the new Irish republican movement.[41] The event put movement history on all the evening news programs in Boston and gave Bill what he called "the credibility" to visit the republican groups in Northern Ireland.

The college offered an unusual setting for labor education because it included so many neighborhood activists and students of color who staffed community-based agencies. It seemed like a promising place to open some lines of communication between that world and the largely white world of organized labor. When Pat Reeve became associate director of the Labor Studies Program, she shared my interest in using history to raise questions about exclusion and discrimination. Pat's ambitious course, "Getting a Seat at the Table," used some of the revealing new labor history on race and gender identities to push beyond a discussion of discrimination to a debate about inclusion and power sharing. Using difficult interpretive literature, she encouraged "students to grapple with the past as a means of addressing moral questions in the present."[42] Instead of presenting historical studies based in a scholarly community as received information, she used critical debates about race and gender as stimuli for discussion within a classroom based community of inquiry, where students learned to question their own culture and experience, and confront the problems they faced in a labor movement that lacked a demonstrated commitment to power-sharing within its ranks.[43]

New Opportunities for Teaching Movement History

Things were changing in labor education across the country. The old guard that served the house of labor in the Cold War years had given way to a new generation of labor educators influenced by the social movements of the sixties and by the popular education movement's effort to democratize adult learning. One important example of this shift came in 1987 at the prestigious Harvard Trade Union Program, established in 1942 during the heyday of industrial relations as a field. The TUP had survived as a ten-week executive training session for top local and national leaders while being housed in the Harvard Business School. Even after the program left the "B School," it was protected by the labor law scholar Derek Bok when he was president of Harvard and by the influential labor economist John Dunlop, who had been U.S. secretary of labor.

One of our own students, Celia Wcislo, attended the program and suggested that I visit the director and offer to teach labor history for the program. She thought there was plenty of room for improvement. One visit with the director foreclosed that possibility. He told me how much he disliked the new labor history and its harsh treatment of union officials. A year later he retired and was replaced by Linda Kaboolian, an activist in the AFT from Michigan, who asked me to teach the core course in labor history, not to celebrate the institutional survival of unions, but rather to problematize the institutional history and focus students' attention on strategic decisions made—and unmade—in the past. Encouraged by this invitation, I decided not to ask students to borrow knowledge from a history bank where I worked as a teller, but to follow Freire's suggestion that education dialogue begin with problem posing.[44]

Each year for the next decade I taught an often diverse group of trade unionists who came to Harvard from all over the United States and from other nations. At first, I wondered if my radical labor history book and my critical approach to teaching movement history would offend some of the union officials in the class. I adopted a participatory approach in which each student presented a class report on some historical problem, often a case study of some controversial issue. By democratizing the course, and opening up to all voices and opinions, my own voice became one of many, and by no means the only one, drawing critical lessons from the past. The class became a safe place to study current labor problems in historical context. It became a learning community where each student could share a discovery about the past and address a question about a critical choice that once had faced the labor movement.

The new labor history excited many of these trade union students, because it allowed them to discover a hidden past, one in which radicals played a far greater role than they expected; it also allowed them to see a labor movement that often opposed the triumph of "free market" economics, conservative politics, and competitive capitalist values. Indeed, much of that history counters the pessimism that informs contemporary scholarship.[45] These students were eager to learn because they worried deeply about the fate of their unions, which, some Harvard professors told them, were on the verge of extinction unless they changed and abandoned their old adversarial ways. Overwhelmed by data and analysis of labor's current plight, they found in stories about labor's past what one woman student called "a beautiful contrast." Another trade union student summarized the feeling of others when he wrote: "This class has rejuvenated our energy to continue our efforts to regain the power the American labor movement possessed in the past."

Teaching history at the Harvard Trade Union Program created new opportunities for applying a problem-posing approach to the past in union based educational settings. My favorite students at Harvard were the brilliant miners who left the coal fields to join the talented national staff assembled by Richard Trumka, the young reformer elected to lead the United Mine Workers in 1981. I met Trumka when he came to Harvard for a showing of John Sayles's film *Matewan*, which we introduced to a audience of trade unionists and students. He liked my approach to UMWA history and asked me to come down to Beckley, West Virginia, for two days to teach labor history to one hundred organizers. I agreed in a heartbeat, and proposed using the participatory approach to worker education developed by Les Leopold and Mike Merrill at the Labor Institute in New York. I prepared a packet for the session which included a historical chronology that placed UMW history in a national context listing important events and development. I asked them to compare this time line with statistical information represented in graphs that included variables related to the expansion and decline of the union's membership. After my slide lectures focusing on how and why the mine workers' movement grew, the organizers broke up into groups to discuss the historical information I gave them and to address the questions I posed.[46]

The sessions were lively and well received. Trumka wanted a reprise. He invited me to do a similar presentation focusing on the hard work of union organizing for the UMWA International Executive Board in Washington, which was about to invest in a new outreach program. The invitation represented a rare chance to teach labor history to union leaders with pressing concerns about rebuilding their movement.

When I arrived in the dusty old UMWA offices in Washington, Trumka introduced me to Jesse Jackson, who was there to offer the board his support for the union's bitter strike against Pittston Coal Group in Virginia, a story recounted in chapter 9. Hearing the coal miners from all over North America testify their loyalty to Jackson's progressive vision was a memorable experience.

I immediately volunteered to work with UMW staff on the Pittston strike, an experience that deepened my relationship with Rich Trumka and some of his gifted, committed staff. With his support, I was able to act as co-chair of the Boston area Pittston strike support committee and build new working relationships with a range of trade union officials, including the president of the State Federation of Labor. In his visits to Boston during the Pittston strike, Trumka did a world of good for my efforts to win union support for the kind of labor education we offered. When he agreed to address our tenth anniversary event in 1990, he had become a new hope for thousands of rank-and-file activists inspired by his honest assessment of the crisis facing unions and his earnest call for a social movement unionism to replace the old ways. Trumka's speech at our dinner in the local electricians' hall charged up our audience of students, graduates, and supporters, emphasizing what we could learn from labor's ordeal and from the black workers' movement in South Africa. His appearance and endorsement of our efforts marked a turning point in our struggle to win union support for our version of workers' education and its role in creating the new labor movement Trumka advocated with power and eloquence.

Besides this political boost, Trumka's support offered crucial opportunities to test the belief we shared about the importance of historical consciousness in the movement building process. Indeed, in subsequent years I have heard numerous union leaders of all kinds call for "more labor history." They want more of it in the public schools where students are being trained to be obedient workers without any sense of their rights, but also for their own members who no longer come from union families and who lack any sense of the struggle that helps them understand why workers need an aggressive labor movement. At a time when the AFL-CIO and some of its affiliates are mobilizing their members for ambitious organizing drives, their leaders fear the case for unionism will not be made in a very compelling way. It is not history in an academic sense they want to convey to their members; it is a sense of the past that helps young people feel like actors in an old morality play, like inheritors of a tradition. Sometimes when they ask me to do history for the members, what they really seem to want is a kind of sermon on values and traditions to revive their passive congregations.

During the 1990s, as the winds of change blew through the house of labor, radical teachers reached a wider audience when they called for critical education that empowered rank-and-file members. Addressing the University and College Labor Education Association in 1990, John Russo of Youngstown State University called upon us to replace the old servicing model of worker training with an organizing model designed to encourage meaningful participation by union members. "Rather than taking advantage of membership knowledge and skills in instructional activities," he said, too many labor educators held on to the traditional delivery methods dependent on the teacher as trainer and expert, because those in charge felt "threatened politically" when the members examined past practices and explored alternative strategies. Speaking in the George Meany Center, the AFL-CIO's official school for workers in Maryland, Russo challenged labor educators to shed their fears and run the risk of upsetting our patrons in union offices. Besides pushing the membership to develop their own strategies, he called upon labor educators to tackle the most controversial issue of all: the lack of union democracy in many unions that functioned much like one-party states. These efforts might be seen as disloyal, he said, but they were necessary if unions expected to revive themselves by mobilizing their members. Like local union members, labor educators should adopt an organizing model of unionism to replace the old servicing model.[47]

For the past decade I have taken a problem-posing approach to teaching labor history to union members, an approach that asks them to think together about what went wrong in the past and what in that past still offers them hope. The dialogue that ensues usually leads to free discussions about what is still wrong in the present. Many students have been willing to make sharp criticisms of the movement in rendering historical judgments, even about controversial issues like anti-Communist purges and the AFL-CIO's Cold War foreign policy. They have also used historical cases to analyze sensitive matters and controversies often too explosive to discuss in their current manifestations, especially patterns and practices of racism and sexism within unions.

Evaluations returned by over four hundred students in the Harvard Trade Union Program who took the history course over the last decade repeatedly emphasized the importance of learning from the movement's "mistakes" including, above all, the mistake of exclusion. These reports, said one trade union student, were critical, "in that we could look back and determine what we considered mistakes," and they were "creative in that we could use history as a way of thinking about new strategies. . . ."

My role as a history teacher is to share some of what I have learned from other historians to serve as an intermediary between my scholarly community and the learning community I am trying to create with worker students.[48] This task does not depend much upon delivering prepared lectures drawing on the bank of historical knowledge. Instead, I have been drawn more and more to history telling, to narrating the movement stories I believe are most pregnant with meaning. My job is to provide a kind of master narrative of movement history and then ask the students to share in the story telling, to report on certain chapters in labor's untold story. I must push the learning process beyond narrative reporting by selecting meaningful stories and posing difficult questions about their meanings. But even when worker-students choose not to address my often loaded questions, they convey wisdom in the very ways they tell the story, especially when they connect their report to their own histories and those of their fellow workers. As I have matured as a teacher and storyteller, I have become convinced of what Alan Dawley says when he argues that we understand "narrative, whether as history or myth, as memory or prophecy" as a "precondition for historical agency." Whether the goal is redemption or revolution, Dawley argues, "the sense of connection to the past provides identity and momentum, while the belief in an altered future gives hope and purpose." Such narratives can encourage "people of all ranks to engage in strategic thinking" about their past and their future.[49]

My efforts as a teacher of history have paralleled those of a whole new generation of labor educators, some of them veterans of sixties' social movements and some of them products of union struggles. At this point, it is difficult to evaluate the impact of the educational opportunities we have offered union members and movement activists over the past decade or so. Maybe some day historians will look back and say, as Myles Horton did when he looked back on popular education in the 1930s, that what we learned from each other sparked the efforts of union people to survive the crisis of our time and build a stronger movement for the next time.

Part Two

TELLING MOVEMENT STORIES IN PUBLIC

Appreciating bright moments in movement history: Laura Foner reciting a speech given at the Women's Trade Union League's founding convention for a History Workshop commemoration in Boston's Faneuil Hall, 1983. Photograph by the author.

CHAPTER **4**

Commemorating Moments of Solidarity in Massachusetts Labor History

In 1982 Herbert Gutman addressed the Organization of American Historians about his experience of sharing the new social and labor history with union workers, through a seminar funded by the National Endowment for the Humanities.[1] It was a bittersweet encounter because he realized, as never before, how working people had "had been cut off from their past, deprived of access to the historical processes that shaped their lives, the lives of their parents and the nation at large." One of the trade union participants in Gutman's history seminar was an Alabama industrial unionist named A. S. Lemart, who had built his union, helped to integrate it, and served as a statewide labor official. "A quiet, dignified, largely self-educated Southern trade union leader, democratic in his instincts and demeanor," this man was stunned when he discovered "the thwarted efforts by white and black unions to build democratic and protective unions in his own father's youth." Lemart was "the direct heir of experiences important to his everyday work as a trade unionist, yet those experiences were totally closed off to him."[2]

Gutman argued that Lemart was a lot like Mathilda Teoli of Lawrence who told a reporter that her mother Camella had never revealed the very dramatic role she played as a teenager in the great Bread and Roses strike of 1912. They were both victims of an "amnesia" that affected most Americans during decades when mainstream culture celebrated "American-ness" by "defining it narrowly and identifying it with achievement and assimilation," said Gutman. "The tension between individualist and collectivist ways of dealing with dependency, inequality, and exploitation" remained under cover until a few people began to share closely-held life stories—people like Nate Shaw, the militant Alabama sharecropper who spoke about a life full of race and class tension. The civil rights and women's movements created new tensions in society and stimulated

101

curiosity about past conflicts, but most people, according to Gutman, remained enthralled by the old historical synthesis celebrating a tension-free America. In 1982 these tensions between individualism and mutualism "appeared to be of interest mainly to antiquarian leftist 'social' historians."[3]

Herb Gutman's attempts to bring labor movement history to the labor activists like A. S. Lemart left him worried that the new history of the 1960s and 1970s had "bypassed most of the people in the audience." It was almost as though it had been written in a foreign language.[4] Hoping to transcend a fragmented, localized social history, Gutman worked with Alfred Young to organize a conference to discuss how social and labor historians could construct a new synthesis to replace the old one.

More than fifty of us gathered at Northern Illinois University in 1983 in a surprisingly gloomy frame of mind, sharing in one way or another Gutman's concerns about the effectiveness of our efforts. Some even questioned the relevance of labor history when union workers voted for Ronald Reagan, when union leaders twiddled their thumbs while the house of labor crumbled, and when AFL-CIO head George Meany thumbed his nose at critics. A feeling of self-doubt prevailed at the DeKalb conference because, as one participant observed, working-class history had been nearly orphaned by the contemporary state of the American labor movement."[5] As labor historian Leon Fink put it a few years later, our generation of radical scholars seemed infected by the political pessimism of the Reagan-Bush era. In the 1950s Cold War scholars loved to dismiss the relevance of radicals and explain "why *they* lost." Then, in the 1980s we, the aging radicals of the 1960s, expressed an "equally confining cynicism" about "why *we* lost."[6]

Labor historians also seemed to be lost in their own world unable to bridge the "yawning gap" between themselves and the world of the people they presumed to describe. Indeed, few were even "rubbing shoulders with the people or events" they were interpreting. Unlike the labor intellectuals of the progressive era, Fink declared labor historians of our era had been unable to connect "personally and politically," with the union people they studied, at least not in an "institutionally creative" way.[7]

During the soul-searching conference of labor historians at DeKalb, I spoke with Steve Brier who had begun working with Herb Gutman to make social history available to union workers and to a wider public. Frustrated by only being able to reach a few trade unionists at a time, they assembled a team to write a new synthesis incorporating the fragments of social history already unearthed. Brier had visited Sweden where he discovered the remarkable worker history projects created by the "Dig Where You Stand" movement, through which local groups had involved large numbers of workers in active projects to "recapture their own pasts."[8] He was hopeful that "popular history techniques" might be more widely adopted in the United States. I shared his optimism based on our first efforts to adapt British History Workshop methods to Massachusetts people's history. Brier and I felt a little out of place in a conference of labor historians who seemed to have given in to the pessimism that had swept over American intellectuals in the Reagan era. Our experience rubbing shoulders with union workers told us there was a hunger for history out there.

Celebration and Evaluation

Those of us who participated in the Massachusetts History Workshop discovered in social history a medium through which to carry on a conversation with the retired workers who attended our gatherings in Lynn and Lawrence. We were encouraged enough to pursue a more ambitious workshop with clerical workers, but we also hoped for more trade union involvement and support. We appreciated the grants we received from the state humanities council, but we chafed a bit trying to meet the academic criteria required for funding. Academic humanists did have something to offer the public, but most of the folks in our workshop lacked academic credentials. In any case, we wanted to work with local communities not as emissaries from the academy but as collaborators in joint enterprises to study the past. We were also interested in creating less academic, more celebratory occasions to recall moments in the past when workers' solidarity appeared and unexpectedly relieved the tension between mutualism and individualism.

Of course, we were aware of the dangers inherent in commemorative history events. The People's Bicentennial Commission celebrated the American Revolution in 1976 as a triumphant moment in people's history, without considering the consequences of the Revolution for women, slaves, and native peoples. History Workshoppers in Britain worried about their own celebrations being simply "backward looking" commemorations that affirmed the enduring spirit of the common folk.[9] The Bread and Roses Pageant of April 1980, which proceeded our workshop in Lawrence, also exuded this kind of spirit, emphasizing popular unity and neglecting cultural complexity. Many neighborhood oral histories commemorated the good old days, before urban renewal, and reflected the residents' "defensive pride" as well as the strains of "parochialism and ethnocentrism" that came with the assertion of identity.[10] I had seen plenty of this in the series of neighborhood histories produced by the mayor of Boston for the Bicentennial in 1976. Indeed, my own oral history of the South End, a celebration of ethnic tolerance in the highly segregated city, missed some internal conflicts within that diverse neighborhood.

The labor movement attracted most of our attention as historians and activists, but its adherents were hardly in a mood for public celebration. Facing an onslaught from employers and Republican government officials, they retreated further into their shells like great old snapping turtles who, in David Montgomery's metaphor, struck out at their enemies when provoked. In union circles there was little interest in a past that often recalled earlier moments of conflict and defeat. Many hard-pressed labor officials wanted to forget a contentious past and present a more cooperative face to employers who demanded more productivity in the face of "foreign competition."

Nonetheless, our little history workshop group believed there was a need for celebrations that recalled earlier moments of solidarity like the ones we discussed with workers in Lynn and Lawrence, the times when workers created the kind of movements that now seemed to be missing from the scene. The challenge for us was clear. As Michael Frisch put it to other progressive oral historians in 1982, it was necessary to move beyond "the static celebration of the past to . . . a mutual and active exploration of values."[11]

Women and Unions

Our 1982 workshop on the lives of Boston clerical workers was a celebration of individual and collective strivings by women in office jobs. At the same time, speakers evaluated the problems those workers faced in labor unions whose leaders placed no value on office work and the women who performed it. Many of us in the workshop had supported efforts by feminists to organize clerical workers in our own time, and to incorporate the values of the women's movement in a reformed labor movement. One of our members, Libby Bouvier, had written a fascinating dissertation on the inspiring efforts of the Boston Women's Trade Union League to take up the same challenge during the progressive era. One of the workshop participants, Ros Feldberg, had written an excellent article on early office organizing efforts that emphasized the league's contribution.[12] We knew that the league had been founded at the American Federation of Labor Convention in 1903, and we thought it would be exciting to return to the site of that event at Boston's Faneuil Hall for a commemoration of the WTUL's founding.

But we wanted to proceed only if we could win union support. A labor leader, Nancy Mills, liked our idea and agreed to seek that support. She had recently been elected on a reform slate with two other women to head Service Employees Union Local 285, a large statewide organization of government and hospital workers. Mills agreed that a commemoration of the Women's Trade Union League would be a good way to revive the memory of an earlier generation of progressive women, like Boston's own Mary Kenney O'Sullivan, who pioneered in the effort to open the labor movement to women workers.

Mills gained an endorsement from the Massachusetts AFL-CIO Women's Committee for the eightieth anniversary of the WTUL and then from the state labor council. As a result, contributions arrived from other union locals. We decided not to seek a humanities council grant because we now had the union backing we needed, including donations from the teachers, glaziers, airline mechanics, and pipefitters.

The Women's Trade Union League commemoration, held in Faneuil Hall during International Women's Week in March of 1983, was well attended by women unionists, feminists, and other activists. Word-of-Mouth Productions, a group of women performers with a union orientation, dressed in costume and acted out speeches of WTUL organizers as people came into the hall. Dark and dusty Faneuil Hall, "the cradle of liberty," was a perfect theater of memory for Laura Foner and other performers to recite WTUL speeches and sing old songs. There were few places left in Boston, or other cities, in which to reenact scenes like this.

The event, titled "Brave and Free," reminded the audience of what the league stood for and how many of its demands were still being pursued by a successor group, the Coalition of Labor Union Women (CLUW), another cosponsor. The keynote speaker, feminist historian and novelist Meredith Tax, had written fiction and nonfiction about the league, and she was explicitly critical of the unions' treatment of women.[13] Praising the WTUL's efforts to bring women into the labor movement, Tax called for a continued struggle to expand unions to meet the concerns of women by adding "cultural and emotional components" to its appeal. "One thing is clear to anyone who studies labor history," she said to the "Brave and Free" gathering. "A labor movement that is also a women's movement is a whole other ball game from the male lodges that have been the normal form of labor organization in the U.S."[14]

AFL-CIO president, Arthur Osborn, attended the Faneuil Hall meeting and didn't seem too pleased with Tax's talk. But the event had been sponsored by "his women's committee," and he gave a speech stressing the steps unions were taking to reach out to women at work. The workshop had broken through to gain union backing and financial support and a certain degree of credibility for our recuperative historical work. We had celebrated a moment of unity in the history of the labor and women's movements, but we also had put that moment in tension with the subsequent history of union exclusion and gender bias. Our next commemorative effort again sought union support to celebrate a far more controversial moment in Boston, and in U.S. labor history—the exhilarating May Days of 1886.

Labor Day and May Day

During the early 1980s, as AFL-CIO leaders reeled under assaults of corporate enemies and Reaganites, they revived the celebration of Labor Day, a ritual that had atrophied in the prosperous years during and after World War II. Attempts to bring back the old Labor Day parade met with some response in cities like New York where, in 1982, 150,000 unionists jammed Manhattan's streets to protest President Ronald Reagan's anti-union policies and to celebrate the centennial of the event.[15]

The Massachusetts AFL-CIO revived the holiday as well, but after a few efforts to do so, trade unionists returned to long speeches and cold eggs at the

Boston Labor Day Breakfast. By contrast, the Labor Day Bread and Roses Festival in Lawrence attracted large crowds—even without much union support—by returning to an older protest theme that recalled the memory of a militant strike. Traditionally, Labor Day celebrations sought to demonstrate the loyalty and patriotism of trade unions, whereas the new festival emphasized a more multicultural kind of Americanism, celebrating the contributions of women and immigrants as well as unions. Indeed, the Bread and Roses Festival was explicitly based on a moment in labor history shaped by the radical Industrial Workers of the World, rather than the conservative American Federation of Labor, and therefore it seemed to recall, not so much the loyalist rituals of Labor Day, as the ritual protests of May Day.

I had been fascinated with the history of May 1 ever since I researched its history in Boston with two of my graduate students, Hugh Carter Donahue and Jama Lazerow. It was a moment of remarkable convergence when the great eight-hour movement reached a climax and united all kinds of workers in what Boston labor reformer George McNeill called "one great solidarity."[16] In 1983 Eric Hobsbawm published his essay on how workers invented May Day as a tradition. "As it happened," he wrote, "the First of May was initiated at a time of extraordinary growth and expansion of the labor and socialist movements of numerous countries, and might well not have been established in a less hopeful political atmosphere." May Day was "fortuitously associated" with the "symbolism of spring," which suited the high expectations of the young labor movements of the 1890s. "It thus became rapidly transformed into a highly charged annual festival and rite," repeated annually to "meet the demand from the ranks."[17]

For reasons described in the next chapter, May Day in the United States became associated with the Haymarket bomb explosion and "riot" in Chicago on 4 May 1886, with the red scare and the suppression of the eight-hour movement that followed, and, of course, with the memory of the anarchists convicted of the crime and executed in 1887. After Haymarket, writes Robert Wiebe in his history of popular democracy, "urban police expanded their surveillance over the street life of the poor," who had once enjoyed "remarkably free use of public spaces." To be able to "use what had once been open to them, lower-class men found themselves increasingly at odds with the law" and also found it more difficult to make "political statements in public." Indeed, "clearing the streets had a deadening effect on lower-class men," who had used public demonstrations and other rituals to "secure their places in democratic politics."[18]

During the progressive era, local elites, commercial boosters, and public officials dominated public space and sponsored numerous civic celebrations and historical reenactments to shape public consciousness of the past. "Dissenting groups that fell outside the boundaries of the public and its history, as defined by civic officials," found it difficult, according to David Glassberg, to challenge this elitist "apportionment of ceremonial space and time or to offer alternative formulations of collective history and communal identity to the public."[19] Furthermore, as civic celebrations focused more and more on shaping historical memory, pageants celebrating the past were used for "patriotic and moral exhortation," not to recall traditions of protest.[20]

After a brief revival by the American Federation of Labor in 1890, May Day became an entirely socialist or anarchist holiday celebrated between 1907 and 1917. After World War I, May Day marchers were subjected to intimidating harassment. While May 1 became the workers holiday in many other nations of the world, an occasion to recall those who died for the eight-hour day in 1886, it was far more difficult to celebrate in the United States where Labor Day tended to replace the memory of May Day.[21]

The association of May 1 with American socialism and anarchism was problematic enough, but then, after the Russian Revolution, the identification of May 1 with Communism obliterated the historic resonance of the holiday in labor movement history: that is, as a moment of triumph for the great eight-hour movement that had significance to all workers, even those on distant shores. It was more American to celebrate the gift of leisure on September 4 each year than to recall the sacrifices made for shorter hours on May 1.

I had been strongly influenced by David Montgomery's interpretation of the original eight-hour-day movement as the product of "a unique class aspiration." He saw it as an effort that united all kinds of workers and provoked "unanimous opposition from employers"—an interpretation that seemed valid for Boston's labor history.[22] The labor movement's abandonment of the aspiration for shorter hours in favor of higher wages and better benefits seemed to be a sign of progress, but as the work week gradually lengthened and more young people entered the labor force, it seemed worth recalling a time when workers had created a liberation movement to free themselves from the tyranny of an oppressive workday.[23]

Furthermore, it was time to challenge the hold of anti-Communism over historical interpretation and commemoration—to challenge the official "apportionment of ceremonial space and time" for workers history. The way the Lawrence Bread and Roses Festival reinvented Labor Day as a workers celebration suggested that some kind of pageant might serve to highlight the significance of May Day, not as a socialist or communist holiday, but as a workers holiday created at a time when a new generation of labor activists were calling on workers of the world to unite. In South Africa, Nicaragua, and the Philippines a new kind of social-movement unionism erupted—a third force that could not be controlled by the U.S. State Department and its AFL-CIO agents or by the Kremlin and its agents. Militant workers in these nations naturally appropriated May Day as their time to call for international worker solidarity.

Inspired by these world currents, radicals in Massachusetts revived May Day to express international labor solidarity with the black trade unions in South

Africa. On 1 May 1985 they organized a spirited antiapartheid demonstration at Harvard to protest the university's investments in Shell Oil, a company that had large operations in South Africa. The demonstration attracted local union support because it was endorsed by the United Mine Workers, then in the midst of its own international boycott against Shell Oil, which, besides its South African investments, held stock in the union-busting American coal corporation A. T. Massey.

The events surrounding the demonstration are described in the preceding chapter as part of a political drama in which union radicals struggled with AFL-CIO officials who denounced our ideology and denied our legitimacy. They were furious about the fact that we had won support for the anti-Shell rally from important AFL-CIO affiliates.[24]

After the successful Harvard protest, which linked U.S. workers' struggles with those of the South African antiapartheid movement, the same activists organized an occupation of a Boston shop that sold South African gold coins. At that rally Carol Doherty, the president of the state teachers association, gave a speech she asked me to write on the history of May Day as a demonstration of international workers' solidarity. As we returned to the picket line around the coin shop, I asked the trade unionists if they would support a centennial celebration of the first May Day in the following year. The response was surprisingly enthusiastic, largely because the South African workers had reinvented May Day despite all the Cold War baggage attached to it.

What I had in mind was inspired by the historical pageant John Reed organized in Madison Square Garden to recreate the drama of the 1913 Paterson silk workers strike led by the IWW. The pageant successfully brought together workers and intellectuals to recreate a labor event.[25] I had worked with a few radical dramatists in Boston who might play a role in such a reproduction. One of them was Maxine Klein, the Tony Award–winning director who resigned from her tenured position at Boston University to protest against President Silber's regime. In 1977 she directed a wonderful production of Howard Zinn's play about Emma Goldman's life. That same year, Klein used a public lecture I gave on the 1886 general strike to write an episode for her popular historical drama "Boston Remembers." The scene was set in Faneuil Hall at a Knights of Labor strike meeting on the night before the great May Day protest.

The History Workshop group was ready to facilitate a cultural production but we wanted the unions to take some ownership of the commemoration. Our union supporters said we would fail to get official support if we simply wanted to honor the anarchist or the socialist traditions associated with May Day. We agreed that the aim of our pageant was to restore the meaning of May Day for the American labor movement—the meaning it held before the Socialist International declared it a workers holiday in 1889. Indeed, one of our most avid allies was Bobby Banks, a business agent from the Ironworkers' Union who wanted to revive the labor movement and to recall the leading role construction unions played in the great eight-hour movements of the 1880s.

He joined our planning committee, along with Mark Erlich, the Carpenter historian. Tommy Evers, the head of the State Building Trades Council, loved the idea of the Faneuil Hall event. He admired Eugene Debs and James Connolly, the Irish socialist executed for leading the Easter Rising in Dublin. Tommy wasn't afraid of offending anyone, and he was willing to ally with anyone who wanted to revive the spirit of the labor movement. Ironically, the enthusiasm for the May Day event came from the trade unions with the most conservative leaders. Evers not only pledged funds from his organization, but offered to seek support from the state AFL-CIO, of which he was a vice president. The event immediately became a controversial issue. The president of the state labor federation, Arthur Osborn, thought the History Workshop was a "leftist front group" and that Marty Blatt and I were trying to trick building-trades unionists into supporting an event with a hidden socialist agenda. Our ironworker friends knew we were radicals but they were not afraid of being duped by the likes of us. With Evers's endorsement, the celebration generated enthusiasm in the building trades, whose agents were asked to ensure a good turnout at the pageant.

Seeing this appropriation of the May event by the trades, Osborn proposed a compromise. He would speak if the event took place on May 2 and not on May Day. We agreed and welcomed the endorsement of the state AFL-CIO. As a result of efforts by the building trades, over five hundred people, mostly labor union members, filled Faneuil Hall on 2 May 1986 for an event we called "Labor Remembers: The One Hundredth Anniversary of the Great Eight-Hour Strike."[26] Once again, the historic venue added meaning to the event. Boston trade unionists had met in Faneuil Hall exactly one hundred years before to debate and to endorse the general strike. The Little Flags Theater dramatized the event by performing a scene that reenacted, from actual testimony, the stormy debate over the strike vote that had taken place at the hallowed hall in 1886. Learning from the Bread and Roses Festival in Lawrence, we included a variety of cultural performances in addition to the dramatic reenactment. These performances, not usually seen at union events, included the original eight-hour song sung by "On the Line," a chorus of fifteen women union activists, poems offered by electrician Susan Eisenberg, and a version of "We Shall Not Be Moved" sung by vocalist Cheryl Holmes, who made a strong connection between the civil rights and labor movements.

Mark Erlich and I presented a slide show on the historical significance of May Day and of the Great Upheaval of 1886. The theme of our presentation was "freedom and solidarity," linking the struggle against the tyranny of the endless workday to the rituals of mutuality and habits of solidarity the labor movement cultivated in its best practice. Mark emphasized the leading role of his union, the carpenters, and its leader, P. J. McGuire, in the eight-hour movement, and announced the publication of his book on the carpenters' history in Massachusetts.[27] I discussed the American origins of May Day as an international workers' holiday suppressed in the United States, but celebrated in many other nations. Events far away made my job easier. The day before in South Africa, a million black workers had struck to make May Day a national holiday.

Building trades union leaders applauded our event. It attracted coverage on the evening TV news, which featured our most reluctant participant, AFL-CIO president Arthur Osborn. The media exposure earned us no credit with him. As far as he was concerned Marty Blatt and I were using history as a different means of doing politics. Worse, he blamed me for provoking a fight within his own council and for creating a situation in which he felt obliged to speak—against his will—at a public event whose organizers he distrusted. He put out the word through his aides that he would not appear with me in public again.

Black and White Unite and Fight

Our next commemorative project did not make Osborn feel any better about the History Workshop or my role in it. He came from the local at the Raytheon plant where Patriot and Cruise missiles were manufactured and naturally tended to be sensitive about leftists who criticized the Cold War and who argued that the United States and AFL-CIO policy kept the conflict alive. His own union local had been created out of a bitter fight with the Left-led United Electrical Workers in 1949. Along with the UE, which remained active in Massachusetts during the 1950s, there was one CIO union that allowed Communists and progressives to criticize the Cold War and McCarthyism: the United Packinghouse Workers Union (UPWU).

One of these UPWU leftists, Jim Bollen, lived in Lynn and helped us with our first workshop there. I also knew Jim as author of a pamphlet on a remarkable packinghouse workers strike in 1954–55 in which he had played a leading role as chief shop steward in the Colonial Provision plant in Boston's Haymarket district. It had been long branded a "red strike" in official circles, because Bollen and others in the union had been involved in the Communist Party, but among the strikers and their allies the Colonial struggle was known as "the long strike." The strikers held out for fourteen months and endured even after their union was decertified through one of the first Taft-Hartley "elections" in which only strike breakers were allowed to vote.[28]

I thought "the long strike" should be recalled and remembered, not as a "red strike," but as an extraordinary demonstration of worker solidarity. I asked Jim Bollen to help the workshop organize a reunion of those members of Packinghouse Workers Local 11 who had waged the struggle in 1954–55 and who had survived to make their local one of the few successful biracial institutions in

Boston. For Jim, a dedicated socialist, it was easy to say yes; he was one of those for whom remembering was a political obligation.

We both thought that the Colonial strike story needed retelling in more public ways. At a time when many of the city's unions reflected the racial segregation and racial polarization highlighted by the fight over desegregation in the 1970s, this story offered an example of black and white Bostonians finding common ground. During the city's busing wars of the mid-seventies Bollen said that the union's symbol of a black hand grasping a white hand was torn off the local's union hall by vandals. I thought Bollen's story of the strike was a kind of redemptive narrative—in which a living remnant of CIO social unionism survived through the Cold War and into the racially polarized 1970s. Local 11 redeemed the promise of democratic, inclusive unionism that emerged from the CIO struggles in the late 1930s.[29]

The idea of a Colonial workers reunion also appealed to Bollen because the packing plant had just closed after a heroic fight by the workers and their community allies to keep it open. Its multiracial membership formed a strong labor-community coalition that put significant pressure on the city council and City Hall to save the jobs. The owners ultimately closed the plant, but the unity and creativity of the Colonial workers allowed them to maintain a positive group identity, to hold on to a good feeling about their union, and to win more benefits for compensation and retraining than any other group of "dislocated workers." We thought a celebration of the long strike in 1955 would also serve as a reunion for two other generations of workers who sustained their union local until the plant closed.

To make sure that workers participated in the planning, workshop members met with a committee of Colonial workers including old-timers and the militant young steward who helped organize the fight against the shutdown. We received another encouraging grant from the State Humanities Foundation to fund a history workshop and reunion for the Colonial workers on 27 March 1988. Nearly two hundred former Colonial workers and their families assembled at the Electrical Workers Hall in Dorchester to hear brief talks by the veterans of the 1954–55 strike and to hear comments from the floor by a range of unionists.

In a small way, we hoped to counter the impression, commonly held in our deindustrialized region, that unions were somehow to blame for plant closings—either for asking too much or for not fighting hard enough to keep the shops open. The private company that owned Colonial had disappeared, along with the jobs it created, but only after the union had struggled to keep those jobs in the community, urging the city to use its powers of eminent domain to seize the plant and reopen it under worker ownership. The city failed to respond, but even after the local died as a formal institution, it lived on in people's memories. Several workers we interviewed said the union was "like a family."

The company and the city had failed them, not the union. We hoped the event would help show the public, and the rest of the labor movement, that the Colonial plant closing not only cost the city and the workers several thousand jobs, it also cost the city a remarkable democratic institution that black and white workers had created and nurtured over fifty years of struggle.

Collaboration and Reclamation

After our first history workshop with the Lynn shoeworkers ten years earlier, we moaned about not having videotaped the moving testimonies and dialogues we had heard in Hibernian Hall. We were left only with a pretty little booklet about the dialogue that took place in Lynn. We decided to videotape the Colonial reunion and make it part of a visual production about Local 11 and its testing in the 1954–55 strike. We were aware that printed public history reached a limited audience and so we wanted to produce a video to seek a wider audience, especially young people in public schools. The Local 11 story seemed like an ideal way to explain why people of various races and nationalities fought so hard to create and defend their unions.

After the workers' reunion, Jim Bollen arranged for me to videotape an interview with Shelton Coats, who had been elected the first African American president of the Colonial local after the strike. It was now a local that included former strikebreakers, many of them black. As Coats recalled:

> After the strike I was asked to go back to work with strikebreakers. We had to make friends with them. During the strike I noticed that very often the Company would turn away whites and hire blacks. The blacks knew nothing about a union. They were paid only $1.20 an hour. They brought blacks in for cheap labor, long hours and low pay. When I went back, the [replacement] workers knew about me. The older union workers talked to the strikebreakers about me and they listened. They found my election as president very encouraging.

Many years later, Shelton Coats spoke in a personal way about what it meant for a black worker to be elected leader in a largely white union local. "Blacks didn't have much confidence in blacks because we didn't think we had power." But, he continued, "I found out that you can get power by working in people's interest and being honest. The power I had came from blacks and whites." When he walked back "on the line" after fourteen months on strike, he heard the veteran white strikers tell the black former strikebreakers: "There's Shelton. He's our leader now." For the next thirty years, Coats gave back to the local some of what he had received. What he valued in the union was a feeling of being "close knit." As a black man, he said, "you had a chance to present yourself and your ideas and people would accept them."

When Coats retired, the members elected a new president, a Polish immigrant named Herbie Bardasz. At the History Workshop's reunion for the Colo-

Celebrating a victory in the long strike at Colonial Provision Company, Boston, 1955: Leaders of United Packinghouse Workers' Local 11. *Third row center:* Shelton Coats; *third row, third from right,* Jim Bollen. *Photograph courtesy of Jim Bollen.*

nial workers in Dorchester, Bardasz spoke with tears in his eyes about the meaning of history. "I had to learn my past," Bardasz said. "I learned it from Shelton Coats. And this is what I learned from him: You can cooperate with the employers all you want, but you will never be a member of their club. It comes down to this: You have to fight for your people; they will fight for their profits."

Thinking back on my interview with Coats I am reminded of what Sandro Portelli said about his experiences interviewing black and white residents of Harlan County, Kentucky. "There's gonna' always be a line," an African American woman told him—meaning a line between intellectuals and the people they engage in their work, a line between the observers and the observed. But as Portelli says, there are those folks who, while recognizing a "degree of difference" between us and them, nonetheless choose to speak to us across whatever line separates us.[30]

None of us in the workshop had any filmmaking experience, but we had been able to videotape the reunion and various interviews, including discussions with Jim Bollen and Shelton Coats. Cynthia McKeown was working at my college on a effort to protect non-union workers against unfair terminations, and she told me that she made videos for cable TV. When I told her the Colonial strike story, she agreed to make a video for Boston cable access television at virtually no cost. I gave her our taped interviews with Local 11 veterans and lots of still photos from Jim Bollen's collection, and sketched out a narrative line for the film. Then Cindy and other volunteers produced a thirty-minute video production about Local 11's "long strike," entitled *Glory Days,* which aired on Boston cable television in May of 1988 with the strikers providing the narration with their own voices. Collaborating with Cindy and Barbara Lipski on their production of *Glory Days* offered a first impression of what could be accomplished, and what could not be accomplished, by telling movement stories on film.

Collaborations and Reclamations

Another collaboration emerged from the Colonial workers' reunion. Jim Bollen and I decided to write a scholarly history of the strike based on his original story and on my research into oral history and printed sources.[31] A condensed version of our essay also appeared in an ambitious effort to present Massachusetts labor history in a book called *Commonwealth of Toil* that I coauthored with Tom Juravich and Bill Hartford. The Colonial strike saga epitomized the kind of story-driven history we wanted to feature in order to reach a public audience including high school students and union members. The book included over one hundred illustrations to offer a visual text to the storytelling. It was well advertised and distributed thanks to the effort of Massachusetts AFL-CIO's secretary treasurer, Robert Haynes, one of the ironworker officials who had supported our May 2 centennial in 1986, and thanks to the support of state senate president Thomas Birmingham, a former labor lawyer. Over five hundred copies were sold at one state labor convention, and books were sent to every school and public library in the commonwealth.[32] The kind of people's history the workshop advocated was beginning to reach its public.

Haynes had recently asked me to integrate stories from *Commonwealth of Toil* into the booklet distributed to the high school children of union members to help prepare them for the AFL-CIO scholarship competition with awards of $400,000 each year to college-bound students. He also asked me to assist the union representative on the state board of education who wanted to add labor history to the new social studies curriculum standards.

We were encouraging teachers to tell "labor's untold story" to young people, who, much to the chagrin of their union elders, remained uneducated about the sacrifices union activists made to fight against poverty and fear and to fight for justice and dignity. At a time when so much attention and funding was devoted to preparing children for jobs through "school-to-work" programs, we hoped our book would promote more study of the problems of work, along with the solutions workers proposed to those problems.[33] Besides this, we hoped *Com-*

monwealth of Toil would emulate the work of the American Social History Project created by Herbert Gutman before his death in 1985. Our work, like the *Who Built America?* projects, sought to place workers at the center of the American story—to show how workers' struggles for equality and dignity were "not peripheral or marginal wrong turns down dead end streets, but rather defining characteristics of national development."[34]

Other collaborations also emerged from the History Workshop's attempts to tell working people's stories in public places. Our interaction with African American workers during the "long strike" project encouraged us to reach out into the black community where, we knew, people's history work had been taking place very energetically since the time of the school desegregation movement. Elizabeth Bouvier and I offered a couple of public workshops on how to do family history during Black History month. Ruth Batson, the civil rights leader who headed the Museum of African American History, asked us to do another session at the African Meeting House on Beacon Hill. Through Batson I met Robert Hayden, the historian of Boston's black community and a leader in the struggle for equal educational opportunity. We shared an interest in the history of the Brotherhood of Sleeping Car Porters in Boston, which Hayden inherited directly from his grandfather, a fifty-year man with the Pullman Company. He had begun to reach out to black railroad retirees as part of an effort to celebrate their union leader, A. Philip Randolph, who was to be remembered with a bronze statue in Boston's Back Bay railroad and subway station.

The funding for the Randolph memorial resulted from the efforts of State Representative Byron Rushing, who represented the South End, where the porters had lived and worked. An activist in the Northern Student Movement and first director of the Museum of African American History, Rushing wanted a monument to the modern civil rights leader in Boston, a city with many statutes commemorating white abolitionists. In 1988 a beautiful bronze likeness of A. Philip Randolph was placed at Back Bay Station in the South End. Hayden asked me and some of my students to help to organize a turnout of retired porters and waiters for the dedication of the Randolph statue.

Representative Rushing wanted something more—a permanent educational exhibition to honor the lives and labors of the black Bostonians who worked on the railroads. Hayden received funds from the Transit Authority to interview surviving porters and dining car waiters and to select relevant photos and artifacts for a group of six permanent panels to be erected in the station—a public presentation of movement history in the corridor leading to the bronze likeness of Randolph. I proposed the selections from Bob Hayden's interviews to be displayed on the panels, along with one hundred photos, and wrote narrative text to link the voices and images together. It was an exciting chance to write people's history for a permanent public memorial, and specifically, to write about the remarkable confluence of the socialist, labor, and civil rights movements embodied in the career of A. Philip Randolph. It was also an unexpected opportunity to collaborate with the leading popular historian of Boston's black community.[35]

The Workshop has survived. Recently we planned a project to create a website for students and teachers interested in the photos, posters, leaflets, and manifestos of the many radical and progressive movements spawned in the Boston-Cambridge hatchery during our time. The effort is now in the hands of workshop stalwart Libby Bouvier and a new member, Chris Idzik, who became active while he was teaching in a public high school. He then joined the staff of the internationally recognized Facing History project, which was expanding its educational work on the Holocaust to raise historical consciousness about various oppressed groups. Chris now teaches history at the esteemed Boston Latin School in a position created by Facing History. In this role he involves his students in documenting and interpreting local social movements.

The group meets less often now and sets its sights on much more modest goals with much longer time limits. Many of us are far more involved now in doing people's history in other institutional and political venues. For example, Libby Bouvier, who joined the History Workshop in 1982 and kept the group together in recent years, needed to devote much of her free time to parallel work on the ambitious Gay and Lesbian History Project. She helped produce the project's stunningly successful public exhibit at the Boston Public Library in 1996, which drew an estimated fifty-five thousand visitors (the largest number in history). She co-edited the superb lesbian and gay history book, *Improper Bostonians,* published two years later by Beacon Press. Libby has taken advantage of the greater support that has emerged for people's history and community documentation in recent years—far more than existed when we started the History Workshop in the 1980s. She is involved as a professional archivist in documenting four underrepresented groups in Boston—African Americans, Asian Americans, Latinos, and the lesbian and gay community.

My role in the workshop diminished as I became more involved in doing history with and for the labor movement. In this work and in various public history projects I have drawn consciously and unconsciously upon the experimental efforts we made in the History Workshop to share the history we knew with workers and to celebrate the history they chose to share with us.

This experience influenced recent collaborations with workshop cofounder Marty Blatt, who ceased participating in our projects after we organized our reunion for the packinghouse workers in 1989. He carried on parallel efforts as an education specialist for the state secretary of labor during Michael Dukakis's last gubernatorial administration and as an advocate for people's history on the state humanities council. He then became the historian at the Lowell National Historical Park and, after years of productive work, he became the chief of cultural resources at the Boston National Historical Park where he produced a dramatically successful centennial event honoring the erection of the famous brass relief that stands above the Boston Common and recalls the heroism of the African Americans soldiers who served in the Civil War with the Massachusetts 54th Regiment. In both positions Marty spoke out with a clear voice on the issues facing the emerging professional field of public history, which faced constant pressure to publicize the contributions of institutions and officials rather than those of local communities and movements for change.[36]

While he worked at the Lowell National Historical Park, Blatt labored with tenacity and creativity to make sure that workers' history, including the experience of slavery, was part of the important new exhibit opened at the old Boott Mills in 1991. It is the only national park exhibit that in any way captures the experience of American workers. Marty also brought a History Workshop sensibility to bear on the exhibit with excellent videotaped interviews with textile workers recalling their experiences in the mills.

As part of this effort to mount the Boott Mills exhibit he asked me to join with two other historians as advisors in the production of a multi-image slide show to introduce visitors to the museum displays on the industrial revolution. I argued strongly for an interpretive script that problematized the first century of industry in America. Marty thought the slide presentation designed for the original visitors' center was too romantic about Lowell's golden age as a model factory town and too simplistic in its celebration of technological and entrepreneurial progress. So he was inclined to agree with my proposal which derived directly from the way I taught about the industrial revolution in New England using classic texts like Leo Marx's *Machine and the Garden* and more recent works like John Kasson's provocative *Civilizing the Machine* and the pathbreaking *Women and Work* by Thomas Dublin, who joined us an advisor and supported a controversial approach to the show. The final product, a short but visually spectacular slide show called "Wheels of Change," is based on a script which recalls the great social and moral debates aroused by industrialization beginning with Jefferson and Hamilton and ending with Andrew Carnegie and Eugene V. Debs speaking about the benefits and costs of the American system of manufacturing. One consequence of progress was industrial conflict graphically represented by the death toll of workers who died in the bloody strikes of the late nineteenth century.

Overall, the public response to "Wheels of Change" seemed positive, even enthusiastic, until Marty received a letter from an attorney in Studio City, California, who denounced the presentation as propaganda—"blatant, ugly, stupid and overt." He even called on his U.S. senator to "identify those responsible" and to investigate "their backgrounds."[37] Our idea that the consequences of the industrial revolution were debatable proved more controversial than we had imagined. Concerned about this extreme response to our people's history of industry, which was viewed by hundreds of visitors each year, I asked to review the written comments left by viewers. A park ranger sent along photocopies from a logbook that included many positive responses, like one from a man who applauded seeing for the first time "a workers' view of industry."[38]

My collaboration with Marty Blatt continued in a National Park Service project to recognize historical sites that represented workers' memories of labor and industrial history. Some of their efforts are described in the next two chapters as attempts to rescue working-class memories blocked off from their potential inheritors.

Conclusion and Evaluation

Two years after Herb Gutman died in 1985, his effort to "reclaim the past for the public" was praised by Russell Jacoby in a book bemoaning the disappearance of public intellectuals. The author consigned Gutman's work to a "cultural world almost abandoned"—a world in which intellectuals still spoke to the public, and were not yet pulled under by the "tides of professionalism."[39] A decade later, Jacoby's pessimism may still be warranted because professional historians live in a different world than rural and urban working people. As a result, the public is presented with academic history no longer connected to traditions of memory. Disconnected from memory, historiography has turned reflexively in on itself and no longer plays a role in shaping public identity.[40]

And yet, many historians have refused to abandon the cultural world Herbert Gutman envisioned. Those of us who participated in public history work were not the only ones seeking to escape an "imploding" profession dominated by "self-referential" practices. Instead of continuing to look inward, many of those who practice our craft have expressed a desire to turn outward toward our publics. In doing so, historians have discovered that even in this present-minded time, our fellow citizens are curious about their past and about what has been forgotten.[41]

The loss of collective memory has created a strong need for recuperative history. "The passage from memory to history has required every social group to redefine its identity through the revitalization of its own history," says the French historian Pierre Nora. "Those who have long been marginalized in traditional history are . . . haunted by the need to recover their buried pasts." And, as a result, Nora declares, "the demand for history has largely overflowed the circle of professional historians."[42]

In the United States, where important places of memory have been destroyed and where important moments of solidarity have been forgotten, working people are left with oral traditions and with a few histories that incorporate popular memory. Oral history has, however, preserved important popular memories, including those of people in struggle against their masters. These memories are important to historians who believe their art and craft is based on recording, preserving, and interpreting such recollections. Historians can do more than study memorials as artificial representations. They need not abandon the quest to understand "lived experiences that memory bears into the present." We can still, as Patrick Hutton believes, practice history as "an art of memory," and still regard "living memory" as the grounding of our interest in the past, the past as it was actually experienced.[43]

Commemorative people's history events may be criticized as nostalgic celebrations, or dismissed as a romantic escapes into the past. But if visiting the past is often like traveling to "foreign country," we can visit there without taking a vacation from reality. We can return to our lives in the present with a better set of maps about where we want to go in the future. We can return with a more grounded moral critique of what appear to be the inevitable forces of progress. Popular memory has long served as a wellspring for radical criticisms of the present and alternative visions of the future.[44] "The communities of memory that tie us to the past also turn us toward the future as communities of hope," Robert Bellah observes. "They carry a context of meaning that can allow us to connect the aspirations for ourselves and those closest to us with the aspirations of the larger whole, and see our own efforts as being, in part, contributions to the public good."[45]

The Massachusetts History Workshop sought to recall the communities of hope and the moments of solidarity working people created in times when they aspired to an important place in the society and a central role in the democracy. In creating what Workshop founder Raphael Samuel called "theatres of memory," we embraced and celebrated their aspirations, hoping they might enhance our own and those of our fellow citizens.

Keeping movement memories alive: Lucy E. Parsons, wife and comrade of Haymarket martyr Albert E. Parsons. *Photographs and Prints Division, Schomburg Center for Research in Black Culture, Astor, Lenox, and Tilden Foundations, The New York Public Library.*

Remembering Haymarket: Chicago's Labor Martyrs and Their Legacy

> Chicago is a city of factories. Chicago is a city full of workers. But no statue has been erected in memory of the martyrs of Chicago and no one, or almost no one, remembers that the rights of the working class did not spring whole from the ear of a goat, or from the hand of God or the boss.
>
> EDUARDO GALEANO, *The Book of Embraces*

On a rainy day in May 1886, as a squad of police marched to disperse a protest rally in Chicago's Haymarket Square, a ferocious explosion cut through the uniformed ranks. The bomb blast of May 4 that killed several policemen, the wild gun fire from police revolvers that took the lives of fifty or more workers, the sensational trial of the anarchists accused of the bombing, the public hanging of the four anarchist martyrs on Black Friday 11 November 1887, and the controversial pardon of the remaining defendants—all these dramatic events were remembered by workers engaged in the labor and radical movements for the next fifty years. During that time movement people were deeply divided about how to remember the Haymarket martyrs: as innocent victims of the grand struggle for the eight-hour day or as irresponsible anarchists who provoked a "red scare" that crippled the whole labor movement.

The Memory

The memory of Haymarket that so divided its custodians did not remain as powerful in the United States as it did in other places, like Mexico, where May Day was celebrated as an occasion for remembering the martyrs of Chicago. It was "one of the first in a series of instances of American working-class martyrdom" readily "blocked" from later generations of working people, according to Michael Kammen. Institutionalized efforts to shape public historical consciousness obliterated memories of opposition to the government among immigrants and other dissenters. Recollections of Haymarket struck discordant tones when sounded against the "mystic chords of memory" Abraham Lincoln thought he heard "stretching from every battlefield and every patriot grave, to every living heart and hearthstone, all over this broad land." Indeed, it was assumed by most

native-born people that "immigrants ought to adopt American traditions, customs, and ceremonials, by shedding their 'alien' memories like so much dead
skin." In the process, says Kammen, working people in the United States found
it difficult to recall heroic deeds of martyrdom that in other places, "helped to
provide an energizing focus for a sense of collective identity among powerless
social groups."[1]

I became interested in the memory of Haymarket when I was asked to attend
a 1992 meeting of historians, folklorists, preservationists, and others at the
Lowell National Park to discuss the criteria by which labor history sites would
be nominated as national landmarks. Les Orear and Bill Adelman of the Illinois
Labor History Society spoke of their long efforts to commemorate the events at
Haymarket Square that had aroused so much passion and division in Chicago.
The square itself was a poor candidate for a landmark because it had been
bisected by the Kennedy Expressway and because most of the old union buildings in the area had been destroyed. National Park Service criteria clearly required sites with "architectural integrity."

Orear and Adelman then spoke about the world-renowned gravesite memorial to anarchist martyrs in Chicago's Waldheim Cemetery, which, they said,
should surely qualify as a significant landmark, except that the criteria of the
landmarks program *excluded* cemeteries and monuments![2] Like Waldheim,
many labor history sites of importance are the final resting places of those
martyred in our extraordinarily violent history of labor-capital conflict. When I
was asked to write an introduction to the labor history theme study for the
National Landmarks Program, it struck me, sadly, that some of the best-known
sites in labor history were monuments to victims of massacres. Many of these
sites were nominated by local groups as candidates for national landmarking:
for example, the site of the Lattimer massacre in eastern Pennsylvania where
sheriff's deputies killed nineteen Slavic miners in 1897, the Union Miners'
Cemetery in Mt. Olive, Illinois, where Mother Jones is buried with four union
miners killed during the 1898 Virden lockout, and the monument to the victims
of the 1914 Ludow massacre in Colorado.[3]

My introduction to the labor history landmark study focused on these kinds
of sites and on a discussion of the difficulty of marking places of memory that
exist in tension with the desire of elites to celebrate memories of national unity.
Haymarket represented the kind of memory that conveys "what social reality
feels like rather than what it should be," to use John Bodnar's terms, the kind of
memory that by its "very existence threatens the sacred and timeless nature of
official expressions."[4]

After completing my own essay about "marking labor history on the national
landscape," I became more interested in what the French historian Pierre Nora
called *lieux de mémoire*—sites which lie, he said, at "the intersection" of history
and a dying "tradition of memory." Society creates "lieux de mémoire," Nora
wrote, "because there are no longer 'milieux de mémoire,' real environments for

memory."[5] I presented my study of Haymarket as a *lieu de mémoire* at a conference in France organized to explore the application of Nora's ideas to U.S. history. That paper evolved into this chapter, which explores the exceptional power of Haymarket as a memory, preserved and reproduced by anarchists and others in the labor movement, a memory of special importance not only to immigrant workers in the United States but to workers in other nations. The events themselves are reviewed in their special temporal and spatial contexts, examined for their dramatic contents, and then evaluated as stories. These stories were retold in familiar melodramatic forms and staged in what Raphael Samuel called "theatres of memory." In these arenas "unofficial knowledge" could be passed along and used as part of a secular religion important to radical movements.[6] The special significance of the Haymarket martyrs monument in Waldheim Cemetery is discussed as one of those theaters.

The City

The "milieu de mémoire" in this story is the booming city of Chicago in the 1870s and 1880s, "hog butcher, steel maker to the world," a city segmented along class lines after the Civil War as militant immigrant workers confronted aggressive entrepreneurs; it was the site of the first May Day general strike in 1867 when ten thousand workingmen, led by the molders at the McCormick Reaper works, took direct action for the eight-hour day. Social revolutionaries like Albert Parsons, a Confederate soldier later radicalized by Reconstruction politics in Texas, gained a following among Chicago workers in the years after the brutal repression of the 1877 railroad strike by the police, state militia, and federal troops.[7] One historian even describes a "socialist hegemony over the local labor movement" in these years. Immigrant socialists were far more visible in public than the secretive Knights of Labor and their largely English-speaking leaders. Chicago's vast immigrant working class (76 percent foreign born in 1884) included many newcomers who responded to socialist ideas, especially when articulated by trade union organizers.[8]

After joining the Marxist International Working People's Association (IWPA), Albert Parsons and other social revolutionaries affiliated with Michael Bakunin's breakaway Black International in 1883. While remaining loyal to the teachings of Karl Marx and the principles of communism, they broke with the Second Socialist International because of its emphasis on electoral politics. The Chicago revolutionaries agreed with Johann Most, the bombastic German anarchist, on the need for armed insurrection to overthrow the capitalist state. They also shared his enthusiasm for dynamite as the great equalizer, but unlike Most they believed in the revolutionary potential of the labor movement. The "Chicago idea" placed "the union at the center of revolutionary strategy and the nucleus of the future society," writes Paul Avrich, the historian of anarchism.[9]

Socialists and communists of the IWPA influenced Chicago's German and

Bohemian immigrants, who constituted many of the forty thousand members of the Central Labor Union (CLU), a dual union formed in 1884 by revolutionaries disaffected with the moderate leadership of the Knights of Labor and the craft unionism of the new Federation of Organized Trades and Labor Unions led by pragmatic men.[10] These social revolutionaries, who would later be called anarchists, looked back for inspiration to the Paris Commune, the anniversary of which they celebrated each year in March with remarkably popular ceremonies. In 1879 a "monster" rally attracted 100,000 people to the lake front where a surviving Communard spoke. Nourished by a rich social and cultural life, which included armed self-defense groups (the workers militias), countless picnics and dances, and a vibrant proletarian theater, these ceremonies took place annually for thirty-seven years and "became more elaborate every year," an example of how radical workers created an enduring memorial tradition.[11]

The groundswell of enthusiasm for the eight-hour day among Chicago's unskilled and unorganized surprised even the revolutionaries. Though the shorter workday seemed like a mild reform to them, the radicals in the Central Labor Union took leadership of the new movement. In 1884 the Federation of Organized Trades made 1 May 1886 the date for a nationwide general strike, but its leaders acted reluctantly, as did the Knights of Labor. The social revolutionaries filled the void. IWPA women such as Lucy Parsons and Lizzie Swank-Holmes organized in the needle trades, while Albert Parsons, Michael Schwab, and other socialists spread the eight-hour fever to other trades. Skilled organizers and passionate orators, they injected drama into movement culture with daring actions that showed "a flair for the theatrical."[12]

The socialist Central Labor Union caught the rising wave of eight-hour militancy and organized a demonstration on Easter Sunday 1886 in defiance of Christian values. A few days later on that first May Day, eighty thousand striking workers marched down Michigan Avenue demanding "eight hours for work, eight hours for rest and eight hours for play."[13] On May 3 Chicago police shot and killed three pickets at the McCormick works, and that night Albert Parsons and his anarchist comrades met to plan a protest rally in Haymarket Square. That meeting, on the evening of May 4, attracted a smaller crowd than expected—perhaps three thousand—to hear Parsons and other radicals.[14] The city's mayor, concerned about the violence that erupted at McCormick's, had ordered a large squad of police to preserve order. He attended the rally and left, believing the crowd to be calm and orderly. After Parsons spoke and departed, rain threatened to fall and the crowd began to disperse. Only three hundred people remained in the large square as the anarchist Samuel Fielden finished his remarks denouncing the law as being "framed for your enslavers." Suddenly, alarmed at Fielden's inflammatory language, two detectives hurried to the local police station where 176 police had been ordered to stand ready.

The Event

Soon a squad of 130 police marched out on the square in a military formation. The police captain asked Fielden to disperse the crowd and he agreed. Just as he stepped down from the hay wagon he used as a speakers' platform, someone (a perpetrator was never identified) threw an explosive device into the police ranks. The officers drew their pistols and began firing wildly, shooting blindly for five minutes. Seven police and an unknown number of rally participants and bystanders fell dead or wounded. One reporter estimated fifty civilian deaths. Sixty law officers were wounded and one of them died later. One policemen was killed by the bomb—six others died in the frenzied gunfire from their fellows' revolvers.

The Haymarket police riot lasted only a few minutes, but the explosion and what followed created the most powerful memory in U.S. labor history. And, unlike any other incident in nineteenth-century working-class history, except the Paris Commune, the Haymarket tragedy made an enduring international impact and became part of an oppositional memory constructed by workers outside of the United States where the official memory sought to criminalize the martyrs.

The chaos in the square provoked the first serious "red scare" in America. The *New York Times* editorial was typical: it called for a Gatling gun solution to the outbreak of anarchy and for the use of "hemp" in "judicious doses." In Chicago, where a state of martial law existed for two months, hundreds of men and women, mostly immigrants, were rounded up and interrogated. Employers and their allies seized on the bombing to discredit the eight-hour movement and the Knights of Labor, whose leaders failed to escape blame by denouncing the anarchists. Chicago's law officers and its press constructed a narration of what happened in the square to absolve the police of responsibility. They manufactured evidence of a horrible dynamite plot aimed at the complete destruction of Chicago.[15]

The official interpretation of the Haymarket "riot" justified a massive assault on labor and radical movements in Chicago and elsewhere. As John Higham wrote in *Strangers in the Land:* "For years, the memory of Haymarket and the dread of imported anarchy haunted the American consciousness. No image prevailed more widely than that of the immigrant as a lawless creature, given over to violence and disorder."[16] The bombing provoked a wave of anti-immigrant and antiradical repression, including an Illinois "criminal syndicalism law" denying free speech to anarchists.[17]

The memory of Haymarket caused awful problems for mainstream labor and socialist party leaders. The conservative Knights of Labor head Terence Powderly refused to plead clemency for the anarchists—a plea made from many foreign quarters, including a group from the French Chamber of Deputies.[18]

The German American leaders of the Socialist Labor Party denounced the Chicago anarchists and drew a lesson: given the "overwhelming superior strength" of the employers and their allies, any appeal "to physical force could only incur bloody defeats" and retard the growth of socialism. American Socialists, even those like Joseph Buchanan who ardently defended the Haymarket "boys," reached similar conclusions. "The Chicago bomb" convinced Buchanan that until a working-class majority voted and was cheated out of the results, revolutionary action could not be justified. "Men who will not vote right," he used to say, "will not shoot right."[19]

Samuel Gompers, president of the new American Federation of Labor, also condemned the anarchists' methods and blamed them for killing the eight-hour movement and for causing all unions to suffer. But Gompers also appealed for the convicts' lives on the grounds, he later wrote, that "labor must do its best to maintain justice for radicals or find itself denied the rights of freemen." In his clemency plea, Gompers warned the governor of Illinois not to create a memory that would be of use to the "revolutionary movement." Executing the Chicago anarchists would cause "thousands and thousands of labor men all over the world" to look upon the radicals "as martyrs," "executed because they were standing up for free speech and free press." This is exactly what happened as "labor men" invented a memorial tradition out of Haymarket, against the wishes of official leaders who wanted to forget the "catastrophe."[20]

The Hangings

However, trade union and socialist party leaders who disassociated themselves from the Haymarket martyrs discovered that memories of the Chicago anarchists and their travails were widely shared and deeply held among workers in many nations. Protests "swept the European continent" on 11 November 1887, the date when Albert Parsons and three anarchist comrades went to the gallows. Peter Kropotkin, the well-known Russian anarchist, reported no city in Spain and Italy worth naming "where the bloody anniversary was not commemorated by enthusiastic crowds of workers." In these places, he said, "The commemoration of the Chicago martyrs has almost acquired the same importance as the commemoration of the Paris Commune."[21] When Gompers visited European cities in 1895 he noticed "in nearly every labor hall there were pictures of Parsons, Spies, Lingg, etc., and with an inscription: 'Labor's Martyrs to American Capitalism.'" On later visits, he saw "the same pictures still there."[22]

Why did the memory of the Haymarket martyrs endure? The events themselves provide a starting point. The bombing was the most sensational news story of the era: The hunt for suspects also attracted intense press coverage. The spectacularly publicized trial of the eight anarchists accused of the "bombing" created a remarkable drama of its own, including a jailhouse romance between defendant August Spies and the daughter of a prominent Chicago businessman.

Faced with the overwhelming power of the state in determining their fate and their memory, the defendants and their supporters plotted a narrative of their own, reversing everything the prosecution charged. "In their narrative interpretation [which became central to the working-class memory of Haymarket] . . . their persecution and even their execution were paradoxically empowering acts . . . that proved all their ideas to be true," Carl Smith writes. In the oppositional memory of Haymarket, the condemned men were recalled as martyrs who died for democracy and freedom while the state relied upon "lies, force and violence to hold it together."[23]

The trial and the hangings of Albert Parsons, August Spies, George Engel, and Adolph Fischer, along with the suicide of Louis Lingg (who killed himself by exploding a dynamite cap in his mouth), produced a "drama without end," because, Smith explains, even those who condemned the anarchists had adopted their view that "urban industrial society [w]as a ticking bomb." After the hangings a prominent Chicago minister said no event since the Civil War had produced "such profound and long continued interest and excitement." These events attracted attention because they occurred in a "free America and [in] a time of peace" and because they evoked "an apprehensive concern"—a fear that they were but a first phase "of a widespread discontent upon the part of millions of poor people of this and other countries."[24]

The press was obsessed with the anarchists, and some journalists, like the cartoonist Thomas Nast, portrayed them sensationally as demonic bomb throwers. But at the same time, the publicity generated curiosity about the anarchists and what they looked like. Some of the many drawings in the newspapers depicted them as normal human beings.[25] In this melodrama the anarchists themselves played compelling theatrical roles, particularly Albert Parsons, who acted with power and passion in ways that many found unforgettable. Joseph Buchanan, whose rich life as a labor agitator involved many important events, vividly remembered Parsons's boldness many years after his execution. "Every man who has passed the half century mile post has stored away in his memory cabinets pictures which illustrate important events—mayhap crises—in his past life," he observed. "Sometimes they steal out from their hiding-places unbidden, and they lead the thought procession back to other days." In that "small cabinet" where Buchanan "stored the few pictures" he called "my tragedies," one often stole out: the scene recreated his audience with the governor of Illinois when Buchanan made one of the last clemency pleas for "the Haymarket boys." First, he read a letter from Spies, who offered to die in place of the others and appealed only to "the judgement of history." Buchanan then turned to a short note from Parsons that he had not yet seen in which the condemned man asked that if he was to die, he be granted a reprieve only so that his wife and two children could die with him. Everyone in the room gasped and Buchanan nearly broke down.[26] Partly through such dramatic gestures, Parsons and his comrades found their way into "the memory cabinets" of many labor activists.

The Haymarket story reached a sensational climax on 11 November 1887 with the hanging of the four anarchists—the "Black Friday" long remembered in labor and radical movements. Perhaps the intensive media coverage of the executions (especially the graphic on the cover of *Leslie's Weekly*) perpetuated the event's memory. Public hangings were intended to dramatize punishment and memorialize pain.[27] The popular press in this era expressed a morbid fascination with hangings and the instruments of execution that it exhibited during the Haymarket trial.[28] However, the sheer drama of the story and the publicity it attracted does not fully explain the power of the Haymarket memory, which may be highlighted by a comparison with an equally sensational story of labor violence and public ritual.

Only a decade before the Haymarket incident, the state of Pennsylvania concluded a civil war in the anthracite fields with the public hangings of twenty Irish coal miners—the Molly Maguires. The Mollies' fight with coal companies and their armed forces was far more bloody and dramatic than the Chicago events of 1886 and 1887. The executions of the Irish miners were more gruesome and witnessed by far more people than the Haymarket hangings. Court cases leading up to these hangings produced the dramatic testimony of the Pinkerton agent and informer James McParlan. The trials attracted national press attention even though they took place in the mine fields, as did the executions on Black Thursday 1876, when the first ten miners were hung in a "deliberate demonstration of the state's power to exact the ultimate penalty," in the words of J. Anthony Lukas. It was "an awful day of retribution remembered for generations in the coal patches of Pennsylvania, in mining camps, and in Irish American communities across the land." The Molly Maguire saga remained "popular" in part because, as Lukas suggested, "the affecting stories of Molly after Molly walking to the gallows in the pale light of dawn, often holding a single rose sent by a wife or girl friend . . . stirred people's morbid curiosity."[29]

The memory of those executed miners remained alive in the hard coal country of eastern Pennsylvania for other reasons as well. The martyrdom of the Irish miners symbolized the injustice experienced by immigrant workers in America. In the 1970s a movement appeared to obtain a posthumous pardon for the Mollies' alleged leader, Jack Kehoe. The effort was successful. On 21 June 1980 exactly one hundred years after Black Thursday, a plaque was erected on a wall of Schuylkill County Prison, where, it says, the largest mass execution in Pennsylvania took place with the hanging of "alleged" Molly Maguire leaders.[30] How does the preservation of this memory compare with how the Haymarket was recalled?

The Mollies and the Haymarket "boys" represented the two most notorious cases of "working-class martyrdom" in U.S. history, but the story of the Irish miners was more effectively "blocked" off from later generations than the saga of the Chicago anarchists. The coal miners were tried and executed at the end of a great depression when the labor movement was defeated, whereas the Haymarket defendants were arrested during the "great upheaval" of 1886. As result, their ordeal could be seen as part of something greater, indeed a formative event for the international labor movement, which was dedicated to a universal demand—the eight-hour day, a cause that gave their deaths heroic meaning. The Mollies died for a secret movement of Irish Catholics condemned by their church. They perished after the eclipse of the Fenians, who might have made them martyrs, and were executed during the rise of the parliamentary Home Rule movement in Ireland whose leaders dreaded the memory of peasant terrorism.[31] Even the Ancient Order of Hibernians renounced "Mollieism" to escape the wrath of the Catholic church, whose bishop in Scranton had excommunicated the Mollies. Terence Powderly, the Irish Catholic leader of the Knights of Labor—another secret order—complained of being branded "a Molly Maguire, and in fact a Communist," and strenuously disassociated the Knights from the Mollies.[32] Indeed, few demanded pardons for the condemned Irishmen, and many of their prominent compatriots believed that they were guilty. In the Haymarket case the defendants were presumed innocent even after "proven guilty"—an innocence proclaimed by important public figures like Congressman Robert Ingersoll, Senator Lyman Trumbull, William Dean Howells, Henry Demarest Lloyd, and Illinois governor John Peter Altgeld.

The Martyrs

The innocence of the Haymarket martyrs seemed to make them especially tragic victims. Their heroism and stoicism added to their allure. Seeking to explain why the Haymarket episode "made such a powerful and lasting impression," one historian turned to Peter Kropotkin's observation that while others had died for labor's cause, none had been "so enthusiastically adopted by the workers as their martyrs." The moral qualities of the defendants appealed to workmen who believed the victims to be "thoroughly honest" as well as innocent. They "had no ambition," said Kropotkin, and "sought no power over others." Dedicated to their fellow workers and to their principles, they refused to plead for clemency on their own behalf during the entire year they awaited death. Even on the scaffold, "they hailed the day on which they died for those principles." As Kropotkin wrote one year after their execution: "Such men can inspire the generations to come with the noblest feelings."[33]

But the anarchist movement did not depend solely upon inspiration to keep memories of Haymarket alive. The martyrs' families and supporters ritualized the act of remembering and began to do so immediately with a funeral many witnesses would never forget. After struggling with city officials who prohibited red flags and banned revolutionary songs, the anarchists led a large parade silently through Chicago's working-class neighborhoods on the long walk to Chicago's Waldheim Cemetery, a burial place for many of the city's German Jews. On Sunday 13 November 1887 thousands of workers marched in a funeral procession behind the bodies of the anarchists, past a half-million people who lined the streets to watch. Only when they reached the cemetery outside the city limits did they begin to sing "the Marseillaise"—the tune Parsons sang before his execution.[34]

The mourners made Waldheim a "monumental memory site" partly because they were barred from access to the real "milieu de mémoire"—Haymarket Square.[35] In his guide to the area for the Illinois Labor History Society, William Adelman describes the tempestuous history of this Square—a quintessential urban public space that like most markets, was a common gathering place for farmers, small traders, and plebeians of all sorts. It was so large that the Chicago anarchists chose it for the May 4 protest because they actually believed twenty thousand people would attend their rally. Nearby stood union halls so filled with eight-hour strike meetings the evening of May 3 that the anarchists planning the protest rally had to gather in the basement.[36]

Soon after the Haymarket riot, the conservative *Chicago Tribune* started a fund drive to erect a statue in the square to memorialize the fallen police officers. The paper was owned by Cyrus McCormick, whose militant workers spearheaded the eight-hour movement. Many industrialists contributed and a statue of a policeman with an upraised arm was dedicated on Memorial Day 1889. The statue, which symbolized the authoritative memory of the bombing, would experience a troubled history. In 1903 part of the inscription was stolen and later a streetcar operator ran his train off the track and knocked the statuary policeman off its base. The driver said he was tired of seeing that policeman with his arm raised in the air.[37]

The police statue symbolized an important activity for the forces of law and order: restricting urban public spaces from use by an insurgent working class.[38] The labor movement could not reclaim the square itself for a memorial to mourn the workers who died there. But those who sought to preserve the memory of the martyrs could challenge official apportionments of "ceremonial space and time" by commemorating the anarchists' death every November 11 at Waldheim Cemetery.[39]

The Monument

In the years that followed the executions, the official story of the riot was tarnished when the very same Chicago police who led the charge on the square were discredited by charges of corruption. In 1893 the AFL's Chicago Trades and Labor Assembly joined radicals and progressives, including the famous defense attorney Clarence Darrow, in asserting that the defendants had been denied a fair trial and in demanding a pardon for the three anarchists who remained in prison. On 25 June 1893 thousands of unionists again converged on Waldheim to dedicate a statue at the gravesite. Many foreign visitors from the Columbian Exposition boarded special trains to attend the ceremony nine miles

Memorializing hallowed ground: photograph of Albert Weinart's 1893 Haymarket monument, Waldeim Cemetery, Chicago. *Photograph courtesy Illinois Labor History Society.*

from Haymarket. The statue, inspired by a lyric in the "Marseillaise," was forged in bronze in the form of a hooded woman laying a laurel wreath on the brow of a dying worker. It resembled earlier art in the French republican tradition in which strong female figures symbolized liberty and justice.[40] The martyrs' followers created a place of memory with a monument at Waldheim in order to advance the work of remembering.[41]

The day after the dedication, the new populist governor of Illinois, John Peter Altgeld—himself a German immigrant—pardoned the three other Haymarket defendants and ensured his own political demise. The governor's statement—a remarkably radical one for a public official—blamed repressive police action for the bombing tragedy, claimed evidence had been fabricated, and accused the trial judge of "malicious ferocity."[42] This courageous statement added enormous power to the memory of the Haymarket defendants as innocent victims of a "judicial hanging." Altgeld himself, "the forgotten eagle" in Vachel Lindsay's poem, was in fact remembered, perhaps longer than any other governor, as a politician who put truth and honesty above ambition.

These events heightened the significance of the Haymarket martyrs' grave as a site of memory. "Waldheim, with its hauntingly beautiful monument, became a revolutionary shrine, a place of pilgrimage for anarchists and socialists from all over the world," writes historian Paul Avrich. For decades, it drew more visitors than the statue of Illinois's favorite son, the martyred President Lincoln. Always ready to repress radicalism, the Chicago police drew more attention to the site by placing "restrictions on the annual memorial ceremonies" and threatening to ban them entirely—a sign of things to come.[43]

Besides physical sites like monuments, Nora suggests, there are "lieux de mémoire" created to "maintain anniversaries, organize celebrations, pronounce eulogies" through ritual and through ritualized storytelling—all ways of defending "privileged" memories that "without commemorative vigilance" would be swept away by history. Like monuments, written and oral narratives reflect, as much as they create, the will to remember.[44]

The Story

The martyrs' lives and deaths provided a redemptive narrative for a whole generation of radicals who told the anarchists' story repeatedly in speeches and writings that appeared in many languages.[45] After the Chicago trial Emma Goldman "devoured every line on anarchism I could get, every word I could get about the men, their lives their work." Their execution "crushed her spirits" at first but then caused her "spiritual rebirth," giving her a "burning faith, a determination to dedicate myself to the memory of my martyred comrades, to make their cause my own."[46] Abraham Bisno of the Cloakmakers Union recalled 1887 dramatically as "the time the anarchists were murdered by the authorities of the law." Bisno's intensive discussions and "studies" of the Haymarket case and "every item of evidence" helped him "develop the capacity to lecture upon social questions" and to "address large meetings in the year of 1888, making for the formation of labor unions among our people."[47] Eugene V. Debs, who became a socialist after being imprisoned for leading the great Pullman rail strike of 1894, prayed at the martyrs' graves after his release from jail, just before he went to downtown Chicago to greet by a parade of a million workers.[48]

Debs's prayer represented the persistent religious symbolism in anarchist memorials to the Haymarket martyrs who were put to death in what the anarchist writer Votairine de Cleyre called "Chicago's Calvary." The trial and execution became a conversion experience for many of her fellow anarchists. The annual memorials to the five martyrs on November 11 created a bond for the shattered anarchist movement and provided "moral coherence" in a chaotic capitalist world. These rituals passed along the "shared experience" of the events of 1886 and 1887, which gave ethical meaning to life and death for many individuals who were radicalized during those years.[49]

No one in that remarkable "traveling community of radicals" worked harder to keep the dead alive in memory than Albert Parsons's widow. Lucy Parsons dedicated her life to preserving the legacy of her martyred husband and his comrades. She became a cause célèbre in Chicago when the police chief vowed to prevent her from speaking in public. Her fame grew outside of Chicago when in 1889 she published *The Life of Albert Parsons*, a remarkable book that held a "weird fascination" for one reviewer who wrote that "few stories in our literature hold such dramatic power as this . . . a tale of chivalry so exalted, with an ending so tragic and pathetic," that it seemed like a classic romance.[50] Throughout the grim nineties Lucy Parsons continued memorializing the martyrs during her speaking tours, especially on November 11 when the hanging was remembered in many cities. In 1897 her rival Emma Goldman spoke at the commemoration in Chicago, taking Lucy's place in the limelight, but in 1903 a new edition of Albert's biography appeared and his widow resumed her speaking tours.[51]

Through her agitational work Lucy Parsons contributed to the cult of martyrdom surrounding the Haymarket anarchists. But she wanted to do more than memorialize the victims of a "judicial hanging." She intended to preserve the memory of their radical ideas and strategies for the labor movement. She worried that "the class solidarity of the Great Upheaval" had collapsed "and dissolved into memory" and she tried, as does historian Bruce C. Nelson in *Beyond the Martyrs*, to bring the "Chicago idea" of direct-action unionism out of the gallows shadow, out of the courtroom stage setting, out of the context of tragic storytelling. Like other radicals at the turn of the century she bemoaned a labor movement now "stuck in a union mire" because trade organizations were concerned only with shorter hours and higher wages, not with a vision of a new society.[52]

Lucy Parsons and her comrades resurrected the "Chicago idea" and made it part of a usable past for the Industrial Workers of the World, whose founding convention in Chicago she attended in 1905. Haymarket would often be recalled by Wobblies, like William D. Haywood, who presided at the IWW's first meeting. He later wrote of the bombing, trial, and hanging as "the decisive events in shaping his radical convictions." He was haunted by August Spies's last words uttered just before he was hung from the gallows: "There will come a time when our silence will be more powerful than the voices you are strangling today."[53] The men and women who revived the "Chicago idea" through the IWW "pledged to honor" the memory of the Haymarket martyrs—a promise they kept in an energetic "In November, We Remember Campaign," which linked the 1887 executions to the death of other radicals.[54]

The First Day of May

The memory of the martyrs also endured because many workers associated their deaths with the celebration of May Day and with the struggle for the eight-hour day—the issue that led to the choice of May 1 as a workers holiday by the 1889 International Socialist Congress in Paris. The Marxist champions of May Day had been active in the protests against the Haymarket executions and were well aware that the martyrs' memory was linked to the May 1 general strike of 1886.[55] Many Italian immigrants in the United States observed May Day as "la pasqua dei lavoratori" (the Easter of the workers). Some of them learned of the Chicago martyrs for the first time in picnic songs and in speeches by charismatic anarchists like Luigi Galleani who often referred to the incident as an example of how American democracy could be as oppressive as European tyranny. Radicals recalled that all the Haymarket defendants were immigrants, except Parsons, and predicted that their fate awaited others in this so-called land of liberty.[56]

The remembrance of the Haymarket martyrs on May 1 was more than ceremonial. Their martyrdom became a keystone in constructing a homily of supreme sacrifice for workers' movements on the ascendancy in many capitalist nations during the 1880s.[57] Confronting aggressive employers, hostile churches and newspapers, and militarized police forces, these movements needed issues like the eight-hour day, tactics like the mass strike, and heroes like the Haymarket martyrs. Movement builders found all these things in the tragic Chicago story.

More than at any time in the subsequent century, radical movements identified across national boundaries—sharing common issues like the eight-hour day, fighting common struggles for trade union legality, and using similar tactics like the militant strike. The Chicago martyrs became their common heroes. Revolutionaries excited by the worker insurgencies of the 1870s and 1880s exerted a remarkable influence on labor movements around the world; and among them, the anarchists of the Black International exercised an outsized influence. Consider the example of Mexico, where the great May Day march in Mexico City would be referred to "as the annual demonstration glorifying the memory of those who were killed in Chicago in 1887."[58] The enduring connection between the Haymarket martyrs and May Day in Mexico derives from the anarchists, many of them Spanish immigrants, who acted as *obreros intellectuales* and organizers of many early trade unions.[59] At ten years of age Enrique Flores Magon first heard of the four men hung in Chicago when his father spoke of them as martyrs. Magon imagined "the bodies dangling to and fro at the ends of ropes" like the men who were hanged from trees in his native land.[60]

Mexicans also created places of memory to recall the Haymarket events. Traveling near Mexico City on May Day 1923, an American poet, together with D. H. Lawrence and his wife Frieda, witnessed a scene in which people laid a cornerstone for a statue to "The Martyrs of Chicago" whose murder—described during a rally as "shameless and villainous"—could still rouse "all Mexico" to protest. At this point, while immigrant anarchists and syndicalists were driven underground in the Unites States, their Mexican comrades remained important in the labor movement as founders and leaders of the Confederación General de Trabajadores. Later, Diego Rivera's mural in the Palace of Justice depicted the four anarchist heroes in a grander site of memory.[61] Perhaps, the Mexican memorials to "los mártirios de Chicago" reflected one more effort by those "architects of national identity," including Rivera, to define "Mexico in opposition to the United States," as if to say: "We're Indian, they're Anglo. We're Catholic, they're Protestant. We have history, they have no memory."[62]

In the United States labor radicals found it more difficult to perpetuate Haymarket rituals. During the early 1900s anarchists maintained November 11 as a memorial day, but the occasion lost its power to attract pilgrims even before World War I. After 1890 anarchists and socialists failed to revive May Day as an occasion for remembering the martyrs—that is, until another sensational murder trial in 1906 promised to send three more labor radicals to the gallows. Pinkertons and law officers kidnapped Bill Haywood and took him with two other union militants to stand trial in Idaho for the dynamite murder of that state's former governor. The labor and socialist movements roused themselves in furious protest. They revived May Day in 1907 as an occasion of mammoth demonstrations, especially in New York where over 100,000 immigrants marched all day, and even in Boston, hardly a radical labor town, where nearly as many rallied on the common.[63]

The "spectacular show trial" in Idaho not only allowed the socialist movement to resurrect May Day, it provided a powerful occasion for remembering Haymarket. The events of 1886 and 1887 were invoked in the Haywood trial by Clarence Darrow, the defense attorney who had helped win a pardon for the surviving "Haymarket boys," and by Eugene Debs, author of the inflammatory tract "Arouse Ye Slaves," who recalled Haymarket in a threat that infuriated President Theodore Roosevelt. "Nearly twenty years ago," Debs wrote in the

Appeal to Reason, "the capitalist tyrants put some innocent men to death for standing up for labor. They are now going to try to do it again. Let them dare! There have been twenty years of revolutionary education, agitation, and organization since the Haymarket tragedy, and if an attempt is made to repeat it, there will be a revolution and I will do all in my power to precipitate it."[64]

Haywood and his comrades were acquitted, May Day was recreated as a memory day, and in 1908 Lucy Parsons, carrying copies of the martyrs' *Famous Speeches,* made such a successful tour of eleven western cities that she decided to reprint the collection. Her tours became even more popular as the IWW preached the Chicago idea of direct-action unionism and reclaimed through dramatic free speech fights the public space closed down to radical labor after Haymarket. But Lucy Parsons also spoke to mainstream union members—for example in New York City where early in 1911 the Central Federated Union endorsed her talks before AFL locals. Then in two cross-country tours she sold ten thousand copies of the new edition of the Haymarket anarchists' *Famous Speeches.* In November, after her return to New York, she and Bill Haywood "spoke to packed November 11th meetings."[65] At a time when many unions fought desperate struggles with the courts and the police and when the AFL adopted a "strong anti-statist outlook" and a posture of "semi-outlawry," trade unionists remembered the Haymarket tragedy as part of a state assault on the labor and eight-hour movements, and, like Abraham Bisno, recalled the anarchists as innocent victims of that assault.[66]

A few years later, when anarchists, socialists, and Wobblies faced extinction amid the furies of war, there were other trials to remember—the McNamaras, Mooney and Billings, Carlo Tresca—and other victims to mourn, the women and children murdered at Ludlow, along with the Wobbly martyrs Joe Hill and Frank Little and their comrades massacred in Everett, Washington. The IWW began a new campaign to "remember" these victims in "Black November," but in the next decade, after the destruction of the labor left, few occasions survived in which movement heroes and heroines could be honored.[67]

May Day celebrations were targets of state repression during World War I. Some laws actually banned the flying of the red flag that used to appear at the head of May 1 parades. During the red scare just after the war, May Day marches were violently attacked in several cities.[68] In any case, this holiday had little hope for a revival in the patriotic fervor of the time, a time when the official culture created a very different holiday in May. Memorial Day, at the end of the month, created for the Civil War dead, now became an occasion for honoring soldiers killed in France and for recalling memories of World War I.[69] May Day, as a time of remembering the Haymarket affair, suffered from outright suppression, while November 11, the memorial day of the hangings, faced a different fate in the court of official remembrance. After 1918 this day in November would be celebrated as Armistice Day, a major creation of "patriotic culture"—a veneration of the very state the martyrs had violently opposed and of the soldiers who had died for that nation-state.[70]

The History

Haymarket faded from working-class memory in the deeply repressive era of 1920s. Only private memories of Haymarket survived in individual "memory cabinets." "The act of remembering" Haymarket became an individual one, as is all the real work of remembrance.[71] The memory of 1886–87 events now passed into recorded history. The Haymarket affair became a parable for the conservative interpretation of American history. In his influential six-volume history James Ford Rhodes concluded "that the punishment meted out to the anarchists was legally just." Another prominent historian concurred and added that the "wretches" who assumed "an impudent front" during the trial were found guilty and "merited" their "punishment."[72] Thus did authoritative, academic history seek to negate the radical, proletarian memory of Haymarket.

But one historian unlocked the cabinets of private memory and made old movement recollections of Haymarket part of recorded history. In 1936, during a revival of progressive U.S. historiography, a young historian named Henry David published the first scholarly work on Haymarket that dismissed previous historians' judgments as "historically false." He demonstrated that the seven defendants could not have been guilty of murder given the evidence offered. He even questioned the possibility that the bomb could have been thrown by some other anarchist. The historian went on to challenge the interpretation of labor officials who blamed the anarchists for the failure of the Knights and the eight-hour movement. A scholar who studied at Columbia University, David absorbed the popular memory of Haymarket from Lucy Parsons; from George Schilling, the brilliant Chicago labor leader; and from his own immigrant father, who had an extensive personal knowledge of the American and European revolutionary movement; they passed their memory of the Haymarket directly to the historian.[73] Alfred Young, the radical historian of the American Revolution and its memory, studied with David after he became a professor at Columbia and remembered him saying that his father was a Russian revolutionary who named his son after Henry David Thoreau. Young recalls his professor as someone who took him under his wing and who showed that a "left person and a Jew might make it in the academic world."[74]

In 1937, a year after David's book appeared, a revived labor movement, with a historically conscious left wing, recalled the memory of 1887. In November union activists and leftists celebrated the fiftieth anniversary of the Haymarket executions in the Amalgamated Hall in Chicago. It was a year during which the cycle of conflict in the city turned again to anti-union violence. History seemed to be repeating itself. Lucy Parsons and others related to the martyrs spoke at the anniversary and at Waldheim. The presence of representatives of the embattled Spanish Confederación Nacional de Trabajo (CNT) represented the last vestige of the old international anarchist movement. Parsons referred to the newest tragedy in Chicago labor history. Just a few months before, the same city police who killed three strikers at the McCormick Works on 1 May 1886 shot down ten pickets at the Republic Steel Works on 31 May 1937–Memorial Day.[75] For a short time, the memory of Haymarket became useful to the new industrial unions of the Committee of Industrial Organizations and to the Communists who led some of them.

The press and the authorities blamed the bloodshed on Memorial Day 1937 on a "Communist riot," just as they had done after the Haymarket riot. But after a congressional committee viewed a suppressed newsreel of the shooting, the police were accused of killing peaceful strikers. Once again, a battle ensued over the memory of working-class martyrs in Chicago, and once again, influential voices sought absolution for innocent workers accused of being red rioters by the shapers of public opinion. Unexpectedly, the public response to the Memorial Day massacre helped create more protection for workers' rights and civil liberties. As a result, the memory of working-class martyrdom took on a different, less potent meaning. Cognizant of labor's violent past, and the effect of police actions at Haymarket and after, Chicago union leaders came to believe that workers' interests could only be protected by controlling or influencing the government. The Democratic mayor of Chicago repented for his decision to send police to guard Republic Steel's South Chicago mill on Memorial Day and offered labor so much support that one of the strikers wounded by the police supported the Mayor's reelection campaign in 1939. As Democrats and as citizens, workers began to invest in "the state" because the government seemed to be standing by them in industry and in society as a whole.[76]

The Cemetery

When Lucy Parsons was buried with her husband, her son, and her beloved comrades at Waldheim in 1942, so was one of the last carriers of the "Chicago idea" of revolutionary unionism—an idea based on anarchist and syndicalist hostility to the capitalist state. A few years before her death, Lucy had joined the Communist Party, which now became the principal interpreter of Haymarket and its place of memory, Waldheim Cemetery—this despite the party's hostility to anarchism.[77] During the popular front, Albert Parsons and the "anarcho-syndicalists" of 1886 fit into the pantheon of Communist Party heroes as "martyrs of class struggle who gave their all for the emancipation of the working class"—heroes that included some who traced their political lives to Haymarket, notably "Big Bill" Haywood, who before he died in Moscow, asked that half of his ashes be buried in the Kremlin Wall and the other half "scattered at the site of the Martyrs Monument." In 1942 Jack Johnstone, a prominent Chicago

Communist and respected labor organizer, asked to be buried with the Haymarket anarchists; so would other party leaders in later years, including William Z. Foster and Elizabeth Gurley Flynn, who as a teenager had been inspired by Lucy Parsons at the IWW founding convention.[78] By sharing sacred ground and by writing labor history that linked anarchists, Wobblies and Communists in a kind of popular front, party intellectuals attempted to absorb the memory of Haymarket within their own tradition.

But during World War II, when the Communist Party disbanded, Waldheim faded as a site memory. It now embodied a "memorial consciousness" that barely survived because "the intimate fund of memory" had disappeared.[79] The avant garde Chicago poet Kenneth Rexroth captured the moment well in 1942, the high tide of national unity during World War II. At Waldheim, he wrote with a heavy heart, of Emma Goldman who was buried there that year, and of

> The philosophers of history,
> Of dim wit and foolish memory,
> The giggling concubines of catastrophe—
> Who forget so much—
> Now in Waldheim where the rain
> has fallen careless and unthinking
> For all an evil century's youth,
> Where now the banks of dark roses lie,
> What memory lasts Emma of you
> Or of the intrepid comrades of your grave,
> . . . of "mutual aid,"
> against the iron-clad, flame-throwing
> Course of time?[80]

Rexroth wrote at a time when, in a complete negation of the spirit of 1886, American labor union leaders, including the Communists, took a "no-strike pledge" for the duration of the war. The Haymarket anarchists no longer served as heroes for a labor movement whose leaders had abandoned old anti-statist traditions. Many union officials, especially the immigrants who rose to power in the new unions, had decided to forget the bloody past of police and military repression, to regret their ancestors' militant radicalism, to block out memories of their rejection as immigrants—all in order to embrace a new version of "working-class Americanism" in which unions (with their ethnic membership) would take their place as a legitimate interest group in a pluralistic society.[81]

By this time those who had experienced Haymarket had died. The oral tradition through which stories of Haymarket had been transmitted barely survived in Cold War America. It was a time when, Marianne Debouzy says, memories of working-class radicalism sank into oblivion as individuals were silenced and as left organizations were dismantled or outlawed, making it difficult for people to share oppositional memories.[82] During the 1950s the grandson of Oscar

Neebe, one of the Haymarket defendants pardoned in 1893, traveled to Mexico where he was shocked to learn that his grandfather was a revered proletarian hero. The memory of Oscar Neebe had been suppressed within his own family, which had suffered "many persecutions for Haymarket." Neebe's grandson inherited only his grandfather's name with no knowledge of his famous role in labor history.[83] Years later the descendant saw that memory reclaimed by the custodians of Chicago's venerable labor history. During the centennial of the Haymarket "riot" the city's famous radio personality Studs Terkel interviewed Neebe's grandson along with the historian Bruno Cartosio, who spoke about the surviving memory of Haymarket in Italy. Later Cartosio wrote of the Neebe family's memorial history. He thought it illustrated how memories that seem to have been forgotten, because they are not recorded, are actually remembered in private, available for telling to those willing to do the asking.[84]

The Reclamation

The memory of Haymarket was reclaimed in the 1960s by a new movement whose antiauthoritarian ideas were quite compatible with the beliefs of the Chicago martyrs. Like the anarchists of 1886, some antiwar radicals of the late 1960s believed in the propaganda of the deed; they declared war on a state that made war on Vietnamese insurgents and their supporters. On 4 May 1968, as antiwar demonstrators prepared for militant protests at the Democratic convention in Chicago, someone defaced the police monument in Haymarket Square. On 6 October 1969 the statue was blown up. The Weatherman faction of the Students for a Democratic Society took credit. An enraged Mayor Richard J. Daley promised to replace the edifice. On 4 May 1970—the anniversary of the 1886 bombing—a new statue was dedicated to the police.[85]

While this violent struggle to memorialize the Haymarket victims pitted 1960's anarchists and the forces of law and order, the old voice of the labor movement arose taking its own stand on this site of conflict. The Illinois Labor History Society was formed in 1968 by union progressives like Les Orear, who worked for the Packinghouse Workers and by labor historians like Bill Adelman, a labor educator. When the Teamsters and a few other unions contributed funds to rebuild the police statue blown up during the 1968 "days of rage," the Society was contacted by Bill Garvey, who edited the Steel Workers' union newspaper. He was dismayed that the scores of workers killed by the police in the 1886 riot had been totally forgotten in the controversy about the memory of the lawmen who died there. In 1969 he joined Labor History Society members in forming a Haymarket Workers' Committee to plan a memorial event in the Square to the innocent union members who lost their lives there simply by coming out to protest the shooting of fellow workers striking for the eight hour day. Garvey rented a hay wagon as a speakers' stand and asked radio personality

Honoring labor's fallen soldiers: Studs Terkel speaking at the first Haymarket Square commemoration, Chicago, 4 May 1969. *Photograph courtesy Illinois Labor History Society.*

Studs Terkel to keynote the memorial. The Labor History Society did not oppose the reconstruction of the police statue, but it demanded a compensatory place in Haymarket Square to mark the death of the workers who had gathered there for a peaceful protest in 1886. In 1970 Les Orear joined the Illinois State Historical Commission and persuaded its members to erect a memorial plaque in the square to honor the union dead. It was dedicated on May 4 of that year, but it was soon ripped down by vandals and never restored.[86]

The struggle over Haymarket's divided memory escalated even further. On 6 October 1968 the newly dedicated police statue was bombed again.

Mayor Daley ordered round-the-clock security at the cost of $67,000 a year. Such protection became too costly, so city officials moved the official Haymarket icon indoors to police headquarters. On 4 May 1972 local anarchists and members of the IWW demonstrated at the site and attempted to erect on the empty pedestal of the police statue a papier-mâché bust of Louis Lingg, the anarchist who had cheated the hangman in 1887 by committing suicide in his jail cell. Once again, the Chicago police appeared to clear the square.[87]

After the passions of the sixties and seventies cooled, Paul Avrich wrote his masterpiece, *The Haymarket Tragedy*. Meeting the highest scholarly standards, Avrich's book, published in 1984, focused on the personalities and passions of the anarchists themselves, a focus very close to the core of popular memory. He quoted extensively from the speeches and writings of the participants to capture their passion and eloquence, and to show that "their words can speak to the present generation across a gulf of a century, with undiminished relevance." To Avrich, "[t]he struggle of the 1880s—the struggle for economic security, social justice, personal liberty—is the struggle of today."[88] Like Henry David, Avrich attempted to cross "the gulf" between "memory and history" posited by Pierre Nora in his work on *lieux de mémoire*. Both of these historians understood how the memories of subordinate groups survived and the ways in which they could be recovered and incorporated in alternative historical interpretations.

The memory of the Haymarket martyrs never became the subject of the intensive and creative reconstruction devoted to the memory of Emma Goldman, a martyr of another sort, a person whose own convictions were shaped by the tragic events of 1886. Goldman's memory, revived and reshaped by the women's movement, received official support from academics and foundations who contributed to a process likened to "canonization." Recent representations of Emma Goldman emphasize the "innocence of her ideals," as contrasted with the cruelty of her persecution. According to Oz Frankel, this effort allows her memory to be placed in a broad American tradition and a "constitutional discourse" about the limits of dissent. "Exonerating old enemies" of the state may, he argues, be "a feature of the American way of forgetting and remembering."[89]

The memory of the Haymarket martyrs was not "tamed" by historians. On the centennial of the event in 1986, a number of excellent historical publications preserved the original values and intentions of the martyrs: for example, a special issue of *International Labor and Working Class History* and a centennial scrapbook edited by David Roediger and Franklin Rosemont for the old Chicago socialist publishing house, Charles H. Kerr.[90] An important essay by Bruce C. Nelson explained that events of 1886–87 held significance "beyond the martyrs" whose ordeal was either memorialized religiously by the left or criminalized by the right. Nelson, who would soon publish a superb social history of the Chicago workers of this period, emphasized the significance of anarchism as a popular movement in the late nineteenth century.[91]

However, the public work of commemoration in Chicago did take place within a broader discourse about civil liberties and workers rights.

Unable to mark the actual place where the workers died in the square, the Labor History Society acquired the deed to the Waldheim monument from the Pioneer Aid and Support Association of friends and family, which had had it constructed in 1893.[92] It then maintained the site, which still attracted visitors from around the world. When the History Society organized a centennial event at the Cemetery in 1986, it even persuaded the Chicago Federation of Labor to endorse the commemoration. As Les Orear recalled, a younger generation now led the labor movement. These union officials were more open to the idea of honoring anarchists as innocent victims and less worried about identifying themselves with the memory of radical martyrs. But this was much too tame for a small band of anarchists who remained active in Chicago; they picketed the event because it was not organized to honor the martyrs as anarchists. Instead, it recalled the sacrifice of worker activists in the popular struggle for the eight-hour day.[93] Indeed, Chicago Mayor Harold Washington used the occasion to proclaim May Labor History Month, following the precedent of Black History Month in February. Rather than referring to the anarchists as men who died for their beliefs, he spoke to commemorate "the movement towards the eight-hour day, union rights, civil rights, human rights" and to the remembrance of the "tragic miscarriage of justice which claimed the lives of four labor activists."[94]

Finally, in 1997 the monument at Waldheim gained official memorial status as a national landmark, but only after the directors of the labor-history theme study persuaded the park service to lift its ban on marking cemeteries and graves. Robin Bachin wrote a fine historical treatment of the site that preserved the memory of the martyrs with integrity, rather than taming it in order to make a case for the site as a significant one in the history of civil liberties.[95] In her nomination of the Waldheim monument to the park service, Bachin argued that this famous site of memory had meaning for movement history. "Haymarket has provided a symbol through which various groups have been able to create a usable past and shared pride in radical heritage." Indeed, she added, "activists worldwide continue to invoke the Haymarket martyrs in their struggles for civil rights." The long, patient work of the Illinois Labor History Society reached a successful climax as more than a thousand people came to Waldheim on 4 May 1998 for the official ceremony. The AFL-CIO presence was noticeable. Eight trade union leaders spoke—representative of a younger generation that had not inherited the criminalized memory of Haymarket.[96]

However, unlike Waldheim Cemetery, Haymarket Square itself would remain unmarked, like many other sites of violence in American history. After the explosive events of the 1960s the site was neglected and forgotten, except by the Illinois Labor History Society. In 1982 Harold Washington became the first black mayor of Chicago after running against the old patronage system and its abuses, including police brutality. As part of the centennial anniversary in 1986, the Labor History Society proposed to Mayor Washington that the city recognize the martyrs of 1887 with a memorial park in the square.[97] When Mayor Washington died in office, hopes for a Haymarket Square memorial faded, but not for Mollie West, a Chicago radical and survivor of the 1937 Memorial Day massacre, who clung to her belief that labor history sites, like Haymarket, can provide meaning for working people with no memory of struggles for social justice. She continued to advocate for a Haymarket Square memorial, but she could only imagine its construction through an act of resurrection: "We're waiting for Mayor Washington to come back," she said in 1993. "If he was here, this would've been done by now."[98]

"Memory implies a certain act of redemption," writes John Berger. "What is forgotten has been abandoned . . . [and] with the loss of memory the continuities of meaning and judgement are also lost."[99] More than any story told in American labor history, the Haymarket story preserved a memory of workers innocently victimized, of martyrs whose death gave meaning to the sacrifices made for labor rights and working-class empowerment, and of visionaries who created a labor movement to radically change capitalist society. Those who retold the story in this way rendered a harsh judgment on a city ruled by fear, a judiciary controlled by tyrants, a democracy defined by property.

A place of memory in Southern movement history: Dr. King leaving the Lorraine Motel in Memphis moments before his assassination. *Photograph courtesy Wide World, Associated Press.*

CHAPTER 6

Releasing Silenced Voices and Uncovering Forgotten Places in the American South

> [T]here is no denying the fact that Americans can be notoriously selective in the exercise of historical memory. Surely there must be some self-deceptive magic in this, for in spite of what is left out of our recorded history, our unwritten history looms as its obscure alter ego, and although repressed from our general knowledge, it is always active in the shaping of events.
>
> RALPH ELLISON, *Going into the Territory*

It is often said that historical memory has endured to a far greater extent in the South than in any other region of the country. Some attribute this quality to southerners' love of "a good tale" and to their gift for telling it. "They are born reciters; great memory retainers; diary keepers, letter exchangers, and letter savers; history tracers, and debaters, and—outstaying all the rest—great talkers," remarked Eudora Welty, one of the South's finest writers.[1] The southern cultural proclivity for storytelling has preserved many memories, but so have highly organized memorial efforts in public places, like the ones devoted to the Lost Cause of the Confederacy and its fallen heroes which are unparalleled in the United States. The power of that memory shaped white southern identity for years until the civil rights movement and sympathetic historians, like John Hope Franklin and C. Vann Woodward, challenged the old myth of the Lost Cause and the Solid South.[2]

I became fascinated with the region's dissenters and with its radical movements while studying southern history with Woodward. I was intrigued by how dissonant memories were represented in the region's recorded histories and by how they were neglected or distorted. I also became interested in how an adjutant general of the Sons of the Confederacy like Covington Hall could recast the memory of the South's defeat into a romantically radical call for its people to throw off the chains of Yankee colonialism.[3] As Jacquelyn Dowd Hall shows in her essay on Katharine Du Pre Lumpkin and her sisters, "the party of remembrance" could not control how The Lost Cause would be interpreted by free thinkers who might tell stories to emancipate southern history from white supremacy.[4]

The way southerners remember is "bound up in place," wrote Eudora Welty. Many white novelists, from Faulkner to Styron, and after, have anchored their stories in vividly drawn southern places, places often haunted by ghosts of the past. But black novelists like Margaret Walker have been just as conscious of place.[5] A good example is Zora Neale Hurston's *Their Eyes Were Watching God,* a novel in which the author reconstructs Eatonville, Florida, as a beloved community created by black people, a little like the places recalled nostalgically by white writers.[6]

This attachment to place which helped shape the identity of black and white southerners could be oppressive. "As the historically dominant group in southern society white Gentiles became accustomed to 'placing' individuals as a way of ordering a chaotic and often violent region," David Goldfield explains. Placing drew upon a long list of characteristics like family name, birthplace, religion, occupation, and education; and its most important function was to keep black southerners in their place. "Placing also depended on conformity to the customs of a given rural area, town, or city at a particular point in time," says Goldfield. "To know one's place and to act accordingly was important for getting along in the South, especially before the civil rights era."[7]

William Faulkner was acutely sensitive to how "Southern culture developed ingenious devices for preserving its image of itself as a whole, harmonious organism," including "an amazing capacity for not seeing what was clearly before its eyes," according to a recent biographer. A powerful example is the fact that people with even one African or mulatto ancestor (with "one drop" of black blood, as the saying went) were declared black even when they looked white.[8] Faulkner knew the powerful ways in which southern communities dealt with people who refused to perform their assigned roles. He wrote at a time (the 1920s and 1930s) when white southerners believed they were getting "people into their proper places again after two or three generations when people and things were disastrously out of place."[9] Faulkner presented a more complicated picture by creating unforgettable characters who were "damaged" by southern history, destroyed because they questioned their place in the social order. Still, like many other regional intellectuals, he never abandoned a sense of the South as a special place. Anyone who has read *Absalom, Absalom* remembers the anguished words of the protagonist saying of the South: "I don't hate it. I don't hate it."[10]

Besides anchoring identity, a sense of place became useful in constructing collective memories. Southerners energetically created and passionately preserved "places of memory," or what the French historian Pierre Nora calls *lieux de mémoire*—sites given special meaning after real environments of memory (*milieux de mémoire*) had disappeared.[11] Powerful sites of memory exist in the South—public monuments, and grave stones, and the battlegrounds of more than one kind of civil war. The most visible symbols were created by the official custodians of southern identity: antebellum plantations and towns like Colonial Williamsburg (an amazing historical reconstruction), battlegrounds, forts, and state capitols of the Confederacy, not to mention sacred peaks like Lookout

Mountain in Tennessee and Stone Mountain in Georgia, where in 1915 the United Daughters of the Confederacy commissioned a gargantuan sculpture showing three fathers of the Confederate Nation on horseback—President Jefferson Davis with generals Robert E. Lee and Stonewall Jackson—and where, in the same year, the modern Ku Klux Klan was resurrected with the ritual cross burning. Stone Mountain Park is now a major tourist attraction along with the nearby "AnteBellum Plantation" exhibit, a "romantic reconstruction" of life in the Old South.[12]

Nora uses the French word *lieux* so as to include not only physical places of memory, but also substitutes for "spontaneous memory" like "devotional institutions" (museums and archives) and memorials to the dead (monuments and cemeteries) as well as festivals and ceremonies that serve as replacements for spontaneous rituals.[13] Few *lieux de mémoire* were preserved, restored, or created by powerless people: people like Southern poor whites who risked so much to join the labor movement, and whose history was all but removed from the mental and physical landscape; people like the poor blacks who risked even more to join the civil rights movement and whose history has been more successfully preserved through recent struggles over places of memory.

The monuments to the Confederate soldier represent commonplace *lieux de mémoire* that helped to establish a memory of the South as a nation and a special place. One study of the monuments examines how women in the Daughters of the Confederacy led the effort to collect funds for ever more impressive monuments in "conspicuous places" like public parks and courthouse squares rather than cemeteries. These statues honoring the southern cause were intended to counter the national history of the Civil War as a war to put down a treasonous rebellion. As the commercial New South emerged, these memorials to the Confederate dead were constructed to honor self-sacrifice at a time when self-serving avarice seemed to be undermining southern values. Ironically, the monument-building became a commercial competition in which some local boosters even ordered their military statues of Italian marble from a Connecticut Yankee firm.[14]

The celebrations of Confederate Memorial Day at these sites reached massive levels in many places; these events were used to promote conservative politics and the idea of the Solid South. Confederate memorial celebrations began to wane by the 1910s as the veterans died off and the Sons of Confederate Veterans found the Lost Cause less important as a ritualized memory.[15] In 1929 Faulkner described the stone Confederate soldier in his imaginary town of Jefferson as a monument to a haunted past, a figure whose "empty eyes" gazed "into wind and weather." These statues represented "petrified" moments or fragments of history that had been "torn away from the movement of history, then returned, . . ." as Nora puts it, "like shells on the shore when the living sea of memory has receded."[16]

These *lieux de mémoire* attract attention even now. The West Indian novelist

V. S. Naipaul wrote recently that the monument to the Confederate war dead in Charleston, South Carolina, expressed the "pain of defeat"—a defeat "going against every idea of morality, every idea of a good story, the right story, the way it should have been: the tears of the Confederate memorial are close to religion, the helpless grief and rage . . . about an injustice that cannot be rehearsed too often."[17]

The ways in which symbolic sites could be used to perpetuate useful memories can be seen in the history of another monument located in New Orleans, a city that lacked Confederate military tradition, a city whose influential whites "had to look elsewhere for a history that would justify their attempts to dominate blacks," writes Lawrence Powell. They found it in the 1874 battle of Liberty Place, where the reactionary White League led over eight thousand armed men in a coup attempt against the radical Reconstruction government. The battle came to symbolize the white city leaders' version of the Lost Cause myth. Crescent City elites manipulated the memory of the battle to promote social unity through rituals like yearly pilgrimages they organized to the graves of the White League dead.[18]

It seemed that this *lieux de mémoire* would fade in importance until another social crisis revived the tradition of the gentlemen's mob. In 1891 veterans of the original Liberty Place battle called a mass meeting to denounce the acquittal of eleven Italian immigrants accused of a "black hand" murder of a police officer. Appealing to southern "manhood," leading citizens roused a lynch mob, stormed the jail, and murdered the Sicilians. This "riot" caused international concern, but it also helped the White League Monument Association in its foundering efforts to raise money for a marker around which the New Orleans power elite could, as Powell explains, manufacture a tradition of Civil War valor they lacked. It became a rallying point again and again: in 1898 to celebrate the disfranchisement of black voters under the guise of eliminating corruption; in 1934 to denounce the populist Governor Huey Long, whose radical programs frightened the old power brokers; in 1948 to support the reactionary Dixiecrat Party of Strom Thurmond.

Until the 1960s public memory of the South remained petrified in concrete symbols and marble statues standing "against the day," Faulkner wrote, "against the day when our Southern people," who resisted "inevitable changes in social relations," would be "forced to accept what they at one time might have accepted with dignity and goodwill, say, 'Why didn't someone tell us this before? Tell us in time?'"[19]

Since then, a far more dynamic sense of place and space has emerged in the South, because the civil rights movement disrupted the old South's habit of "placing" people and of recording events; it created new places of memory—often on top of the old—and it released voices long suppressed in southern history. For example, in New Orleans during the 1960s, civil rights protesters appropriated Liberty Place for demonstrations *against* segregation. The National Association for the Advancement of Color People resolved to demolish the monument and in 1974 the mayor ordered the addition of a bronze plaque to the monument saying that the white supremacist sentiments expressed on the memorial were "contrary to the beliefs of present day New Orleans." After a revived Ku Klux Klan began to rally in Liberty Place, the city's first African American mayor tried to have the obelisk removed in 1981, creating a howl of protest from white voices, including former Klan leader and state representative David Duke. The monument was later taken away from the square to protect it from vandals and to remove it as a point of controversy. Its fate remains undecided, its meaning still contested.

The monumental history of the South has been dominated by the elites and dedicated to the memories of generals and politicians. The only poor whites memorialized are represented in those statues of Confederate soldiers, the loyal infantrymen in gray who served the Lost Cause of a new nation. A survey of potential labor history landmarks for the National Park Service included few extant sites that could signify the lives of these forgotten men and women who toiled in the fields and the factories, the mines and the mills that produced the region's wealth.[20]

Few of these structures survived and even fewer were preserved for their national significance or architectural value. Workers passed through the coal and textile towns, the turpentine and timber camps, the dockyard and railyard districts leaving few material traces of their lives. Long gone are the storefront meeting halls and the holiness chapels where workers congregated, "the unsteepled places" they made "their own" and where there was room for free voices to discuss "democratic experiments," as E. P. Thompson once put it.[21]

It is easier to find places where they died and were buried than places where they lived, worked, and associated. And this is why so many gravesites and cemeteries were nominated by local groups for the national labor history landmarks project mentioned above. Earning a living in southern industry usually meant dying prematurely, because few unions and workplace safety laws existed to protect workers. The public remained ignorant of horrific workplace fatalities except when an "accident" or "disaster" hit the front page of newspapers—like the mine explosion at Monogah, West Virginia, that snuffed out hundreds of lives in 1907.

It should be possible to find and mark the sites where these workers died or where they were buried. But most of the old mines are closed and the miners' graves are difficult to find. They were not marked with hard stone like the resting places of those who owned property and enjoyed standing, but rather by softer headstones from which the sands of time soon eroded the names of the dead and the times of their lives. One of the sites nominated as a national landmark is Mt. Cavalry Cemetery in McAlester, Oklahoma, where a mass grave holds the remains of thirty-two Mexican immigrant miners who died in a gas explosion at the Bollen mine on 17 December 1929. With the help of donations solicited by Will Rogers and funds contributed by the Mexican government, a grave site was dug for twenty-four of the Mexicans. It was marked only by a single wooden cross. According to park service criteria, this cemetery would not qualify for landmarking.[22]

It was also difficult to find markers of important union struggles in the South. An exception is the monument in Waco, Texas, at the grave of Martin Irons, who led the Knights of Labor in a victorious strike over the Southern Pacific Railroad in 1885. The memorial to Irons was erected at a time when labor and farmer movements were powerful in the Southwest. It was a time when they enjoyed popular support in their fight against enemies as hateful as SP owner Jay Gould, who boasted that he could "hire one half of the working class to kill the other half."[23] The interracial movement-building of the Knights and the People's Party in the South seems to have occurred in a time out of mind.

But in surprising ways, a memory of that "populist moment" has been passed down through the generations, as Manning Marable explained in a fascinating reflection on his family history. Looking back as a movement intellectual on his great-great-grandfather's life, he recalled stories his grandmother told him of how Morris Marable arrived in Alabama as a slave in 1854, took his freedom, and became a landowner and the operator of a cotton gin used by black farmers. Morris's lifelong quest for freedom led him into the protest movement organized by the Farmers' Alliance. During the 1890s he joined the People's Party and was elected sheriff of his small town by black and white farmers. According to family legend, writes his descendant, Morris Marable was "intensely proud of his office and carried out his duties with special dispatch," keeping a small Bible in one coat pocket and a revolver in the other, always prepared. But he was not prepared for the collapse of his "dream of freedom" in the nightmare of political repression, lynching, and disfranchisement that followed after the populist movement was destroyed.[24]

There are no monuments to heroic figures like Morris Marable who led people's movements in the South. For many years it was difficult to find the grave of West Virginia's working-class hero Sid Hatfield, the sheriff in Matewan who helped organize coal miners and opened fire on Baldwin-Felts gun thugs when they invaded his town in 1920, a story colorfully reenacted in John Sayles's motion picture. Unseen by moviegoers were the even more dramatic events that followed: Hatfield's acquittal by a sympathetic jury, his murder by a Baldwin-Felts death squad as he went to stand trial for another indictment, and then, in reaction to the assassination, the astounding march by thousands of armed coal miners to liberate captive coal counties from the gun thugs. The fallen union hero could not even be buried in his home state. His remains lie in an obscure cemetery across the Tug Fork River in Kentucky.

Hatfield's memory endured, even though his resting place remained largely unknown. It survived because West Virginia miners told his story over and over again and because places of memory survived: the town of Matewan, the court house at Welch where "the good sheriff" was assassinated as he went to stand trial, and the battleground around Blair Mountain where in 1921 the miners army faced the coal operator's forces in a confrontation bordering on civil war. The filmmaker John Sayles heard stories about the Matewan massacre while hitchhiking in West Virginia, but when he returned to make a film about the event, he discovered that the memory had been discredited by decades of bad press. "The media of the time painted the Matewan massacre and the mine wars that followed as the workings of an out-of-control mob," a continuation of the bloody Hatfield-McCoy feud that was portrayed simply as a crazy war created by misguided family loyalty. But the causes of these "backwoods feuds" were deeply rooted in economic and political struggles. The release of Sayles's popular film *Matewan* in 1987 was a turning point for many local residents, according to a report in the *Charleston Gazette*. It was the first time they saw their history "portrayed in a sympathetic, even heroic, light." Plans are being made to make Matewan a historic site, because, as the mayor put it, "there's a story here to tell." Important things happened there, he said. "This is where people stood up to the coal operators and things began to change."[25] The release of Sayles's film also recalled Sheriff Sid Hatfield's heroism and led the United Mine Workers to erect a new gravestone marking his final resting place.[26]

In a superb analysis of oral traditions in "bloody" Harlan County, Kentucky—the cockpit of the Appalachian mine wars—Alessandro Portelli explains the importance of a surviving place of memory. He describes the "Battle of Evarts" in which three deputy sheriffs and a striker were killed while many were wounded. This incident, which took place in 1931, provoked visits from northern intellectuals, as well as newspaper accounts and a congressional investigation, partly because the event occurred during the depths of the Depression when labor violence and civil liberties became important national concerns. This event also made history; that is, it was recorded in written histories and memoirs. The Evarts events survive in a few individual memories as well as in the official and historical record, but Portelli could not find evidence of it in the communal memory, partly because the actual site of the battle has changed beyond recognition. What Portelli calls the "communal space referent" has, in the words of one local resident, been "washed away . . . and burned out." The more dramatic "Battle of Crummies" a decade later is remembered in Harlan County even though it failed to make history and remained unknown and unrecognized, even in union histories. The 1941 conflict (so out of phase with the national emphasis on unity in the face of World War II) has remained part of "communal memory" because it relies on the building where four striking miners were killed by machine gun fire; this little company store is "a visible place of memory that keeps the storytelling alive."[27]

Many sites of memory in southern workers' history have been washed away or burned out, but this was not the only problem we faced in preparing the labor history survey for the National Historic Landmarks program. Besides cemeteries, the criteria for selecting sites seemed to rule out many places important in workers' memories, like the company store in Crummies. The program aims to "identify, designate, recognize, and protect buildings, structures, sites and objects of national significance." To qualify, nominations must be associated with "events that have made a significant contribution to . . . United States history," with "the lives of persons nationally significant," with "a great idea or ideal of the American people," or with a distinguished architectural type.[28]

What is the national significance of a store in Harlan County where a few miners were gunned down in a strike or a "riot"? What, for that matter, is the historical significance of any strike in the coal fields, strikes often ignored in history books? What great idea or ideal of the American people is represented in these conflicts and in the obscure sites where they took place? What is the broad pattern of U.S. history to which these events and their participants contributed?

One answer is that these conflicts created unusual spaces in which democracy could flourish. Richard Couto argues that while the concerns of southern coal operators were those of capital—concerns about competition, about profit and survival—the coal miners contributed something "curiously missing from the stock of capital's human parts . . . memory and conscience."[29] Coal miners' strikes in the Appalachian South, he writes, created unusual "free spaces"— defined by Harry Boyte and Sara Evans as "the environments in which people are able to learn a new self-respect, a deeper and more assertive group identity, public skills, and the values of cooperation."[30]

Couto extends this communal notion of free space to include a "sense of connection with the past"—with efforts to achieve a democratic change that is part of a longer historical process not rooted entirely in a particular place. In the southern coal mining region, even in places where the United Mine Workers have not survived, the union has been remembered because it created spaces for free speech and free assembly, which had not existed in coal camps where the company controlled access to "places of public discourse."[31] There is a parallel between how many West Virginians, including some blacks, recall the labor movement—as a force for freedom, as a protector of civil liberties—and how many African Americans remember the civil rights movement.

In 1991 Cecil Roberts, vice president of the United Mine Workers of America, drew upon this memory in testifying before a congressional committee on behalf of a proposal to make Blair Mountain in West Virginia a national park site. I assisted Roberts in preparing his argument for marking the location of the great battle between the coal miners' liberation army and the armed forces of the coal operators. Though no structures of historical significance or architectural integrity existed on the hallowed mountain, it was the site of events significant to the "broad national patterns of United States history," according to the Park Service landmarking criteria.

Roberts' testimony took on an urgent tone because the anti-union coal company A. T. Massey planned to strip mine on Blair Mountain.[32] The United Mine

Workers' leader explained how he inherited the memory of the miners' march to Blair from his father who as a boy watched a private airplane bomb the marching miners under the orders of the anti-union sheriff. He admitted that labor history is a "highly political" subject and that violent events like the Battle of Blair Mountain make it controversial. But, he suggested, conflict has made American history and has been memorialized in countless Civil War battlefield sites. Roberts argued that the mountain was sacred ground in another kind of civil war: a war between advocates of workers' rights and defenders of property rights. He bolstered his case with references I suggested from labor history, notably David Corbin's excellent book which reinterpreted the 1921 miners march as a fight for civil liberties instead of an act of sedition. The armed miners acted not as seditious rioters, Roberts testified, but as "patriots" redeeming their state from the rule of terror.[33]

The case of Blair Mountain as a historical site, worthy of preservation, required an argument for the national significance of the 1921 battle. In making the case, Roberts drew not only on what he learned by reading history and talking to old coal miners but also on what he heard by listening to his grandmother talk about Mother Jones staying at their house and his great-uncle talk about the miners march. He "learned early on that if you look at the battle of Blair Mountain as one event, then you miss the significance much as you would if you examined the Battle of Gettysburg without considering its role in the Civil War as a whole." The West Virginia miners were actors in more than a battle scene. They played on the national stage. Their armed march, Roberts declared, was a preeminent event in the "great struggle for industrial democracy" during the World War I era.[34]

The American public is accustomed to visiting Civil War battlefields, but even on these hallowed grounds, landmarking has caused serious controversy and political conflict.[35] Memorializing workers who died in other civil wars will rekindle painful memories and even provoke new conflicts about old issues. The recent furor over historical exhibitions at the Smithsonian Institution demonstrates how some controversies (over Western expansion and Hiroshima) can even become national affairs. But those who have taken on the task of presenting difficult themes at historic sites have also elicited a positive response from members of the public who appreciate candid remembrances of disturbing events.[36]

Cecil Roberts's sense of a conflicted past filled with contested places finds its way into the work of only a few southern writers, like Denise Giardina, who wrote a novel about the miners march to Blair Mountain.[37] Most recent fiction set in the South evokes a sense of place in a less critical way than it was evoked in the writing of Faulkner or, more recently, of William Styron. According to Hans Bungert, modern southern fiction centers on places used to celebrate family and family traditions, like the annual grave-cleaning in one of Clyde Edgerton's novels. The "family seems to have become the place where a sense of history is acquired, ..." but it offers a "narrowed" sense of the past in the hands of these writers. Regional writers no longer seem as challenged by what Bungert calls "[t]he collective burden of the region's past and the task of reconstructing the past of the South in the present." Southern writing continues to be a "literature of memory," but the memories involved are not as old or as tragic as they used to be.[38]

The memory work of black writers is different. It cannot rely so easily on places of memory for celebrations of family. As Toni Morrison has said: "There is no place you or I can go . . . to think about . . . or summon the presence of; or recollect the absences of slaves; nothing to remind us of those who made the journey and those who did not make it." Morrison's novels tell us of southern blacks who cannot recall family history with pure nostalgia or remember their home place with a proud sense of ownership. While there is often no actual place we can go to think about slaves or about blacks as sharecroppers and domestic servants and convict laborers, the literature created by African American writers is a "place we can go" to "summon the presence" of slaves and their descendants.[39] In Nora's terms, these novels and poems constitute *lieux de mémoire* based on the duty to remember. White southerners could often rely on their written history to present the past as they "would have liked it to have been"—to use Ralph Ellison's words—whereas southern blacks have often relied upon memory rather than history as a means of preserving their identity as a people. Blacks struggled to prevent white-dominated history from negating their collective memory. In response, writers like W.E.B. Du Bois preserved the black historical memory of the Civil War and Reconstruction against white historiography and what he called "the propaganda of history."[40]

African Americans express a more complex sense of place than white southerners. Black writers have resisted the easy equation of a sense of place and a sense of self made by white writers in the South. Ralph Ellison believed that place and identity were "intricately involved" and that a scene often told much of a story—so much so that he said: "Geography is fate." But, he insisted, African American identity is "too often reduced to a simplistic idea of scene" or "explained *merely* in terms of place." Thus, the dilemma described by the character in his great novel: "I am invisible, understand, because people simply refuse to see me. . . . When they approach me they see only my surroundings, themselves or figments of their imagination—indeed, everything and anything except me."[41]

Americans of African descent struggled to create their own place within space rigidly defined and controlled by white men. The struggle is illuminated in a recent study of the effort whites made to keep blacks out of certain places on streets and sidewalks in Danville, Virginia. When blacks refused, at great risk, to yield to white people, they were asserting their citizenship, because the use of public space was essential to that role. In 1883, Jane Dailey explains, white men "repossessed the town—politically and physically—through violence" in a bloody confrontation on Main Street in which four black men died as the city's white minority negated the rights of the black majority and "re-inscribed the boundaries of black 'place.'"[42]

It is painful for blacks to recall important places in their history, like the towns destroyed by white racial pogroms—places like Rosewood, Florida, the subject of a feature film. It was a place ignored by history and kept secretly in black memories until recently when former residents "found their voices."[43] The Greenwood section of Tulsa, Oklahoma, home of novelist Ralph Ellison and historian John Hope Franklin, was also destroyed by a white mob in 1921. The oral tradition of white Tulsans emphasized the relief efforts after the destruction of Greenwood. In the black oral tradition, the tragic memory was reconstructed as a story of survival and renewal. The "segregation of memory" in Tulsa highlights how "notoriously selective"—in Ellison's words—"the exercise of historical memory" can be.[44]

An earlier example of the segregated memory has been explored by the historian of populism, Lawrence Goodwyn, who described a rare case of interracial cooperation in a part of East Texas where poor whites and blacks combined to elect independent candidates, like the sheriff Garrett Scott, a white man, and his lifelong political ally, the district clerk, a black man named Jim Kennard. Both men joined the radical People's Party and were reelected throughout the 1890s. The Populists enforced the law fairly until 1900 when local Democrats in the White Man's Union assassinated Kennard and another black Populist and then surrounded the county jail where a wounded Sheriff Scott and his deputies, black and white, held out for five days until they could retreat.[45]

Sheriff Scott's memory was preserved by his defiant family and by black constituents, even after he was driven from the county. But the defeat of interracial Populism left independent blacks and whites with "literally no political place to go" except into "the party of white supremacy." "To this day," Goodwyn wrote seventy years later, the White Man's Union "as a memory . . . enjoys an uncontested reputation among Grimes County whites as civic enterprize for governmental reform." This memory of bloody events in 1900, like the elite memory of the Liberty Place battle in New Orleans, played the "redemption" theme—one that has well served white power in the South since it was first employed to justify the defeat of black Reconstruction. The prominent African American memory of events in Grimes County emphasizes the black exodus following the shootings, a fact entirely missing from the white oral tradition.[46]

As a displaced people, southern blacks sought to construct a sense of Africa as a place of origin. Memories of Africa survived through oral traditions. But many black writers "charged the word *Africa* with meaning" that did not depend on memory, according to Mevin Dixon.[47] The Greenwood section of Tulsa, for example, is referred to in one memoir as "Little Africa"—a place built, defended, and rebuilt by black pride.[48] This sense of a meaningfully imagined place was also projected to the free states of the North, to the free black colonies of

Ontario, to the "exodus" for Kansas, to the all-black towns of the Indian Territory, and later to the Communist idea of a "black belt nation" in the South.

Besides this imaginative projection of "free space," there is a more literal black "recollection of what territory remained unsubdued, perhaps unsubduable, by Jim Crow's regime of remembering." These are the words Karen Fields used to describe her grandmother's memory of black Charleston. In this memoir, Mamie Garvin Fields recalls her life in the city's free spaces, like the black carpenters' union hall, where community events took place, and the picnic spot near Lemon Swamp that had been "a notorious hiding place of those freedmen, who after the Civil War resisted efforts Northerners made to place them back on their own plantations as wage laborers." She recalled it as a place where her great-great-grandfather hid as a slave waiting for General Sherman's liberating army to arrive in South Carolina. It was the last place he saw his wife. It was also "a place [in] which she played as a child," writes Fields, "enjoying the delicious horrors of its darkness and its quiet, and near which she acquired part of her adult character, from kin who had been slaves."[49]

This is a particularly beautiful articulation of the connection between geography and memory, between history and personality; it is also to be found in other works of southern oral history, like *All God's Dangers,* which captures one of the most powerful voices in the twentieth-century South—that of the African American farmer Ned Cobb, whose memories were recorded and presented by Theodore Rosengarten. This stunning narrative (in which Cobb is called Nate Shaw) reflects the will to remember, and more: the importance of freely speaking one's own mind and working on one's own place.

"I had no voice," Ned Cobb recalled, "had no political pull whatever." He could only labor according to the white man's "rulin's." But he never lost his pride of ownership (his labor mixed with the land) or his desire to speak. "Don't nobody try to tell me to keep quiet and undo my history," he declared. If the "big white ones" kept dragging out the old fear of blacks getting power and getting voice—the same old conservatism that's "been plundering me and plundering the colored race of people since I was big enough to know" as Ned put it—then he would say to them: "I'm tired of it, I don't want to hear all that. Anything tries to master me I wish to remove it. And for God's sake don't come messin' with me. If there's a better life for me to live, any more rights I can enjoy, get out the way and let me enjoy em or let me go down."[50]

This remarkable voice is now part of southern history thanks to an intergenerational joint enterprise in movement history. During his first meeting with Dale Rosen and Ted Rosengarten in 1968, Ned Cobb identified himself as a part of the "advanced guard" of the civil rights movement, a man, an "agency of prophecy," who had made his stand with the Alabama Sharecroppers Union in 1932 and paid dearly for it. Soon after Cobb's arrest and imprisonment for defending the union in a shoot-out with white lawmen, the Communist-led movement of sharecroppers was suppressed.

When "the movement" returned to the South in the 1960s, it was a "wonderment" to many, but "expectable" to Ned Cobb. He told Rosengarten about his grandmother's memories of white people who "had come from the North after 'the surrender' to help black people secure their freedom." They left with the job undone but "would return to complete it." They would come again in the 1930s as Communist organizers and then in the 1960s with the civil rights movement—come to change the conditions that bred hatred and fear. "To his way of thinking, social and economic salvation would bring about a change in human personality," Rosengarten wrote. So "the movement in all of its eruptions" would mean a "turnabout on the southern man, white and colored" when, Ned imagined, whites would stop feeling superior and blacks would no longer feel inferior. This is what Rosengarten learned from listening to the man telling the history of his own life, standing, as he did, between the two generations, "separating them and linking them."

> Even across three life times the velocity of change would frustrate a snail. But if a person cannot hope to savor the ultimate victory, he can improve himself by taking part in the movement of his day. Such participation does not have to be voluntary or self-conscious. Everyone may benefit from victories won by a few—victories over disease, over manual labor, over economic exploitation. The standards people live up to become a force against backsliding. Ned's father could never have been re-enslaved, and now his children would never accept segregation.[51]

After Ned Cobb served his prison sentence, he chose to remain in Alabama on his farm rather than joining the black exodus to the North. Like Hartman Turnbow, the civil rights movement hero who refused to leave Mississippi, Cobb knew his state, its land and its people. Both men were moved to stay in place by their sense of heritage. These experiences suggest that a "strong black identity and a southern sense of place did not necessarily conflict with one another," according to historian Jimmie Franklin. "Indeed, one could argue that attachment to place may have fostered a genuine spirit of protest in some black southerners."[52]

Recent oral histories of African Americans such as Ned Cobb have made an impact resembling that of the testimonies of slaves recorded in the 1930s which altered southern history by offering a view of slavery from the perspective of those enslaved. The "alternative truths" of other defeated groups, like poor whites, have also helped "disarrange" the governing narrative of southern history plotted by white elites. Even in places like Harlan County, where the terrible defeats discouraged public testimony and where patterns of paternalism endured, oral historians like Alessandro Portelli have discovered counter-memories of resistance surviving among southern poor whites.[53]

For example, consider one of the most powerful uprisings in all of U.S. labor history: the massive general strike of southern textile workers in 1934. It began on Labor Day, the first one celebrated in some company-dominated mill towns. Workers' hopes were raised by President Franklin D. Roosevelt, whose National Industrial Recovery Act promised a northern standard of wages and hours for the industry. Those hopes were soon dashed when employers refused to abide by the law. The strike blew up in Alabama, stormed through the Georgia and Carolina Piedmont like a hurricane, and then took off up the east coast shutting down mills from Rhode Island to Maine.

The "uprising of '34" shocked southern elites, who expected loyalty from white workers based on company paternalism and the favoring of whites to the exclusion of blacks in textile employment. Poor white mill hands lived in tightly controlled company towns, accepted the benefits of corporate paternalism, worshiped in conservative Protestant churches, and shared a southern regional identity with their employers presumably based on white supremacy, Victorian morality, and hostility to Yankees, especially to labor organizers.

The great 1934 textile strike originated *within* these new southern places—these industrial mill towns of the Piedmont—where the ruling ideologies had remained unchallenged. Company towns could not simply endure unchanged, when faced with the strain of industrial competition and the added pressure of the Great Depression. The southern country folk who settled in these places raised voices of protest rarely heard in public. For example, during the strikes of 1928–29 young female workers behaved like "disorderly women" and expressed all kinds of opinions and desires in ways that bore little resemblance to the traditional voice of southern womanhood.[54]

By releasing a "multiplicity of voices," historians of southern women have upset the interpretive models governing the study of women's history in America. Earlier studies based on a feminist theory of sisterhood that transcended race and class do not fit the southern experience. Nor does the New England model that posited a growing separation of home and work as a result of industrialization. And the doctrine of separate public and private spheres for men and women does not explain the behavior of "disorderly women" on the picket lines or of the Atlanta labor organizer O. Delight Smith—a woman whose work took her into public life and into many places reserved for men. Contrary to prevailing myths, not all southern women remained in the separate spheres assigned to them by a Victorian canon of domesticity. In telling their stories, historians of southern women have, in Jacquelyn Dowd Hall's view, offered a more complex view of women's lives than the governing theories of women's history allowed.[55] A wonderful example of this new work and the "multiplicity of voices" it has released is *Like a Family: The Making of a Southern Cotton Mill World,* written by Hall and her colleagues in the Southern Oral History Program. It places women at the center of that world.[56]

The account of the 1934 general strike in *Like a Family* also challenged myths about southern distinctiveness—especially the myth that poor whites were docile and individualistic in contrast to northern workers. The textile workers' protest was a "moment in history that laid bare longings and antagonisms ordinarily silenced, distorted, or repressed."[57]

The strike was extremely violent. Seven strikers were killed by the National Guard at Honea Path, South Carolina. They were mourned by a massive funeral march of ten thousand people, but then they became victims of "social amne sia"—seemingly forgotten in collective memory. No one in town wanted to talk about the strike and the killings. The strikers and their families were discouraged by the strike's defeat or intimidated by the fear that their past would haunt them. Others were loathe to recall the terrible divisions the strike caused. Some ministers denied slain strikers burial in church cemeteries, causing some families to stop attending services in those places of worship. "It just tore the churches up," one resident remembered. The son of a mill superintendent said the story of the massacre would "never be told" in Honea Path because "it was brothers against brothers . . . another Civil War."[58]

But now the story has been told and the voices of the strikers and their opponents have been heard, thanks to the work of the Southern Oral History Program and the authors of *Like a Family* whose research revived private memories and made them more public. At first, when Professor Hall and her colleagues in the Southern Oral History Program began interviewing textile workers, they discovered "silence" about 1934, "not memory"—a silence born of fear, frustration, and defeat.[59] But gradually the story unfolded in the release of silenced voices stimulated by historians and filmmakers producing a documentary about the suppressed memory of the strike. *The Uprising of '34* was shown on public television all over the nation on Labor Day 1996, except in South Carolina, one of those places where a kind of conspiracy developed to hide a bloody secret involving class warfare.[60]

Despite the banning of their film from public television, filmmakers George Stoney and Judith Helfand stimulated the public recovery of the strike's memory in South Carolina. Their project was the result of deliberate effort by activists and researchers to "study this watershed moment in Southern labor history"—a moment of which the "popular memory . . . had been lost—silenced by fear, distorted by the media, and omitted from school textbooks." Many strikers "had told no one—not even their own children—of their part in the uprising," and "remained unwilling to discuss their actions over a half century later." Something dramatic happened in Honea Path when filmmakers began interviewing participants in the 1934 strike. Once they found their voice, the descendants of strikers insisted on discussing the history of the strike and erecting a monument in a public place to the fallen strikers.[61] A young woman named Kathy Lamb led this commemoration effort after learning about the strike and its casualties from the filmmakers. At an emotional screening of the documentary film before a community audience, she said: "It is time to remember, to heal, and to honor these lost loved ones and those who were wounded." She hoped something like this would never happen again, but, she added, "it is part of our history and must not be forgotten."[62]

This kind of mobilization of memory and reclamation of public territory is rare among southern poor whites, especially among those who broke out of their place and joined the labor movement. Such activity betokens a growing consciousness among many groups that the disappearance of certain memories requires "commemorative vigilance."[63] Recuperative memory work has been more common among southern blacks whose civil rights struggle mobilized memories of oppression and created places of memory to mark its own passage.

The civil rights movement boldly envisioned a South of newly freed spaces to be shared by one and all. No one gave voice to this utopian sense of place better than Martin Luther King in his greatest speech. In rich tones and poetic rhythms, King reflected on the "hallowed" place to which they came in 1963, the Lincoln Memorial, and the place from which they came, "the dark and desolate valley of segregation." Anchoring his thoughts in the oppressive reality of famous southern places, he invoked many sites of memory sacred in the memory of white supremacists and "the lost cause" of a nation based on slavery. "Some of you have come from areas," he declared, "where your quest for freedom left you battered by storms of persecution and staggered by the winds of police brutality." Placing his hopes in the South, he urged the "veterans of creative suffering" to continue the work—to "[g]o back to Mississippi, go back to Alabama, go back to South Carolina, go back to Louisiana . . ." and to make real "the promise of democracy."

And then he concluded, urging the throng not to "wallow in the valley of despair," but to share his dream that "one day out of the red hills of Georgia the sons of former slaves and the sons of slaveholders will be able to sit down together at the table of brotherhood . . . that one day down in Alabama, with its vicious racists . . . that one day down in Alabama little black boys and little black girls will be able to join hands with little white boys and white girls as sisters and brothers." Martin Luther King's utopian vision of the South—a place where "the crooked places will be made straight"—was rooted in the American dream of the lyrical "Sweet Land of Liberty" in which freedom rang from the hills of New Hampshire to the curvacious slopes of California. But King dreamed of more than that. "Let freedom ring from Stone Mountain in Georgia," he exclaimed as the crowd erupted, thrilled that he would claim for freedom this sacred place of white supremecists.

The current marking of civil rights movement sites in the South, often scenes of terrible attacks on peaceful citizens, suggests that other sites of conflict can be recognized in public even though they remind us of a troublesome past. For example, Kelly Ingram Park in Birmingham, now part of a nationally recognized Civil Rights Historic District, is located across the street from the Sixteenth Street Baptist Church where four young girls died as a result of a Klan bombing in 1963. The park includes several memorial sculptures associated with "death and violence" and a statue of Dr. Martin Luther King.[64] These places of memory were marked as a result of long campaigns by historically conscious black citizens.

In Memphis a struggle took place between blacks, who wanted to preserve the motel where Dr. King was assassinated as a National Civil Rights Museum, and many whites who wanted to tear it down and remove a place of memory important to the black freedom movement. A black radio station and the American Federation of State, County and Municipal Employees, who supported the black sanitation workers' fateful strike in 1968, led a fund drive that raised money from hundreds of ordinary citizen to make the Lorraine Motel a public place of memory. The director of the new Civil Rights Museum, Juanita Moore, described the movement's transformative approach to the southern phenomenon of "placing." "I think the people of Memphis are very proud of the fact that they have moved past thinking of Memphis as the place where King was assassinated to a place where you can come to learn more about the civil rights movement, as you pay your respects to King and his memory."[65]

Throughout the South "there are significant public efforts to recognize the legacy of the civil rights movement at all levels of the federal government"—including new historical place markers like Maya Lin's stunning civil rights monument and additions to the national park system, nominations to the Register of Historic Places, and so on, even at the state and local level.[66] This dynamic reclamation of public places and private voices is particularly intense in the South. There have been two conferences and many publications on the South as a place, and much greater recognition in public of the diverse traditions and experiences of southerners. The curators of a controversial museum exhibit on slavery in Richmond, Virginia, responded in this way to the criticism that they were "rewriting history." They admitted the truth in this allegation and added that "correcting the public's belief in absolute history" was part of their responsibility as southern historians.[67]

Perhaps, as a recent president of the Southern Historical Association said, the last three decades of historical work have enabled those who have returned to the South to better comprehend the complex culture of the region, a culture that "blacks helped to mold and that they often shared with whites around them." There is also among African Americans a spiritual and physical return to the South, as some, in the words of the rhythm and blues song, depart the cities, "Leaving on That Midnight Train to Georgia."[68] Maybe, as historian Nell Irvin Painter suggests, the rewriting of southern history "is why African Americans now reflect a willingness to claim the South as their territory"—because their history is now recognized as essential to a meaningful definition of the place.[69] But, as Carol Stack shows in her book, *Call to Home*, about African Americans returning to the rural South, the prodigals can go back to remembered places without regressing to old ways of life. "You can definitely go back in time," one repatriate told her. "You can go back. But you don't start from where you left. To fit in, you have to create another place in that place you left behind."[70]

Today's southerners seem to have inherited mainly segregated memories of their separate places. Ned Cobb put it sharply when he recalled that rich and poor Caucasians called the South "white man's country." Even when poor whites sometimes saw things the ways black people saw them, they always thought they were in a "a class above the Negro." These "little ones thought they had a voice," he added, "but they only had a voice to this extent: they could speak against the nigger and the big man was happy for em to do it." But, Cobb added, "they didn't have no more voice than a cat against a big man of their own color." He noticed that rich and poor whites did not "hang together in every respect. . . . I've had the big white ones talk to me against the poor ones; I've had the poor white folks talk to me against the big ones." He even found some poor white people that would go along with black people to "an extent."[71]

Countermemories of places in the South shared by blacks and whites are preserved by a few people, like Manning Marable who continues to tell the story of his great-great-grandfather, the populist sheriff in rural Alabama elected by blacks and whites a century ago. The extent to which poor whites would go along, and even follow the lead of southern blacks, has been explored more deeply in recent scholarship than it was in the past when conventional wisdom held that southern racism determined the behavior of all black and white workers. In this view, class identity never became important in southern history. The labor movement remained segregated while the civil rights movement emerged without any connection to white workers and their unions. But newer studies, many based on the oral histories of black and white workers, suggest a more complex view of the region's labor history.

Racism is always present in interracial encounters, so the first task is to document its presence. But, as Rick Halpern argues, it is also important to elaborate the "ways and circumstances in which workers either subordinate their prejudice to the project of building an alliance with 'others' or capitulate to those feelings" and remain within their own enclaves. There are more examples of racial border-crossing by workers in the South than in any other region. There were crossings on the New Orleans docks, for example, and in other places as well: the Louisiana cane fields and piney woods, the cotton fields of the Arkansas Delta, the mines and mills of the Birmingham district, the tobacco factories of North Carolina, and the meat packing houses of the Southwest.[72]

There is no need to construct a myth of interracial unity based on class consciousness, when we can study actual examples of the "extent" to which white workers left their enclave to ally with blacks, and vice versa. Social relations and racial attitudes may not have changed much as a result of these leave-takings, but other changes did take place. Industrial unions, especially the United Mine Workers and the CIO, needed to "make a *religion* of racial unity"—as one activist recalled—in order to succeed; and when they did succeed, union contracts worked against endemic discrimination in southern workplaces and generated, according to Halpern, a "rights consciousness that encouraged black workers" to defend and extend unionism. "When the union came, it was just like being reconstructed," Ruby Smith remembered of her days as a Winston-Salem tobacco worker. Movement historians have learned much from studying these tense alliances in which blacks often played a leading role and often insisted on taking their unions into the community, allowing the CIO to become a "general social movement in a number of localities." In other words, for a time the new union movement and the nascent civil rights movement worked in concert. White workers often reacted against black gains in industry, however, and when the CIO's "Operation Dixie" failed in 1948, partly as a result of the assault on Left-led unions, "the CIO ceased being a labour *movement,*" says Halpern; "and this, in turn, deprived civil rights activists of political and social space in which to operate."[73]

Anti-Communism and anti-unionism have silenced those who remembered these efforts to cross what seemed to be the eternally closed borders of the region's racial enclaves. There are now places we can go to remember the martyrs of the civil rights movement, the many blacks and the handful of whites who gave their lives to create new, shared spaces in southern life. But there is little other than oral tradition left to recall those workers who suffered and died taking the first tentative and ever so dangerous steps down a road not taken in southern history. They deserve more. There should be monuments to the black Populists murdered by the White Man's Union in Grimes County, Texas; to the socialist H. L. A. Holman beaten to death in nearby Van Zandt County for preaching interracial unionism to timber workers; to the four white trade unionists who died defending an African American organizer named Sol Dacus in Bogalusa, Louisiana; to Frank Weems, a black member of the biracial Southern Tenant Farmers Union slain by deputies and riding bosses in the Arkansas Delta.[74] Those few who dared to create free spaces for democratic experiments in the South deserve their places of memory, if not for what they accomplished in the past, then for what their efforts mean for the future.

A People's History of
The Great Depression
Monday, 10/25 at 9pm on 2

THE MEMBERS' MAGAZINE
OCTOBER

'GBH

Programming the Great Depression for public television: cover of WGBH program guide, 1993. Photograph by Dorothea Lange. *Courtesy of WGBH-TV Boston.*

CHAPTER 7

Seeing the Past with "Movement Eyes": Making Documentary Films about People in Struggle

The visceral impact of documentary film can be enormous. I felt it for the first time when I watched *Point of Order*, the gripping expose of the witch-hunting senator, Joseph McCarthy. Too young to remember the deranged anti-Communist from Wisconsin, I could now see and feel his creepy mendacity. As a young Democrat, I could also admire the principled courage of his bow-tied inquisitor, Mr. Welch, asking: "Senator, have you no shame?" The film made me thankful for the few courageous liberals who stood up to McCarthy.

Movement Documentaries

A few years later, *The Inheritance* inspired me even more. The star of the show was the great union leader Sidney Hillman, who saved the immigrant clothing workers from the sweatshops and tenements and led them into the promised land created by the New Deal. By the time I saw this first union documentary, liberal stars were falling from the sky, even the best and brightest of them, the experts who took the nation to war in Vietnam. At the same time, New Left historians targeted Hillman as one who was coopted by "corporate liberalism"—the cooperative ideology of business, labor, and political leaders determined to defuse class conflict.[1] What the *The Inheritance* lacked politically, it possessed visually and musically. I can still picture scenes of foreign-born clothing workers building an industrial union led by socialists, and I still recall the sweet voice of Judy Collins on the soundtrack, singing "Carry It On."

A decade later, a New Left generation of filmmakers made movement history meaningful to a wider public. Barbara Kopple's knock-out documentary *Harlan County, USA* captured the tragedy and the hope of movement history. The labor movement's descent into gangsterism is epitomized in the murder of union reformer Jock Yablonski by gun thugs paid by the president of the United Mine Workers. The rise of the Miners for Democracy, in Yablonski's wake, betokens the union's rebirth.

Radical America published an interview with Kopple in which she recalled beginning her project with an investigation of the Miners for Democracy movement. Soon, she realized that nothing in the world was going to stop her from telling that larger story of "bloody Harlan" and the strike taking place there at the Brookside mine. After years of hard work, she told the story from the perspective of "rank-and-file people." Rather than use a narrator, she let the miners speak for themselves.[2] *Harlan County, USA* appeared during a time when Hollywood became fascinated with the working class, producing films that romanticized blue-collar lifestyles while muting class conflict. "For Hollywood's new breed of film makers," wrote Lyn Garafola in a review of movies like *Rocky, Mean Streets,* and *Blue Collar,* "the working-class is ultimately a pretext" for offering images of "vague discontents while discrediting the politics of change."[3] Against the studio myth of the working class, *Harlan County* showed us the real people, cinema verité.

Barbara Kopple won an Academy Award for her documentary, but other filmmakers also produced good films putting movement history on celluloid, giving us pictures of the Non-Partisan League in North Dakota, of Finnish Communists in the Mesabi, of the Wobblies in the mines and mills, and of militant women in the CIO whose lives were depicted in *Union Maids* and *With Babies and Banners.*[4] These films were much appreciated by students and teachers of movement history, but they circulated largely within New Left circles and in the classes of some union educators. Then, in 1987 movement history finally found a public and touched a nerve in the body politic. The broadcast of *Eyes on the Prize* on public television took documentary filmmaking and movement history-making to new heights and to new audiences.

Eyes on the Prize Films

I remember sitting spellbound at a screening of *Eyes on the Prize* at the Kennedy Library in Boston in 1986. The program we saw that night began with Fannie Lou Hamer singing "Go Tell It on the Mountain" with the Mississippi Freedom Party delegation at the 1964 Democratic Convention. Then we see a bloodied Reverend C. T. Vivian angrily condemning Birmingham police and shouting at them: "We are willing to be beaten for democracy and you misuse democracy." Cutting to an interview recorded years later, the filmmakers give us Vivian reflecting on the past and taking us to the heart of the matter: "It was a clear engagement," he declares, between his people seeking the fullness of their personalities and those who would destroy them. One could not walk away from that, he said. "This is what movement meant," he concluded. "Movement meant that finally we were encountering on a mass scale the evil that had been destroying us on a mass scale and you do not walk away from that." After this unforgettable introduction, narrator Julian Bond tells us how in the fifties and sixties Americans fought "a second revolution. . . . It was a hard fight challenging America's basic beliefs" in inalienable rights, liberty, and justice, and in the principles of democracy. And then we hear young voices singing the series theme: "The one thing we did right, was when we started to fight. Keep your eyes on the prize, hold on."[5] This was movement history in all its power and glory.

After the screening we heard from Henry Hampton, the creator of *Eyes*, who mortgaged his house to get the funding together through a Boston-based enterprise he called Blackside. He talked to us about what he wanted his films to convey to his fellow citizens. He hoped to show them how the civil rights movement tested our nation's democratic principles, to show them how much activists were willing to sacrifice for freedom. But Hampton wanted the *Eyes* films to get beyond the stock images of police dogs attacking defenseless protestors. Rather than simply feel sorry for the movement's martyrs, viewers would be impressed by their larger goal: fulfilling the promise of democracy. What mattered most to Henry Hampton was revealing what he called "the intelligence behind the movement" and what it took, besides courage and conviction, to undertake "the enormous process of dismantling apartheid in this country with relatively little violence."[6]

Eyes accomplished this and more: it helped millions of Americans see our recent past through movement eyes. When we see the Albany activists fighting for their rights, we can, if we wish, see that they are fighting for all of us. When we hear them sing, we can feel their power. In one of the most exciting sequences of movement footage ever recorded, the Albany freedom fighters clap and rock while they sing: "Ain't gonna' let no body turn me around, gonna' keep marchin', marchin' to the freedom land." Then, Bernice Johnson Reagon, an Albany activist, explains how much of the "movement's business had to do with nurturing the people" through song, the "bed of everything"—the "concentrated essence" of "our peoplehood."[7]

Even though only a few whites are seen on the front lines, Hampton wanted white viewers to share the movement's sense of purpose and accomplishment. Julian Bond could not preach this in his narration; it was something you could only feel by seeing the pictures captured by television cameras that pointed out from the movement people toward their oppressors, so that viewers share the activists' angle of vision.[8] Blackside's education director, Judy Richardson, who had been a movement activist in the Student Nonviolent Coordinating Committee, later said that the goal was to create films that would actually "show ordinary people involved in the movement" and make it easier for viewers, old and young, to "see themselves as those kinds of people—people who make change."[9]

Who was this man, Henry Hampton, who talked to us so quietly and eloquently about putting the movement on film? Born in 1940, he grew up in awe of his father, chief surgeon at the black hospital in St. Louis, a distinguished man who hired a student of Frank Lloyd Wright's to build a house for his family in the white suburbs. Hampton later said he inherited some of his father's determination to "never let anybody control him." He wanted to be economically secure without working for anybody. One morning in 1955 young Hampton awoke and could not move his legs. He had been stricken with the polio virus. A young man with broad shoulders and strong limbs, he now faced a life without the athletic pursuits he loved. He turned then to reading and debating, things highly prized by the Jesuit teachers in the Catholic school he attended. As a premed student in college he joined in civil rights protests, "tenuously at first." His parents were ambivalent about his activism; they wanted him to become a doctor.

After trying graduate school Hampton dropped out and moved to Boston where he began working as communications director for the Unitarian Universalist Association (UUA). In 1965 he went to Selma, Alabama, when James Reeb, a Boston UUA minister, was beaten to death after the first march across the Pettus Bridge had been turned around. The trip changed Hampton's life. As he joined the thirty-two hundred marchers who finally crossed the bridge and marched triumphantly on to Montgomery, he made what he called the only prophecy of his life: "This," he said to the marchers next to him, "would make a great film." He returned to Boston and produced a few films for the UUA while participating the the association's Black Caucus and in the local civil rights movement taking on the problem of northern school segregation.

In 1968 Hampton took a world tour with UUA people and visited South Vietnam just before the Tet Offensive. He came home thinking differently about his work and quit his job with the association. "The world was just too big," he recalled. "Too much was happening to get caught up in the denomination thing."[10]

That year he founded Blackside, Inc., and began producing films for business and government. When *Roots*, the television "docudrama" about slavery, generated an enormous television audience, Hampton got support from the distributor, Capital Cities Communication, to make the film on the civil rights movement he had imagined at Selma. But production lagged and the funder pulled the plug. Blackside plunged into a bleak time and by 1983 only Henry himself remained—weighed down with a $100,000 debt. Refusing to quit, he edited his civil rights material into an eight-minute sampler and showed it to Ruth Batson, the soul of the Boston civil rights movement, who told him: "You've got to make this." Soon, other people around the country were saying the same thing, and by 1984 Hampton had raised the money he needed to finish his series and make his dream come true.[11] In 1987 millions of Americans were able to see the civil rights movement as a national accomplishment, to see that "the African American struggle for the expansion of democracy in our land was a liberating gift to us all," as movement historian Vincent Harding put it.[12]

Eyes I was a uniquely successful venture in the history of documentary filmmaking, partly because Hampton and his talented team of young filmmakers had such a powerful, coherent story to tell. The movement appears as the moral engine that carries viewers on a freedom train from the streets of Montgomery to the bridge at Selma—always gathering momentum, always taking on new passengers.

Historian John Bracey later criticized the films for leaving out "nationalist and radical alternative to integration" and for ignoring the sharp ideological debates within the Movement—topics that might have seemed to take the train off track. Hampton and company made some amends in their second series, *Eyes II,* when they produced programs about Malcolm, Black Power, and the Black Panthers. Nonetheless, Bracey thought the second series, like the first, was dominated by Martin Luther King and his philosophy, and by footage created largely by the white news media for white audiences. Of course, these media ignored black revolutionaries who questioned the "basic premises" of U.S. society, rendering them more or less invisible to documentary filmmakers.[13]

Eyes II did succeed, according to Bracey, "on its own terms" by presenting "the struggle for racial justice" with impressive visuals and interviews.[14] One program in the series impressed me deeply, because it recreates the two incidents of violence I remember most vividly from those frightening years: the murder of Panther leader Fred Hampton by the Chicago police and the uprising of the incarcerated at Attica Prison. These events were the subject of a gut-wrenching film in the *Eyes II* series by Louis Massiah and Terry Kay Rockefeller, called "A Nation of Law?"

After her work on *Eyes II,* Rockefeller became series producer for Blackside's next big project: *The Great Depression.* I had worked with *Eyes II* producers on the program about the Boston school desegregation struggle and had expressed interest in their new series on the 1930s. In the spring of 1990 Terry Rockefeller called and asked me to meet her at Blackside, so we could talk about the new series.

Union Side Films

By then, I had gained some experience in two history film productions about the labor movement that brought me face-to-face with the difficulties of putting workers history on the screen. The Public Broadcasting System balked at programming on the labor movement. A 1990 study reported that "PBS prime time programming devoted to the lives and concerns of the business elite [was] on average 10 times more prevalent than programming devoted to workers."[15] AFL-CIO affiliates protested the class bias of public television but without much success. As the National Endowment for the Humanities pulled back from progressive film projects, producers naturally approached organized labor for funding support, but PBS refused to broadcast films funded by unions, whom they viewed as "special interest groups." One exception was a fine film about the Homestead strike, *The River Ran Red,* produced by Steffi Domike and Nicole Frateaux, supported with funds from the Steelworkers Union, and broadcast on Pittsburgh Public Television.

The two films I helped produce on labor movement history never received foundation money or public television access. The first film, described in the chapter 4, was *Glory Days,* the video Cynthia McKeown produced in 1988 for our History Workshop about "the long strike" in Boston's Haymarket during the 1950s. With virtually no budget, Cindy and Barbara Lipski made a wonderful little film for a local audience that accomplished just what we hoped: telling an unusual story of worker solidarity using the words and images of the workers themselves. *Glory Days* was a typical labor documentary with "talking heads" reminiscing and "talkin' union" over stills of picket lines and rallies with upbeat music in the background. But it succeeded in telling a story that needed telling about interracial unionism in a segregated city.[16]

A year later I met Barbara Kopple at a strike support rally for the coal miners then locked in a struggle with the Pittston corporation. She recalled her interview with *Radical America* and told me about her new film on plant closings in the Midwest. I had been talking to the director of organizing for the United Mine Workers, a former student named Ron Baker, about making some films about the union's history that the organizers could use. I asked Barbara if she wanted to make these kinds of films. She immediately conceived a much larger project: a full-scale documentary film history for the union's 1990 centennial. Though her Harlan County film still rubbed the sores of many people who'd fought the union's internal wars during the 1970s, the union president, Richard Trumka, admired Barbara's work and generously funded the project we proposed. He asked me to make sure the history was done right.

Out of Darkness: The Mine Workers' Story was produced on an insane production schedule, but it was done in time to premier at the union's centennial convention. Narrated by miners themselves in every kind of coal field accent, the 100-minute video pulsated with Tom Juravich's exciting soundtrack, and featured the state-of-the-art special effects by producer Bill Davis, who made videos for MTV. Those of us who worked on the film and were invited to the convention premier watched nervously as the long video played in a ballroom at Miami's bizarre Hotel Fontainbleu. We were thrilled when hundreds of union delegates stood and applauded for five minutes in the dark as the credits rolled and Tom sang his rock-and-roll version of "Which Side Are You On?"

In making this video, Kopple wanted to break out of the labor documentary genre that relied on old still photos and the talking heads of elderly workers and academic commentators. So she insisted on injecting the union's history with episodes of the recent Pittston strike victory, which produced yards of exciting television news footage. It also gave Barbara a chance to use her impressive interviewing skills in real-life settings. This rhythmic interaction of the past and

Filming coal miner interviews during the Pittston strike: the author with Barbara Kopple, Norton, Virginia, 1990. Photograph by Bill Davis. *Courtesy Cabin Creek Films.*

present made *Out of Darkness* special. UMW people were thrilled with the video, and they made sure it was broadcast on local television stations in the coal fields.

As historical advisor and associate producer I did my best to put some tension into the film by making sure UMW dissidents found a place in the film production. We used old pieces from *Harlan County, U.S.A.* to show how corrupt the union had become. The UMW people supported these decisions as well as Barbara's efforts to foreground women's voices and experiences. She made the film, under serious artistic constraints, as a way of extending her commitment to democratic forces in the United Mine Workers, whose leadership came to the fore in the inspiring Pittston strike described in chapter 9.

At the same time, Kopple was finishing another labor documentary about a similar strike that occurred a few years earlier—a strike of union meat packers in Austin, Minnesota, that had ended in a devastating defeat for the insurgent local, P9 of the United Food and Commercial Workers Union. One afternoon, after we finished working on *Out of Darkness,* she asked me to join the UMW staffers to look at rough cuts of this P9 film at her studio in New York City. She told us how nervous she was that the film would alienate union people because of how it portrayed tensions among the strikers. The clip we saw was an emotionally wrenching sequence in which two brothers talk about the strike with one deciding to cross the picket line. Kopple was in his truck interviewing him on the frigid morning he crossed the line in Austin. We didn't know what to say, except that we were upset by what we saw. The finished film, *American Dream,* won another Academy Award for Barbara, but it embittered union people who supported the strikers, because unlike *Harlan County,* the new film ended up taking the side of the national union and its spokesmen and implying that the local militants were tragically misled.[17]

Blackside Films

My limited union-side filmmaking experience did little to prepare me for working at Blackside. In our initial conversations about Henry Hampton's new series on the Depression, Terry Rockefeller explained that there were some rules about filmmaking at Blackside that might make it difficult to put 1930s social movements on the screen. Without understanding, I pitched a lot of ideas to Terry and her staff at that first meeting: beginning the series with how workers experienced Ford and Fordism, emphasizing the self-help practices and cultural traditions that helped people survive during the Depression, dramatizing the CIO as the largest social movement of the era, appreciating the real threat posed by fascism and the real contributions made by the radical left, capturing the power of boxer Joe Louis as a popular figure, getting my friend Ralph Fasanella on camera to talk about Fiorello LaGuardia and how he saved New York, and so on.

Rockefeller and her team seemed interested in many of these suggestions, probably because they had already begun to research some of these same stories. They also found my approach to movement history congenial. She had studied history at Johns Hopkins, where she nourished her desire to do history from the bottom up and to show how social movements shaped history.

In the summer of 1990 Terry Rockefeller asked me to join the original team of academic advisers who had been meeting to plan a pilot program for the series. At one of our first meetings on Shawmut Avenue in Boston's South End, Henry Hampton explained that Blackside and its filmmakers now faced the challenge of making films about Americans of all races and ethnicities. It was a chance to explore new ground and gain another kind of credibility. Historian Nell Irvin Painter declared Hampton and company ideally suited to the task; in fact, she said, Blackside was uniquely prepared to make this a series of films "about the 1930s that speaks to the 1990s"—to create an unconventional series, a people's history of the Depression informed by the new social history (and the social movements that motivated it). The series could be infused with current multicultural sensibilities, Painter argued, and need not reflect the old historiography of the period with its emphasis on economics, electoral politics, federal programs, and the legendary New Deal personalities.

The first sessions with Blackside staffers and historians that summer provoked stimulating discussions about putting the best of the new scholarship on television and about capturing a diversity of experiences and voices never seen before in Depression-era documentaries. Hampton exerted a quiet presence in these meetings, listening with remarkable patience and interest to suggestions by historians which, I later learned, were usually unsuited to film treatment. He set a tone in which open discussion flourished and those of us without filmmaking experience were encouraged to think visually. A fine tolerance of opinions prevailed in this multicultural setting, where whites could speak freely about presenting black people on film and vice versa. *Eyes* veteran Judy Richardson said one day that Blackside was a bit like SNCC, where everyone—from producers to interns—talked everything through "movement style."

After one of these meetings in Blackside's cramped offices I compared impressions with historian Robin Kelley, who had just published his superb book *Hammer and Hoe*, about Alabama Communists during the Depression. We both shook our heads in wonder at how much trouble Hampton took to include historians in the process and the way in which he insisted that his producers take us seriously. The process was, as Robin said, "amazingly democratic" because Hampton set the tone and "really listened." Our previous experiences as film consultants had often been perfunctory. The producers simply needed some academic input to satisfy their federal-funding requirements. It was different at Blackside because Hampton respected scholarly history, and embraced movement history. However, he also demanded much more from us than ideas about what was important in the past. More than once he would say, this seems like "good history," but will it make good television? Will Americans care about these people and their stories? Are we going to preach to them or are we going to pull them in to the film, even against their will? Henry drew upon a gut sense of what audiences would watch and what kind of people and stories they would care about.

After our initial meetings about the pilot program and series contents in 1990, we heard the distressing news of Henry's cancer. It hit him that Thanksgiving as he sat on plane headed for a vacation. He told the writer Wil Haygood about the experience. "It began small enough, a cough. Then came the sonnets of pain in the lungs. Friends told him he was working too hard, that 'The Great Depression' was already taking its toll." But hard work had never weakened Hampton; his problem was far deeper; oat cell cancer in his lungs. Hampton called his staff together "to tell them the work must go on, and not to worry about him." The work did go on, but as senior producer Terry Rockefeller recalled, everyone "worried openly about Henry, [feeling] uncertain and afraid."[18]

Summer School

In the spring, my consulting role grew when Rockefeller asked me to help her plan a "school" on the thirties for the production staff, modeled on the successful educationals Blackside had created for the *Eyes on the Prize* filmmakers. The Blackside School, which would be attended by the series producers and associates, offered an opportunity to join an important history-making venture, a movement-inspired project that might reach millions of people, a quantum leap beyond the audience I had ever imagined reaching in my own projects.

The school we planned lasted six days. Veterans of 1930s radical movements mingled with the famous New Deal historians Frank Friedel and Arthur Schlesinger, and younger radical scholars. Leo Seltzer, who made leftist documentaries in the thirties, told us about the newsreel footage of the period. Historians Alan Trachtenberg and Maren Stange told us the stories behind the famous still photos of Dorothea Lange and Walker Evans. Steve Fraser, the biographer of Sidney Hillman, helped me explain the CIO to producers, and Tom Juravich came to sing movement songs of the Depression years. I asked the proletarian painter Ralph Fasanella to show us slides of how he depicted the Bronx in the thirties, hoping his sensibility and his memory would color our show on the New Deal in New York during the LaGuardia era. Fasanella captivated a room full of producers and historians when he showed us his paintings of scenes from the city of his youth. Talking fast and wisecracking in his pure Bronx dialect, Ralph delighted everyone, including Henry Hampton, who astounded us all when he appeared at some school sessions, weak and wan—showing us how much he cared.

Columbia historian Alan Brinkley, author of a fine book on mass protest movements in the 1930s, started the school by warning us how much more difficult this series would be to make than *Eyes on the Prize*. He reminded us of how fragile democracy seemed in the worst Depression years, of how deeply suspicious many were about democracy's ability to survive the crisis.[19] Sobered by Brinkley's remarks, we all strained to hear the soft-spoken words of movement historian Vincent Harding, who struck a different chord. Still recovering from heart surgery, he apologized for his weakened state and then looked to Hampton and said it was a miracle that they were both present there together when only a few months before they were both surgical patients at Boston's Beth Israel Hospital. They had both survived life-threatening illnesses and were reunited on another project.

In his soft-spoken, heartfelt remarks to the Depression school that summer Harding, who had been an important inspiration to the producers of *Eyes*, said: "Tell a story of the Great Depression that could only be made by the company that had already made *Eyes on the Prize*." Series producer Rockefeller recalled this as a key moment in her thinking about how Blackside, with its unique history, should tackle a period as well known as the 1930s and take on major problems in "mainstream history." What it meant to her, she told me recently, was paying attention "to everyday citizens and the power they have to make change, looking for evidence of movement (not just for African Americans' civil rights but for full human rights), taking stock of and presenting the American public in its full diversity, even if reporters and newsreels of the day had not." These became what she called "the checkpoints" to which the filmmakers would hold each other accountable—the standards for testing each treatment, script, rough cut, and final cut.

Harding tackled the central problem of the Depression series as Hampton saw it. We lacked a central theme like the one the movement provided for the first *Eyes on the Prize* series. Pondering the assortments of pitches historians made for various stories, Hampton even wondered quite candidly if any of them would add up, if audiences would ever know what the series was about. The films would not be about people suffering the effects of the Depression, because Blackside did not see poor people as victims of history. Nor would the programs be about desperate people being saved by government programs, because Blackside films showed ordinary people who were "socially aggressive." So how would the filmmakers focus their stories?

Vincent Harding said that *Eyes* should be the guide to the new films about the Depression. Everything we saw on film about the movement in the 1960s "was built on something" that came before. In both decades ordinary people did "magnificent things" to expand democracy. For Harding, who grew up in a deeply religious West Indian community in Harlem, those stories revealed the "spiritual resources" people drew upon to do such extraordinary things in the midst of awful crisis.[20] After recovering from heart surgery, he met with high school teachers who used the *Eyes* series in their classrooms. He hoped they could help students understand the freedom struggle as much more than an attempt to gain rights for black people, helping them see how it filled "the need for a continuing and creative national movement for the expansion of democracy." America needed this in the 1960s, and Blackside documented those struggles. America needed the same thing in the 1930s, and so the historical project remained the same. Harding was saying something most academic historians would not say: that movement history could give people hope.[21]

As a movement historian and activist I found Vincent Harding's argument compelling, but it probably seemed a bit too philosophical to the filmmakers who were simply looking to put great stories from the thirties on television. As Rockefeller later recalled, the production team left the Depression school with various impressions of 1930s history, but not with the shared understanding that they would make a series that confirmed Harding's view: the belief that movement history gave people hope by showing how collective struggles advanced democracy. For individual documentarians, especially those without movement experience, the production process was one in which they were, in Rockefeller's words, "educated by witnesses for whom the 1930's had been a triumph of survival, common action, and change."

Stories of Struggle and Survival

The Blackside Summer School left me energized and hoping for some kind of continuing role in the Great Depression series. I asked Terry Rockefeller to bring me in on the project as a team member so that I could work with her and the other producers on a regular basis during my sabbatical year. To my great delight, she agreed and encouraged me to become as involved as I dared and as much as the producers allowed. Terry asked me to coordinate research for the series and to exploit my network of oral historians to find witnesses. Blackside's porous process of filmmaking soon allowed me to join in meetings about story ideas, discussions as fascinating to me as they were frustrating to the producers who wanted to get on with their shows.

Though Hampton was skeptical, Rockefeller decided to make Henry Ford and Fordism the subject of the first film so that the series would begin in the 1920s and forecast the coming of the Depression. She convinced the highly acclaimed documentarian Jon Else to make the film. He had been a SNCC volunteer in Mississippi and a producer in the *Eyes I* series. Else believed in the power of the Ford story as a set up for the coming of the Great Depression. We talked intensively about the new literature on Ford and how his legendary reputation virtually defined Americanism in the twenties. Else devoured the new labor and social history on the auto industry and was especially taken with the interpretation offered by Stephen Meyer in his excellent book, *The Five Dollar Day,* which helped shape the treatment of the film that became *A Job at Ford's.* The producer was enthusiastic about using Ford's colossal River Rouge production complex as a setting for his story. It was the most impressive site in industrial America, an awesome power station of mass production where iron ore from the Mesabi Range was offloaded and then thirty-three hours later a freshly painted Model T Ford would roll off the line. The Rouge became far more than a brooding visual setting for the film; it became a determining force that asserted its own character like a genie Ford let out of his magic lamp. As a SNCC and Blackside veteran, Else was inclined to tell the Ford story from the bottom up, working the experience of Fordism against the legend of the Great Man, the most popular figure in 1920s America.

When the producers began discussing how the eight-part series should end, I jumped in, as one could in Blackside meetings, and proposed that the last program return to Ford's Rouge plant, where the series began. The Great Depression films could conclude there in 1941 as the United Auto Workers strikers lay siege to the Rouge, literally surrounding the huge complex with their automobiles: the makers of Ford's products and the products themselves had returned to silence the roaring dragon of production. Ford had become a kind of public enemy to many Americans by denigrating President Roosevelt, defying New Deal laws, and accepting a medal from the Nazi government. In the 1920s, said Antonio Gramsci, "Fordism" became synonymous with Americanism. But in the late 1930s it became something quite different because a new more inclusive Americanism emerged.

"Fordism Is Fascism." So said the union picket signs at the Rouge in 1941. Proclaiming unionism as Americanism, the United Auto Workers forced a democratic election at Mr. Ford's place. The workers voted for the union and forced the old man to recognize the UAW.[22] In challenging Ford's authority and in debunking his legend, the auto workers' union needed to win the support of the company's most loyal workers: the African Americans. The movement of young people in Detroit's black community off of Mr. Ford's plantation and into alliance with white workers coincided with the birth of the modern civil rights movement in Motor City. Here at the crossroads of movement history, at the coming together of the young CIO with the even younger civil rights movement, there was a great story—a story that laid the groundwork for the stories already told in *Eyes I.* Orlando Bagwell, the supervising producer for the series, liked the idea of *The Great Depression* series as the first part of a trilogy that previewed the civil rights epic, following *Eyes I* and *II.* For a little while this story about the "Siege of the Rouge" even caught the eye of Henry Hampton.

After a successful round of chemo, Henry had returned to the company and the project, and those of us who were new to the Blackside family could now see how he worked. He would say to the producers: "Now in three sentences, tell me what your film is about? What is your story? Where is the conflict? Why will I care? Do you believe in it? Tell me again." And tell it they did . . . again, again, and again.[23]

I wrote up a film treatment for an episode concluding with the big 1941 strike at Ford's Rouge works, and then received a similar interrogation from Hampton. After we talked he told me the show wouldn't work for various reasons. First of all, the team had decided that the series should end two years later during World War II, when the Depression had ended. He was less interested than I hoped in an ending that depicted the birth of a new kind of civil rights movement within Detroit's black working class. It might make the 1930s series look too much like the familiar *Eyes on the Prize* programs. He wanted viewers to see the society as a whole in the ending. Hampton was also concerned that a return to the Rouge plant in Dearborn during a strike would leave the impression that Blackside had produced "a labor series."

Indeed, he worried openly about how labor and the left would be treated in our programs, and warned us about the indulgent use of radical icons and images of the era: the folk songs, the strike footage, the Communist demos, the radical speech makers—all the idioms of Depression-era socialist realism. My guess is that Hampton did not want his producers to make romantic films about 1930s American Communists during the conservative Reagan-Bush era, at a time just after Soviet Communism had fallen. Nonetheless, he listened thoughtfully in the early advisors' meetings when Robin Kelley and Gerald Gill made excellent cases for the importance of Communist activity in places like Harlem and Birmingham. Ultimately, those of us who advocated for those kinds of stories about 1930s radicals faced the same acid test Hampton used to judge all the other proposals made for the series. Our heroes and heroines wouldn't make it as film subjects simply because they fought the good fight for social justice.

Eyes on the Prize succeeded as public television because it did not sermonize or propagandize. The series made the Movement part of the American story, part of a human drama that could engage a wide range of viewers, even those unsympathetic to social protest. As a result, Blackside helped make the civil rights movement part of the "cultural DNA" of the nation, in the words of his collaborator Jon Else. Hampton wanted to do something like this with stories of struggle and survival from the Great Depression—to paint an inclusive picture of a nation in crisis, something that got at the heart and soul of a people. One reporter likened Henry to "something like the uncle of an extended family charged with keeping the scrapbooks and photo albums, whose mission is to maintain the family narrative" and to make sure that all family members are included.[24] This characterization is an apt metaphor for Hampton's concern with America's wholeness and with the fate of what he called "the democracy."

The series producer of *Eyes I,* Judith Vecchione, captured Hampton's point of view when she wrote the prefatory lines of narration about how the civil rights movement struggled "to make America be America." These words represented Henry Hampton's sense of movement history as stories of "pain and joy" that help "guide us through this grand, tragic—and unfinished—American chronicle, the struggle of Black Americans for equity and the continuing challenge to redeem democracy in America." In conveying his values to his producers, and asking them to share those values, Hampton acted less like a filmmaker than someone Vecchione called a "visionary." Indeed, he never treated his producers simply as filmmakers with technical expertise and artistic talent because he saw filmmaking as a calling that required social conscience and a sense of vision.[25]

Finding Footage, Checking Facts

Besides pitching story ideas in team meetings, and struggling to write them up in film language, I was engaged to perform other less exciting tasks. The producers needed someone to comb the historical literature in order to help plot and document the stories they were assigned to film. In other cases, they needed to find new stories that met certain filmmaking criteria. And of course they required pictures, preferably newsreel footage, as well as live witnesses who would testify on camera. I learned how to search film archives and used oral history networks to find witnesses.

The series producers also wanted someone to do "fact checking" to ensure the accuracy of the producers' treatments and "rough cuts." This mundane work proved to be important, because when the events were not captured on camera, the producers were tempted to use photos or cuts of newsreel footage that resembled or represented something that happened in the story they were telling. They took great risks when they did this, as we learned from a painful case in point.

While we were producing *The Great Depression,* we all watched a gripping documentary film about black GIs who liberated Nazi concentration camps during World War II. *The Liberators* received high praise from many people notably Jesse Jackson, who was fostering a new dialogue between Jews and African Americans. But then a writer in the conservative magazine *Commentary* charged that the producers had played fast and loose with the facts, wrongly placing the black tank unit at Buchenwald. The black soldiers had actually liberated a different camp not shown in the film.[26] The halls at Blackside buzzed with talk of the controversy. Some people accused the critic of trying to subvert a noble effort at finding a bit of the past that Blacks and Jews could share. Steve Fayer, the series writer, told me that these charges, though disturbing, might be true because many producers refused to get stuck on the historical facts when they impeded dramatic story telling. Filmmakers wanted historians to be advisors, not fact checkers who would hold their feet to the fire.

At Blackside, there was no fooling around when it came to standards for authenticity. In our first meeting, a filmmaker, not a historian, laid down the rules. Jon Else wrote us a memo in which he acknowledged the temptation to use visuals or interviews that approximated the events being featured, especially in telling stories from the 1920s and 1930s "for which so few witnesses and so little footage exist, stories in which women and people of color were more often than not invisible to the newsreel cameras." Still, he insisted, "Everything should be what the audience believes it to be." Viewers would be asked to trust the films we would make and so Blackside producers would be expected to honor that trust. "Because historical documentaries carry a unique burden of assumed credibility, because they are based on scholarship, and because of their extensive use in schools," Else explained, "we must adhere to a rigorous standard of accuracy, especially when borrowing from fiction to structure well-told documentary stories with drama, resolution, tragedy and humor." The programs we would produce had an "added responsibility," because they would have a long afterlife. They would become part of the historical "literature" of the nation, and probably would be "read" by far more people than books about the Depression. "The programs we produce today will become the stock footage of tomorrow, over which we have no control, and which must be as correct as we can make them now if they are to be of much real value in the future."[27]

Dramatic Storytelling

There was a constructive role for a historian to play in the documentary film-making process. I could apply my research skills and historiographical knowledge. I could even contribute my ideas about the best stories to tell. I also believed that the narrative writing skills we practiced as historians would be useful in composing film treatments and scripts, and in writing the voice-over narration. I quickly discovered, however, that filmmakers went about the business of storytelling in their own ways, very different than the ways I learned to write history. I also saw that at Blackside these ways of telling stories were well practiced and well taught.

Series writer Steve Fayer laid out the Blackside formula that had worked so well in many of the *Eyes on the Prize* episodes he had written or cowritten with producers. He made it clear how our stories differed from narratives in academic history: "We are not doing treatises of historical surveys but stories we have carved out of an historical period"—stories that offered much more than "understanding" in an intellectual sense. In a memo on dramatic storytelling, he wrote that our stories had to have "*visceral* as opposed to strictly intellectual payoff." Even PBS viewers who wanted to be "informed" were "still very interested in *action.*" Fayer asked producers and advisors to remember that they were not being asked to cover the history of a period. "We are telling stories from the history," he added. "And stories do not work very well without dramatic structure." Like the producers of *Eyes,* those working on *The Great Depression* would frequently be asked: "Where is all this going? Where's the payoff?" As a litmus test for a script, Fayer suggested posing these questions: "Is this story unfolding with some drama and suspense? Are you giving them a PhD Thesis or a good novel, with dramatic ebb and flow, with gathering storms and raging storms? . . . Have you given the audience a reason to keep watching, even though they may know the final outcome?" To help answer the last question Fayer cited the powerful film about gay activist Harvey Milk, whose story grips the viewer even though his assassination is foretold.[28]

What was this "dramatic structure" our stories should take? The answer was compelling in its clarity: Tell your story with the kind of act structure used in Greek drama. If possible, tell it in three acts. In Act I the problem or conflict is introduced, in Act II, the conflict reaches a climax, and, finally, in Act III action resolves the conflict. Fayer, the writer, put the formula in more modern show business lingo by quoting the legendary song-and-dance man, George M. Cohan, who was also a writer and producer. Get your hero up a tree, and confront him with a dramatic problem, Cohan had said; then in the second act, throw stones at him, "almost stone him off his perch"; and finally, in the third act, "get him down out of the tree." Although I had never consciously adopted this structure in my writing, I realized that it had been present in most of the novels and plays I had read since childhood, and less intentionally in many of the historical narratives as well. Still, I wondered, how would the complicated history of the 1930s fit into such a tried-and-true formula. Would fact fit into the form writers used for fiction?

It was difficult for historians to select and develop stories with these criteria in mind. My first treatment for a potential "labor show" presented the CIO as the era's largest social movement, but even though I wrote in the present tense with references to visual images, the proposal read like a chapter from a labor history book rather than like a plot for a stormy novel. The treatment also lacked the sense of place so important to many of the *Eyes* programs that took the viewers to Albany and Birmingham, to Gary and to Attica and made the setting a dramatic part of the story. And despite Fayer's warning, I put "so many characters" in this show that it would be "difficult for the audience to care about any of them."

If my ideas were going to be helpful, they needed to be presented within Blackside's framework. I could make a case for the CIO as the most important social movement of the 1930s in historical terms. But a working story about the labor movement needed to fit into a dramatic structure and it needed to present witnesses on both sides of the class struggle. Finally, the story required a local setting so viewers could experience a sense of place—but local events also had to connect to national developments.

Finding the CIO Story

Given these formidable requirements, it was difficult to choose two union stories from 1930s, a decade filled with dramatic confrontations between workers and bosses. Lyn Goldfarb, the producer assigned to the labor show, had helped to make a film about one of them, the Flint sit-down strike against General Motors in 1937. *With Babies and Banners* centered on the role of the Women's Emergency Brigade in the Flint strike; so Goldfarb did not want to do another film on the event that had become the stock image of labor in the 1930s. Instead she wanted to make another kind of film, featuring working women in the thirties.

We began researching the great 1934 textile strike. The walkout involved thousands of women who appeared with unusual clarity in photos and footage, but we soon encountered what would be an endemic problem: a lack of eye witnesses willing to go on camera. I was not surprised by this difficulty given what I had learned from the Southern Oral History Program's attempts to record memories of the general strike, attempts that encountered a "social amnesia" born out of the uprising's devastating defeat and the ongoing divisions left in its wake.[29]

The technical dilemmas of the research were matched by the problems of finding a film language in which to place our ideas about movement stories. When Lyn Goldfarb and I spoke to Hampton about labor history, he reacted as though we were speaking in code. And in retrospect, I think we were. We talked about the stock ingredients of union stories, and it sounded formulaic: bad conditions and bad bosses provoked strikes, picket-line violence, and then, predictably, the union's triumph. This script seemed natural enough to union-side filmmakers, but it didn't impress Henry. He was a businessman in the entertainment industry who had heard plenty of stories about how unions seemed to slow down production and jack up costs. And as an African American, he also knew how unions discriminated against blacks and how very few of their white leaders or members supported the civil rights movement.

At one point, as Lyn and I struggled with how to make our pitch for labor history, Hampton stopped me on the stairs, and said: "Am I going to have to beat you and Lyn up over this labor show?" He would not tell us what to do, but he was clear about what we should not do: remain caught in the traditional genre of labor films, as in *The Inheritance,* in which unions heroically march toward a better world. He had just squirmed through a PBS television documentary on Walter Reuther's life that simply seemed like union propaganda. I agreed that the film's central conflict—Reuther's struggle with the auto giants—came through as one dimensional and lacking in dramatic tension. Even Walter Reuther's old left-wing rivals now had nothing but praise for the UAW chief.

To appeal to the unconverted and to create dramatic tension, a Blackside labor film would include bosses as well as workers. In *Eyes* Hampton made sure we heard the voices and saw the faces of sheriffs and other segregationists whose testimonies enhanced the significance of movement history by showing the viewers how much the movement threatened power elites. This kind of "testimony against interest"—Hampton meant against our interest as progressive filmmakers—also helped the viewers understand the stakes involved in social conflict.

For a time, though, I wondered if we would make a labor show. When we spoke to Hampton about the places where the CIO created some interracial unity (our best example was the Chicago stockyards), he was very skeptical. He wanted to hear the witnesses and see the footage rather than listening to us talk about cooperation between blacks and whites. He needed to be convinced that Blackside could do a union-side film without drifting into propaganda.

Fortunately, the team had decided early on to do a film on the Southern Tenant Farmers Union, the interracial protest movement that swept across the Arkansas Delta in the mid-1930s as sharecroppers demanded the payments due them under the New Deal Agricultural Adjustment Act. This was story that could *show* how the labor movement stretched the color line. The STFU story was being produced by Dante James as one part of a program on the Depression in rural America. Hampton wondered if this would be just another "liberal cause" presented in documentary form, but James convinced him that he could make a genuine Blackside film about this union. As the STFU story went forward, we searched high and low for a story of rural America to pair with this dramatic tale of Arkansas sharecroppers standing up for their rights. We considered various possibilities like the Dust Bowl, the Tennessee Valley Authority, the New Deal on the Navajo Reservation, but we could not find a story with the newsreel footage and live witnesses we required.

The labor show remained in limbo, storyless in Blackside terms, just like the show on art and culture in the 1930s whose producer Rick Tejada-Flores tried to figure out how to depict artistic subjects within the "dramatic structure" the other programs adopted. The series soon came up short of funds. The corporate donors who contributed to *Eyes* were not very interested in underwriting a series called *The Great Depression*. As a result, one program needed to be eliminated from the series. In the reorganizing process, it was decided that Dante James would be asked to combine his southern sharecropper episode with a story about industrial workers in order to create a "labor show."

Having retold the STFU story in my first book, I was eager to contribute to this episode and to share my experience of interviewing H. L. Mitchell, the union's cofounder. Contacts I had made through Mitch helped us locate several STFU veterans including the other socialist founder, Clay East; organizer Charles Stith; and folk singer John Handcox, the spindly preacher's son who added lyrics to a gospel tune and gave "We Shall Not Be Moved" to his movement and to the movements that followed. When the production team interviewed Handcox in 1992, the aging troubador was not able to speak clearly on camera. Dante James made a brilliant decision: he started audio tape and asked the old troubador to sing his movement songs, unaccompanied. And sing he did. He sang his signature song about not being moved by oppression, and his other tunes "Raggedy, Raggedy Are We," "Roll the Union On," and "Mean Things Happening in This Land"—which would become the title of a labor program filled with Handcox's haunting voice. "We Shall Not Be Moved" would be the theme song of the STFU segment, and it would be reprised during the second part of the film on the CIO, and during the coda, which took viewers ahead to civil rights movement of the 1960s.

In a sense, the STFU story had been there waiting for Blackside to tell it. It was more than a union story; it was a movement story that prefigured the civil rights crusade to come. It was dramatic because in mean places, black sharecroppers and their white allies stood in harm's way. There were practical advantages to the story as well. Because the STFU became a liberal cause, photographers had taken excellent photos. The *March of Time* newsreel series even reenacted the union's story, which, though set in the Delta, linked directly to the national scene. Most important, it could be fit into Blackside's dramatic structure. It begins when hopes are aroused by the New Deal in the Delta, and it creates a sense of concern as landlords steal federal benefits, evict sharecroppers, and stalk their secret meetings. It offers a sense of release as the union wins a strike in 1935, but then produces a sense of crisis when terror descends on the Delta croppers in 1936, and, despite the entreaties of Eleanor Roosevelt, the president refuses to meet with an STFU delegation when he comes to speak in Arkansas. The story ends tragically with grainy black-and-white images of the STFU's African American remnants huddled in a forlorn roadside demonstration after their union has affiliated with the CIO—the "Joe Louis of the labor movement"—only to be weakened by internal tension and defeated by planter repression. As we see this heartbreaking footage, we hear the aged, wavering

Speaking across the racial divide: Norman Thomas addressing tenant farmers in the Arkansas Delta, ca. 1936. *Photograph courtesy Southern Tenant Farmers Union Papers, University of North Carolina.*

voice of John Handcox as he sings "No More Moanin'. No More Moanin'. There'll be no more moanin' after awhile. And before I'll be slave, I'll be buried in my grave. There'll be no more moanin' after all."

This sad ending invited us to create a companion story of a CIO victory. We explored a potential story with historian Zaragaso Vargas about a victorious strike of Chicana pecan shellers in San Antonio. But that story had to center on Communist leader Emma Tenyucca, who was frail and unwilling to be interviewed on film. Our best hope seemed to be in Chicago, where the CIO organized an interracial union of meatpackers. Drawing on Liz Cohen's exciting book, *Making A New Deal,* I researched the film potential of the story. Studs Terkel and Les Orear, a union veteran and activist in the Illinois Labor History Society, directed us to excellent witnesses, former activists like Congressman Charles Hayes and Victoria Kramer, a Communist union organizer. Kramer had not talked about the role of the Communist Party in the back of the yards when she appeared in *Union Maids,* but now she seemed open to the idea.

The packing town story also allowed for a depiction of the Memorial Day massacre in Chicago, one of the most dramatic events of the Depression years captured on newsreel. Lyn Goldfarb had recorded fine interviews with participants in the horrific 1937 shooting. I could even imagine the film ending in 1939 when thousands gathered from all over Chicago region for a memorial service. This celebration of CIO victories was the subject of a wonderful photo that faces Cohen's last chapter, "Workers' Common Ground," over this caption: "The mix of faces assembled here—men and women, white and black, of all ethnicities reflected the new unity among industrial workers that helped make the CIO a success."[30] Unfortunately, we lacked enough newsreel footage to make the Chicago story come alive visually.

As we searched for another labor story with cultural diversity, I realized that we could tell the biggest CIO story of all—the surprisingly untold saga of the steel workers' struggle for industrial democracy. Initial research uncovered a wealth of newsreel footage and some exciting witnesses. Furthermore, the story involved two great antagonists—John L. Lewis, the lion of labor, and Tom Girdler, the tiger of the steel industry—two unforgettable characters about whom witnesses spoke with passion and conviction. It was the life-and-death struggle between these two great forces that frustrated President Roosevelt in 1937 when he said the Little Steel strike made many Americans wish a plague on both houses.

Fortunately, the producer, Dante James, was receptive to the steel industry focus because he had been raised in a union family. His father had settled in Grand Rapids, Michigan, after migrating from the South, and there he became a millwright in a diesel plant represented by the United Auto Workers. The son of an involved union member, Dante grew up "committed to labor." Though trained as a television engineer, James wanted to shape the content and message of visual production. At Washington's public television station, he got his big break: to be solo producer of a documentary on the gifted black vocalist Marian Anderson.

Telling the CIO Story

I wrote a long treatment of a CIO story focusing on the steel workers for James. It didn't work. "This steel story's a mess," he said, putting aside my "treatment." And then he said: "Now *tell* me the steel story." I talked it through in a few minutes. This is how the story unfolded, almost of its own accord.

First, the setting: The steel industry as it was in Aliquippa, Pennsylvania, the "perfect company town," built by the hard-driving steel man Tom Mercer Girdler in the 1920s. I learned about the town from a union steel worker who took one of my history courses. In 1987 Pete Eritano told me that the last of the "ten heroes of Aliquippa" had just died; these were the men who had taken their dismissal case against Jones and Laughlin Steel Company all the way to the Supreme Court in 1937. It was their case that made history when the Court ruled in their favor and upheld the constitutionality of the National Labor Relations Act. The collective memory of these events remained strong in Aliquippa, as I discovered through initial telephone interviews with the local people identified for me by Eritano and the Steel Workers retiree organization. They had great stories to tell about life in "Little Siberia."

In Act I viewers go to Aliquippa and learn about life in the totalitarian town Tom Girdler built in the 1920s. Surprisingly, they see scenes of people working in the mills, not bread lines of the unemployed. They will learn in this show that the labor movement in the Depression was about justice as much as it was about jobs. We learn that Girdler developed a tractable workforce of immigrants and blacks who remained loyal to Jones and Laughlin Steel until the New Deal set off a flurry of organizing. But these efforts ended in brutal defeats as the old craft union failed to overcome company-town tyranny. This can be seen in the most dramatic newsreel footage of strike violence ever recorded in the 1930s. Then, into Girdler's totalitarian world enters the great antagonist, the brooding John L. Lewis, who vows to organize the steel industry as he forms the Committee for Industrial Organization in 1935. End of Act I.

In Act II the confrontation between the antagonists deepens as we see the Steel Workers Organizing Committee of the CIO organizing blacks and immigrants in Aliquippa and other steel towns and helping to reelect FDR in 1936. We hear Girdler's utter disdain for Lewis and Roosevelt. Events move quickly in early 1937 as we see the Flint sit-down victory, the sensational capitulation of the U.S. Steel Corporation to the CIO, and then the Supreme Court's surprising decision to uphold the Wagner Act and to restore the jobs of ten steel workers fired by Jones and Laughlin in Aliquippa. Within a few days the town's workers strike triumphantly against J&L and turn the tide against Girdler and his minions. The law is finally on their side.

This whole sequence of events creates the feeling within the labor movement that anything is possible, that even Tom Girdler and the toughest anti-union companies can be defeated. But then we discover what Hampton called a "ticking bomb." Tom Girdler is assembling an armed force, purchasing guns and tear gas along with thousands of propaganda pamphlets branding John L. Lewis a Communist. He is determined to defeat and destroy the CIO.

Dante James was unfamiliar with the history of the steel industry or the CIO, but at this point he smiled, and said: "It fits like glove!" He could now visualize the story and see it gaining dramatic energy. Next, we see pickets gathering at Girdler's South Chicago steel plant on Memorial Day 1937, we hear them talk confidently about the government finally protecting their right to peaceful picketing. (Studs Terkel had identified several people we could interview who were present that day at the bar called Sam's Place before they went out with holiday gaiety to picket Girdler's plant.) Then we see the suppressed Paramount footage of the Memorial Day massacre as Chicago police fire on a crowd of fleeing pickets, many of them shot in the back as they run for their lives. End of Act II.

Finally, the resolution in Act III. The Little Steel Strike ends in a total victory of Girdler's forces, but the LaFollette Committee investigates the Memorial Day massacre and blames the industry for violating civil liberties. The National Labor Relations Board ultimately intervenes, restores thousands of fired workers to their jobs with back pay, and orders the Little Steel companies to hold democratic elections in their mills and plants. The steel workers get organized politically, and soon the days of Girdler's company town are over. Democracy has come to "Little Siberia."[31]

The steel story's underlying dramatic structure did not emerge until Dante asked me to *tell* it orally. Then, he saw it. As we made the film, the story became clearer and stronger, offering up a naturally dramatic narrative structure. The discovery of the inherent drama in this story reminded me of a remark John Sayles made about filming *Matewan*, another exciting union story. Even when his team was "neck deep in the technical demands of making the movie," the "strangest and nicest thing" would happen: "the story" would just pull the filmmakers out of the production process and make them "pay attention." For Sayles, it was as though "the movie was already asserting its character, letting us know what it was supposed to be, like it was out there all the time just waiting, waiting up in those hills for us to find it."[32]

Some philosophers argue that historians construct stories artificially from fragments of a past that have no inherent meaning. They say we create our narratives much as novelists do.[33] Finding our steel story in Aliquippa was an experience of *discovering* a narrative embedded in the past rather than one of constructing a plot to make sense of a senseless past. Historians do draw— perhaps unconsciously—upon the literary form used in novels. Like traditional tellers of tales and writers of fiction, historians believe that "action inevitably takes the form of a story lived in a beginning-middle-end sequence," according to Alan Dawley.[34] Since the great novels provide perhaps the best "rules for storytelling," we should consider them as we tell our real-life stories because these rules are not merely literary constructs. A dramatic structure exists in the way we pass through life, because stories are not only told: they are also lived.[35]

Dante James's film *Mean Things Happening* depends on the inherent drama of the CIO story in the Great Depression. However, the telling of the story required creative decisions, for example the choices of where to begin and end the episode. As labor history filmmaker Elsa Rassbach remarked, in deciding on the "beginnings and endings of our stories, we are creating narrative structure." In showing the winners and losers in the end, we are making the kinds of judgments that storytellers must make. In documentary filmmaking, screenwriting conventions usually require the identification of protagonists and antagonists as well as a "story line" that takes an audience through the ritual experience of identifying with characters and their dilemmas, experiencing their shared sense of crisis with its climax, and then seeing the resolution of their story. As I worked more closely with the producer, writer, and editor of the labor show I began to realize that historians and filmmakers did share something in common in their efforts to "reconstruct the past."[36]

Henry Hampton thought our steel story was a good one, partly because we pitched it not as another episode in labor-management conflict but as a chapter in working people's struggle for civil rights; it also contained dramatic tension created by characters and values in conflict. It included testimonies that worked against the interest of the filmmakers, like the hard-edged words of Tom Girdler's very elderly son. Finding him in his Florida retirement home through a steel industry archivist was my biggest research discovery. Girdler held on to his father's bitter resentment toward the labor movement and the New Deal. He testifies against the interest of the filmmakers; he provokes emotional tension with his chilling remarks. Geoff Ward, the maestro of documentary screenwriting, reviewed the series and described Girdler as "the eerily unrepentant son of Tom Girdler, the Republic Steel magnate whose mindless intransigence helped bring about the deaths of ten unarmed strikers and the wounding of many more in what came to be called the Memorial Day massacre of 1937."[37]

Despite Hampton's skepticism about union-centered films, he found the labor show compelling. He even surprised us by suggesting that we close the film with a very inspiring speech by Victor Reuther about how "democracy has to stand on two feet," the political and industrial. In order for "participatory democracy to be meaningful," says the old union fighter, workers should have a say in determining the conditions under which they sweat it out every day. They should have enough set aside to live dignified lives when they are "too old to work and too young to die."

Mean Things Happening worked for Hampton for several reasons; it was clearly sympathetic to the workers' movement, but it was good television. It had enough drama to grip viewers even if they were unsympathetic to unions. The narration was factual, not judgmental, thanks to Steve Fayer's firm hand as a series writer who made sure we wrote our scripts to show, not to teach. Moreover, the tragic sharecropper story and the victorious steel worker story illustrated the larger stakes involved in conflicts between workers and owners. Besides wages and working conditions, employers and employees fought over the definition of property rights and human rights. In this way, Hampton could see the labor movement of the thirties as a civil rights movement as well as a vehicle for union power. The STFU and the CIO appeared as forerunners of modern struggles for full citizenship and equal rights, he remarked to a reporter. He had discovered in the filmmaking process that many of the tactics—strikes, sit-ins, protests—and many of the organizational structures adopted by the civil rights movement and chronicled in *Eyes* "were learned by blacks and laborers in the 1930s and used to change not only business practices but also the entire society."[38]

Viewers and Reviewers

Just before broadcast time in the fall of 1993, Hampton was less concerned with the parts of the Depression series than he was with the whole. After the success of *Eyes,* he wondered if the lack of a central theme in *The Great Depression* would limit the new series' appeal. He wasn't sure, but at a party on the eve of show time he told us each "to place our own value" on what we had done.

The public response exceeded our greatest expectations. *The Great Depression* aired on PBS stations in November 1993 and attracted a good audience, 60 percent higher than the normal prime-time ratings for public television. Over 22 million viewers saw some part of the series on the 280 PBS stations. The previous success of *Eyes on the Prize I* and *II,* and the popular response to Ken Burns's *Civil War* series, helped create public interest in this kind of programming.[39]

Very favorable newspaper and magazine reviews also helped. In Boston, where the series reached nearly 400,000 viewers, the *Boston Globe* reviewer wrote: "The Great Depression uses the same basic methodology of story telling that worked so well in the previous [Blackside] series—great narrative voice at once dispassionate and mournful (this time it's Joe Morton), eyewitnesses rather than analysts commenting on events, eye-popping archival footage marvelously restored, off center case studies, and last but by no means least, a spectacular sound track of period music ranging from Woody Guthrie to Billie Holiday." The series maintained a "strong and confident point of view—no 'on the one hand on the other hand' pablum here." The programs reflected real sympathy with the poor and oppressed without being hymns to Roosevelt and New Deal liberalism; and they "seemed entirely free of cant"—a tribute to Hampton's insistence that we tell the stories, not use them as pulpits.[40]

The reviewers readily identified the series' overarching theme: how ordinary Americans save a democracy in peril while they are saving their own lives. One of them quoted Hampton's worries about the difficulty of "drawing a dramatic narrative" from the sprawling historical events of the thirties, and then praised him for solving the problem. "His solution, . . ." said the *Nation* reviewer, "is Noah-like, selecting discrete stories of individuals or local movements (they represent all regions of the country as the film, like a verse from a Woody Guthrie song, travels effortlessly from coast to coast) and gathering them all into the ark of a grand theme, Stories from a Generation's Struggle for Democracy."[41]

The labor show which centered on this struggle cast it in terms of a confrontation between two ideas of democracy: one based on property and entrepreneurial liberty and another based on liberty and justice for all, regardless of economic status. One reviewer thought this philosophical dilemma made *Mean Things Happening* the "most thought-provoking of the seven hours."[42]

Vincent Harding's idea about ordinary people saving and expanding democracy had been transformed into a successful theme. The producers did much more than evoke this well-worn theme with newsreels and interviews. At a time when Americans were losing faith in government, and even in democratic principles, at a time when the Reaganites had discredited the New Deal and its legacy, they allowed viewers to see what was at stake in an age when democracy was mortally threatened by the failure of corporate capitalism and the success of fascism, imperialism, and genocidal racism. "Hampton and his producers have superbly dramatized a period when democracy was tested more severely than perhaps ever before in American history," wrote *Time* magazine's reviewer.[43]

Documentaries, like feature films, tend to "highlight individuals rather than movements or impersonal processes that are the subject of a good deal of written history," says one knowledgeable historian, but it is possible "to make films that avoid the glorification of the individual and present the group as protagonist."[44] The producers of *The Great Depression* films made this possibility a reality. The great political figures of the era take the stage—FDR, Fiorello LaGuardia, and John L. Lewis—but the little people are the real saviors of the democracy.

The series made good use of the children and grandchildren of the Depression generation as commentators and observers; they became part of the American family album Henry Hampton seemed to be keeping. Jon Else's evocatively written introduction to the series brought the history of the thirties home by presenting it as the experience of our parents and grandparents. After reading epic narratives like Lincoln's Gettysburg address, Else wrote these words: "Somewhere in the hardest of hard times with America slipping away, our parents and grandparents found the courage to fight their way out." As you see striking footage from the period, the narrator continues: "Nothing turned out the way they planned. Some lost their nerve, and some gave their lives. But by the time the Great Depression was over, they had done better than simply save America—they had made a new America."[45]

Jon Else's narration, combined with Lillian Benson's artful edit of visuals and interviews, pulled in many viewers and impressed reviewers like Lewis Cole, who wrote in the *Nation*: "For me, it was a personal gift that within the first ten minutes the documentary managed to convey another, more visceral, appeal of the era: For people like my parents, it was a moment of dauntless youth, the time when they embarked on history's great adventure of collective action, their heroic attempt to exchange socially and spiritually the crippling isolation of American life for the inspiring wonder of human solidarity."[46]

Cole praised the films for educating people about the "possibility of activism and the realities of social conflict," but he also offered serious political criticisms of *The Great Depression* from the left. First, he perceived a "lack of attention to the spontaneous solidarity shown by workers," in which "they put their class interests above their prejudices." There were, he said, "legions of such instances" in the 1930s. He was correct, of course, but few of these spontaneous moments were recorded on film. Cole did appreciate the organized expressions of solidarity we featured in the series. He called the first part of the labor show an "arresting" dramatization of the "conflict between the land-owners and the struggling sharecropper union" that captured the "danger faced by these intrepid, unknown heroes," and he saw in the second segment about the steel workers "a study in class consciousness."[47]

Second, *The Great Depression* failed to probe "the relation between radical ideas and the mass actions brought vividly to the screen in sometimes three-dimensional diamond-like clarity" in the old newsreel footage. I shared the same disappointment that the series had captured the excitement, but not the political process, of movement building. Documentary filmmakers emphasize action over thought, and therefore slight issues of motive and conviction. How-ever, as a historian interested in these issues, I failed to find acceptable ways to write political ideas into narration. Witnesses could speak of their ideas and motives, but the narration could not be made to speak for them. Since the producers decided not to use historians as explainers and interpreters, the witnesses became the historical interpreters. What witnesses often recalled were the dramatic actions in which they participated, not the values and ideas that compelled them to action.

Third, said Cole, the series gave "scant attention" to "people and causes associated with Communism," people like Harry Bridges and Paul Robeson, and causes such as the Scottsboro boys case and the Spanish Civil War. He had grown up in a Communist family and had "always assumed his parents' almost romantic affection for the heroes and dramas of the thirties . . . sprang solely from the period's radicalism."[48] He expressed frustration that even after talking at length with the producers, he could not fathom how story decisions and choices were made in the mysterious Blackside production process. It is unfor-tunate that he did not participate in the long debates over story ideas, including a number about Communists that failed, for filmmaking reasons, to produce results.

In some cases, the voices of Communists could not be heard because wit-nesses refused, even after all these years, to speak on camera about their experi-ences. In other cases, their stories didn't fit into the series' thematic structure, heroic stories like that of the Abraham Lincoln Brigade in the Spanish Civil War, already the subject of a fine documentary called *The Good Fight*. Or else they appeared outside the focus of a particular episode, for example Dante James's segment about the "Don't Buy Where You Can't Work" campaign in Harlem which was initiated by activists in the black community and later joined by the Communist Party.[49] Another problem was financial. Lacking the funds to pro-duce a program on culture and the arts, we missed a superb opportunity to explore the leftist Popular Front and the appeal of American Communism for artists like Paul Robeson and writers like Richard Wright. Finally, as we consid-ered the role of the CP in the labor movement, we simply could not examine the subject fully and fairly, not just because former Communists were reluctant to testify, but also because a full treatment required looking not only at the ways in which party members helped build the movement but also at how they pursued their own agenda, sometimes causing bitter divisions—within the Southern Tenant Farmers Union, for example, which had been organized by members of the Socialist Party.

The Communists are given their due in the first program where they are the central actors in the conclusion of Jon Else's Emmy award–winning program on Henry Ford and his workers. In the rough cut of his film Else had the Communist "Internationale" playing over scenes of the funeral of three party members killed by Ford's men during the 1932 Hunger March. This was too much for Hampton, who worried that the series would sound too leftist and look too much like a mere reflection of radical images from the "Red Decade." Instead, the first show ends with the "Star Spangled Banner," which was also played at the Communists' funeral service.

Unlike the critic Lewis Cole, Hampton did not assume the drama of the Depression era sprang solely from its radicalism. During the making of the series, producers who worked on Eyes told me of his discomfort with figures like Malcolm X and the Black Panthers, who are profiled in Eyes II, and the black Communist Angela Davis, who is not. They said Hampton was afraid viewers wouldn't understand ideological figures who sounded so divisive. He wanted to tell stories that brought Americans together, as he believed the story of Dr. King and the nonviolent civil rights movement did. Therefore, some Great Depression producers may have worried about pursuing stories on 1930s revolutionaries. But Hampton was not a censor. He liked to create what he called "creative discomfort." His discomfort with episode 1 of the series, a show that oozed class conflict, didn't stop Jon Else from depicting the Communists as heroic martyrs whose deaths end the first program on an ominous note of fear and anger.

As a team member involved in agonizing discussions of what stories could work in the filmmaking tradition created by Blackside, I accepted the compromises and omissions that resulted, even though it meant being disappointed by how much of the movement history of the Great Depression we could capture. As far as the left is concerned, the Socialists received more attention than the Communists, who were far more important in movement building. The program on 1934 shows newsreels of the San Francisco general strike, but misses the chance to portray Harry Bridges, who represented the best of what Communists contributed to the struggle for survival in the Great Depression. The producer Lyn Goldfarb was eager to tell stories of CP heroics, but for filmmaking, rather than ideological reasons, she became far more enamoured with the romantic tale of Upton Sinclair's socialistic 1934 campaign for governor of California. Bridges brilliantly engineered the most important strike victory of the early 1930s and changed the lives of thousands. Sinclair lost the election. So focusing a show on his gubernatorial campaign, even though it forecast modern electioneering, was not the choice most movement historians would have made. Still, as a result of that decision Lyn Goldfarb made an entertaining and moving film that captured in its own way the romance of a movement crusade.

There were other imbalances and inadequacies of even greater magnitude. The shows weave together, often brilliantly, black and white story lines, but the multicultural sensibilities we brought to the series did not produce strong episodes about Latinos, Asians, or Native Americans, even though potential stories were aggressively sought by the research effort I coordinated. Terry Rockefeller was most disappointed by our failure to tell sustained stories of women's struggles. If we could do a whole program on Fiorello LaGuardia, she thought, we should have been able to do a great show on Eleanor Roosevelt.

The most difficult thing for a historian to accept is that making films is so different from writing books. The Darwinian process of story selection and the Draconian process of film editing makes comprehensive coverage an impossible dream. Historian Robert Rosenstone, who has contributed to many films, including Hollywood features like *Reds,* says that scholars are often dismayed by the choices film producers and script writers make. But even those who serve as academic advisors are never asked, he adds, to go "into the editing room, where the decisions on putting the film together are made, where the final meaning of the film is created."[50] I was invited into the editing suites at Blackside where I sat with Dante James and his editor Jon Neuberger, and I talked with them while they watched and cut miles of tape. I was drawn into their storytelling problems, problems I had never faced as a writer of historical narrative. As a result of this experience, I came to accept the gaps in our films, even the missing stories of radicalism that distressed Lewis Cole.

The Great Depression did not feature movement history in some of the ways I hoped it would, but it remained true enough to the character of *Eyes on the Prize* to show how 1930s protest movements reshaped and redefined America. It showed how those movements "sought and won a measure of democratization of existing society," to use Richard Flacks's words, so that formerly powerless people could exercise their voice in the decisions that affected their lives. In making those movements part of a "narrative of democracy" these films about the 1930s did speak to the 1990s and to a mood of civic despair.[51] In *Democracy's Despair* Michael Sandel argues that our confused and "multi-encumbered" citizens have been rendered "storyless" and therefore "unable to weave the strands of their identity into a coherent whole." He says that "political community depends on the narratives by which people make sense of their condition and interpret the common life they share."[52] I believe this is true and that it helps explain much of the positive response by viewers and reviewers to *The Great Depression.*

However, the task we chose was not simply to produce films that fit into a revived and unified narrative of democracy. The series took shape in the midst of a very heated debate about "whether multiculturalism would be the undoing of America," to use Terry Rockefeller's words. Indeed, she made sure that when

Arthur Schlesinger Jr. spoke to our school for producers about Franklin Roosevelt he was also asked to explain his opinion that "multi-ethnic dogma" had undermined the purpose of our national history by replacing "assimilation with fragmentation."[53] Another historical advisor, Robin Kelley, spoke for many at the school when he challenged Schlesinger's interpretation of cultural politics. The debate ended at the school that first summer of production, but it remained in the background of our discussions about storytelling.

In final form *The Great Depression* was hardly a celebration of multiculturalism, because, for one thing, many ethnic and minority groups were absent from the newsreel footage we needed to tell our stories. In any case, rather than celebrating separate identities, the films explored the sense of "two-ness" experienced by people of color, by African Americans who expressed racial pride as Joe Louis whipped those "hopes of the white race" and who, at the same time, embraced Joe as an American hero knocking out his Italian foe and then his German opponent who had entered the ring with the blessings of Mussolini and Hitler. Seeing the final show when the Depression ends and Americans come together to be an "Arsenal of Democracy," viewers can recall from the previous program why our Congress failed to enact an anti-lynching law and can see why our government confined Americans of Japanese descent to concentration camps.

The programs were not the stories of assimilation and integration Schlesinger might have chosen to advance "the historic idea of a unifying American identity."[54] Nor were they the celebration of New Deal liberals and their policies he had provided in his *Age of Roosevelt* books. Instead, the producers told stories that reflected the ambiguity of New Deal democracy. Henry Hampton shared Martin Luther King's dream that Americans could redeem the promise of democracy, but he was painfully aware of how the democratic rhetoric had been used by the tyrannical majority—and not only in the segregated South. His insistence on probing the contradictions in the New Deal and the limits of democratic expansion in that era helped the producers capture what Ralph Ellison meant when he wrote: "American democracy is a most dramatic form of social organization. . . . No matter what kinds of narrative, oral or written, are made in the reconstruction of our common experience," Ellison declared, no matter how much we yearn and thirst for "a rational social order," there is no way of disguising the fact that we, as a people, are "in a constant state of debate and contention."[55]

Although Hampton received most of the attention from reviewers, series producer Terry Rockefeller deserved most of the credit for resolving the myriad problems, large and small, that plagued the project. No one believed more in carrying on the sense of family created at Blackside during the *Eyes* productions, and no one did as much to cope with the dysfunctions of quasifamily life or with the difficulties of pleasing a demanding but sometimes mystifying father

Presenting the Great Depression films to the public: the author (*center*) with Terry Kay
Rockefeller and Henry Hampton, 1993. Photograph by Harry Britt. *Courtesy University
of Massachusetts Boston.*

figure like Henry. She was the one who fought hardest to find stories about
women and about underrepresented groups, but when they failed to material-
ize, she found a way to make sure those faces were seen and those voices were
heard telling other stories. She made sure the producers hit the historical markers and still developed the big theme of how ordinary people redeemed democracy in the struggles of the 1930s. Because of Rockefeller's own rich understanding of social history, *The Great Depression* really revealed ordinary people
doing extraordinary things. Under her direction, the show took off from the
"catastrophic events" and human suffering they caused, and then depicted the
ways people tried to overcome them. She made it possible for Hampton to say
that even with all the depressing scenes of hunger, suffering, and oppression
depicted in the films, it would be possible for viewers to look closely and "see
some redemption there."[56]

Henry Hampton died on 22 November 1998 as Blackside producers were
finishing a new series on African American artists called *I'll Make Me a World.*
When we gathered at his memorial service at the old abolitionist church
on Arlington Street, the Blackside family he had created was reunited and

joined with scores of other folks from Boston's human rights community. We held hands to sing, once again, the movement song "Eyes on the Prize" as we mourned the passing of a wonderful mentor and visionary filmmaker.

After the memorial service, we walked across the common to the African Meeting House on Beacon Hill, where Blackside folks gathered to talk things over movement style. There, where I first met Henry Hampton at an oral history workshop, it occurred to me that his death might mark the end of an era, a kind of golden era of socially conscious documentary filmmaking.

When I spoke to Henry Hampton for the last time, we talked about how filmmakers were experimenting with new kinds of documentaries. He said the new series Blackside projected on the black arts would have to find new forms of expression. The lives of African American artists might not fit into the old story-driven treatments Hampton's producers had used to put social history on film. We discussed the creative ways documentarians were exploring the past and the memory of the past. We both admired George Stoney's film *The Uprising of '34*, which plumbed the depths of remembering and forgetting about the class violence of the Depression years. We agreed that the documentary captured what is richest in oral history, the art of dialogue, which connects people across generations and cultural spaces in a joint enterprise to seek meaning from the past.[57]

I look back on my Blackside experience with a deeper understanding of how the work of filmmaking differs from historical writing. The demands of telling stories through pictures and live witnesses present quite different challenges to filmmakers than the ones we face as writers of historical narrative. The compromises filmmakers make would often be unacceptable to historians. "Woe be to those elements of history which can neither be illustrated nor quickly summarized," writes Robert Rosenstone of film scripting and editing. Yet I agree with his view that this often brutal "thinning out process" can make for better storytelling, as long as the result remains within the bounds of historical accuracy. Indeed, what I learned from Blackside people about what makes a story work as human drama has been very helpful in my subsequent historical writing. The dramatic structure implicit in the best history books is often similar to the structure we adopted explicitly to tell our stories from the Depression years. In any case, I decided that, despite the "trade offs" documentary filmmaking requires, we historians can, as Rosenstone maintains, participate in the decision-making process without losing our "professional and intellectual souls."[58]

Indeed, these experiences may make us better writers and teachers of history. Telling stories on film made me more aware of the limitations of written history and more excited by the possibilities film offers for "representing the past"— possibilities, says Rosenstone, "that could allow narrative history to recapture the power it once had when it was more deeply rooted in the literary imagination." Telling history with pictures, sounds, and oral testimonies does not mean sacrificing the truth, he adds, but it does mean understanding that the "truths conveyed in the visual media may be different from, but not necessarily in conflict with, truths conveyed in words."[59] It is even possible that collaborating with filmmakers will help historians to write their stories with more soul, to tell stories that appeal to the mind's eye, stories that touch the heart as well as the intellect.

Part Three

LEARNING FROM MOVEMENT HISTORY

Bringing movement politics to voters: Mel King campaigning for mayor in the South End of Boston. *Photograph © Richard Sobol.*

CHAPTER **8**

Why Movement History Matters:
The Politics of Class and Race
in Boston

In March 1972 a group of black parents with children in the Boston public schools sued the city's school committee for deliberately segregating their children from white students. The plaintiffs could not challenge southern-style segregation statutes, but their attorneys found a clear record of the school committee's resistance to desegregation. Committee members overtly defied the desegregation guidelines laid out in the state's Racial Imbalance Act—a law enacted in 1965 in response to school boycotts organized by the civil rights movement. Ironically, Massachusetts had been through all this before when the legislature, influenced by the abolitionist movement, abolished mandated school segregation. This effort overrode the historic separate-but-equal decision rendered by the courts in the noted Roberts case of 1850.[1]

The Busing

A century and a quarter later, the drama was replayed. And on 21 June 1974 Federal Judge Arthur W. Garrity concluded that the defendants, the elected school committee responsible for the Boston public schools, had "knowingly carried out a systematic program of segregation affecting all of the city's students, teachers and school facilities and have intentionally brought about and maintained a dual school system." Therefore, he ruled, "the entire school system is unconstitutionally segregated."[2] Garrity then issued a controversial desegregation order requiring crosstown busing of children between Boston's highly segregated neighborhoods. When the plan was implemented on September 12, the day began quietly at eighty schools, but violence erupted in South Boston, where crowds chanted "Niggers, go home" and then stoned afternoon buses carrying black children. The battle of Boston had begun. It would become a world news story, creating media images as memorable as those of whites protesting school desegregation at Little Rock Central High School in 1957.

In a city gripped with the fear of race war, black parents, and their white supporters, mobilized to defend their children while some white residents boycotted the desegregated schools and joined neighborhood organizations dedicated to resisting the court order. When a Haitian immigrant was nearly beaten to death by whites in South Boston on October 7, rioting erupted in Roxbury and the governor called out the National Guard. Racist graffiti appeared everywhere in the Athens of America. Judge Garrity was burned in effigy on the Boston Common, where on the old bandstand a poster was hung that read:

THE CITY IS OCCUPIED
A BOYCOTT EXISTS
A TYRANT REIGNS
LAW IS BY DECREE

The conflict over busing in Boston provoked a wave of doubt on the part of liberals who had strongly supported the civil rights movement's crusade to desegregate the South. Though opposed to school segregation, these critics blamed Judge Garrity's order for placing an unfair burden on the city's working-class whites, who had their own history of oppression. The Boston journalist Alan Lupo, who wrote the first book about busing in 1977, concluded that the "city was imprisoned by its own history." Its people had failed to learn from that history, had failed to learn about the oppression of white working people of immigrant origins who were now held solely responsible for race discrimination. After he observed a tense standoff between white protestors and the police trying to protect black children in school buses, Lupo wrote with bitter irony of this confrontation between Boston's community of color and its white Catholic community. And where, he asked, were the Yankees, "the ones who brought the slaves and who fought on both sides of the issue of freedom and equality, the ones who enticed immigrants and then spat on them"? They were nowhere to be seen that day. They were safe in the suburbs having left a dubious legacy to those who inherited their Boston.[3]

When some white parents took their kids out of the schools and others left the city in what was called "white flight," observers like Lupo saw their worst fears confirmed. In a later edition of his book on busing, he complained that the integrated school system had not delivered improved quality. A decade after the court order, the school system had changed from 70 percent white to 70 percent children of color, with parents voicing numerous complaints. There was confusion over school assignments, there was poor leadership and "increased criminal violence by blacks, replacing the white and black violence that marked the early years of busing." There was a perception that "an already failing system was getting worse."[4]

Lupo's reading of history was shared by other critics of busing, and it reflected a growing disillusionment with the protests of the sixties and the policies they had created.[5] The far right was on the offensive, attacking all forms of affirmative action against racism, and neoliberals were bemoaning the unintended consequences of reforms intended to promote equality. No redemption could be found in the history of Boston's desegregation struggle, only consternation.

Common Ground

This regretful reading of history received powerful sanction in 1985 with the publication of J. Anthony Lukas's enormously influential book *Common Ground: A Turbulent Decade in the Lives of Three American Families.*[6] I eagerly awaited its publication, having followed its progress through the long years of research when Tony Lukas interviewed scores of participants, even some of us who had been involved in *Radical America's* editorial statement on the history and politics of the desegregation struggle, described in chapter 1. As a famous *New York Times* writer, Lukas had been sympathetic to the student and antiwar movements. He was one of that generation of liberal journalists who zealously questioned official versions of the truth and the phony objectivity the media projected. Furthermore, unlike most liberals, he seemed very concerned with the problem of class, which he called the "dirty secret in American life."[7] Like most everyone who read *Common Ground*, I was engrossed in the dramatic ways Lukas used social history and oral history in telling his saga.

Common Ground earned rave reviews and received the Pulitzer prize. It was, said rapturous reviewers, the "riveting stuff of genuine tragedy," which read like a novel and at the same time, offered "a dispassionate reconstruction of events." A "model of thoroughness and balance," it would be the last word on Boston's busing ordeal.[8]

I found the book moving and disturbing at the same time. As a student and teacher of Boston history, I was awed by Lukas's skill in making the past come alive, but as an observer and participant in the antiracist struggles of the time, I was offended that he devoted only a few paragraphs to the racial violence that had frightened and hurt so many people in Boston during the fall of 1974. Even more worrisome was the writer's conclusion that "the price" of busing wasn't worth paying.[9] He painted a picture of a struggle that "originated in righteous claims, but degenerated into a grotesque convulsion that benefitted no one," in the words of one of the few critical reviews.[10] My feelings were shared by others in the activist community, and they were magnified when we saw how important the book became as a definitive history. Not only was *Common Ground* being taught in the nation's education schools, it was being widely quoted by liberal politicians and policy makers disillusioned with racially divisive policies that seemed to be splitting the Democratic Party and driving angry white working men into the Republican Party of President Ronald Reagan.[11]

Lukas's doubts about the price to be paid for school desegregation arose out of his class analysis of the conflict. The legal struggle over school segregation waged in Judge Arthur Garrity's federal courtroom "often resembled an Irish morality play, fought out between various conceptions of what it meant to be Irish in contemporary Boston. It was a family feud." On one side were "the two-toilet Irish"—Judge Garrity, Mayor Kevin White, Senator Edward Kennedy, and their WASP allies in the *Boston Globe* and the suburbs. On the other side were the "little people" in the white neighborhoods who felt betrayed by "their own"—the same working people who abandoned the Kennedy Democrats and joined the Reagan Republicans. It wasn't necessary to emphasize the racism of the white folks who opposed busing, Lukas wrote, because "class resentment did more than anything to feed the fires of white resistance in the inner-city neighborhoods."[12]

I decided to write about *Common Ground* after a moving conversation with Ruth Batson, a pioneer of the civil rights struggle who headed Boston's Museum of African American History. She was deeply disturbed by Lukas's book. "Look at what he's done to our history," she said. "He's left our movement out of his story, left out the struggle that was carried out for so many years by black people in Boston." As she later told a *Globe* columnist, she feared the book would "forever distort" the history of desegregation in the city.[13]

What, I wanted to know, would that history read like with the movement put back in? I already knew many episodes of the movement story from activists I had interviewed or spoken with informally. I also had read several chapters of it in a remarkable book produced by Boston's most important community activist and civil rights leader, Mel King. His personal history of social change in the city was produced by Boston's movement-inspired South End Press in 1981, but his book *Chain of Change* never reached the kind of audience Tony Lukas's reached.[14] What, I wondered, would the story look like if conveyed through the movement eyes of Mel King?

Mel King found no place in *Common Ground,* which featured portraits of five white leaders, including Mayor Kevin H. White, Judge Garrity, Humberto Cardinal Medeiros, *Boston Globe* editor Thomas Winship and the anti-busing city councilor from South Boston, Louise Day Hicks. Lukas presents Mrs. Hicks as an opportunist "who didn't really have anything against black people." Staunch for labor and the Democratic Party, "[h]er invective focused on 'the special interests,' 'the Establishment,' 'the outside power structure,' 'the rich people in the suburbs,' 'the forces who attempt to invade us.' . . . You know where I stand," she told her supporters, who knew she stood for the racial status quo. "Boston for the Bostonians," she proclaimed, aiming her anger at suburban elites who issued court orders and published liberal newspapers. Lukas claimed that "[b]y Bostonians she meant 'the workingman and woman, the rent payer, the home owner, the law-abiding, tax-paying, decent-living, hard-working forgotten American.' "[15] But black Bostonians felt excluded from Hicks's Boston, restricted to their neighborhoods, their low wage jobs, and their segregated schools. Lukas included no portraits of African American leaders who had shaped the desegregation struggle, the court order,' and the community response: movement actors like Ruth Batson and Mel King, who is briefly mentioned by Lukas as someone whites found "an unnerving figure."[16]

Mel King

I came to know Mel King when I lived in the South End of Boston, a diverse area of working-class homeowners and lodgers. In 1972 he had been elected to represent the district in the state legislature. It was easy to be sucked into the winds of protest that blew through this storm center of poor people's struggles against urban renewal. King was usually at the center of the storm in this neighborhood that helped make Boston a "contested city."[17] I worked with a group fighting the conversion of lodging houses into luxury apartments and in the process began to collect oral histories with neighborhood residents and activists who told me about the neighborhood's multiethnic, live-and-let-live tradition.[18] South End schools were already quite diverse so court-ordered busing aroused no opposition there in contrast to the militant white resistance that emerged in a few white areas.[19]

King grew up in the South End's dense New York Streets area, the child of West Indian immigrants. In the 1950s he would see the neighborhood targeted for destruction by the bulldozers of urban renewal, like the old West End and other "urban villages" that awaited a similar fate. He attended the Abraham Lincoln School made famous in Mary Antin's novel of immigrant success, *The Promised Land*. The school was "a little United Nations," King recalled, one of the few racially integrated schools in Boston. He went to a black college in South Carolina, and when he came home one summer was thrilled to hear Paul Robeson speak. The man's bearing and his vision inspired the young King, made him "ready for the work to come." After college he returned home to earn a master's degree in teaching, and then when he tried to teach in Boston, he encountered "the fantastic and fanatical racism" that black people faced in the public schools. At the same time, he suffered from overt discrimination while seeking housing for his family. These experiences set him on a determined course to combat racism in Boston, a city that arrogantly proclaimed itself enlightened when it came to race relations.[20]

The Black Education Movement

Seeing the history of the black education movement in Boston through the activities of Mel King puts the "tragedy" of busing and the city's racial conflict in the context of movement history; it also puts the consequences of desegregation in a different light than the one Anthony Lukas shed on the story. During the

1960s, Boston's highly segregated schools and neighborhoods became targets of protest efforts that would lead to significant changes in city politics. In 1961 the NAACP sued the Boston Housing Authority for practicing de facto segregation. The courts found the BHA guilty. The public schools suffered from neglect by the city's business leaders and from the retrograde and blatantly racist practices of politicians who maintained control of the school committee and school department.[21] In 1960 Citizens for Boston Public Schools (CBPS) formed to protest these conditions, and a year later, it endorsed four candidates for school committee. The two whites won and the two blacks lost; one of the latter was Mel King.

In 1962 the Northern Student Movement, initiated to support civil rights struggles in the South, joined some black churches to set up tutorial programs for black children in inner-city schools. In the same year, the CBPS, the NAACP, and CORE all published reports critical of segregation in Boston's schools and joined forces to pressure the school committee. When the committee refused to acknowledge de facto segregation, students boycotted the system. Roughly nine thousand students (about one-quarter of the student body) participated in the Stay Out campaign of 1963 while many attended freedom schools modeled after those in the South. The civil rights movement in Boston kept the pressure up on all fronts. At the same time, Mel King led a STOP day and asked people to walk off their jobs to protest racial segregation, police brutality, and other forms of discrimination. The NAACP and other established black leaders opposed the idea of a work stoppage and called their own demonstration, a memorial to slain civil rights leader Medgar Evers. But the two groups did come together in a "gesture of solidarity," marching through the South End while singing "Freedom, Freedom" and "We Shall Overcome" to a rally on Boston Common.[22]

In response, the school committee became more intransigent. The chairperson, Louise Day Hicks of South Boston, had been elected to "keep politics out of the schools" and at first appeared open-minded, but in 1963 she emerged as a leader of the white resistance to desegregation. That fall she campaigned for reelection as a defender of segregation and the "neighborhood school." Indeed, Hicks "identified herself as the budding symbol of northern intransigence toward civil rights demands," according to Peter Schrag, author of the revealing book *Village School Downtown*. She also identified herself with Mayor James Michael Curley's populist legacy and against Boston's blue-blooded WASP establishment. She campaigned "on behalf of small people who never expect to make it big." Hicks led all candidates in the 1963 election. Mel King failed to come close in his second bid for the school committee.[23]

During the mid-sixties, civil rights protests in Boston included parent boycotts, student strikes, speaking out at school committee hearings, picket lines, marches, and the creation of "freedom schools," including one at the South End Settlement House where Mel King was "principal." This agitation (highlighted by Martin Luther King's appearance on Boston Common) led to the passage of the state Racial Imbalance Law in 1965, which mandated school desegregation but prohibited busing as a solution. After a brief lull, boycotts continued, notably at the Gibson School described by Jonathan Kozol in his famous book, *Death at an Early Age.*

A new phase of the struggle began. Black activists now demanded "community-controlled education" and created voluntary plans to bus black children to suburbs and to open private schools in Roxbury. But at the same time, the black education movement continued to challenge the school committee, encouraged by the statewide law aimed at improving the racial balance in schools. Movement leaders accused Louise Day Hicks of using the "fear-laden issues of busing and race for her own political advantage," to ensure her reelection to the school committee in 1965. Hicks again topped the field, but Mel King won far more support than he had previously in his bid for office, finishing sixth in the race for five seats on the committee. The black community was becoming highly politicized. For the first time in the city's history, a greater percentage of black voters than white voters went to the polls in the primary election.[24]

In 1967 Mel King became director of the New Urban League, which hoped to promote further organizational development in Boston's black community. Louise Day Hicks decided to campaign for mayor on her segregationist record. Her candidacy threatened the new image of Boston promoted by former mayors Collins and Hynes and their allies in the downtown business and banking establishments.[25] City elites were relieved to see the emergence of a more acceptable liberal candidate, Kevin Hagan White of West Roxbury. A Williams College graduate, and a new type of Irish politician, he appealed to the successful professional classes more than to the working-class folks in neighborhoods like South Boston, Louise Hicks's "hometown." White campaigned against Hicks as a Kennedy liberal who would restore racial peace. He sought support from black voters and presented himself simultaneously as a reformer, like New York City's glamorous mayor John Lindsay, as well as progrowth leader who would continue plans for the New Boston. After an intense, bitter campaign, White beat Hicks by less than five thousand votes. He won because he received over fifteen thousand black votes. A registration drive and a push to get out the vote had led to an unprecedented 68 percent turnout among blacks. In the same election Thomas Atkins became the first African American elected to an at-large city-council seat.[26]

As mayor, Kevin White began to build a patronage machine modeled after Richard Daley's organization in Chicago. It included an important arm in the black community.[27] To Mel King, the incorporation of black loyalists into the mayor's administration represented a continuation of the "service stage" in African American political development, which involved "taking the white power structure's handouts rather than organizing the community to demand satisfaction of black needs." He believed that Mayor White wanted to prolong this situation through traditional patronage arrangements, but that black political activists had come too far to return to a state of dependency on the Democratic Party and City Hall.[28] The protest movement against racism in the schools paralleled other community-based empowerment efforts, which, taken together, represented a new "organizing stage" that had begun to emerge in Boston's neighborhoods.

The Organizing Stage

Community groups immediately challenged the probusiness development policies of the White administration aimed at improving the downtown area, which was becoming a leading center for the concentration of capital. While City Hall fostered a "New Boston" for banks, businesses, hospitals, and private colleges, the neighborhoods remained poor and suffered from the conversion of affordable housing into "luxury housing."

The South End, a battleground during this stage of urban renewal, produced a strong neighborhood advocacy group, CAUSE, and two tenant unions, one of them a Hispanic organization. In 1968 CAUSE members, including Mel King, occupied a Redevelopment Authority office in the South End to protest inadequate relocation plans. Then they picketed a parking lot in the South End where the Redevelopment Authority had bulldozed livable buildings, displacing one hundred families. When CAUSE members blocked the parking lot, twenty-three were arrested, including Mel King. Protestors then encamped on the site. Their Tent City became a symbol of popular resistance to the city's probusiness housing policies.

Besides the problems of discrimination in schools and housing, people of color suffered from pervasive discrimination in the labor market. After decades of being restricted to low-paying service jobs, Boston's growing black population gradually began to secure employment in industry during the 1950s, but then the city's manufacturing shops began closing. The new hi-tech jobs that opened up in the suburbs remained off limits to people of color. Government employment, which provided opportunities for many blacks in large cities, remained virtually all white in Boston. Though some new job opportunities opened up for blacks between 1950 and 1970, their earning power remained relatively unchanged. After twenty years of "progress" they still earned two-thirds of what white workers received. Blacks had not experienced the occupational mobility of white ethnic groups, according to historian Stephan Thernstrom, because of systematic racial discrimination.[29]

The White Administration coincided with a period of prosperity. New jobs were created in downtown offices, in new stores, and in the city's numerous education and health care institutions, but these positions were occupied mainly by educated suburbanites. After suffering from the recession of the seventies, white construction workers hopped aboard the new gravy train created by Boston's building boom, but their success was not shared by inner-city residents of color excluded from the unionized construction industry. In 1968 the first black activists confronted the construction industry, forming the United Community Construction Worke;⁻ (UCCW) to fight against discrimination by contractors and unions.

The assassination of Martin Luther King in April of 1968 led to angry protests in Boston's black neighborhoods. In the aftermath, activists created a Black Unified Front (BUF) which included many important groups, though not the National Association for the Advancement of Colored People, whose leaders were apparently offended by the group's nationalist politics. The Front demanded community-controlled development funds. Mayor White listened but then tried to co-opt the BUF by forming his own group, the Boston Urban Foundation, with the same initials. Frustrated with City Hall's determination to control development policies, Mel King and others laid the groundwork for the emergence of community development corporations in Boston's neighborhoods. This work quickly moved to what King called the "institution-building stage" when he and other urban planners secured funding for a state Community Development Finance Corporation.[30]

The movement for community-controlled development conflicted with Mayor White's desire to strengthen City Hall and his own organization in Boston's black neighborhoods where activists were moving toward independent political activity. In 1971 Boston's only black City Councillor, Thomas Atkins, decided to challenge Mayor White in the preliminary election. Atkins received a protest vote, but White won the votes of most people of color who guessed, correctly, that he would once again face Louise Day Hicks in the final runoff. After pushing very hard for Black and Latino registration, Kevin White won the election by a big margin. His victory did not depend on voters of color as it had in 1967. The mayor began to build a stronger base in white working-class areas that had been solidly for Hicks, and where he was known as "Mayor Black" because of his promises to voters in Roxbury. Independent political leaders in the black community assumed that since White was now confident of African American electoral support, he would pay less attention to their concerns and more attention to the worries of white voters.[31] When Judge Garrity issued his school desegregation order in 1972, Mayor White hoped to avoid being caught in the middle of the conflict that would ensue.

The traumatic conflicts over court-ordered busing, described at the outset of this chapter, created a profound sense of crisis in the city. When the white attacks on school buses began, black people feared for their lives and many doubted if City Hall and the virtually all-white police force would protect them and their children. Given the enormous risks involved in desegregating the schools, Mel King and his allies wondered if they "were doing the right thing" by supporting busing. After all, many of them had emphasized the need for community-controlled schools with funding equal to what white neighborhood schools received. Many leaders of the black education movement, doubting the possibility of equal treatment in the city of Boston, had focused their energies on busing some black children to quality schools in the suburbs in a community-controlled program called METCO.[32]

Mel King found his own dilemma resolved when he talked to a black student being bused to South Boston High School. "We have to go," she declared. "If they run us out of that school, they can run us out of the city." For this student, and for many other people of color, busing was not "just a matter of education; it was an intensely political experience" from which hundreds of young black people received a very practical education.[33] Ruth Batson expressed pride in the black children, and also the white children, who went through hell to attend desegregated schools. She saw the children not as victims, pawns in the game played by more powerful forces, but as heroes and heroines of their own story. "I thought that the kids who went through this were just wonderful kids. They weren't kids with great marks or anything. They were just kids who were determined. There was a movement. And they felt part of a movement."[34]

Even youngsters connected with the anti-busing movement were changed in unexpected ways. Tony Lukas wrote sensitively about one of the white students on the firing line, Lisa McGoff, a leader of the "Last White Class" at Charlestown High School. She was changed as a result of her experience. Unlike earlier graduates of the neighborhood high school, McGoff had gained an opportunity to meet and relate to people of color. Forced segregation had deprived earlier generations of that opportunity and that possibility for human growth. Lukas described her mother, Alice, as being agonized by her daughter's "seemingly irreconcilable emotions." For years Alice McGoff had crusaded against Judge Garrity's "judicial tyranny" with Charlestown's militant anti-busing group, Powder Keg. But even while fighting "forced busing," Alice McGoff "had watched with mounting admiration as Lisa assumed leadership at the school (which included peacemaking), managing through force of personality to restore some vestige of solidarity and tradition," Lukas wrote. "Her child was a determined young woman now, armed with the courage of her convictions. Some Powder Keg members might complain about Lisa's role at the school, suggesting she had somehow sold out to the 'pro-busers,' but Alice defended her, proclaiming a mother's pride."[35]

The busing was an intensely political experience for many people in Boston: for the black leaders and parents who rallied at Freedom House in Roxbury to maintain calm in the black community and to prepare children for what awaited them in desegregated schools and also for the white protestors who joined organizations like ROAR (Restore Our Alienated Rights) to resist what they saw as judicial tyranny. The conflict also produced a group of political leaders who would play leading roles in postbusing Boston. Ray Flynn, then a state representative from South Boston and strongly supported by ROAR, emerged as one of the leaders of the antibusing movement.

In 1975 Representative Flynn seemed interested in challenging the incumbent mayor White who had lost his support in many white areas where the resistance to busing was strongest and where people blamed City Hall for helping to implement the desegregation plan. White was defensive. He complained that he was "sharing too much of the busing burden."[36]

Flynn chose not run for mayor in 1975 and so ROAR lacked a strong candidate. In fact, it was the black education movement that produced viable candidates like State Senator Bill Owens, who had organized the antiracist rally in the fall of 1974. A Boston public school teacher and counselor named John O'Bryant, who had managed Mel King's campaigns for school committee, decided to make his own bid to become the first African American elected to the committee. He ran well in the preliminary and made the final list of candidates. After the primary, the newspaper of the South Boston Information Office carried a letter of warning: "Wake up Southie," it read. "Do you realize you gave 834 votes to John O'Bryant who is a pro-buser? . . ." The writer continued: "I was in the army with O'Bryant and believe me, he's not IRISH. He's a black man from Roxbury and believes in forced integration and Forced Busing." O'Bryant lost in the final election, but in the next election he succeeded, after struggling for nearly two decades to change the school system.[37]

O'Bryant became the first black person elected to the Boston School Committee in thirty-five years, while at the same time, Louise Day Hicks and John Kerrigan, two outspoken opponents of desegregation, lost bids for higher office. A year later, O'Bryant formed the Black Political Task Force to encourage further political participation. The desegregation struggle also brought along with it a movement to desegregate the work force, especially the lily-white staff of the Boston schools; it encouraged parents to hold schools more accountable to them and less to the patronage bosses; it forced other powerful institutions in the city to address the problems of public education.[38] Finally, the campaign against separate schools created possibilities, long denied, for white parents and children to get to know and even to cooperate with parents and children of color.

Other progressive developments flowed out of the busing crisis. Independent black politics gained momentum rapidly in the late 1970s as a new generation of black political activists came of age during what Mel King called the "organizing stage" of community development.

Mayor White managed to keep his interracial coalition together despite major community protests against his policies in an inner-city class struggle over housing. He proved far more adept than most of his contemporaries at responding to crises that threatened to rip apart his probusiness coalition. While other liberals gave way to "cop mayors" like Frank Rizzo in Philadelphia, or to black mayors like Coleman Young in Detroit, Kevin White stayed the course and continued to build up a patronage machine second only to the Daley organization in Chicago.

In 1975 White won reelection to a third term over a more conservative white politician who had alienated most blacks, but after the election the mayor had to cope with more discontent among African Americans. Boston had become a more dangerous city than ever before for people of color. Even after the stoning of school buses subsided, racist attacks continued. Black homes in white neighborhoods were attacked. In 1979 twelve black women were murdered in six months, provoking angry cries about a lack of concern by city and police officials. A black high school football player was shot down on a field in white Charlestown and permanently paralyzed. And the police shot and killed three black men without being brought to justice.

In 1979 Mel King decided to challenge Mayor White in the preliminary election. He charged that employment conditions for people of color had actually worsened in the private sector. The city added fifty thousand new jobs after 1970 but by the end of that decade, 65 percent of the new jobs belonged to suburban commuters. One federal government study showed that minorities were underrepresented in many clerical and sales jobs that required minimum training and few specialized skills, even though they were better educated than their counterparts in other cities. Mayor White took credit for a modest increase in minority representation in city jobs, but he could take no credit for minority hiring that resulted from court suits against the police, fire, and school departments, which had remained lily white during his first two terms. He stood aside during the bitter struggle of the United Community Construction Workers (UCCW) to apply "the Philadelphia Plan" for minority affirmative-action hiring in the construction industry, a fight that also ended up in the courts.

In 1979 Mel King and other community activists developed a Boston Jobs for Boston Residents program to address the employment needs of white men and women who lived in the city as well as the needs of workers of color. The program demanded that a minimum of 50 percent of the total work force, craft by craft, be composed of Boston residents on all publicly funded or subsidized development projects in the city. A minimum of 25 percent had to be minority workers and a minimum of 10 percent women. King's negotiations with City Hall over the policy broke down—one of the many reasons he decided to take on Mayor White in the 1979 preliminary election for mayor. When King made the jobs residency policy an issue, White responded first with an executive order on minority hiring and then with an order establishing the hiring goals King had proposed.

King was also a key leader in the campaign for district representation that would allow for more school committee and city council representatives from communities of color. The Boston People's Organization, created by Mel and his supporters, took movement politics to the next stage and achieved a victory in 1982 with charter reforms that replaced at-large elections with district representation that, in turn, produced greater minority representation on the school committee.[39] This victory laid the groundwork for a breakthrough in independent political action, a unification of the city's many social movements into Mel King's Rainbow Coalition.

The Rainbow

The Rainbow Coalition developed a comprehensive agenda for community development through community empowerment. Its politics were infused with King's idea that urban politics needed to be about more than City Hall's distribution of resources. As his associate Marie Kennedy put it, this idea was based on the need to redistribute control over decision-making in city life.[40]

With the news that Kevin White would not run for reelection, the Rainbow Coalition decided to organize a campaign to elect Mel King mayor. King's preliminary campaign generated a new kind of excitement in Boston politics and a new sense of possibility in the progressive community. Hope was also engendered by the successful mayoral bid of Harold Washington in Chicago. Washington's campaign was based on community mobilization and organization against City Hall run by the old Daley patronage machine. It was also a campaign based on an effective multiracial, multiethnic coalition. When Mayor Washington came to Boston in midsummer to endorse King, the Rainbow campaign surged forward in its recruitment and fund-raising activities. Visits by Andrew Young and Jesse Jackson added even more enthusiasm to the campaign and solidified King's black support. Soon the polls showed that Mel King had a chance to make the final run-off because most of the newly registered voters were people of color who planned to vote for him.

After an enthusiastic grassroots campaign, King finished in a dead heat with the other top finisher, State Representative Ray Flynn of South Boston, an old foe in the battle over busing. King nearly doubled his percentage of the total vote he had received in his 1979 run for mayor. He swept the Black community with 90 percent of the vote, and he carried Asian and Latino precincts with big majorities. His campaign dramatically boosted voter registration in minority areas, where twenty-three thousand new voters registered in the three weeks after his preliminary victory. Besides this, King had galvanized many other liberal and radical groups with his idea of a Rainbow Coalition, a coming together of the various social protest movements that had surged through Boston for two decades.[41]

Ray Flynn maintained his anti-busing, anti-abortion stance and took no chances on alienating his core constituency, white voters whose resistance to school desegregation was strong. He refused to recognize Boston's racist past or to use the term *racism*. He insisted that the issues were economic not racial—the same in South Boston as in Roxbury. But Flynn also wanted to expand his base, to create a new coalition that would allow him to govern effectively if he was elected. He did not want to be seen as a single-issue anti-busing candidate. As an at-large city councilor, Ray Flynn had assiduously cultivated union and community support throughout the city, visibly involving himself in supporting strikes, rent control campaigns, and restrictions on the conversion of rental housing into condominiums. He presented himself as an urban populist supporting the neighborhoods against City Hall and downtown business interests.

The Mayoral Campaign of '83

The press loved comparing the two contestants who would square off in the final mayoral contest, "the craggy faced Irish battler from South Boston" and the "brawny, bald, bearded activist" from the South End. "The two men were the most left-ward in the race, both running on a promise to shift money and urban planning energies away from glamorous downtown and harbor front development toward rebuilding Boston's neglected working-class neighborhoods." The two candidates' "populist appeals were so evenly matched" that *Time* magazine could not distinguish them.[42]

Each candidate still lived in the "rough Boston neighborhood where he was born and raised." Both men's fathers had worked on the Boston docks and both had attended public schools. Left unsaid was the fact that Mel King went to one of the city's few integrated schools, in the South End, while Ray Flynn starred in three sports at all-white South Boston High School. The two "rough" neighborhoods the candidates came from responded very differently to Boston's historic busing crisis. While white mobs stoned school buses full of black children in South Boston, parents in the South End formed escort groups for the white kids being bused into their schools. King and Flynn were both raised in poor, working-class neighborhoods, but more than the murky Fort Point Channel and Amtrak yards separated the wide-open, multiracial South End from the all-white, intensely parochial neighborhood Ray Flynn had represented in the State House.[43] *Time* magazine also ignored what distinguished the grassroots coalitions King and Flynn created. The core of each candidate's coalition took shape during the busing conflict that polarized the Hub in the mid-seventies, and in many ways the 1983 campaign was fought along some of the same battle lines drawn during the desegregation conflict.

Throughout the campaign King insisted that racism was still a political and social problem of the highest order. It was hurting white as well as black citizens. He reached out to white citizens and appealed to their best instincts. He often reminded leftists and militants in his campaign to treat people in white areas as potential allies, as "people the same as you and me." He expressed outrage at the way demagogues constantly reminded the Boston Irish of their oppression, but, instead of creating something positive out of their people's anger, used it to create a "hostile defensive mentality." He actively sought white supporters, but not by assuring them that people of color had exactly the same problems, or by ignoring the divisive issues of racism and bigotry. He used his

Boston Jobs residency program to appeal for unity between white and minority workers in the city.[44]

A broad multiracial alliance of the new social movements born in the sixties and seventies gathered under King's rainbow. He linked the issues raised by these movements in what he called the "chain of change" and took what he humorously called "a whole left approach." This gave the Rainbow Coalition a decentralized, movement quality. The candidate enhanced this feeling by consistently referring to the "we" of the campaign and by looking beyond the elections to the long process of popular empowerment. It was the first time since the antiwar demonstrations of the early 1970s that so many movement activists could come together in a common cause—to work together in a multicultural coalition that brought together a range of issues and offered a progressive program to an entire city.

The Real Problem

Flynn wanted the city to forget busing and racial conflict. He aimed to bring the city's neighborhoods together around "ground floor economic issues." "The real problem is economic discrimination," he said in an important TV debate. Although Flynn based his coalition on a traditional white anti-busing, anti-abortion constituency, he also attracted significant support from liberals and leftists who liked his economic populism and the opportunity his candidacy offered to capture City Hall for the people in Boston's working-class neighborhoods.[45]

Some of Flynn's supporters were movement activists, former student radicals who moved into white working-class areas like East Boston and Dorchester to start organizing projects, community newspapers, and, in Dorchester, a Tenant Action Committee. In 1973 they created the Dorchester Community Action Council (DCAC) to fight for rent control and against the neighborhood deterioration that affected both tenants and homeowners. The council was organizing whites who often believed that neighborhoods deteriorated *because* blacks moved in, but instead of confronting those views, the organizers decided instead to emphasize the institutionalized racism of bankers and real estate interests who busted up white neighborhoods and then victimized the blacks who followed. This "class conscious" strategy deliberately avoided the divisive issue of race.

In 1976 DCAC merged with the citizen action group devoted to energy problems. The new organization called Fair Share adopted an energetic door-to-door canvasing approach in Boston and blue-collar towns like Chelsea and Waltham. Mass Fair Share, headed by Michael Ansara, a former SDSer at Harvard, built up a large statewide membership by hiring student canvassers on a commission basis and received good publicity for its local campaigns on street repairs, playgrounds, schools, housing, taxes, and utilities. The approach was derived from the ideas of the famous community organizer Saul Alinsky, who believed in the importance of chosing reasonable targets for local groups, so that they could see some successes flowing from their efforts.

Fair Share continued to organize in racially troubled Dorchester. In this tense setting, it set up a number of block clubs in a black and Hispanic area that had become polarized in the aftermath of busing and it tried to build alliances between blacks and working-class whites on issues that transcended race. Fair Share decided not to take a position on busing, which was very much resented in white neighborhoods.[46] Charlotte Ryan, a community organizer who worked in Dorchester at the time, told me that while many individual organizers in Fair Share were personally concerned with fighting racism, they did so in a private way. They agreed with their leaders' decision to avoid divisive racial issues for the purposes of organizing. Ryan shared this view of organizing when she began her work in Dorchester. She also opposed the school busing plan because it was divisive. As a person of Irish working-class origins and a member of a trade union family, she immediately adopted the populist view that you could "unite people around common economic grievances without addressing racism directly." However, after working in the black and Latino sections of Dorchester, Charlotte Ryan changed her thinking about racism. "Like other white people," she told me, "I didn't see how the world was divided on race and I didn't have the door slammed in my face all the time just because of my race. People of color couldn't choose whether or not to make racism an issue, like the white organizers did. If you were black in Boston you couldn't escape the issue."[47]

Populist Appeals

Ryan supported Mel King in 1983 while her Fair Share associates backed Ray Flynn. So did other former radicals in the tenant unions and the trade unions, including the militant leader of the Hotel Workers Local 26, Domenic Bozzotto. These movement activists engaged in a public debate about the meaning of populism, an issue which now divided Boston's progressive community.[48] I had already been arguing with populist intellectuals about the historical lessons to be drawn from the past, and I attempted to apply my interpretation to the campaign underway in the city.[49]

The economic populists who supported Flynn embraced an older notion of an exploited class that incorporated poor and working people of all kinds, including small property owners, against the forces of monopoly and the enemies of democracy. They believed that poor blacks and whites shared common problems, common interests, and common enemies. But, this view, I argued, ignored the history of racism in populist movements and the ways in which populist thinking usually avoided racial problems by seeking economic common ground on which poor whites and blacks could stand together.

In my view, Flynn's appeal for economic unity and his fear of divisive issues like racism harkened back to earlier populist and reform movements that emphasized good government and economic justice as the best antidotes to discrimination. These movements advocated economic democracy but not social equality, which implied race mixing and integration. It was much easier to attack Wall Street and assume that all oppressed people would be united by common economic grievances than it was to take up the difficult struggle for equal rights. "The historic lesson of the populist movement" and of other reform movements was, in my opinion, that racism could not be covered up "by using exclusively economic demands for racial unity." Ray Flynn's socialist and progressive advisors repeated some past mistakes by assuming that racism and other forms of discrimination could be avoided as political issues and that economic reforms alone could bring people together. They even argued that Flynn, a former opponent of school desegregation, would be better able to reach out and heal the city's wounds than a leader of the civil rights movement who had dedicated his life to overcoming racial division.[50]

Mel King articulated a very different kind of populism. His was not an economic appeal that reduced social problems to questions about distributing resources in "fair shares."[51] He wanted to redistribute the power over decision-making because in a representative democracy like ours, majority rule often disfranchised entire communities, as it had Boston's small black population. Democracy could easily produce gross forms of inequality. So, instead of a populism aimed at redistribution, King envisioned a new populism based on a transformation of government and politics. He wanted to move beyond representative democracy to participatory democracy— a guiding principle of many of the sixties radical movements whose veterans came together in the Rainbow Coalition. Such a populist movement not only addressed the grievances of poor people against the rich and powerful; it also aimed to change the way poor people thought about each other and about power. It envisioned the birth of a new labor movement, based on the idea of creating new jobs and sharing them rather than on the old practice of protecting them from non-union competitors. Mel King's "transformative populism" was a visionary politics way ahead of its time in 1983.[52]

In the final election, Flynn defeated King by a two-to-one margin, carrying 80 percent of the white vote and only a small fraction of the vote cast by people of color. However, King's election-night gathering seemed like a victory party. Mel had received 20 percent of the white vote, more than Harold Washington received in Chicago or Andrew Young in Atlanta, even though King ran a more radical campaign in a more overtly racist city, and his campaign had empowered people of color and motivated an upsurge of voter registration among African Americans, Asians, and Latinos. The campaign had also forged a vibrant coalition of people of color, women's groups, gays and lesbians, and other progressive movements who would now play a much larger role in city politics. Though he had lost the race, King declared that the Rainbow Coalition had not been defeated. He thanked the crowd for allowing him to lead such a movement through "what historians will recognize as a turning point in the social, cultural and political history of Boston." Indeed, the emergence of movement politics had come a long way since Mel King first ran for the school committee in a campaign that, as he recalled, did not "excite any great interest."[53]

Flynn's Governing Coalition

When he became mayor Ray Flynn hired many of his leftist backers as staffers. Critics called them the Sandinistas in City Hall. The energetic mayor announced his desire to represent all of Boston's neighborhoods. He was seen in all corners of the city, at every kind of meeting and wake, and at many disasters, large and small. He visited a black family attacked by white youth and appealed for calm in a desegregated housing project. He also strongly supported the militant struggles of the multiracial Hotel Workers union. Ray Flynn needed to create a coalition that could govern a city, a city whose political landscape was changing in part because of the social movements that came together in King's Rainbow Coalition. Some of Flynn's supporters said that the mayor "had learned a lot" through the "hard years of suspicion and conflict" that followed the busing conflict, that he had been personally changed by the experience from being a defender of a white neighborhood to being an advocate of working people of all races.[54] Later on, he even joined an anti–Ku Klux Klan march in Georgia, provoking some of his old supporters in South Boston to accuse him of being "used by some of the more radical members of Boston's civil rights brigade."[55]

During Flynn's administration more people of color were employed in the city and on construction jobs, partly as a result of affirmative action policies, but they kept wondering how much had changed for them: they kept worrying about the growing poverty in their neighborhoods and about Flynn's neglect of the desegregated schools. In 1986 activist leaders in the black community expressed their position affirmatively by calling for a plebiscite favoring the separate incorporation of an area of Roxbury to be called Mandela and to be controlled by its fifty thousand residents, overwhelmingly people of color. Only 25 percent of those voting favored the creation of Mandela, but the separatist movement reflected serious alienation from Mayor Flynn's populist coalition.[56] Members of both the white and black establishments reacted to the Mandela plan "with more than anger," Alan Lupo observed. They felt "hurt by those they were helping," and just when things in Boston seemed to be looking better. Personally offended, Mayor Flynn threw his political machine into the fray to defeat the poorly organized movement, while "Mel King, as was his wont, prodded the powers that be" for "behaving like racists who were angry that uppity blacks were resenting and rejecting being patronized."[57]

The Good Old Days

During Mayor Flynn's first term Anthony Lukas's book *Common Ground* took the city by storm. Mayor Flynn and his progressive allies embraced the book as a testament to the failure of movements and policies that made race and racism central targets. They seemed to share Lukas's dim view of busing's conse quences: racial conflict and resentment without real improvement in the public schools.[58] As mayor, Flynn all but wrote off the public schools, which now seemed a concern mainly of poor children of color and their parents—people without much voice in City Hall.

Lukas's class analysis was appealing to liberals who endorsed his view that the white working class had absorbed an unfair "burden" of desegregation. The white suburban elites had escaped responsibility, and therefore, Lukas argued, the best solution to the problem of school segregation would have been a metropolitan desegregation plan that would have integrated schools on the basis of class as well as race.

This solution impressed newly class-conscious liberals as well as populists, but it was angrily rejected by civil rights–movement activists. Leaving aside questions of practicality, they charged that the proposal for metropolitan school desegregation ignored Boston's civic responsibility to its public schools. Tom Atkins, the lawyer who brought the case before Judge Garrity's court, addressed the matter this way: "the Supreme Court made it abundantly clear that 'the scope of the violation determines the scope of the remedy.'" In Boston "the copious record compiled in federal court established that *Boston* officials ma- nipulated *Boston* boundary lines, discriminated against blacks in filling *Boston* faculty and administrative ranks . . . deliberately assigned black and white *Boston* students and staff in a racially segregative manner, discriminated in the allocation of *Boston* educational resources . . . deliberately overcrowded *Boston's* black schools when white schools were under-utilized, and deliberately cited *Boston* schools so as to take advantage of *Boston's* residential segregation."[59]

Mel King commented critically on the racial assumptions behind the class- conscious solution Lukas proposed for the school segregation problem. With an edge in his voice he spoke of *Common Ground's* popularity among readers who saw the busing order as "a way in which the so-called preferred people" in the suburbs would be allowed to escape "the burden of the desegregation process." His message to them was: "Black people are not a burden." He denounced this thinking as "a mean and vicious way" of characterizing the city's people of color, as a kind of unwanted burden. "We were, and in fact are, an opportunity," he declared. Desegregation was an opportunity for people who live in this city "to open up and act in the most humane way possible. And they blew it." King concluded that Boston citizens had an opportunity to say, Let's have a city where, in Old Testament terms, "all the tribes were welcome," and not say the responsibility was on someone else. "The responsibility was right here, and the opportunity was a great one."[60]

Many politically powerful people failed to appreciate the ways in which desegregation had led to school improvements. Though constantly troubled, these institutions had already educated a new generation of citizens who had found some way out of their segregated neighborhoods, playgrounds, and housing projects.[61] It was easy to invoke a popular folk memory of the mythical "good old days" before busing when neighborhood schools existed with stricter classroom discipline, the days before "white flight." But much of this talk was "misplaced nostalgia," according to a recent assessment. Before the busing order, Boston's schools were in bad shape, worse for blacks than whites, but in generally poor condition. In fact, statistics show marked improvement in student achievement in the years since busing. Other studies show that white flight from desegregated schools was not the reason for the decline of white students.[62] A 1995 survey indicated that 85 percent of Boston's parents were satisfied with the "controlled choice assignments" that had evolved out of the 1974 desegregation plan, and that 75 percent had no desire to return to a plan that mandatorily assigned their children to neighborhood schools, as in the "good old days."[63]

Divided Memories

Bitter memories of court-ordered busing remain strong among many white Bostonians, and for many parents, including many people of color, the accomplishments of the black education movement may be unclear or even unknown. It is an older generation of civil rights activists in the black community and their allies who carry the memory of what difference the movement for educational equality made. They know how much was accomplished in Boston after educational apartheid was dismantled. And they know how little would have been achieved if institutional racism had not been confronted head on. It was this moral and political imperative Mel King carried into citywide politics after the busing conflict.

Bostonians can look back on the exciting election of 1983 in two very different ways. It can be seen as most city leaders would see it—as a turning point in the city's race relations when Raymond Flynn of South Boston created a new kind of governing coalition that reached out into communities of color and took on issues that helped heal the city's open wounds. For Flynn and his supporters it was a kind of "populist moment" when a local guy mobilized the working-class neighborhoods to take City Hall and give it back to the people. Or the mayoral election of 1983 can be seen, as it is here, not as "a moment of triumph" but as a "moment of democratic possibility."[64] For King and his followers political empowerment is not usually gained in the electoral arena. Nor do elections radically alter who gets what in terms of public resources and in terms of the opportunities public policy can create. They simply decide who governs on a short-term basis. In Mel King's eyes, community-based struggles for control must be waged to ensure any real democracy and equality in how the government functions. He said later that those movements are rarely able to coalesce and effectively take control of government. When they try and fail to do so in the electoral arena, "people go back to their own struggles."⁶⁵ And that is as it must be. A coalition of movements is only as strong as its constituent elements. Its strength comes from their strength.

King was unable to keep the Boston Rainbow Coalition together after the 1983 campaign, but that practical example of unified movement politics remained an inspiration to others, notably to Jesse Jackson who adopted its form and much of its content in his 1984 and 1988 presidential campaigns in the national Democratic primaries. The second campaign was won by a Massachusetts politician, our Governor Michael Dukakis, who espoused a "disinterested" managerial liberalism which distanced him from the class-conscious liberalism of the New Deal and from the race-conscious liberalism that appeared during the mid-1960's.[66] By contrast, Jackson's Rainbow campaign brought movement politics into the national arena just as Mel King brought it into the urban arena in Boston. Jesse Jackson articulated with passion and intelligence the concerns for social justice and economic equality that the labor and civil rights movements had injected into national politics during earlier times.

Even after more than decade of retreat from those politics, and even after the Reagan Revolution spread racial resentment and dismantled the welfare state, a civil rights activist and radical populist gave people of color a reason to have hope in politics. He even captured the hearts and minds of thousands of angry white working-class voters hurt by conservative politicians and their policies, hurt by what Jackson called "economic violence." His 1988 primary campaign took everyone by surprise and suggested that "simmering beneath the surface" of electoral conservatism there might be "a radical antagonism to the new politics of inequality."[67]

I thought then that Jackson's campaign represented something more. Like Mel King, he took on racism, the Achilles heel of previous populist campaigns which had called for economic justice but refused to attack racial inequality. In 1988 Jesse Jackson became the nation's first prominent black populist consciously building on the legacy of the civil rights movement and its accomplishments. His campaign represented another exciting moment of democratic possibility when citizens could vote for economic justice *and* social equality.[68]

The movements created two or three decades ago to fight for civil rights and neighborhood survival, for community empowerment and radical social change in cities like Boston are no longer as vital as they used to be. Even the community-based institutions created by social movements struggle to survive in a more conservative political environment that discourages citizen action. But perhaps the historical experience of these forerunners will be of value to the leaders of social change in the future. Someday, when they are strong enough, these new leaders will come together to form a coalition to decide who governs. Then, white people in the city will find themselves in a new position within coalition politics. Perhaps movement history will offer some counsel.

Few movements in U.S. history have actually involved white people learning from black people's struggles. The Rainbow Coalition in Boston was a product of that social learning, and Mel King was as much a teacher as a political leader. In the early 1960s, he helped initiate a black education movement that led to the school desegregation process in the 1970s. That challenge to the status quo created an activist core in the black community with Mel King at its center; it was a core of inspiration for many other protest movements that soon emerged. In 1983, King's Rainbow campaign mobilized the Asian and Hispanic communities, as well as other neighborhood groups and various social movements composed of white people who had learned their own lessons from the black freedom struggle, a struggle that itself had "gone through all the stages of developing consciousness and competence" and had reached a point at which it could become the center of a wider coalition of movement people.[69]

This account of movement history in Boston is based upon the narrative of Mel King, who lived that story. He believes it is unfinished, still unfolding, like "a chain of change still being forged." Mel's story of Boston told of "changing relationships, between people of color and white folks; between have-nots and have-a-lots; between men and women." It was, and is, a story with a moral. "If as a community we are prepared to lead others through the experience of learning to cooperate, dealing honestly with painful prejudices and tensions built into this society, and learning to bend enough in times of need so that the whole is more flexible and resilient, we will be able to do more than control our own community," King wrote. "We will be able to influence larger sections of the city, bringing together an array of potential allies." "Further movement" in our kind of society will be filled with conflict-producing tensions, but movement people have to work through them to "come together" and move "out of their isolation" to challenge conditions that exploit them all. Somewhere in the future, Mel King believes, lies a city of hope in "which all the tribes are welcome."[70]

Raising the Ghost of Mother Jones: strikers' families mourn their dead and fight for the living. A protest march at Pittston Coal Group offices, Greenwich, Connecticut, 28 June 1989. Photograph by Elaine Osowski. *Courtesy United Mine Workers of America.*

CHAPTER 9

Planting the Seeds of Resurgence:
The United Mine Workers
Strike Pittston Coal in 1989

During the spring and summer of 1989 I eagerly followed the news of a strike taking place in the far southwestern corner of Virginia, where 1,700 coal miners were fighting to save their union and their way of life. Their walkout against the Pittston Coal Group soon became a kind of last stand for a labor movement battered and bruised ever since the air traffic controllers lost everything in their 1981 strike. I helped form a Boston area strike support committee and participated in a campaign against the Shawmut Bank, whose vice president sat on the Pittston Board of Directors. I learned more about what was at stake when I visited UMWA headquarters in March to make a labor history presentation to the Executive Board. I heard the union president, Richard Trumka, denounce the escalating court fines that threatened to bankrupt the national union, and I listened to Jesse Jackson liken the strikers' moral courage to that of the black freedom riders. Like many others, I felt drawn to the "war zone," where massive civil disobedience was under way, to see what novelist Denise Giardina called the "Appalachian Intifada."[1]

When I arrived at Camp Solidarity the miners in charge told me that at least fifty thousand people had already visited to support the strike. It had become a place for movement pilgrims to camp, to picket, to rally, to disobey judge-made law, and to call upon a higher law that condemned corporate greed. On the way back, I wrote about the visit for an insurgent labor newspaper: "There's a feeling running through Camp Solidarity. It's a 'They're coming for us next' feeling." I camped out near Mike Dunbar, a roof bolter in an Exxon mine in Illinois, who told me how threatened the Virginia state police were when he and his Illinois buddies turned up on the picket lines blocking roads with their trucks. "I don't want this at home," he said. "We've got to stop it here." Buzz Hicks, the president of the local at the Moss 3 treatment plant—which the miners occupied—

put it this way: "We've got people suffering badly here. So let's go ahead and fight the fight here. Let's just have it all out right here while we're at it. Maybe this will show these large companies that we're going to stick together."[2]

Sitting around the fire at Camp Solidarity with miners from my home state of Illinois made me think about how other encampments have marked out people's struggles in our history, like bonfires of solidarity in the national epic of "dog-eat-dog progress." I thought about the many strike encampments in miners' history, like Cabin Creek and Ludlow, that we were showing in a documentary film I helped Barbara Kopple produce for the UMWA's one hundredth anniversary. I thought about the citizen encampments in Washington—about the Bonus Marchers of 1932 whose tent colony was destroyed by the U.S. Army under General Douglas MacArthur, and Resurrection City, which grew up from the Poor People's March after Dr. King was murdered. Camp Solidarity was part of that stream in our history, an encampment where people came together and overcame the fear of facing the future alone.

As I left Camp Solidarity I talked one more time with Buzz Hicks and asked him what it meant that tens of thousands of union workers had made the pilgrimage to the Clinch River Valley. He squinted under the beak of a camouflage cap that said "No Guts, No Glory: UMWA," and said: "We've come to the point where we don't even call it a strike any more. It's a people's movement. We're telling our people, 'Hey, if this thing ends tomorrow, we've got people out there who need our help.' And, he concluded, 'I don't think you'll ever see another situation arise in this country where one labor union will have to stand alone.'"[3] Here was a story to tell of movement history in the making.

When Richard Lewis Trumka became the president of the United Mine Workers of America in 1982 at the age of thirty-eight, he inherited a union with a reputation for "bitter political infighting" and a declining membership. A third-generation coal miner with a law degree and lots of charisma, Trumka wanted to "turn the members' attention to external threats," including the rapid growth of non-union western coal. In 1984 his team negotiated a national contract with the Bituminous Coal Operators Association (BCOA) and won ratification without a national strike for the first time in twenty years.[4]

But soon after signing this contract the UMWA struck against the renegade A. T. Massey, and the union plunged into a bitter struggle that would test Trumka's promise as a leader. Massey refused to sign the new BCOA agreement because it wanted to end payments to the 1950 pension trust fund; it also demanded separate contracts for all of its subsidiaries so that it could trim labor costs to fit each company and free itself of obligations to hire laid-off UMWA members in the new, non-union mines it opened as subsidiaries.

The strike began quietly and then all hell broke loose when Massey hired replacement workers for all 2,500 union miners. War raged along the Tug Fork River on the West Virginia–Kentucky line, recalling the legendary days when Sid Hatfield shot it out with the Baldwin-Felts gunmen at Matewan and when the UMW's armed forces marched up Blair Mountain on the way to liberating Mingo County. Massey spent $200,000 a month on security, including helicopters and an armored personnel carrier; it built miles of chain-link fence as well as cement observation posts occupied by uniformed guards. Scab coal trucks traveled with state police riding shotgun, but only risked running coal during the day. When attacks on the replacement workers began, UMW officials from Washington tried to calm the strikers. With the strike in trouble, Eddie Burke, regional director from Charleston, decided to try a new tactic: civil disobedience. For several weeks in early 1985, "[h]undreds of miners and their family members blocked roads near Massey mines with marches, sit down demonstrations, and parked vehicles, halting production, generating the most favorable publicity to that date, transforming the strike and bringing the company to the bargaining table for the most serious negotiations of the strike."[5]

But the miners' actions also provoked court fines and injunctions that reduced picketing. Organizers dispersed fewer pickets to the mines, and lawyers resolved the strike. The injunctions, coupled with the union's emphasis on legal action, limited "the miners' participation in their own strike." The UMW carried on an impressive corporate campaign including an international boycott crusade, but Massey stuck to its guns. The violent dispute lasted for fifteen months. In December 1985 the National Labor Relations Board finally held that Massey's refusal to bargain as a single employer constituted an unfair labor practice. Trumka took this decision as a sign of victory and called off the strike. The company reduced its royalty payments to the 1950 Pension Fund, and the UMW was forced to accept a labor contract less favorable than the national agreement.[6] The Massey strike taught bitter but powerful lessons to the United Mine Workers, who would be better prepared for the next battle.

Preparing for War at Pittston

In less than two years a similar conflict emerged when the Pittston Coal Group withdrew from the BCOA and stopped paying into the industry-wide health insurance fund for retirees. Pittston's new coal division president, Mike Odum, said he wanted contract concessions, like the ones Massey achieved, because his firm, unlike most BCOA members, needed to compete in international markets. The company intended to shave $5 to $6 a ton from the costs it incurred under the old BCOA agreement.

The new UMWA-BCOA national agreement, signed on 30 January 1988, gained some job security, won a modest 6.8 percent wage increase, and established an unprecedented Education and Training Trust Fund to pay for retraining and educating unemployed miners and their dependents. The rank and file ratified the agreement and again Trumka secured a national agreement without a strike. But Pittston rejected the new pact. The union engaged in some fruitless bargaining with a management team; it was clear Pittston would allow its old contract to expire on 31 January 1988, thus provoking a strike, because the UMW refused to allow members to work without a contract.

Pittston's new management increased salaries for top executives and decided to decrease labor costs. It had already busted the Teamsters union in its Brinks armored-car division and had reduced the union mining force by four thousand.[7] But its executives wanted more. They wanted out of the BCOA agreement and concessions in a new contract that would cut labor and health care costs. The company also aimed to run coal seven days a week and wanted to escape from the costly health care fund.[8]

Trumka had been tracking Pittston's corporate strategy for three years, fearing another Massey strike in which the employer would try to break the UMWA. On 27 January 1988 Pittston confirmed his suspicions when it announced that in the event of a strike permanent replacements would be hired. The union offered to work under an extension of the old contract, but Pittston refused. When the existing agreement expired on January 31 the company ended pension contributions for working miners, eliminated arbitration of disputes, and refused to check off union dues. It also cut off health benefits to 1,500 widows, retirees, and disabled miners.[9]

This last action would become a central moral issue in the strike, arousing deep anger in the coal fields and moral condemnation from the churches, but at the time, it attracted little attention. Eight years had passed since President Reagan broke the air traffic controllers strike and replaced the entire workforce. Since then, organized labor had been bludgeoned with countless demands for concessions justified by the ruthless "bottom line" calculus that seemed to dominate "corporate culture."[10] The new business stars were men like Frank Lorenzo, then locked in a deathly struggle with the unions of Eastern Airlines. Contract strikes seemed not only futile but disastrous. The striking International Paper workers in Jay, Maine, had been replaced by scabs who would then vote to decertify their union. Even the most militant, creative strategies, like those employed by the P-9 local of Hormel packinghouse workers in Austin, Minnesota, ended in a bitter defeat despite a national solidarity effort of heroic proportions.[11]

A strike of a few thousand miners in Appalachia seemed like a sure loser to experts in the coal industry. Pittston was confident that a strike could be isolated, that some of its union employees would cross the line and come back to work, and that the courts would limit pickets and protect replacement workers. Trumka was not about to be provoked into a fatal strike. He "could see the demise of Lewis's union yawning before him, one debilitating strike at a time: First, Massey, now Pittston. If Pittston won, other companies would follow— until his whole union and its cherished national contract unraveled."[12]

Richard Trumka was a new kind of labor leader—the son of a coal miner, he earned a law degree and returned to the mine his father had worked in the little Pennsylvania coal patch known as Nemacolin, where he had grown up hearing stories about scabs and gun thugs, about people being evicted from their houses and living in tent colonies during strikes. When he took some of us around his hometown, he pointed out the Catholic church and said that that was the only place his parents, people of immigrant descent, felt they were on equal footing with the foremen who ran the mine owned by a big steel corporation. Trumka was a passionate speaker and a dramatic storyteller of the old school. He wanted to make the most of the UMW's cherished traditions and habits of solidarity, but he hoped to make them relevant to the new challenges facing his members—still the shock troops of the American labor movement.[13]

He had unified a bitterly divided union and was enormously popular with the members. He believed they would follow him even if he broke with tradition. He decided to keep the Pittston miners on the job, working without a contract. But if the union was going to force Pittston to accept a new contract, it needed a new strategy or it would be Massey all over again. Together with Vice President Cecil Roberts and a remarkably gifted staff, Trumka planned a multifaceted strategy. Since it would be difficult to win the strike on the picket line (though quite possible to lose it there), the union needed a corporate campaign against Pittston to pressure the employer on a national level and, because of the company's export business, on an international scale as well. Unions had been using corporate campaigns and boycotts for some time, but these tactics, though employed expertly in the Massey strike, had not produced a victory. Nor did the corporate campaigns against Hormel and International Paper save those strikers from losing their unions and their jobs.[14]

The brutal concessionary strikes of the eighties convinced Trumka that a total mobilization of members and allies was needed to win. Those union leaders who had not empowered their own members or aroused allies had been isolated and defeated. But militancy was not enough. The Massey strike demonstrated that even aggressive UMWA picket lines could be decimated by court orders and violated by heavily guarded strikebreakers who could become permanent replacements. Trumka knew that unless he was willing to take big risks, defeat would be certain. He drew two lessons from recent movement history. From the eighties he learned that playing by the rules meant defeat for striking unions; and from the sixties he learned that nonviolent movements could mobilize and energize ordinary people and win support from the public and the media. All this pointed toward civil disobedience and legal defiance and building something like a 1960s protest movement around the strike.[15]

Still Trumka, a creative labor lawyer, wanted to use laws when they would help the union. If the UMW struck Pittston over the contract, the courts would regard it as an economic strike (according to the National Labor Relations Act), and, therefore, would allow Pittston to hire permanent replacements for the strikers. With disastrously high unemployment in Appalachia, the company could easily find those replacements, and, if it held out long enough, it could impose a defeat on the UMWA like the one Ronald Reagan inflicted on the air traffic controllers. So union lawyers immediately filed unfair labor practice charges against Pittston with the National Labor Relations Board (NLRB). If the board ruled against the company then, in a strike over unfair labor practices, Pittston would not be allowed to hire replacements permanently. On 23 March 1989 the NLRB agreed to hear the unfair labor practices charge, and the union prepared for a strike.[16]

During the fourteen months Pittston miners worked without a contract, they suffered all kinds of harassment from company managers trying to provoke a strike. The union attempted an inside strategy trying to slow production and pressure Pittston while its members were still on the job. It didn't work. As one of the union organizers recalled, "These coal miners were proud of their work. They were used to working 110 percent and were willing to keep productivity rising. They hated Pittston for cutting off health benefits to their elders and for harassing them in the mines but they just couldn't keep themselves from working full bore and feel good about it."[17]

While the inside strategy bogged down, the union's outside strategy patiently prepared miners and their families for a new kind of strike, a strike the likes of which the UMWA had never seen. In late 1988 and early 1989 the union brain trust grappled with how to avoid a strike like the Massey walkout, which had remained an isolated conflict publicized mainly for its violence. Marty Hudson, an aide to Vice President Cecil Roberts, would be the strike coordinator, with strict orders from the president: "This strike has got to be a strike without violence." Hudson, who had been a picket-line leader at Massey and had watched the violence rage out of control, already knew he had to run this strike differently. Like others involved in the Massey fight, he remembered the good media coverage the strikers had received when they blocked the coal trucks and slowed down operations—that is, before the court injunctions put an end to these tactics.[18] Clearly, the courts would play the same role in the Pittston struggle. Could the union risk defying the courts in an effort to take the moral high ground? Could it win the media over? Could it mobilize the masses of people it would need to keep from losing the strike on the picket line?

Cecil Roberts thought so. Though he was a devoted student of labor history whose family helped make working-class history in West Virginia, he drew on a different history now. He argued that the civil rights movement contained lessons that would help win the impending strike. He had devoured *Parting the Waters,* Taylor Branch's book on Martin Luther King, and carried around a dog-eared copy to staff meetings, where he insisted that everyone read it until they could quote easily from the words of Mahatma Gandhi and Martin Luther King.[19]

One staffer, Gene Carroll, who had worked for the Nuclear Freeze campaign, brought in two peace activists who met with UMW leaders in Washington and told them how civil disobedience could involve entire families and communities, even children and the elderly, and how it could win allies. They talked about ways of occupying offices and blocking roads. On February 18 they conducted a training in Charleston for seventy union field reps from the eastern coal fields. The leaders had to be convinced that civil disobedience would work and that the strikers would not reject it as being "unmanly." Union people were impressed by the training and left to preach the new gospel to the union halls and homes of Pittston's 1,200 miners in southwestern Virginia and several hundred more in West Virginia and Kentucky.[20]

While union staffers and other activists expounded the ideas and tactics of the civil rights and peace movements, others adopted the approaches of the women's movement and community-organizing struggles. The union hired Cosby Totten and Katherine Tompka, who had been underground miners, to organize miners' wives, daughters, and other women in the community to raise consciousness about what was at stake. Together with UMW staff writer Marat Moore they drove hundreds of miles through the coal fields to talk with union members about setting up local women's auxiliaries and then linking them up in district organizations. "They held fund raisers, staged convoys, and established a regular presence at local company headquarters in Lebanon" that started in July of 1988 and lasted for the whole strike. Even before the strike began "the knot of solidarity had been tied."[21]

Pittston's managers wanted a strike, and on 5 April 1989 they got one, but as Cecil Roberts said later, "it wasn't the one they were looking for."[22] On the first day of the strike the battle lines were drawn at McClure mine no. 1, the company's biggest operation. Vance security guards in blue jumpsuits and sunglasses guarded the mine and heard curses rain down on them from the massive crowd of pickets; they were denounced as "gun thugs" like the Baldwin-Felts gunmen who terrorized the Appalachian coal camps in Sid Hatfield's day. Across the road a detail of Virginia state troopers looked on warily at a large group of miners all dressed alike—in camouflage. This uniform had become popular during the Massey strike and it served a useful purpose. During that strike scab truck drivers easily identified people who stoned their rigs by describing their dress. So strikers wore camouflage as their uniform for tactical reasons. But the garb of hunters and soldiers also signified a state of mind, a feeling of solidarity among people ready to wage an all-out war—a war without firearms—to defend their way of life.[23]

From Civil Disobedience to Civil Resistance

The first strike day passed peacefully, but organizers were tense. Pittston's lawyers went to court to stop the mass picketing. On April 12, Donald McGlothin, the circuit court judge for Dickinson and Russell counties, issued his first order limiting pickets to ten. In the meantime individuals took action. Someone shot out a transformer at Lambert Fork, cutting off power to the mine. A scab truck convoy headed for Pittston's Moss 3 coal preparation plant came around a bend in the road and "ran into a barrage of rocks that hit us like a hailstorm," according to one truck driver. "Jackrocks" began turning up on mountain roads, puncturing the tires of coal trucks, Vance security vans, and state police cars. For those unfamiliar with jackrocks, the *Richmond Times Dispatch* explained that these objects, often called "mountain spiders" by miners, were "Nails welded together so they puncture truck tires." "Miniature versions" were "fashioned into ear rings" and were worn proudly by female strike supporters.[24]

It was time to begin nonviolent action in order to maintain discipline and boost morale. The women of the strike moved first. Led by Edna Sauls, president of the Lambert Fork local Ladies Auxiliary, the women who had organized during the previous year decided to occupy the Pittston offices in Lebanon, where they had maintained their tent site and picket for months. On April 18, thirty-seven wives, widows, and daughters of miners confronted a startled receptionist. After a moment of silence, they started singing "We Shall Not Be Moved," the old CIO civil rights song. They expected to be arrested by the police and, in their training they had decided not to cooperate by giving their names: they would all say they were "Daughters of Mother Jones."[25]

The sit-in lasted all night, and the next morning it made headlines across the state. When the women left at 4 P.M., Marty Hudson was delighted. "It let me know what you can do with civil disobedience," he recalled. After this, the women "became the back bone of the strike." Hudson also used their example when talking to the men about the importance of disciplined civil disobedience.[26]

When the women's occupation ended, civil disobedience began on a mass scale. On April 24, three hundred strikers in full camouflage sat down in front of the McClure mine. They locked arms, and when the state police waded in to make arrests, they pulled people apart. There were injuries. James Gibbs, a black coal miner, suffered a broken arm. The actions of the police at McClure angered and even "radicalized" local citizens, according to one reporter. The community mobilization expanded on the following day. To protest the arrests and the brutal treatment by troopers at McClure, a crowd of students from three area high schools walked out of school, and over a hundred of them gathered at Dickinson County courthouse wearing new school uniforms of camouflage. The school superintendent ordered three-day suspensions to those absent without leave.[27]

The next morning nearly five hundred pickets gathered at Pittston's Moss 3 coal preparation plant. Violating Judge McGlothin's order, they sat down in front of a convoy of replacement workers. Again police waded in and hauled off sit-downers as the crowd's anger swelled. John Cox, a district organizer, got on the bullhorn and persuaded people to submit to arrest, keeping a scary moment from exploding into violence. When the crowd started rocking the buses, UMWA District 28 president Jackie Stump ordered them to stop. State police arrested 457 people at Moss 3 that day, including Stump, "whose strong lungs and stern countenance probably prevented a riot that day."[28]

One of the miners told the reporters who had gathered: "They talk about violence and all but look who's getting hurt." The campaign to win hearts and minds to the strikers was in full swing. A few days later the strike made the *New York Times*. It was a short story on the inside pages, but it reported on the seriousness of the strike and it attracted other media to the remote coal fields of southwestern Virginia.[29]

At this moment the union organized its biggest demonstration to celebrate and legitimize this new resistance movement. On April 30, ten thousand people braved a driving rainstorm and crowded onto the Wise County Fair grounds to hear Rev. Jesse Jackson and the strike leaders. Two four-hundred-car caravans arrived from West Virginia and Kentucky. Vehicles were backed up for miles on the roads leading to fair grounds located on an old strip mine. Echoing the themes of his remarkable 1988 presidential campaign, Jackson urged the wet sea of people in forest green to "keep hope alive" even in the hardest times and to unify across all boundaries, including race. When miners went down into the mine every day, and everyone looked alike, workers learned to "live together eight or nine miles underground." If they could do this, he said, "we must learn to live together above ground." Celebrating the fusion of the labor movement and the civil rights movement, Jackson proclaimed: "When we look around today we see the tradition of John L. Lewis and Martin Luther King have come together, and we will not go back." Well aware that civil disobedience had led to so many arrests, Jackson glorified the defiance of unjust laws. He did so not only as a black civil rights leader but as a preacher who could speak in a familiar Baptist idiom to a throng of faithful Christians.[30]

Jackson also stressed the wider significance of the strike. "This is not just your strike; it's the people's strike. Workers everywhere identify with this strike." Trumka picked up on this point, calling Pittston a "turning point for labor" in the United States. He joined Jackson in emphasizing the power of nonviolent protest. It was working. Trumka, in his best stem-winding style, took aim at Democratic governor Gerald Baliles, who had won labor's political support and had then sent state police to occupy the coal fields. Trumka also took pains to distinguish civil disobedience from "civil resistance." The strike involved more than disobeying unjust laws; the strikers were resisting wrongs caused by corporate greed.[31]

They dramatized this by attending the Pittston stockholders meeting on May 10. Union members, who were given small shares of stock, introduced resolutions to embarrass management. One proposal, to allow for secret ballot voting, actually won some support and suggested that some of the Pittston investors might be vulnerable to the union's corporate campaign aimed at Pittston executives in Connecticut and board members around the country.[32]

The union's media message presented the strike as a moral defense of decency and tradition, a struggle for community survival, not for wages. Cutting off benefits became a key issue in the UMWA's public campaign against Pittston. The union made its moral case in a booklet called "Betraying the Trust: The Pittston Company's Drive to Break Appalachia's Coal Field Communities." In 1988 Pittston reported $59 million in profits, yet it was breaking "a delicately forged social pact with the communities" in which it operated just to make more money. Demanding Sunday work and scorning the traditions of a church-going people, it had become just one more "mega corporation with micro vision."[33]

But Trumka knew that the crusade to win the moral high ground would fail if the strikers committed acts of violence. The union's nonviolent strategy would soon be tested. On May 16 Judge McGlothin fined the UMW over $600,000 for violating his order banning mass picketing. He also threatened to add $200,000 for each day it violated his order and $100,000 for rock throwing or other acts of violence. Trumka knew what to do. The UMW might lose its treasury but it wouldn't lose this strike by caving into court orders.[34]

In the Massey strike the union had responded to court orders by limiting mass picketing and ending civil disobedience, but it would not make that mistake now. It mobilized all strikers, their families, and their supporters to challenge judicial rulings. The picket lines were jammed with thousands of people discovering what Richard Couto called "the democratic potential in their own power to say 'No' to corporate power." The actions of April and May involved people who had never been activists but who were now "mesmerized by their newly discovered power to stand up for what they thought was right."[35]

The strikers created a new sense of community in their region. A "culture of solidarity" emerged in the "war zone" as people defended traditional rights with the moral clarity they had learned as evangelical Christians. In these ways, union organizer Marat Moore recalled, people were "harmonically tied to one another." You could feel it, she said, when they sang "Amazing Grace" together as someone was being arrested, or when they sang the old civil rights gospel tune "We Shall Not Be Moved" on the picket line. Standing on the bedrock of their "spiritual commonality," the strikers, overwhelmingly white Virginians, found themselves attracted to the idiom of the black freedom movement. Unpredictably, Jesse Jackson became their spiritual leader.[36]

On May 24, U.S. Judge Glen Williams issued another order to the strikers at the request of the Republican-dominated National Labor Relations Board—an order to stop blocking the Pittston gates and to end a new tactic of impeding coal-field roads with slow-moving vehicles. When the union ignored the order, Williams was incensed. A Republican schooled in the hard-edged politics of southwestern Virginia, the judge called Hudson, Stump, and strike coordinator C. A. Phillips into court to face contempt charges on June 5. When they refused to order their members to stop engaging in civil disobedience and invoked their

Fifth Amendment rights to avoid self-incrimination, Judge Williams sent them off to jail in handcuffs and leg irons. The *Roanoke Times* reported that fines and jailings might not be in Pittston's best interest because the court was creating martyrs, turning the strike into a conflict "like no other in the Virginia coal fields."[37]

Expanding the Strike

It would soon become one of the most unusual strikes in modern history. Ever since the air traffic controllers' strike, labor people had bemoaned the lack of union solidarity that helped employers to isolate and defeat unions. Trumka shared this bitter memory and reflected on it often during the strike. "If we play by their rules," he would often say, "we lose." On June 11 he spoke to a militant rally of fifteen thousand UMW members in Charleston, West Virginia, and called on them to "rise up and fight back."[38]

The next day ten thousand union miners in West Virginia launched a wildcat strike to protest the jailing of the Pittston strike leaders and to show sympathy for the strikers. Mingo and Logan counties, the battlefield in the 1921 civil war, reported 98 percent of the miners on strike. David Evans of Logan County said the workers walked to protest "the excessive fines and the jailings of three union officers down in Virginia. They're going to shut down all the union and non-union mines by the end of next week, . . . whatever it takes to get this settled." Before the week ended the wildcat had spread to six more states involving another twenty thousand miners.[39]

The union now risked even more astronomical court fines; it jeopardized its relations with BCOA members who had just negotiated a new no-strike contract with the UMWA. Trumka told a reporter that he had tried to get the miners to return to work. He said the rank and filers simply refused. "They believe their union is threatened and they walked off their jobs because of that. They genuinely believe the rules are written for them to lose every time."[40]

It was not clear at this point that the UMWA would prevail, but "[i]t had taken a local strike in Southwest Virginia and stirred up a national ruckus." Now the Pittston conflict was big news in the national media. *Forty-eight Hours* had done a segment and one of the strike's most eloquent philosophers, a preacher and retired miner named Harry Whitaker, had appeared on *Donahue*.[41]

At first, civil disobedience seemed mainly a way of ensuring a nonviolent strike, but it became apparent that these tactics also attracted the media. At an early training the peace activists "suggested the union cultivate local heroes, who could personalize the strike for the public so it wouldn't be just another anonymous dispute between the company and the union." The media, struck by the romance of mountain life and culture, locked on to the spectacle of honest, law-abiding rural folk sitting down in front of gigantic coal trucks, kneeling down on a roadside with troopers holding shotguns on them and being carried away to jail by burly policemen.[42]

So far, the union's media campaign was working and Pittston's attempt to make union violence the story line was not impressing most reporters. But the heroics of civil disobedience could easily be overshadowed by violence. And as tense strike confrontations continued during the hot summer months, leaders deepened their efforts to maintain nonviolence. Reporters eagerly searched for evidence of violence, clearly what they expected from coal field strike stories. One story, headlined "A marriage of coal and violence," reported: "Trees are felled across the road. Scab drivers have been beaten up. A coal truck was hit by small arms fire. . . . Somebody fire bombed a mine supervisor's pick up."[43]

The union prohibited alcohol, fire arms, and strangers in picket shacks, and put a picket captain on duty twenty-four hours a day. But disciplined non-violence was a new tactic in Appalachian coal strikes. The miners accepted the new ways only because they believed in their leaders, according to one reporter. On "the picket lines, they say their new style of conducting a strike has perco-lated down from the union president Richard Trumka" who "has brought them a sense of dignity and pride not felt since the glory days of union founder John L. Lewis." One striker put it this way: "We have a smart man at the head of this organization. I have faith in him. All of us do." His ideas won two national agreements, so "you have to believe this is the way to go. If that means non-violent civil disobedience, that's it." The union's strategy seemed to work not only in the media but in the effort to cut Pittston's production. At a Logan County court hearing, a district judge referred to the strikers' "highly sophisti-cated effort to peacefully prohibit trucks" from driving up Pittston's mine road at Slab Fork. A company lawyer replied that the effort was "admittedly peaceful, albeit no less disruptive."[44]

Eddie Burke looked back on this period in June as a time when "crisis" was defused. The month began with Pittston breaking off negotiations, strike lead-ers jailed, the coal field occupied by state police, and another Massey strike on people's minds, but "it ended with the entire labor movement rallying behind the UMW" and hurting Pittston as a result.[45]

The wildcat strikes affected those operators who were supplying or could supply Pittston's overseas customers with metallurgical coal. A Wall Street in-vestment firm's report expressed surprise that the UMW, thought to be weak-ened during the eighties, had fought Pittston to a standstill in two months. "After more than 2200 arrests and $3 million in fines for civil disobedience, the UMW's perseverance is starting to pay off where it counts most—in the financial community which could pressure Pittston to compromise." In June, with coal producers worrying out loud about a long strike, Federal Judge Williams got the two sides back to resume negotiations. For the first time, the top people came from both sides, but they refused to sit at the same table. A mediator took messages between labor and management in separate rooms.[46]

Building a Movement

As wildcat strikes rolled across the midwestern coal fields, imprisoned strike leaders Hudson, Stump, and Phillips were released. The judge who set them free made them promise not to advocate illegal strike tactics. So the heroes of the strike could no longer lead the civil resistance movement. A leadership vacuum yawned in the strike zone. It was soon filled by Cecil Roberts, the UMWA's national vice president, who came down from Washington to direct field operations. Normally, top union officers did not run strikes, but Roberts was different, and so was the Pittston strike.

Born in Cabin Creek, West Virginia, Roberts played basketball in the high school that produced Jerry West and went into the mines like his father. He grew up hearing stories about Mother Jones sitting on his grandparents' front porch when she came to defend the miners in Cabin Creek against the Baldwin-Felts gun thugs who were shooting up the strikers' tent colony in 1912. His great-uncle Bill Blizzard had commanded the union miners' army in 1921 as it marched up from the creeks to Blair Mountain on its way to freeing Mingo County from the coal operators' totalitarian grip. And Roberts's father recalled an unforgettable moment in his boyhood, seeing airplanes rented by the operators dropping bombs on the miners' army.[47] The younger Roberts entered the mines when the UMWA was being reformed and southern West Virginia was a raging storm center of wildcat strike activity. He quickly became a union leader and crack negotiator, but he never forgot his roots. In 1989 he was one of the few national labor officials who used the words "working class" and "class war."[48]

Cecil Roberts arrived in the nick of time, because the "class war" he came to lead in southwestern Virginia was on the brink of violence. "The strikers weren't losing their resolve but some were starting to lose their patience." The UMW vice president took on the difficult task of escalating militancy while keeping the strike activity nonviolent. He constantly told the strikers they were part of something much bigger than a strike against Pittston and a fight with scabs. Like Trumka, he made the whole legal system an issue. In Norton, Virginia, Roberts declared: "It's the system that's really at issue here as much as the contract. The country desperately needs labor law reform that will at least level the playing field."[49]

Roberts boldly defended the strikers' direct action tactics. Wildcat strikers poured into the area from the other coal fields and escalated the "rolling road blocks," which cut the haul to the Moss 3 prep plant by one-third. Speaking to a crowd of three thousand, including many wildcatting midwestern miners, Roberts stood on the bed of a flatbed truck, looked out over a muddy field at the men and women in fatigues, and said: "It's not just a strike any more, it's a movement. Everybody has been wanting to rally around something for years and this is it."[50]

At a big Fourth of July rally, the union introduced the last union leader to have aroused the labor movement and the national conscience. Joining the hundreds who now came to be arrested on the region's back roads, Cesar Chavez exclaimed that with nonviolence, social struggle took on a transcendent, spiritual dimension. "Your commitment to non-violence and the use of passive resistance has captured the attention of organized labor," he declared. "People are attracted to non-violence. They want to come and help you. If the judge likes to put people in jail, let him. He can't put the whole world in jail."[51]

On July 5, Judge Williams, who had already fined Roberts $200,000 for refusing to take responsibility for the road-blocking effort, added another $800,000 to the union's fines, which, it was now apparent, threatened to bankrupt the UMWA. The judge blamed Roberts and UMW leaders for threatening the legal system and creating a situation "bordering on anarchy." On his orders federal marshals were dispatched to aid state police in enforcing court injunctions. As Roberts said, the courts were threatening to fine the union out of existence because members refused to give up their jobs to other men. But the resistance grew. The *Richmond Times-Dispatch* reported that UMW strike supporters who said they were "tourists" clogged the region's coal-hauling roads with their cars, "defying federal court orders against the practice and subjecting the union to $500,000 in daily penalties."[52]

By now the union's stakes in the Pittston strike were enormous. The UMW had risked everything on the outcome, including its actual survival. Federal court fines against the union reached $960,000, which, when combined with state court fines, equaled a total of $4 million. Still, the union's leaders did not waver. As Trumka later said, "we did what we thought we had to do to win the strike." On July 9 he spoke in Charleston and said he was willing to go to jail. "They've done everything they can to me except take away my personal freedom. . . . It's win this fight or be stampeded to death in the very near future." If the fight bankrupted the union, then so be it, Trumka declared. "If we aren't successful," he added, "if justice and legal redress are totally denied here, I submit to you that from the crumbled blocks will arise a movement" just as it had in the past when the UMW faced hard times and had no money. Money did not make a movement. "They can take every dime we got, but we still got the people," said James Hicks, president of the Moss 3 UMW local. "They can take the money out of our pocket but they can't take the union out of our hearts."[53]

At this point, 2,265 felony charges had been filed against strikers and their supporters, many of them out-of-state sympathy strikers. The arrest of law-abiding citizens for blocking traffic aroused special concern. Some had to post $10,000 bonds for minor violations and others were forced to sit in hot buses for long periods of time. Cecil Roberts protested: "I guess you would have to go to China to see it happen, something like this." The most sensational case came on July 12 when police arrested Sister Bernadette Kenney for impeding traffic. She was a nurse driving a mobile unit for dispensing medication. Sister Kenney's arrest received national publicity and aroused even greater religious involvement in the strike.[54]

The incident added moral weight to the union's charge that Governor Baliles had sent one-fourth of the state police to "occupy southwestern Virginia." One of the most photographed picket signs, nailed to a shack outside Moss 3, read: "Governor Baliles! This is South Virginia not South Africa!" The Governor had won the region's traditionally Democratic vote with the support of the UMWA, but according to one report, "Sentiments have run so high against Baliles in the coal fields that the governor has canceled at least one visit" and made no plans to tour the strike zone. A frustrated Baliles wrote to Pittston's CEO, Paul Douglas, expressing disappointment over the failure to bargain and asking for a return to the table because the strike was hurting the growing foreign market for Virginia coal. Trumka joined Senator Jay Rockefeller in a New York meeting with Japanese steel officials to assure them that the West Virginia coal supply was not in jeopardy.[55]

"The nation's worst coal strike since the mid-1970s arrives at a cross roads," the *Journal of Commerce* observed on July 10. "The great majority of the coal hauling" had reportedly ceased in West Virginia, where one company laid off ten drivers who refused to cross picket lines. At this point, the Pittston strike had become even more than a survival struggle for the UMWA, even more than a national test for the labor movement. Sympathy strikes and massive civil resistance helped accomplish what Roberts and Trumka had hoped: making a local strike into a national cause. Labor union members had never seen such bold action on the part of national leaders. Organized support for Pittston strikers reached a level not seen since the farmworkers' boycott of the sixties. Many activists simply felt drawn to the war zone. They wanted to be arrested for the cause, to bear witness for justice and against corporate greed. All through July, reported the *Washington Post,* "Miners and their supporters from around the country continue[d] to pour into Camp Solidarity, the strike's makeshift headquarters in a lush meadow outside Castlewood, Virginia."[56]

To accommodate the wildcat strikers motoring into the region, the union opened a ten-acre parcel of land in Carterton Hollow on the Clinch River owned by a former UMW member who ran a summer camp there. While the wildcat strikers rolled into the camp with convoys hundreds of cars long, other unions began sending delegations from all over the country. The strikers, emotionally drained from their confrontations with scabs and police, at first seemed overwhelmed by the flood of visitors who needed a place to eat and sleep. Seeing "people from all over the country with different accents and different license plates, gave the miners and their families renewed determination." "This strike could really be depressing, but our people have been brought together like never before because of the spirit that comes from what goes on in the camp," said Peggy Dutton, the spouse of a striking miner. "Here is where we laugh, we talk, we love one another. It's a place where we demonstrate how much we care about one another—not just the families on strike at Pittston but all working people."[57]

The women of the strike rose to the challenge and spent every day at camp cooking for the pilgrims. "They spent their own money to come here and help us," organizer Cosby Totten recalled. "Could we let them down?" The women had already been mobilized by the auxiliaries and the Daughters of Mother Jones to feed and care for the local strikers at the Binns-Counts Community Center. The Daughters began "as a traditional UMW women's auxiliary and 'just caught on fire,'" one journalist reported.[58] For months a core group of women prepared for the strike as a struggle for community survival. Linda Addair, a hairdresser in St. Paul who gave up her business and devoted all her time to the strike, explained that the Daughters wanted to avoid slipping back into the "powerlessness" that "ruined the lives" of their grandparents—into what she called "the days of slavery." Like the Ladies Auxiliary in the Flint sit-down strike of 1937 that transformed itself into an emergency brigade, the Daughters "helped transform the strike into a movement of wider dimensions."[59]

Despite all they seemed to have in common, these women did not know each other, because they lived in isolated rural areas. The Daughters brought them together. Being arrested gave them a common experience—and became "a badge of honor," according to Marat Moore—just as wearing camouflage outfits gave them a common uniform. Outsiders found it odd to see strikers dressed in uniforms often worn by right-wing, paramilitary men, but the women of the strike gave their battle colors a new meaning. They wove the colors worn by hunters into quilts, umbrellas, and baby clothes. Camouflage was no longer "simply military or simply male."[60]

The Daughters overcome the isolation of women in mining families, and emerged as highly regarded public activists, like women's auxiliaries had in past strikes. But they did not act on their own advice or "command their own ship" as the militant Women's Auxiliary did in the 1983 Arizona copper miners strike, when the women needed to take leadership of the struggle.[61] Still, when the filmmaker Barbara Kopple and I interviewed Daughters after the strike, they often said that the struggle had changed their lives. They spoke like Anna O'Leary, who explained to Barbara Kingsolver how the Arizona mine strike affected her. "The strike has completely remolded my mind," she said. "I was handed a golden opportunity and I jumped at it." O'Leary realized that people had been working for years to explose the "wrongfulness of the government" when it sided over and over with big corporations. It meant being part of a "world movement" and it was "hard work, but it was worth it." She said she grew from the experience and was "no longer afraid of the future."[62]

The Daughters of Mother Jones helped make the strike what Linda Addair called "a people's movement," and they made Camp Solidarity "the heart of the strike," a point of communion for the strikers and the thousands of supporters who visited during the summer. Camping together on the Clinch River gave them all something to remember, a taste of movement culture from the past, in the present. "On summer evenings, as the heat soaked into the hills, the smell of burning charcoal and the twang of banjos drifted across the wide field," wrote Roanoke reporter Dwayne Yancey. "Kids chased a stray dog named Jackrock. A garbage bag effigy of Judge Williams swung from a branch. An Alabama coal miner brought his bride on their honeymoon," "It was like a hillbilly Woodstock," Eddie Burke remembered. By midsummer, forty thousand people had already visited the camp. Not since the mass strikes of the early 1930s had so many allies participated in direct strike support.[63]

Politicizing the Strike

Although the Pittston strike took place in an isolated part of Appalachia, its leaders put the struggle into an international as well as a national context. They compared the cause to that of workers striking for democracy in South Africa, Poland, and the USSR. They even likened their struggle to the prodemocracy movement in China, which generated intense interest when the army massacred protestors in Beijing's Tienanmen Square early in June. By bringing international attention to violations of labor law, the union hoped to embarrass the Bush administration, which claimed to support the Chinese students, the Soviet coal miners, and the Polish Solidarity movement, even as it opposed trade union rights at home. Trumka often pointed out that only two countries with serious labor laws allowed employers to replace striking workers, the United States and South Africa. It was a "cruel hoax" to tell workers they had the right to strike, and when they did, to replace them.[64]

Trumka believed that U.S. unions had failed to use international labor organizations effectively. He asked staff lawyers to file charges with the International Labor Organization against the U.S. government for failing to prosecute labor law violations during the Pittston strike. The UMW already been more involved in international solidarity work than most unions, especially in South Africa. Trumka wanted to build on this work. In July he addressed an international labor conference to "tell the miners' story" and promote "global labor solidarity." Heads of unions from Belgium and Switzerland pledged their help. The International Confederation of Free Trade Unions had already organized unprecedented support for the strike abroad.[65] Trumka and his staff began laying the groundwork for an ICFTU inspection of the strike zone to heighten pressure on the Bush administration.

For three months, pressuring the political system had seemed totally ineffective. Then, on July 11 the NLRB found Pittston guilty of unfair labor practices. The company had violated federal labor law twenty-eight times and was "failing and refusing to bargain in good faith." The board's ruling made the walkout an "unfair labor practices strike" and thus prohibited Pittston from offering permanent jobs to the strikebreakers.[66] This decision eliminated a key element of Pittston's strikebreaking strategy and aided the union's national campaign against the use of replacements for striking workers. The House subcommittee responsible for labor law began an investigation of the union's charges that workers' rights were being abused in the Virginia strike.[67]

And so the union gained in its effort to make labor-law reform and court bias a national issue. Its leaders also hoped to increase national concern over the health care issue. When Pittston cut off health benefits to retirees, it caused the most publicized of the many health-care-related strikes. It also gave the union a chance to take the moral high ground, and its leaders pressed the advantage in Washington. Senator Jay Rockefeller introduced a bill that would force Pittston to contribute to industry-wide health funds. Later in the summer the *New York Times* focused on the strike and featured health care as an emerging crisis, especially in labor relations.[68]

Whatever long-term hopes the strike inspired, the short-term costs reached intimidating levels. Pittston's lawyers presented Judge McGlothin with new evidence that strikers were violating his orders, and on July 27 he fined the union another $4.5 million—one hundred times what Pittston had been fined after the 1983 explosion that killed seven miners at McClure. In early August the UMW announced it was spending $4 million each month on strike support (while taking in about $500,000 per month from miners not on strike).[69]

In response to a request by Federal Judge Glen Williams, strike talks resumed August 6, but again the two sides met in separate rooms. The union offered a new proposal to discuss more flexible hours but the company stood on its last offer. Chief union negotiator Roberts emerged "disappointed and disillusioned," and *Coal Outlook* worried about the threat of a national strike.[70]

The union's resistance took on a more defiant time. In August, Cecil Roberts directly challenged court authority, daring Judge Williams to jail him. This made news all over coal fields. On August 21, as he came to appear before the federal judge, Roberts gave a rousing speech before six hundred people gathered at the courthouse. "I don't fear going to jail because when you're right, going to jail is okay. There's no use in him trying to say: 'Mr. Roberts, you're leaving here . . . and that's my order.' He might as well put me in jail because I ain't going back. Regardless of what happens today, you keep your heads up, keep your hearts beating like they've been beating and stay on fire for this cause because this is a class struggle between the working class and the very rich."[71]

Roberts's confident words and bold actions stiffened the strikers' resolve. During the weeks he had been in command, Roberts seemed as moved by the strikers' courage as they were by his eloquence. "I've never felt this way about any group of people in my entire life. I think you are the finest group of people in the entire world. The solidarity movement in Poland has nothing on you people here today," he declared before facing the court. The affection and admiration was returned. Strikers told the media that if they put Cecil Roberts in jail, the protests would be violent. Judge Williams shrunk before Roberts's challenge and dismissed the charges.[72]

Defiance of state and federal courts politicized the strike. Roberts often said that if the civil rights movement could successfully defy unjust segregation laws in the 1960s then the labor movement could defy unjust labor laws in the 1980s. In a more traditional way, the strike provoked political anger at incumbent Democratic officeholders, especially Governor Baliles, who was responsible for deploying state police against the strikers. Citizens were angered because the state police had arrested so many people, including many nonstrikers. One merchant erected a sign: "We respectfully refuse to serve troopers during the course of the strike." The House subcommittee found that the use of so many state police along with the federal marshals created "a sense that the coal fields are occupied by a massive security force from outside the . . . region."[73] The Dickinson County sheriff even criticized the governor's use of state troopers and complained about "unofficial martial law." A *Washington Post* headline on August 6 read: "Coal Miners' Discontent Gets Political–Organized Labor Is Boiling with Outrage at Democratic Governor."[74]

Governor Baliles's role in the strike exacerbated union hostility to conservative Democrats; that had been building for a decade because elected officials who received generous support from unions often forgot their commitments to organized labor. Although the union had endorsed the Democratic ticket in 1988, Cecil Roberts had supported Jesse Jackson, and many staffers now favored forming a labor party. As the fall political campaigns began, strikers wanted to take political action. They were angry that the incumbent representative to the Virginia House of Delegates from Buchanan County stood unopposed. Don McGlothin Sr. had over two decades of seniority in the House and had consistently delivered for his constituents, but he was the father of the judge who had fined the union $31 million during the strike. Trumka wanted a union leader to run against the elder McGlothin. Jackie Stump reluctantly agreed, announcing his candidacy on September 18 at the John L. Lewis Building in Oakwood.[75] No one thought Stump had a chance of upsetting a powerful incumbent like McGlothin with a last-minute write-in campaign. Still, the strike movement had shaken up politics as usual in this corner of Virginia.

"Stirring Up the Labor Movement"

The union exerted surprising pressure on Pittston in the coal fields but it could not win the strike on the picket line, at the ballot box, or in the courts. It had cut into the company's sales and profits. Trumka even convinced Australia's mine workers union to prevent their employers from serving Pittston's Japanese customers. Still, the company seemed willing to lose millions to break the union. To crack Pittston the union would need to punish the company's directors and investors with a corporate campaign.

When the strike began, the union initiated an intense campaign against the company at its headquarters in Greenwich, Connecticut, and in other cities where members of its board of directors lived. The union hired Pat Spear to run its campaign in Greenwich. A devout Catholic and community organizer involved in the Campaign for Human Development in Appalachia, Spear mobilized the religious community in Connecticut against Pittston. In late June 12 local clergy sent a letter to Douglas protesting the company's emphasis on union violence and boldly suggesting that he was "like the Pharaoh," who enslaved people and wondered why a pestilence stalked his land. The company dismissed the letter as "absolutely ridiculous." It was harder to dismiss another letter, signed by eighty-six area clergy, condemning Pittston's cut-off of health benefits (it was "not the will of God . . . that . . . persons should be used this way") and calling for a fair contract.[76]

The strikers and their supporters haunted the Pittston executives in Greenwich. "When they went to church, some heard sermons from their priests and ministers against their company," wrote one reporter. "When they commuted to and from work, they ran into strikers passing out leaflets." The minister of the Methodist Church in Greenwich weighed the moral campaign's effect. "I think it jarred the Pittston Company people [who] just kind of assumed this would be a safe haven from the strike. There was just no escape. They just couldn't get away from it."[77]

The union also pressured the board of directors. Along with investors and lenders they were principal targets of the corporate campaign headed by Ken Zinn, who came to Boston in April to begin a campaign against board member William Craig, a vice president of Shawmut Bank. Craig was a good target because his bank had extensive dealings with the public, including unions and city governments. A strike support committee formed to carry on the campaign. The warring labor factions in Massachusetts buried their hatchets, not deeply, but long enough to unify behind the strikers.[78]

On July 12 our Boston area strike support committee invited Trumka to visit the city. He spoke at a spirited union rally we organized at the Shawmut's downtown bank and testified before the Boston city council urging that municipal funds be withdrawn from the bank unless Craig agreed to work for a settlement. On July 26 the city council passed a resolution to remove the city's $20 million from Shawmut Bank because of Craig's links to Pittston and his refusal to work for a settlement. The resolution passed unanimously and made headlines. Boston mayor Ray Flynn was sympathetic to the strikers, so much so that he had visited the coal fields and made a controversial statement comparing the use of state police in Virginia to their use against Solidarity in Poland. Encouraged by these developments, the support committee put added pressure on Craig, picketing his home and encouraging the cities of Somerville and Cam-

Stirring up the labor movement: Mine Workers' President Richard Trumka at a Pittston strike rally, Boston, 1989. *Photograph © Randy H. Goodman '89.*

bridge, along with several unions, to withdraw their funds from the Shawmut Bank. Within a few weeks, $280 million had been withdrawn and the political phase of the corporate campaign began to take its toll on one of Pittston's directors. Meanwhile, the pressure mounted against Shawmut's subsidiary in Connecticut when several unions announced major withdrawals to protest Craig's connection with that bank. The union also pressured the firms of other board members, and some parent companies reportedly complained that Pittston's hard-nosed tactics were hurting them and "stirring up the labor movement."[79]

The UMW's willingness to risk everything in a final confrontation aroused deep sympathy in frustrated labor ranks. Trumka received boisterous responses wherever he spoke, often in tandem with Jesse Jackson. He called upon "people across the country to visit southwest Virginia and see 'a system that doesn't have room for workers in it.'" National AFL-CIO leaders, who had been hoping the UMWA would reaffiliate, saw the groundswell of support for Pittston strikers and for the use of civil disobedience. They also recognized that their affiliates and major media organs like the *Washington Post* had come to see the Pittston strike as a last stand for the UMWA and even for the labor movement itself. On August 30, just before Labor Day, Trumka invited eighteen national labor leaders to join him in blocking the Dickinson County courthouse in an act of civil disobedience. AFL-CIO President Lane Kirkland and Secretary Treasurer

Thomas Donahue, joined the demonstration while a crowd of over one thousand miners and supporters cheered. Trumka and Roberts were convinced, after studying Martin Luther King's example, that a civil resistance strategy would work only if rank-and-file activists knew that their leaders would also disobey unjust laws and take the penalties.[80]

No one could recall any previous example of top union officials engaging in civil disobedience. The arrests received national press coverage and attracted even more union support for the strikers who after five months remained united. Pittston continued to take a beating in the press from politicians like Senator Rockefeller, who demanded government prosecution of Pittston for unfair labor practices. But as the summer waned, a settlement still seemed remote, and with court fines still mounting, some experts began to doubt the UMWA's chances for victory or even for survival.

The strike had become a "cause celebre of organized labor" but it now attracted a lot less attention than it had when tens of thousands of miners wild-catted earlier in the summer. "[T]he strike is bogged down," the L.A. *Times* reported, "attracting few headlines outside the coal country." The Pittston miners now stood in isolation, "clustering in wooden shacks they built at each Pittston mine entrance," the article continued. The arrest of Lane Kirkland and other labor leaders appeared to be a "desperate" attempt to keep the issue alive. Predicting yet another defeat for labor, economist Leo Troy said the UMW would have to accept a settlement on management's terms. The union might invoke its glorious history and its moral appeal to solidarity, but this was the 1980s in the United States. The miners, Troy declared, were "looking at a history that isn't going to repeat itself."[81]

Indeed, even after mobilizing an entire region, creating a powerful resistance movement, and hurting Pittston's production, the union seemed no closer to reaching an agreement. The union needed to do something to keep the pressure on Pittston and to strengthen morale. At this critical juncture strike leaders made a bold plan to seize and occupy Pittston's Moss 3 treatment plant near Carbo, the site of the biggest resistance actions.

Eddie Burke, who organized the operation, had studied labor history and knew what the sit-down strikers of the 1930s had accomplished. Burke and three team leaders spent nearly a month in secret meetings on the plan code named Operation Flintstone after the UAW occupation of the Fisher Body plant in Flint, Michigan, in 1937. The action was organized in military fashion, and on September 16, ninety-nine carefully chosen miners and one clergyman, Jim Sessions, gathered at Camp Sol to receive their secret orders. The groups arrived at Moss 3 on schedule, and Burke led his team through the gate toward the huge six-story structure as the supporters cheered from the road. Worried sick about the possibility of gunfire, Burke shouted over his bullhorn that the group was peaceful and unarmed, and, rather audaciously, that they were Pittston stockholders coming to inspect their property.[82]

Committing acts of civil resistance: Mine Workers' leader Cecil Roberts confronts Virginia state troopers during a sit-in at Pittston's Moss 3 coal treatment plant. Photograph by Ilana Storace. *Courtesy United Mine Workers of America.*

Surprisingly, only three state troopers were in the area. Only two Vance men guarded the plant; they fled quickly. The occupiers clambered up the stairs of the huge facility and in twenty minutes they had locked themselves in the control room. Cecil Roberts assumed command of the crowd outside the plant. He asked them to stay all night to protect the sit-downers inside. As squadrons of police cars poured in through back roads and lit up the night sky in eerie blue, tension grew within the mass of pickets. When would the troopers evict the protestors in the plant? If they tried, could the crowd of supporters stop them?

On the second day of the occupation miners waved cheerily from the plant catwalks and settled down inside, amazed that the police remained at a distance. While the company sought an injunction to end an illegal seizure of private property, the group of one hundred rigged up makeshift showers and set up dormitories in the processing plant. Pittston's Mike Odum denounced this "latest act of violence by the union" and labeled those who occupied his plant "common terrorists." On the third day federal marshalls arrived with subpoenas for Cecil Roberts and Eddie Burke and on the fourth day of the sit-in, Judge Williams gave the sit-downers twenty-four hours to "walk out honorably"—a remarkable concession to the rising mood of popular anger against judicial retribution. If they did not accept this offer of amnesty, the union would be fined $600,000 a day and the union leaders would face jail sentences. Meanwhile, state police made plans to storm the plant. Roberts met with the men inside and said there was an immediate possibility of a police attack on the plant and that they should probably leave. Judge Williams's deadline passed and then the men came out at 9 P.M. cheered wildly by the big throng that had gathered to protect them.[83]

The plant occupation energized the strike community and retied the knot of solidarity, but the national media downplayed the event. The action had not delivered the knockout blow to Pittston, but it had let the company know that the union was still willing and able to strike anywhere at any time without worrying about legal constraints.[84]

Signs of Hope

As the Appalachian hills turned brilliant colors in October, a few signs of hope appeared. On October 2 a bipartisan group of senators introduced a bill to take health benefits to retirees off the table. Two days later the Senate Finance Committee endorsed the plan to salvage two debt-ridden health funds that cover 161,000 retired miners. The plan would be attached to the budget bill as a strategy to ensure it quick passage.[85]

On October 12 a delegation of international labor leaders met with Labor Secretary Elizabeth Dole in Washington and then left for the coal fields. The group, which included a Solidarity member newly elected to Poland's Senate, denounced Pittston's violations of labor law and promised to file a complaint with the International Labor Organization and to work through the International Confederation of Free Trade Unions to discourage Pittston's customers and allied suppliers.[86]

On the day the international delegation visited, Dole announced that she would go to the coal fields herself. On October 14 she convened a first meeting, attended by both Trumka and Douglas, and announced she would soon appoint a supermediator to put federal pressure on the parties to settle. She characterized her tour of the coal fields as "emotionally wrenching." "I saw families against families, brothers against brothers. This is tearing entire communities apart." Dole's comments seemed newsworthy if only because they represented the most sympathetic words unions had heard from a federal official in nearly nine years. In a few days Dole appointed William Usery as her supermediator. He had worked for both Republicans and Democrats, had once been a top official with the machinists, and had "earned a reputation as one of the nation's top labor dispute trouble shooters." If anyone could wrench an agreement out of the warring adversaries, Bill Usery could. But he soon found this strike one of his toughest assignments. The parties, he said, found themselves stuck in a "deep hole full of animosity."[87]

On October 20 the union's campaign against Pittston board members scored a victory when William Craig announced in Boston that he would resign as a vice president of the Shawmut Bank. Craig's resignation marked a turning point. "It sent a very strong message to the board of directors that there was a personal cost" to the strike, said campaign director Ken Zinn. "What we did in this campaign was to take the coal mines to him in Boston and it cost him. Investors must have been wondering about the costs of the strike too. Pittston's income had fallen by 79 percent in the third quarter, from $14.7 million to $3.1 million. Six weeks later the UMW won a suit against Pittston when a federal district judge ruled that the company had violated securities regulations by voting proxies against three proposals submitted by striking miners at the annual stockholders meeting in May.[89]

By now Jackie Stump's write-in election campaign against State Representative Don McGlothin was causing some excitement in the strike zone. The mobilization for civil resistance had been redirected into the campaign just at a time—"crunch time," Trumka later called it—when the strike strategists had exercised nearly all their tactical options. "People told me they'd gotten four phone calls prior to the election," a McGlothin supporter said with amazement. It was one of the best orchestrated campaigns he had ever seen.[90] All of the movement-building energy that Cecil Roberts and his zealous followers had generated in the spring and summer now powered Stump's insurgent campaign. It was the clearest expression of how political the strike had become.

Campaign manager Eddie Burke was shocked when his phone banks reported that 75 percent of the people who called said they would vote for the strike leader. On November 7 Stump won every precinct except the incumbent's home town. "It was a landslide beyond anyone's imagination: Stump 7,981; McGlothin 3,812," wrote an observer. As Stump said to a rally of supporters: "The work has just started because now people throughout the United States have realized that if the politicians that are supposed to help working people don't help working people then we can take them out of office."[91]

Two days later, after news of Stump's election "hit like a storm," contract talks reopened in the Washington area, with Cecil Roberts and Joseph Farrell heading the union and company teams. William Usery, now presiding, began by declaring a news blackout for both sides and insisting on a cease fire in the war zone. The mass picketing and road blocking ended. No trucks were stoned. Most of the state troopers left and nearly all of the hated Vance security guards departed.[92]

Now time seemed to be on the union's side. In November a UPI story predicted that Pittston could lose up to $60 million by the end of the year. One expert said: "Douglas believed the law would take care of everything," but "Pittston apparently misread how fast the courts could move and also underestimated the union's resolve. . . ." UMW officials and the other union leaders had "targeted the Pittston strike as a place to take a stand" and now that they had forced government intervention, the corporation could not expect "a clear-cut victory."[93]

After a week of intensive negotiations that lasted late into the evenings, Usery declared a week's suspension to talk independently with both sides. When the parties returned, a more cooperative atmosphere developed. After eight months on strike and great financial losses on both sides, the parties realized that this might be their last chance to settle and avoid a struggle to the death. The sticking point still seemed to be Pittston's withdrawal from the health care fund. When Usery talked to Elizabeth Dole she said that the government might be able to look into the problem, and this possibility opened up new progress in the talks. Usery set a Christmas deadline to create a sense of urgency, and Trumka joined the talks, a sign of progress.[94]

As Christmas in the coal fields approached, union caravans arrived bringing toys and clothes to the strikers and their families. But the holiday was a somber one. People in the strike zone still endured the hatreds stirred up by the strike. Judge McGlothin, perhaps angered by his father's stunning defeat by Jackie Stump, handed out $33.4 million more in fines in the eighth, ninth, and tenth rounds of criminal contempt hearings and called UMWA members "thugs" and "terrorists." A spokesman for Usery criticized these fines and said they might hurt negotiations.[95]

After a Christmas break the parties reconvened in the Capitol Hilton, and on New Year's Eve, just before midnight Trumka and Roberts reached across the table and shook hands with their enemies, Douglas and Farrell. On New Year's Day 1990 the union and company announced a tentative agreement. Trumka, "who had staked his reputation and the future of the union on the strike's outcome, called the settlement a victory for the entire labor movement." The miners appeared to "score a major victory," *U.S. News* said, "leaving the company with relatively meager gains won only at great expense."[96]

Other reporters saw losses for both sides in that the proposal gave Pittston some of the flexibility it wanted in work rules so it could become more competitive in the international market. The company got fewer work-rule changes than it wanted but it did gain two alternatives to the conventional eight-hour, five-day week and it could now run coal twenty-four hours a day except Sunday during the day. The company agreed to maintain the 100 percent health care coverage the union demanded. On the difficult issue of the trust funds, the company offered to pay $10 million into the funds that covered those who retired before 1976 if it could then drop out. To address the long-term problems of the troubled funds, Secretary Dole agreed to appoint a commission, chaired by Usery, to explore other solutions. On the critical union issue of job security, Pittston and its subcontractors agreed to hire union miners instead of non-union ones. Laid-off union miners would be hired for the first four of every five job openings at Pittston's non-union mines, and subcontractors would provide the first nineteen of every twenty jobs to these miners. It also agreed to limit but not end transfers of coal reserves from union to non-union subsidiaries.[97]

Union leaders intensively discussed the contract proposal with strikers, and on February 20 the Pittston miners ratified it by a 60 percent margin. Trumka announced the results at the AFL-CIO meetings in Florida, and celebration erupted. "One line of labor leaders after another at meetings in Bal Habor said they saw the accord as a break in the long decline of trade union membership." Critics of the labor establishment also saw the strike as a victory and turning point for labor.[98]

Trumka, who knew the strike's costs, said the results were "bittersweet." There had been great suffering, hard feelings, millions of dollars lost along with the jobs of a few union miners. But the UMWA had been saved. And the union had rallied the rest of the labor movement to take a stand at Pittston. He also believed the United Mine Workers had convinced the public that it spoke "for the working people of America." Few labor leaders in the modern era could have made such a claim.[99]

Trumka hoped the Pittston conflict would produce a movement to reform federal labor law. Many who participated in the strike also hoped the movement-building seeds planted in southwest Virginia would grow in other places and generate a revival of the whole labor movement. Participants, supporters, and observers all found much to admire in the strike: the bold, risk-taking leadership of Trumka and Roberts, the solidarity of the mass pickets, the adoption of nonviolent resistance tactics from the civil rights movement, the bold creativity of the Moss 3 sit-down and the Stump write-in campaign, the activity of the women and high school students, the spirit of Camp Solidarity. All of these examples were lessons to bring home, lessons that seemed especially heroic because of the unique context in which they were learned.

It is impossible to recreate the mood of anger and passion the Pittston strike aroused in union labor across the land in 1989. It unleashed a pent-up response to nearly a decade of antiworker Republican rule and even more years of anti-union aggression by employers. It also reversed a trend in which labor union leaders had been tried and found wanting in their leadership of strikes against concessions. Local groups of strikers from Arizona to Minnesota, from Maine to California felt abandoned and betrayed by the national union officials. These struggles had bitterly divided the house of labor and created a sense of dismay almost as destructive as the distress created by union busting bosses. National leaders seemed unable or unwilling to recognize the powerful "cultures of solidarity" that blossomed during these local strikes. Instead of nurturing and supporting such local mobilizations, national officers resorted to legal strategies that never seemed as effective as mass mobilizations.[100] The United Mine Workers retied the knot of solidarity between local strikers and their national unions. They promoted and supported a local culture of solidarity and consciously transformed a strike into a people's resistance movement against corporate greed. In doing so the strikers and their leaders instilled hope in other activists who wanted to reform and revive the labor movement.

Engaging in civil disobedience: social movement unionism in action. Photograph by Sara Brown. *Courtesy Service Employees International Union.*

On Becoming a Movement Again:
The Labor Union Revival in the 1990s

After leading the Mine Workers to victory in the Pittston strike and arousing organized labor, Richard Trumka was being widely touted as a future leader of the AFL-CIO, whose affiliates continued to lose members, bargaining power, and political clout in the 1990s. Some experts were predicting that unionism would soon drop to a dismal 10 percent of the entire private sector workforce. The decline of industrial unionism eroded the power of the economic liberals in the Democratic Party, opening the way for neo-liberals unconcerned with working-class needs and making it even easier for right-wing Republicans and overt racists like David Duke to woo disaffected white workers. In an article written shortly after the Pittston strike, Trumka sounded the alarm and took aim at union leaders who seemed to think that in due time labor's power would swing back just like a pendulum. Instead of waiting passively for the second coming of the New Deal, he urged, union officials had to adapt and change before it was too late.[1]

The transformation of the Pittston strike into a people's movement against corporate greed demonstrated, according to Trumka, some of what it would take for labor organizations to become a movement again. Union leaders needed to activate their members. They needed to look back to movement history to see how unions once embraced a larger range of workplace and social concerns. They could also learn from the social movements of the 1960s like Cesar Chavez's Farm Workers who created a kind of "community unionism." Past experience offered instruction in how to mobilize whole communities and how to create strong coalitions with community groups. He also warned that the law stood in the way of a union renaissance. Since labor law reform had failed, direct action was required. Just as the civil rights movement defied unjust laws to attack racial oppression, a new labor movement needed to confront unjust labor laws that allowed employers to block most union organizing efforts, often simply by terminating activist workers.[2]

But the problem was not simply a legal one. For years AFL-CIO leaders invested little in organizing new workers and remained complacent in the face of decline; they seemed to accept George Meany's old conceit that unions need not "worry about groups of people who do not want to be organized." Just by holding their own, trade unions could exercise plenty of influence in Congress and in corporate board rooms.

Some critics thought the problem went far deeper than complacency. They argued that during the 1940s and 1950s leaders of organized labor discarded the memory of how to organize on a grassroots, community level. Even the progressive industrial unions that organized millions in the 1930s seemed to forget their early history when they were part of a militant social movement. Institutional histories of these CIO unions emphasized their development as a set of vertically structured institutions defined by contracts with certain employers. AFL craft unions suffered from a similar case of forgetting how to organize.[3] In the process of establishing stable centralized unions with viable economic power and routinized political authority, "the labor movement forgot how to build, organize and extend membership," according to Elizabeth Faue. Historians bore some responsibility for these lapses of memory about movement building during the times when women and community leaders contributed mightily to union growth. As the House of Labor crumbled in the 1980s, movement historians helped active unionists recall "the history of the social movement phase of unions," in order to examine old practices and "customs of movement building."[4] By returning to the past, a time before unions became legalized and institutionalized, activists might enlist old ways in making a new future.

Unions had once employed a full arsenal of organizing weapons and had been able to mobilize dues-paying members for certain campaigns; but those efforts seemed less important after World War II. New members came easily in some industries where union contracts brought new hires into the fold. On the other hand, recruiting new members became too costly in some anti-union areas like the South, especially after the demise of "Operation Dixie," the CIO's failed attempt to organize southern industries. Furthermore, organizing, like most union functions, became staff dominated. The members were no longer asked to take responsibility for recruitment. And in a business-union environment, organizing became a part-time business. Being an organizer was not the way to move up in the union hierarchy; nor did the job pay as well as the job of business agent.[5]

As union membership plunged during the 1980s, labor leaders began to take some steps to reverse the decline. International officers pitched staff and money into various campaigns. Sometimes unions competed with one another, leading to negative campaigns in which employers could use the allegations of one union against another. Successes were few and far between. The national AFL-CIO rarely played a role in organizing, which was the prerogative of the affiliates, but its departments tried to coordinate multi-union campaigns in some areas.[6]

Lane Kirkland, who became AFL-CIO president in 1979, soon began to feel the heat from critics who called for more aggressive leadership. One sign of change in the pressure came in 1987 when a number of national union leaders formed Jobs with Justice (JwJ), a coalition of national unions determined to mobilize members and allies on "an old Wobbly principle" that "an injury to one is an injury to all." Those who joined JwJ chapters signed cards pledging to be there at least five times to support someone else's fight. Some local groups created workers' rights boards composed of important citizens to hold hearings on violations of employee rights. In Miami the lively chapter organized a worker abuse hotline and played an active role in winning community support for the machinists locked in a deadly struggle with Eastern Airlines and corporate raider Frank Lorenzo. Jobs with Justice chapters emerged in thirty cities over the next decade. These groups moved into the vacuum left by the moribund central labor councils, which no longer linked unions in common struggles or generated community support; this threatened some AFL-CIO officials, who were disturbed about being exposed and upstaged.[7]

While Jobs with Justice pushed national unions to form community-based alliances that would change the climate for organizing, other groups without official backing kept up the criticism of incumbent labor officials who were reluctant to organize the unorganized. Many of these critics contributed to the Detroit monthly *Labor Notes,* also a communications center for groups battling concessions and fighting for union democracy through caucuses like Teamsters for a Democratic Union and New Directions in the UAW. Obviously, if union officials accepted big concessions without mobilizing members and their allies to fight back, the work of organizing new members would be that much more difficult. The emerging left within the labor movement also used the sense of crisis about falling union membership to criticize AFL-CIO foreign policy, pointing out that its budget for intervening in the labor affairs of other nations was far larger than its budget for organizing on worksites at home.

In response to the sense of crisis about organizing, Kirkland and AFL-CIO Secretary-Treasurer Thomas Donahue created the Organizing Institute. As director they chose a young activist from the Amalgamated Clothing Workers named Richard Bensinger, who freely borrowed from community organizing traditions and who candidly addressed the reasons union officials failed to organize new members. Bensinger recruited young people, mostly from college campuses; trained them intensively; put them in the field on organizing drives as apprentices; and then made them available for union staff positions. The Organizing Institute demonstrated that the labor movement could attract educated, committed young people—this for the first time since the United Farm

Workers strikes and boycott campaigns magnetized idealistic students in the sixties and seventies.[8]

By the early 1990s AFL-CIO affiliates were mounting energetic and costly organizing drives. Employers still used a variety of threats and illegal actions to defeat unions in election campaigns, causing Bensinger and others to call for "blitz" attacks that forced employers to grant recognition based on quick checks of those who signed cards supporting a union. This kind of strategy seemed to work in "hot shops" where workers already felt some collective sense of grievance and had created some preliminary support network, but these situations were outnumbered by those in which non-union workers feared retribution from employers and doubted the veracity of union campaigns. In these workplaces, union organizers needed to invest in a long-term presence and to adopt sophisticated new tactics to overcome the deep fears of employees and the sharp attacks of employers.

New Workers: New Challenges for Organizers

More and more union leaders and activists accepted the necessity of organizing, and began to face the enormously hard work of planning it and making it effective again. A new generation of activists approached the problem with the critical intelligence gained from their own failed campaigns and from their unrelenting opponents. Besides showing a willingness to learn from the experience of struggle and defeat, these unionists seemed to be willing to revisit the past. They were ready to jettison old habits and to borrow tactics from historic movements, including sixties social movements that employed risky direct-action tactics like civil disobedience.

Many organizers believed that new union growth would come mainly from emerging sectors of the workforce, not from the ranks of factory workers and government employees who suffered from the effects of declining employment and mounting employer opposition. One of the biggest organizing challenges for the labor movement lay in the rapidly expanding workforce of private employees in service, clerical, and sales.[9] An AFL-CIO committee presented some of the facts to be faced: 90 percent of the new jobs created in the 1970s came from the service sector, which at the end of the next decade would employ 73 percent of the total labor force.[10] But these workers would earn much less than wage earners in manufacturing, mining, construction, and transportation, and less than government employees.[11] A poll commissioned by the AFL-CIO in the late 1980s assessed workers' receptivity to unions and found that 40 percent of those in sales and services said they would like to see their workplaces unionized, as compared to 25 percent in manufacturing; and yet, only 11 percent of the former belonged to unions as compared to 25 percent of the latter.[12]

This service, sales, and clerical workforce included far more women and people of color (and many more recent immigrants) than the goods-producing sector. These workers had traditionally been seen as "unorganizable" by union leaders who represented white skilled and semiskilled workingmen. Labor history exposed this self-defeating and often self-serving myth, but, as veteran labor reporter William Serrin noted, for the most part, top AFL-CIO leaders did "not care about labor history."[13]

As organizers reported back on the attitudes of workers they met on the ground, the old myths began to crumble. Unorganized women were far more supportive of unionism than men.[14] Workers of color were far more organizable than white workers. When unorganized workers were asked in 1989 if they would join a union in their workplace, 56 percent of the African Americans said "Union, Yes" compared to 46 percent of the Hispanics and 35 percent of the non-Hispanic Whites.[15]

At the same time, union organizers began to question the use of a recruitment model based on the experience of industrial unions whose organizers focused largely on winning elections sponsored by the National Labor Relations Board. In this tradition union organizers appealed mainly to workers' identities as employees paid by a single employer; they usually ignored other identities based, for example, on gender, race, and ethnicity, because this approach seemed divisive.[16]

In any case, during the 1980s union leaders realized that quick victories in federally sponsored elections meant little, unless organizing drives built up enough strength and expertise to carry the new bargaining units over the next hurdle—securing first contracts with employers. This became a horrendously difficult task as many businesses employed anti-union lawyers and consulting firms to defeat union election campaigns, or failing that, to make sure the new union did not win a first contract.[17]

New Ways of Organizing

Out of the crisis new approaches to organizing emerged, often based on a critical understanding of how the NLRB had failed to protect workers and unions. But innovations were also influenced by what organizers learned from other social movements. This was evident in the highly publicized campaigns to unionize clerical and technical workers at the nation's two most prestigious universities, Yale and Harvard, where a large majority of the employees were women. At both universities, union drives benefited from the creativity of lead organizers who adopted a new participatory model of union building. At Yale University organizers broke with the standard model in a 2½ year campaign to bring clerical and technical workers into the Hotel and Restaurant Workers (HERE). They were trained by the veteran union activist Vincent Sirabella to adopt a "rank-and-file organizing strategy" that began in 1980 on a low key without an announcement or the standard leaflets but rather with face-to-face encounters made through house calls, lunch meetings, and social functions.

John Wilhelm, a HERE business agent and an architect of the drive, had been a community organizer and he believed in this approach, which resembled Saul Alinsky's method of creating new leaders through organizing.[18]

At Harvard union organizers had used standard methods of recruitment to reach clerical and technical workers. New York–based District 65 made persistent efforts to organize the medical school, and when it affiliated with the United Auto Workers in 1975, more resources were thrown into the campaign. But progress was slow. The industrial union model of organizing didn't seem to work at Harvard. Frustrated by the UAW regional director, a young organizer, Kristine Rondeau, split off and began organizing an independent union using very different tactics developed with a sensitivity to the needs and concerns of the largely female workers who maintained cooperative working relationships with supervisors in many offices and labs and expressed a good deal of pride and professionalism in their work roles. She adopted a "woman's way of organizing" derived from the women's movement. Instead of organizing around a few issues or agitating "against the boss"—the standard approach—Rondeau and the inside activists who remained at Harvard decided to create a union within the culture of the workplace. The union need not be seen as an outside agent, but rather as an indigenous educational force knitted into the "social fabric."[19]

The Harvard Union of Clerical and Technical Workers (HUCTW) took the high road and tried "to build a community of workers" who felt some ownership over the organization and its strategy for organizing. The organizing campaign would not make a negative assault on Harvard, even though the university spent $2 million in an anti-union campaign. With the generous support of the American Federation of State, County and Municipal Employees, the union eventually took on sixteen full-time organizers, but this wasn't all the administration had to contend with. There was also a "virtual army" of over two hundred volunteer organizers whose "moral fervor" Harvard found difficult to counter.[20]

To build trust between workers and union activists, organizers asked workers about their personal lives. Rondeau believed each worker had a story to tell and that organizing began when people felt safe enough to tell their stories. "The union has to be a place where everybody's story matters," she declared.[21] Building on personal relationships, Rondeau's organizers worked to earn respect by showing that they respected the work that people performed. Rather than emphasizing employees' alienation from their work, the HUCTW stressed workers' need for a collective "voice." At Harvard the union voice was distinctly female, reflecting the many concerns and values of women workers often unheard in traditional union drives. While demystifying the appeal of working at Harvard ("You Can't Eat Prestige!"), the union stuck to its positive message ("You Don't Have to Be Anti-Harvard to Be Pro-Union"). HUCTW won a narrow election victory in 1988.[22]

When resourceful organizers faced employers who were highly vulnerable to outside pressure and internal tensions, as Yale and Harvard were, it was possible for unions to exploit those vulnerabilities. However, organizing lower-paid, less educated service workers in less visible settings was far more difficult, especially when the workforce included lots of new immigrants often unaware of their rights and sometimes very afraid of being deported.

Some unions had organized these kinds of service workers before World War II—for example, hotel and restaurant workers, and janitors in big cities. The hostility of restaurant owners eventually caused the Hotel and Restaurant Workers to lose their waiters, waitresses, and bartenders, except those in big city hotels. The Service Employees International Union (SEIU) had organized service and janitorial workers in several major cities, but during the 1970s landlords began contracting with non-union firms for cleaning services. As a result, employers of unionized janitors began to demand concessions.

In Los Angeles, for example, real estate ownership shifted to large national and international investors who wanted to purchase cleaning services by contract rather than to employ unionized custodians. After a successful attempt to organize contractors and raise wages, the local union of janitors in L.A. lost nearly its entire membership of five thousand as owners shifted to non-union contractors employing Mexican and Central American immigrants recruited through village systems. The local, affiliated with the Service Employees International Union, failed to organize the new workforce and to gain recognition through traditional elections supervised by the National Labor Relations Board.[23]

In 1980 SEIU's national officers were replaced by reformers led by John Sweeney. Though he hailed from a traditional union background and looked the part, Sweeney was an innovator. The son of Irish immigrants, Sweeney was raised in a tightly knit Catholic parish of the Bronx. His father drove a bus and his mother worked as a cleaner and he grew up wanting to honor his family values by becoming a labor organizer. Like many new union leaders of the eighties, Sweeney entered a university rather than a factory. After graduating from Iona College with a degree in economics, he worked for IBM as a market researcher while he waited for an organizing job to open up. He took a pay cut to become an organizer for the Ladies Garment Workers Union. Sweeney then found an organizing job with the Building Service Employees Union and rose through the ranks to become national president of the SEIU.

Publicly soft-spoken and thoughtful, Sweeney was a tough administrator who took on the old fiefdoms in his union, placed young turks from outside in key staff positions, aggressively merged with troubled unions, and expanded the SEIU membership in the 1980s when many other unions sustained big losses. He adopted the updated methods of business unionism, along with the risk-management practices taught in business schools. He increased the national staff from twenty to two hundred and hired a talented, committed staff willing to make change. Many of the leftists who led SEIU locals and held key positions in the national staff hoped to infuse the union with the fighting spirit of the old CIO and to adopt the aggressive organizing tactics used in the 1930s and 1960s protest movements. Unlike most international presidents who watched their numbers fall without knowing how to add new ones, Sweeney raised dues assessments and devoted far more resources to organizing.[24]

Organizing for Justice

In 1987 SEIU janitors in Pittsburgh defeated an employer's demand for concessions by using confrontational "in-your-face" tactics. Based on this experience, Sweeney approved a plan to use direct-action tactics to organize non-union janitors in Denver. The new project, dubbed Justice for Janitors, enjoyed success and was then moved to Southern California where its leaders hoped to unionize thousands of immigrants from Central America employed by cleaning contractors. Justice for Janitors (JfJ) was staffed by young activists and sixties radicals on Sweeney's staff who consciously drew on the history of the civil rights movement for tactical and political instruction. Rather than use the traditional focus on bargaining a contract based on mutual interest, JfJ insisted on union representation as a civil right, much like the black sanitation workers in Memphis who struck for dignity in 1968 during the "I Am a Man" strike that fused the civil rights and labor movements. Borrowing from Saul Alinsky, Fred Ross, and other community organizers, JfJ deliberately sought to create "mini-movements" that gave low-paid custodians an experience of collective struggle they could take into a larger campaign. Its organizers rejected business unionism as too narrow an approach to attract the community support custodians needed to prevail over large employers. JwJ defined a union contract in terms of social justice as well as in terms of economic benefits in an effort to identify unionism with community welfare.[25]

Justice for Janitors also drew tactical lessons from the discouraging experience of union organizers who found that employers could either defy federal labor law or use it to delay representation elections and discourage union supporters. Rejecting the old process of filing for a Labor Board election, JfJ created an attack team led by community activists rather than by vulnerable employees, a team that pressured building owners to cancel contracts with non-union firms. The campaign also mounted corporate campaigns against landlords who engaged non-union cleaning companies and against the core firms who outsourced their business to smaller marginal companies. Instead of petitioning for a federal labor election, activists worked to get union preference cards signed by a majority of workers so that they could then demand immediate recognition of the union.[26]

Sweeney appointed Stephen Lerner director of JfJ. Experienced as an organizer for the Farm Workers grape boycott and then for the Ladies Garment

Workers in the South, Lerner consciously searched movement experience for effective tactics. Unlike those who blamed union combativity for labor's decline, he insisted that the labor movement should learn from history, "take history to heart," and became more, rather than less, "confrontational." "Virtually every great nonviolent social movement in the twentieth century has been built around direct action and civil disobedience," he declared. Effective movements for change "have stood for something so important that large numbers of people have taken enormous risks to support them." Unions needed to become more militant, take more risks, and demand more sacrifices from their supporters. They needed to act more like the civil rights movement which challenged unjust laws with direct action.[27]

Steve Lerner revived the discussion of direct-action tactics, a discussion that had been relegated to the past, because for most labor leaders confrontation tactics involved too many risks, too many costs. His argument resembled that of Piven and Cloward, the famous social movement theorists whose writings had stressed the power of confrontation and disruption for making change.[28] The time had come again for calculated risk-taking, for taking on entire corporations and industries instead of trying to organize single work sites. Unions should organize on a large industrywide scale and take wages out of competition—what the construction and industrial unions had done historically—or else the best organizers in the world would fail to rebuild the labor movement on a shop-by-shop basis.[29]

Large-scale organizing of service workers would not result from labor-management partnerships favored by large industrial unions like the UAW, Lerner argued, because employers of low-wage labor were invariably hostile to unions, just as they were when the first industrial unions used sit-downs and mass strikes to take wages out of competition in the 1930s. This confrontational approach to organizing the expanding service workforce conflicted dramatically with the recommendations of leading industrial-relations experts who preached cooperation and a departure from an organizing agenda that relied on "deep-seated job dissatisfaction."[30] They offered new prescriptions for worker involvement and skill improvement as alternatives to adversarial labor relations, but proponents of nonadversarial approaches focused mainly on "a narrowing core of high wage, high skill jobs" in the larger corporate sphere, according to sociologist Paul Johnston. Few advocated labor-management cooperation in industries with growing numbers of workers in low-wage, insecure jobs—people employed in peripheral firms run by harshly anti-union managers.[31]

In 1989 Justice for Janitors set its sights on the posh office complex at Century City in Los Angeles, where SEIU hoped to organize the immigrant cleaning workers who worked there. The JfJ cadre engaged in civil disobedience and other protests directed against tenants as well as cleaning contractors; its only strategy, said the *L.A. Times,* was "attack, attack, attack." Latino immigrants, often portrayed as fearful and conservative, responded courageously to JfJ's call to direct action. One reporter observed that the union seemed to draw positively "on the traditions and experiences of workers who faced down terror in El Salvador and Guatemala."[32] These immigrant workers were also encouraged by the support of community allies, union staffers, and rank-and-file supporters who took the same risks and planned to protect the "undocumented."

On 15 June 1990, as JfJ mounted a noisy demonstration at Century City, L.A. police responded to employers' calls. Officers waded into the crowd and randomly attacked the workers. Featured on the evening news, this bloody assault aroused public outrage and created pressure on the employers to reach a settlement. Ultimately, the campaign brought over eight thousand largely immigrant workers under SEIU contract in Los Angeles, reviving a tradition of immigrant union organizing long forgotten by business unions. Several students of the JfJ campaign described it not only as an organizing victory but as a "social movement success."[33] It offered another example of why "the union must reinvent itself as social movement in which each member is an organizer," in the words of movement historian Mike Davis writing about a different struggle, in Las Vegas, where aggressive local unions organized low-wage workers by combining "CIO fundamentalism and high-tech, anti-corporate guerilla warfare."[34]

Unfortunately for the new members organized by Justice for Janitors in Los Angeles, the joy of victory turned sour. Some of the new immigrant members of the SEIU local joined with other dissidents to challenge the local's leadership for failing to represent them adequately. These "reformistas" won control of the local's board and were then locked in a paralyzing power struggle with the union president. The reform forces were outraged when the national SEIU office put the troubled L.A. local in receivership and displaced the elected officials, and then divided its large, diverse membership. The old local became a unit mainly of healthcare workers while the janitors were placed in a statewide local headed by the progressive Mike Garcia. The Justice for Janitors organizing drive, run largely by the national office, had focused entirely on mobilization and had not prepared the groundwork for an integration of new members into an existing local.[35]

These problems in L.A. typified the difficulties of pushing an organizing agenda on local unions from the top down. Under Sweeney, SEIU had adopted an old CIO practice of heavily investing in local organizing, but it was clear from the L.A. experience that many locals could not mount ambitious organizing efforts and still maintain member services. Officers in the locals found that the campaigns taxed their resources as well, because they pulled local staff away from servicing and educating members; the drives also required local officials to take political risks. Activating rank and filers to perform the tasks of movement building cut against the grain of generations of trade union practice—practice that rarely involved mobilizing incumbent members or organizing new workers. On the other hand, if the organizing drive depended mainly on SEIU staffers from the outside, the local unions might gain more members but be unable to integrate them or to meet their needs, let alone empower them as union members.

Bill Fletcher, who served as SEIU education and field director, and who went to the troubled L.A. local as Sweeney's troubleshooter, questioned the ends, as well as the means, of aggressive new organizing projects. Staff-driven organizing campaigns, even those that included movement-style confrontations with employers, would not necessarily create a movement culture of mass participatory democracy, Fletcher maintained. Militant organizing efforts could lead to greater "market share" without building a new labor movement committed to the principles of worker empowerment, social justice, and economic equality.[36]

It remains to be seen whether the breakthroughs made by Justice for Janitors can be used to reach others in the vast low-wage, primarily female, workforce composed of African American women laboring in Deep South poultry and catfish operations; Chicanas, Mexicanas, and Latinas toiling in canning, electronics assembling, and commercial cleaning; Caribbeans working in domestic and home care jobs; and Asians working in restaurants, high tech plants, and garment shops. These workers find themselves burdened with enormous family responsibilities; serious barriers in language, literacy, and skills training; and tenuous connections to notions of civil rights. Case studies suggest that community-based organizations, like the Asian Women's Advocates in Oakland and the Chinese Progressive Association in Boston, can meet the needs of this growing low-wage, increasingly part-time workforce. For example, the Garment Workers Justice Centers established in several cities by the newly merged union of needle trades, UNITE, offer resources not usually provided by labor unions, as "bargaining units." Ruth Needleman summarizes these resources as follows: "community roots, an emphasis on one-on-one contact, long term perseverance . . . support during individual crises, and training over an extended period, at a pace well suited to these workers' overwhelming responsibilities."[37]

Community-Based Organizing

Some organizers are aware of historical precedents for mobilizing these kinds of resources. Groups like the Workmen's Circle and the Women's Trade Union League once helped trade unions by reaching out to low-wage immigrant workers. Though they emphasized the struggle for workers' control at the point of production, the Industrial Workers of the World recognized the power of community associations and self-help networks. Similar horizontal forms of organizing reappeared in the early 1930s, notably in community wide mobilizations like the Minneapolis general strike in which women constituted an "army of silent fighters . . . an army without banners."[38]

A group of Vanderbilt scholars drew explicitly upon labor history to argue that unions should return to their social-movement roots by building a sense of community among workers, even when workers lack collective bargaining agreements. According to the study, workers who were relatively new to a workplace and who lacked association with dominant community institutions were attracted to unions by their community building efforts. The authors argued that unions should "reconstitute" themselves as community building agents on and off the job; they said "reconstitute" because they believed that contemporary unions could "derive inspiration and practical models from early twentieth-century unions, which performed a larger role in the community."[39]

The 1980s produced many promising union efforts to create a community presence for the labor movement and to forge coalitions with religious and local interest groups. Sometimes, as in the case of plant closing fights, these local groups took the initiative in representing workers' interests when unions failed to do so, but in other cases, unions sought out community allies to help them in their struggles. In some instances the community "allies" were left wondering if the labor-community coalition was a reciprocal affair, wondering if unions would take support from community allies without giving it back?[40]

So far, few efforts to unionize have sprung directly from independent community based groups. An exception is Baltimore BUILD, described by organizers as "a little bit of church, a little bit of union, a little bit of social service, and a whole lot of politics." BUILD was the product of patient work by the Industrial Areas Foundation which adopted a long-term, institution-building approach to organizing, an approach that contrasted with the short-term, contract-driven tactics of many unions. BUILD put a community face on unionism by using community people as a organizers in one-to-one recruitment efforts and by addressing issues like welfare reform which had been ignored by labor unions. BUILD's campaign for a living wage started from within a community and thus possessed a "moral legitimacy" that union organizing drives often lack, especially when white-led unions organize in black communities. The community organizers of ACORN adopted a similar approach to living wage campaigns in other cities and successfully gained official AFL-CIO support.[41]

Whether union strategies are based on confrontational efforts, like those of Justice for Janitors, or, long-term efforts to create worker institutions in poor and immigrant communities, it seems essential for the labor movement to break down the bifurcation of work and community, a division unions have accentuated by defining themselves mainly in terms of their contracts with employers.[42] It has been argued that such a division between home place and workplace was an essential ingredient of urban life in the United States, dividing men from women, separating work from community. Of course, when the evening whistle blew and workers returned to their neighborhoods and family lives, they did tend to leave the problems and solidarities of the workplace behind them.[43]

However, the new labor history also offers many examples of how movement building drew upon familial and communal solidarities as well as workplace bonds. Even the most volatile workers "created vibrant working-class communities" with "mutualistic ties" that included wider circles of transients in informal organizations. Sometimes these local groupings functioned as what historian Gunther Peck calls "surrogate unions" which could address worker problems in "communal contexts." In this way, informal groups created by migrants and immigrants fulfilled some of the needs of those excluded from trade unions.[44]

Perhaps these historical examples will be helpful to union organizers who are beginning to tap a rich vein of support in new immigrant worker communities. Many newcomers are now more settled and are less afraid of losing their jobs in an overheated economy where the employers' demand for low-wage labor is ravenous. In the winter of 1999 SEIU scored the largest organizing victory since the UAW organized 110,000 General Motors workers after the 1937 sit-down strikes. More than 70,000 poorly paid home care workers in Los Angeles County voted to unionize, most of them women immigrants. In the spring labor won an even more surprising victory at the nation's largest textile manufacturing complex, Fieldcrest Cannon in Kannapolis, N.C., where management had effectively subverted union efforts for decades with all sorts of harassment and intimidation. Organizers for UNITE were even taken aback by the results which they attributed partly to the growing number of immigrants at the plant. Unlike most native white employees, most of these foreign-born workers still live in the same communities, making community based organizing drives an effective approach once again.[45]

However, the promise of community unionism lies beyond successful union recruitment in immigrant neighborhoods. A labor movement rooted in local communities can practice a revived form of what Staughton Lynd calls "solidarity unionism." He has illustrated this kind of localized, "horizontal" movement building in a collection of inspiring historical studies. He believes a new labor movement should be based on community-based movements with indigenous leadership rather than on national institutions which tend to define unionism in contractual terms that depend too much on reaching agreements with individual corporations and on remaining within the limits of what federal labor law allows. Union locals have often been, as Lynd argues, well-springs of democracy and lodestones of solidarity, but they have also become the property of the incumbent members unwilling to reach out to include new groups like immigrants. Local unions will continue to create inspiring cultures of solidarity, but, as the Pittston strike suggests, local struggles need the support of a strong labor movement. That movement also needs progressive national and regional leaders to push hard against the conservative aspects of localism. Beyond the politics of existing locals lies the promise of a new community unionism based on different types of organization that might harken back to the mixed assemblies created by the Knights of Labor and the community based unions of the early 1930s. This kind of unionism could use the resources of national organizations, which might benefit in the long run if they agreed to cede "ownership" to local working people.[46]

Old Wine in New Bottles

Innovative organizing by industrial and service-sector unions has often been initiated by historically conscious progressives and radicals who favor an inclusive approach to organizing all types of employees. In one way or another they have tried to apply the lessons of the CIO to the present. By contrast, the building-trades unions have often been led by conservative business unionists who have usually adopted a more exclusive approach to membership, limiting access to their trades through apprenticeship programs and union hiring halls. As a result, the ranks of the building trades remained highly segregated in terms of race and gender. In recent years their leaders organized few new members. If the logic of industrial and service unionism was inclusion and expansion, the logic of craft unionism seemed to be restriction and protection.

The need to organize new workers in construction rarely arose after World War II, when the various building-trades unions affiliated with the old AFL managed to control nearly 80 percent of the work. Through mutual-gains bargaining, some contractors, often the largest ones, signed agreements that gave them access to well-trained, highly skilled laborers. The contractors agreed to hire only from union halls if the trades agreed not to strike or to provide labor for competing contractors. The National Labor Relations Act (section 8f) allowed for prehire agreements that helped building-trades unions organize contractors without having to worry about competition from non-union labor. Big contractors bid for jobs that included union wages and passed the costs on to customers. The prevailing federal wage-rate law ensured union pay levels for government work. Local unions and their contractor partners benefited from these arrangements and through them constructed impressive joint funds for pensions and apprenticeship training. As a result, construction unions stopped organizing non-union workers in the traditional way. Instead, they depended on their contracts to ensure that new hires would come from the union hall and that new members would be recruited, not through organizing drives, but through the apprenticeship programs they operated with funding shared by union contractors.

However, during the 1970s smaller contractors won more and more jobs in markets dominated by union labor. Larger non-union contractors from the South and West began to bid for jobs at lower costs. They also formed anti-union employer groups to attack the "union monopoly" in public. As construction employment ebbed and flowed with recessions, and as the union market share fell, unemployment grew in union ranks. Meanwhile, craft unions strictly enforced a rule that prohibited union members from working non-union even as this segment of the workforce grew by leaps and bounds.[47]

Untrained, non-union workers were seen as the enemies, the scabs who worked for "rat contractors," according to a recent report about a local construction union on the West Coast. This militant, bunker mentality reinforced a protectionist club system already working to keep women and minorities out of the trades. Even "fellow travelers" from other union locals were viewed with suspicion. "What many union members failed to realize was that their own system of exclusive membership helped train the non-union electrician and create the rise of the non-union contractor," according to Janet Lewis and Bill Mirand, who wrote the case report on a local electricians union.[48]

The same study showed that the local leadership did not know how to respond to a rapid loss of members. Organizing scores of "rat contractors" one by one proved extremely difficult for unions using the standard method of seeking a federally sponsored election. Craft union locals were caught in a bind: their old allies, the union contractors, asked for wage cuts to become competitive with the "rats," but when they accepted wage concessions and increased productivity, unions still failed to restore their market share.[49]

In one of the most powerful construction unions, the International Brotherhood of Electrical Workers, some activists shifted the discussion away from the external threats from non-union contractors and turned it to the union's internal problems. IBEW organizer Mike Lucas began to shake things up by sharing his study of the union's early history. It showed him how organizers had gone out a century before and "sold the union idea, the union spirit, the union principle." They were not selling jobs; they were not asking tradesmen to join the union just to find work; they were asking them to embrace the values of unionism. In many local markets the IBEW gained a "loose monopoly of qualified craftsmen," but it was never secure, and bottom-up organizing continued. After World War II the union shifted to what Lucas called "top down organizing . . . , the securing of work by selling owners, users and employers on the advantages of operating under union agreements." In other words, the union began organizing contractors rather than electrical workers. As a result, the union literally lost the memory of its founding principles, and forgot how to organize.[50]

A few thoughtful IBEW leaders began to argue for a new strategy. "We ensured full employment for the non-union worker," said organizer Jim Rudicil. "Has anybody been teaching non-union workers their rights? Has anybody been turning in non-union contractors for violations of the law? No, because we don't let our people go on to those jobs." Looking again at IBEW history and the union's retreat from organizing after World War II, organizers developed a new program that "salted" non-union construction sites with unemployed union members. Working with historically-conscious trade union leaders, Cornell labor educator Jeff Grebelsky developed the COMET program (Construction Organizing Membership and Training) based on a "revisionist history" of the union and a return to movement unionism in which rank-and-file members organize fellow workers who are not union. Building trades union leaders, who frequently complain that young members lack union values and commitments, swear that the apprentices educated, trained, and placed by COMET are far more active, dedicated trade unionists.[51]

The case study by Lewis and Mirand shows how one IBEW local implemented the COMET program successfully. The union began training apprentices through the program in 1991. It asked them to take jobs with "rat contractors" in order to organize non-union electricians from the "bottom up." Trainers criticized the tradition of seeing the craft union as an exclusive club and tried to change the "outmoded and prejudicial thinking of its own membership toward non-union workers as a first order of business," according to the study. Apprentices or unemployed journeymen received wage supplements from the union for their efforts. "Salts" were trained to spot labor law violations and to blow the whistle on offending contractors. Sometimes their reports resulted in federal charges of unfair labor practices, especially when employers refused to hire or tried to fire union members or when they violated safety laws.

At the same time, the local union officers pursued a top-down strategy by taking legal action against contractors, by stripping them of highly skilled craftsmen (who were offered union membership and employment), and by using media strategies to expose them to the public. The union even took the unusual action of attacking contractors for ignoring environmental laws. With increased bargaining power, the local has been able to organize several project labor agreements, increase its market share to 55 percent, and expand its dues-paying membership at the same time. Non-union contractors screamed bloody murder when confronted with these tactics and challenged "salting" in the courts. But in 1993 the Supreme Court ruled the practice a legal activity protected under the National Labor Relations Act.[52]

Efforts like COMET represent more than new strategies in organizing; they also reflect a historically conscious effort "to construct and project a movement that represents the general interests of working people, and not only a particular group of workers," according to Janice Fine, an expert on the theory and practice of organizing. Union leaders' first attempts to understand their crisis assigned blame to overpowering economic and social trends. This kind of thinking "dwarfs" workers as agents of social change, writes Fine, and it avoids looking inside unions to see what went wrong and to see what conscious choices should be revisited and even reconsidered. Before the mid-1980s, union leaders rarely looked to internal factors—factors union members and leaders could control—as reasons for their decline. Since then union activists have carefully reexamined the histories of their industries and their unions and have made what Fine calls "major strategic corrections." They have adopted different organizing approaches, approaches often rooted in past practice, approaches sometimes informed by the new labor history and its use in numerous labor education and training programs, as well as in college courses. By the mid 1990s the challenge no longer centered on whether movement activists could summon the courage and creative intelligence to remake history; it focused on whether innovation could be moved "from the margins to the center of the labor movement."[53]

By 1994 labor unions had begun to reverse the decline in membership and had improved their win rate in union elections from 47 to 57 percent in one year. Public sector unions enjoyed modest success, especially when they adopted strategies and tactics that "encouraged rank-and-file participation" and "person-to-person contact."[54] Industrial unions even organized new workers in the private sector, where employer opposition remained intense—this according to an analysis of 1994 campaigns that emphasized the importance of conscious planning and "the use of a grassroots rank-and-file intensive, union-building strategy," as compared to the old staff-dominated approach of simply trying to win a federal labor election.[55]

New Voices, New Leaders

The urgent need to meet the onslaught of hostile management and government forces called up a generation of new labor leaders at the local, state, and national levels, leaders willing to break with old habits. Open to cooperation with friendly employers, they were also willing to confront hostile employers and even to use aggressive tactics long abandoned. These leaders were often college educated, sophisticated in how to use the media and how to understand the complexities of labor relations, corporate finance, and government affairs. Unlike the leaders who assumed power in the 1950s and 1960s these officials were not so indoctrinated by Cold War anti-Communism. Some of them even employed militants from inside their own ranks and radicals from outside the ranks in order to revitalize their organizations. Though hardly sixties radicals, they were less threatened by the social movements of that era than the Cold War generation of officials. And though they were virtually all white men, they seemed aware of how important women and people of color were to the future of the labor movement.

Some of these new leaders, like John Sweeney of SEIU, came from fairly traditional union backgrounds, but they responded to the crisis in new ways. Some, like John Wilhelm of the Hotel Workers, emerged from experiences as community organizers. Others, like Richard Trumka of the Mine Workers started out as reformers dedicated to restoring democracy to their unions. Others inherited a different legacy. After the death of his father-in-law, Cesar Chavez, in 1992, Arturo Rodriquez became president of the Farm Workers Union. Chavez was patron saint of the union movement, the one who, with Dolores Huerta and others, made community unionism work, but he had run the United Farm Workers like a boss, purging loyalists and radicals alike and retreating from organizing almost entirely while a rival group, the Farm Labor Organizing Committee, bid for the activist legacy of the farm workers movement. Rodriquez returned the UFW to the fields and to the task of organizing new members.

Ronald Carey was perhaps the most important of these new leaders because he was able to win election, as a reformer, to the presidency of the Teamsters Union in 1991—the strongest, most visible, and most corrupt union in America. The gangster-ridden old guard of the Teamsters union (IBT) had maintained control since the days of Jimmy Hoffa until Carey won support from members who had been hurt by poor contracts that had conceded much to trucking companies. Carey benefited from the take-over of the election process by the federal government, by a split in the old guard's camp, and by the years of persistent and courageous work by the Left-led Teamsters for a Democratic Union. His election was the single most important political event in the revival of the labor movement. It began to change the public's perception of the labor movement; it marked the beginning of an aggressive new approach to organizing by the Teamsters, who hired a radical new director who popularized the saying: "Organizing never stops."[56] Carey's election also helped tip the balance of power in the AFL-CIO toward the critics who wanted to create a new labor movement within the shell of the old.

Nearly two decades of crisis and declining membership had not moved AFL-CIO chief Lane Kirkland far from his business-as-usual manner. When Robert Reich became secretary of labor in the first Clinton administration, he met Kirkland at the AFL-CIO meetings in Bal Harbor and recalled that even though organized labor was "dying a quiet death," Lane seemed nothing like the man of the hour. "He hasn't exactly been a tiger when it comes to organizing," Reich remarked. "Nothing about him suggests the leader of a *movement*." He looked and acted like any other "aging head of a special interest lobbying group in Washington whose main objective is to show how much it has done for them to justify collecting their dues." A member of the Masters, Pilots and Mates union, Kirkland guided labor's ship through a dozen years of rough Republican waters and no one on the bridge challenged his captaincy.[57] At the annual AFL-CIO meetings in Bal Harbor there was never a discouraging word—at least not from the floor where, Bill Serrin reported, the microphones were covered when dissidents rose to speak.[58]

But outside the Beltway, out in the "Rust Belt," far from Bal Harbor, mutinous sounds could be heard within the ranks. Reflecting the bitterness and anger of their members, union leaders blamed Kirkland for failing to lead a strong fight against Reaganism and for failing to provide new strategies for a movement in dire straits.

In 1992, when Bill Clinton was elected president with Democratic majorities in both houses, expectations rose within labor's downtrodden ranks. These hopes were soon dashed by Clinton's failure with health care reform and by his timidity about labor law reform, but, most of all, by his insistence on pushing the North American Free Trade Agreement over the AFL-CIO's passionate opposition. Lane Kirkland became a thorn in Clinton's side, and according to Labor Secretary Robert Reich, the White House offered the cantankerous union leader a chance to step aside. Kirkland angrily turned down Clinton's offer to "seduce him out of office" with an ambassadorship to Poland. "I love my job and I am gonna die in it," he declared.[59] Kirkland vehemently disagreed with Reich's interpretation. History had a different fate in store for the cerebral AFL-CIO head man.

In early 1995 a band of discontented national labor leaders forced him to resign. Secretary-Treasurer Tom Donahue took over and then decided to stand for president against John Sweeney, the ringleader of the coup, who declared himself a reform candidate together with Richard Trumka of the Mine Workers for secretary-treasurer and Linda Chavez-Thompson of AFSCME for a new position of executive vice president. Sweeney criticized the AFL-CIO as a "Washington-based institution concerned primarily with refining policy positions" rather than a "worker-based movement against greed, multi-national corporations, race-baiting and labor-baiting politicians."[60]

The "New Voice" campaign was inspired by the AFL-CIO's lack of response to organized labor's decline. But it also addressed the failure of organization men like Meany and Kirkland to impart any moral fervor or social vision to labor's cause. It was no wonder that many people, including union members, saw it as a lost cause. The reformers called for a return to labor's movement roots. They embraced the moral and tactical example of the civil rights movement, as Rich Trumka and Cecil Roberts had during the Pittston strike. "We shouldn't act as one more special interest group," John Sweeney declared. "We need to act as a social movement that represents working people throughout the society—union members and non-union members alike"—a movement that reaches "beyond the workplace and into the entire community."[61]

In October 1995 the Federation experienced its first contested election in over a century. Sweeney's "New Voice" team of insurgents won leadership of the AFL-CIO with votes from the reformed Teamsters union providing the margin of victory. Claiming a mandate for change, the "New Voice" slate expanded and diversified the executive council. Recognizing the importance of international cooperation, the new leaders scuttled the old Cold War labor institutes, once dedicated to subverting militant unionism overseas, and replaced them with a new international office devoted to promoting solidarity. Acknowledging the limits of the old special-interest lobbying strategies on Capitol Hill, the New Voice leaders returned to grassroots campaigns that showed surprising clout despite the loss of union density.[62]

Declaring an Emergency

Faced with plummeting numbers, the new AFL-CIO leadership declared an emergency and addressed the challenge of organizing new workers. It set up a new organizing department headed by outspoken Richard Bensinger to research targets, teach new strategies, and train organizers for the affiliates. The new executive council resolved that affiliates devote far more of their budgets (at least 30 percent) to organizing. The "New Voice" leadership also considered sponsoring its own campaigns and asked historian Dorothy Sue Cobble to explore the unknown history of Federation organizing campaigns initiated in the time of Gompers. It endorsed an innovative project in Los Angeles (LAMAP) that sought to develop a multi-union, community-based organizing strategy directed at over 700,000 non-union manufacturing workers, a plan that drew upon the history of the CIO in unionizing industrial workers regardless of preexisting jurisdictional claims by established trade unions.[63]

The Organizing Institute's efforts to recruit and train idealistic college students as labor organizers led to the Federation's "Union Summer" Program which offered young people a real-life experience in activism modeled after "Mississippi Freedom Summer."[64] These movement-inspired organizing programs have introduced youthful activists to the labor movement and even brought new talent into the organizing field, but of course these young people are no substitute for mobilizing the incumbent membership to reach out to the unorganized. The most effective organizers are rank-and-file union members who have been trained as part-time volunteers and as full-timers for effective campaigns; for example, in the campaigns of the Communications Workers of America that link organizing with contract fights and build up union strength in the workplace, so that, in a sense, organizing never stops.[65]

In another conscious return to labor's past, the "New Voice" leaders have attempted to revive the central labor councils in nearly six hundred cities. The central labor bodies once exerted a strong presence in many cities by supporting strikes, organizing boycotts, backing labor candidates for public office; they even supported labor parties and played a "key role" in organizing workers, that is, until the AFL adopted rules prohibiting the councils from organizing and competing with the affiliates.[66] For example, in 1918 the crusading progressive John Fitzpatrick, president of the powerful Chicago Federation of Labor, hired the radical William Z. Foster to head an interracial organizing drive in the stockyards. Fitzpatrick himself ran for mayor on the Labor Party ticket a year later and polled over fifty thousand votes.[67]

To a movement characterized by "abiding particularism," the CLCs have represented a potential basis for the national AFL-CIO to mobilize cooperative ventures and reach out to the general public on a local basis. To vertically organized trade unions based on particular trades or industries and on autonomous national organizations, the city councils provided a horizontally organized vehicle for promoting practical solidarity and political unity such as what the Knights of Labor once offered through their remarkable mixed assemblies.[68]

The new executive vice president of the AFL-CIO, Linda Chavez-Thompson, declared that revived CLCs would be the centers of the effort to "create a culture of organizing throughout the labor movement." However, this revival effort faces a formidable historical tradition in which the councils reduced themselves to a role of making political endorsements and contributions. Officers of AFL-CIO unions still oppose an organizing role for the councils, and so these bodies may be less effective at recruiting new members than serving as "nodes in a broader network of progressive organizations that are concerned with work and employment issues. Such was the case in Atlanta where the CLC created an effective organization of local unions and African American community organizations to ensure that local residents would be employed in constructing the stadium for the 1996 Olympics.[69] In Milwaukee, the head of the labor council developed a response to the devastating effects of deindustrialization. He helped create the Campaign for a Sustainable Milwaukee together with community-based organizations; it combined plans for multi-union organizing with proposals for creating new jobs at "living wages" and for revitalizing the urban economy.[70]

The CLCs may be important in creating a more positive environment for organizing in the various communities where unions neglected the alliances they had forged in the 1930s. Jobs with Justice activists who have focused their energies on building the movement-style coalitions with community allies expressed skepticism about whether the moribund CLCs could become anything but turf-conscious assemblies of local union chiefs. After some tense meetings, the new AFL-CIO leaders continued to support Jobs with Justice without abandoning their commitment to reviving the CLCs. They recognized the need to rebuild the labor movement by breathing new life into old bodies while encouraging new more militant efforts to mobilize existing unions and community groups.

Organized labor still faces formidable challenges, internally as well as externally. In the few years that the New Voice leaders have held office there have been setbacks. The militant director of organizing, Richard Bensinger, was replaced in 1998 after provoking some powerful union leaders with his outspoken criticisms.[71] It has been difficult for the national office to persuade affiliates and local unions to devote more resources to organizing and to involve members in the process. Some unions have created a "culture of organizing," but others have not overcome a tradition of inner-directed service unionism.

Toward Social Movement Unionism

The public discussion of the union revival has focused on the results of the specific organizing campaigns, but there are also less visible, longer-term efforts being made as part of the change process. Progressive labor educators have been working in unions and universities, and not just to train leaders and members in their contractual responsibilities (the old service model of worker education). A new "organizing model" of education has been widely adopted; it emphasizes the need for maximum participation by members in efforts to change union culture and to make unions part of a wider movement for social change. Their work has gained far more support from top union leaders in the 1990s than it did in the 1980s, when it was often viewed as negative criticism.

AFL-CIO President Sweeney acknowledged his support for this approach by appointing Bill Fletcher Jr. national education director in 1997. Fletcher believes the old skill-based approach to union education is inadequate. Organizing for keeps "is not solely about strategy and tactics," he told labor educators on May Day 1998. Without a sea change in rank-and-file opinion about what is wrong with the American economy, and what is wrong with the class-biased society, union members would have no desire to organize, no reason to take on intimidating employers. So Fletcher's department is adopting a new Common Sense Economics program "to promote a dialogue with our members about capitalism; about what corporate America is doing to them as workers; about who are our friends and who are our enemies."[72] This approach is a far cry from the old business union ideology that governed the House of Labor, and its corollary that the AFL-CIO stood to protect American workers from Communism.

Fletcher also believes a lack of historical awareness has trapped many union members in a "cone of silence" about the past that prevailed after the purge of the left from the CIO in the 1940s—a silence filled by voices of union leaders who didn't care about a history of conflict and deceived themselves into thinking that labor could have a "love affair with corporate America."[73] He wants to replace the old celebratory approach to union history with a more critical one that allows members to learn from labor's failures while they appreciate its successes.[74] With these goals in mind Fletcher asked me to write a new history for the AFL-CIO education department—one that will incorporate the best movement history of the past three decades.

The New Voice leaders are also more interested in membership education than the old guard, including programs that stress the importance of recruiting and welcoming women and workers of color into union ranks. Although African American working men are now the most unionized group in the workforce (at 23 percent, followed by black women at 18 percent), elected union leaders are still overwhelmingly white men who often find it difficult to share power with minority groups. Union democracy is of course based on majority rule, and in most cases workers of color lack the numbers to elect leaders of their own. The New Voice team has enlarged and diversified the AFL-CIO's executive committee, which now has eleven members of color (20 percent), as compared to only four (or 11 percent) under the old administration. This attempt to be more inclusionary is a positive sign, but, as Manning Marable points out, "the long term question confronting organizing labor" is the same as it was 130 years ago: the question is still "whether it will merge the interests of the black freedom movement with its own agenda for social reform."[75]

Women are the future of the labor movement, according to John Sweeney. In 1960 women represented only 18.3 percent of all union members; by 1994 their share of membership reached 37 percent, but few women had gained important national leadership positions, except in unions like those of the nurses with overwhelmingly female membership. At a state level, more female leaders have emerged in recent decades. In Massachusetts, for example, where women represent 32 percent of all union members, 28 percent of all offices were held by women in 1992, but few of them (14 percent) were presidents and many of them (51 percent) were recording secretaries. Highly successful training programs organized in this state and on a regional level reveal an enormous desire and capacity for leadership among women unionists—a desire often unrequited, a capacity unfulfilled.[76]

Organizing new members is a start since women, immigrants, and workers of color will undoubtedly seek to empower more leaders from their own ranks; but it is only the start. Moving beyond inclusion requires new thinking about union democracy, thinking beyond the outcomes of winner-take-all elections for the very few paid positions available in most unions. Unions need to create far more leadership opportunities in order to reflect the diversity of their members and to attract new members. Some union staffers report that women and people of color are not interested in positions that will require them to live "crazy" lives working way beyond a forty-hour week; it makes sense, as Susan Eaton argues, to create more part-time staff positions with less chance of burning out the people who work them, positions defined less by male notions of authority and more by alternative leadership models based on collaboration and participation.[77] Organizing cannot stop after the first union representation election is won and the first contract is bargained; it has to continue to give life to the union, to create new opportunities for members to express their voices and practice their leadership skills.[78]

The challenge of diversifying unions is closely connected to the challenge of democratizing unions, and both challenges must be met if labor is to add new millions to its ranks. Many unorganized workers still feel that union officers have their own interests, that they "own" the union. Unlike the old guard, the new-age leaders seem less afraid of mobilizing their members, less afraid they will be replaced by rank-and-file insurgents. Many of them seem to have recognized that the labor movement, and their own unions, can "only be saved by unleashing a rank-and-file initiative," write Jeremy Brecher and Tim Costello. "They might prefer to limit change to a militant business unionism which combines top-down control with more vigorous organizing and a greater willingness to strike." But surely, "any substantial revitalization of the labor movement will require a move toward social movement unionism, in which grassroots activism supplants the rigid, bureaucratic character all too typical of American trade unions."[79]

When Ron Carey was removed from the Teamster presidency on charges of election fraud in 1997, reform forces in the movement were deeply discouraged. Carey had led the effort to reshape organized labor's image as one consonant with honesty, integrity, and democracy. This debacle opened the way for the return to national power by the old guard and its leader James Hoffa Jr. a year later. But the end of Carey's progressive administration did not put a stop to the rank-and-file movement for democracy and accountability in the Teamsters. The Teamsters for a Democratic Union still works as an effective and increasingly diverse force for social-movement unionism. Even after the Carey crisis, progressive TDU candidates continued to win against "old guard" forces allied with Hoffa.[80] And in the December 1998 election for the IBT presidency, reform candidate Tom Leedham ran surprisingly well, given the deep disillusionment that followed Carey's downfall. Jimmy Hoffa's son won the election with 54 percent of the vote but he will head a union very different from the one his father ruled from the top down in the 1950s and 1960s.[81]

Despite suffering these setbacks and encountering numerous roadblocks, organized labor is starting to look like a social movement again, attracting student activists, writers and artists, and allies in the churches and universities where pro-labor professors have organized teach-ins for students and have expanded the dialogue between union activists and supportive intellectuals that had been taking place for a long time within labor education circles. Despite formidable barriers to new organizing, women workers in general and workers of color in particular show a strong interest in the labor movement. These are the same workers who dominate large portions of the booming service sector and who hold the future of the movement in their hands.[82] If unions also establish a meaningful presence in communities where these low-wage workers live, if they become community-based organizations, and if they open themselves up to new leaders—if these things happen—then the movement could again take the shape it took in the 1930s when unions represented a way out of poverty and a way into fuller citizenship for the poor and disfranchised.

Even more privileged workers—educated professionals and skilled white men—are worried about their futures in an insecure labor market where employee loyalty means next to nothing. In the lean and mean downsized and globalized economy of the 1990s, more workers are expressing a need for representation—in gaining a collective voice at the workplace. Despite job growth, real wages have declined steadily since 1973.[83] Restructuring and downsizing have eliminated thousands of jobs in wage earning and management ranks, increasing the anxiety over job security. Unlike the shrinking minority of workers protected by union contracts, the vast majority of employees can be terminated "at will" without "just cause." Unless they can prove discrimination based on race, gender, age, or disability, their only recourse is a costly lawsuit.

The expectation of full-time, lifetime employment has disappeared for many employees as employers turn more to the use of "contingent workers."[84] At this writing, there are over 43 million citizens without health coverage, partly because poor people are losing Medicaid benefits "as stringent new laws prod people to move from welfare to work" in low-paying non-union jobs that usually do not offer health benefits.[85] These are a few reasons why the rich are becoming obscenely richer, while more and more people, like the women who received Aid to Families with Dependent Children, are being shoved into the ranks of the "working poor." "The big beneficiaries of our economic expansion have been the owners of financial assets and a new class of highly compensated technicians," wrote Felix G. Rohatyn in the *New York Times*. What is occurring is a huge transfer of wealth from lower-skilled and middle-class Americans to the owners of capital assets and to the new technological aristocracy." This is not the opinion of a labor leader but of a world-renowned financier who is now U.S. Ambassador to France. He went on to add that the "mutual loyalty" of employees and employers has been replaced by a "fear for the future and a cynicism for the present as a broad proportion of working people see themselves as simply temporary assets to be hired or fired to protect the bottom line or to create 'share holder value.' "[86]

So even in a booming economy and a era of conservative political hegemony, there are good reasons why we see signs of a revived interest in union organizing—with all the risks it still entails. There are also indications the new leaders of the AFL-CIO might be able create a vibrant social movement that, in President John Sweeney's words, "represents working people throughout society." The political campaign to make organizing a right, inspired by the civil rights movement, is an important step in that direction.[87] But even if AFL-CIO unions cannot buck the long odds against them and add millions of new members to their ranks, they now offer much more hope that Americans can get help from a strong protest movement willing to reach out beyond the differences that divide workers and take on even the giant global corporations who rule the marketplace and threaten to dominate the course of the next century without significant democratic opposition. Even more encouraging is the rise of a new generation of labor activists inspired by the new social movements of their own time, activists who, when they become leaders, are far more willing to invest power in the working people who have proven time and again in the last two difficult decades that they are willing to learn from their defeats and find new ways of fighting for their rights.

With their backs to the wall, their sense of security shredded, many union members have refused to become quiet victims of downsizing and the struggle to gain the competitive edge. Instead, they have engaged in a process of education and experimentation—a process of social learning. Drawing lessons from painful experiences, many activists have reread labor history, revived certain progressive union traditions, and created new ones. This process of consciousness-raising has reawakened a social-movement impulse among workers much like the one that created the labor movement more than a century ago when U.S. workers took a lead in the international struggle against uncontrolled market forces and rapacious employers—when they formed their own organizations against the might of the state and, through them, asserted new rights as citizens and workers, as brothers and sisters determined to defend the dignity and security of wage-earning families.

Notes

Prologue: Making Movement History

1. For an assessment by a historian who was part of the radical movement in the profession, see Jonathan M. Wiener, "Radical Historians and the Crisis in American History, 1959–1980," *Journal of American History* 76, 2 (September 1989): 399–434. For an earlier critical assessment, by an erstwhile Marxist, see Aileen S. Kraditor, "American Radical Historians on Their Heritage," *Past & Present* 56 (August 1972): 136–53 and my debate with Kraditor, ibid., 69 (November 1975): 122–31.

2. My appreciation for both volumes of *Who Built America?* is expressed in two reviews: James Green, "Conflict versus Consensus in America," and "A Multicultural History," *Boston Globe* (12 August 1990 and 10 May 1992).

For an evaluation of recent textbook treatments of workers and the labor movement that points out remaining shortcomings, see Alice Kessler-Harris and Dorothy Sue Cobble, "The New Labor History in American History Textbooks," *Journal of American History* 80, 2 (March 1993): 1534, who recommend *Who Built America?* "to those who wish to place working people's perspectives at the core of their courses."

3. The accomplishments of labor movement historians in this arena are of special significance. See, for example, the case studies by Richard Schneirov, *Labor and Urban Politics: Class Conflict and the Origins of Modern Liberalism in Chicago* (Urbana: University of Illinois Press, 1998) and Lizabeth Cohen, *Making a New Deal: Industrial Workers in Chicago, 1919–1939* (Cambridge: Cambridge University Press, 1990). Also see the recent national study by Elizabeth Sanders, *Roots of Reform: Farmers, Workers and the American State* (Chicago: University of Chicago Press, 1999).

4. Alan Dawley, *Struggles for Justice: Social Responsibility and the Liberal State* (Cambridge: Harvard University Press, 1991), 151.

5. Eric Foner, *The Story of American Freedom* (New York: W. W. Norton, 1998).

6. See Alessandro Portelli, "Oral History As Genre," "There's Always Gonna Be a Line," in *The Battle of Valle Giulia: Oral History and the Art of Dialogue* (Madison: University of Wisconsin Press, 1997), 9–18, 38–39.

7. Michael Walzer, *The Company of Critics: Social Criticism and Political Commitment in the Twentieth Century* (New York: Basic Books, 1988), 239, 228, 240.

8. Arthur M. Schlesinger Jr., *The Politics of Upheaval* (Boston: Houghton Mifflin, 1960).

9. For a more recent appreciation of Covington Hall filled with wonderful insights, see David

Roediger, "Covington Hall. The Republic of the Imagination," in Paul Buhle et al., eds. *Free Spirits: Annals of the Insurgent Imagination* (San Francisco: City Lights Books, 1982), 178–82, and Covington Hall, *Labor Struggles in the Deep South,* David R. Roediger, ed. (Chicago: Charles H. Kerr, 1999).

10. James Green, introduction, and Carl Sandburg, forward, to *If You Don't Weaken: The Autobiography of Oscar Ameringer* (Norman: University of Oklahoma Press, 1983), xvii–xix, xlx.

11. See James R. Green, "The Brotherhood of Timber Workers: A Radical Response to Industrial Capitalism in the Southern U.S.A.," *Past & Present* 60 (August 1973).

12. See Ellen Carol DuBois, "Making Women's History: Activist Historians of Women's Rights, 1880–1940," *Radical History Review* 49 (1991): 62–64.

13. Ibid., 78–79.

14. Warren Susman, "History and the American Intellectual: The Uses of a Usable Past," in *Culture As History: The Transformation of American Society in the Twentieth Century* (New York, Pantheon 1984), 18.

15. Mary Beard, *A Short History of the American Labor Movement* (New York: Harcourt, Brace and Howe, 1920), 6–7.

16. Richard Hofstadter, *The Progressive Historians: Turner, Beard, Parrington* (New York: Alfred A. Knopf, 1968), 176.

17. C. Vann Woodward, *Tom Watson, Agrarian Rebel* (New York: MacMillan, 1938). For an appreciation of Woodward's work and a dialogue about what it meant to our generation of historians, see introduction and text of "Past and Present in Southern History: An Interview with C. Vann Woodward" by James Green, *Radical History Review* 36 (September 1986), 80–100. Woodward quoted on p. 80.

18. C. Vann Woodward, *Thinking Black: The Perils of Writing History* (Baton Rouge: Louisiana State University Press, 1986), 61–65. And for his remarks on Marxist historians, see ibid., 94–96. He praised the Marxist scholarship of Eugene Genovese but also defended his criticisms of Herbert Aptheker against whom he voted as a part-time instructor for a Yale college seminar on W.E.B. Du Bois.

19. W.E.B. Du Bois, *Black Reconstruction, 1860–1880* (New York: Harcourt Brace, 1935).

20. Philip S. Foner, *The Industrial Workers of the World, 1905–1917, Volume IV of History of the Labor Movement in the United States* (New York: International Publishers, 1965). And see James R. Green, *Grass-Roots Socialism: Radical Movements in the Southwest, 1895–1945* (Baton Rouge: Louisiana State University Press, 1978).

21. George Lispitz, "'Apotheosis of Glory': Surveying Social History," *Journal of American History* 68, 2 (September 1994): 588.

22. Herbert Gutman, "The Missing Synthesis: What Ever Happened to History?" *Nation* 233 (1981): 521, 553, and "Historical Consciousness in Contemporary America," in Herbert G. Gutman, *Power and Culture: Essays on the American Working Class* (New York: Pantheon, 1987), 395–412.

23. Fred Inglis, quoted in Harvey J. Kaye, "E. P. Thompson, the British Marxist Tradition and the Contemporary Crisis," in E. P. Thompson, *Critical Perspectives,* Harvey J. Kaye and Keith McClelland, eds. (Philadelphia: Temple University Press, 1990), 246.

24. Jacquelyn Dowd Hall, "Partial Truths," *Signs* (Summer 1989): 910–11.

25. Jacquelyn Dowd Hall, "'You Must Remember This': Autobiography as Social Critique," *Journal of American History* 85, 2 (September 1998): 441.

26. Ibid., 459, and Hall, "Partial Truths," 911.

27. This phrasing is derived from David Carr, *Time, Narrative, and History* (Bloomington: Indiana University Press, 1986), 10, 16, 61, 65. My thinking on these points has benefited greatly from Alan Dawley's remarks in "Keeping Time in the Twentieth Century," a paper presented to the Organization of American Historians, Atlanta, Ga., April 1994.

28. William Cronon, "A Place for Stories: Nature, History, and Narrative," *Journal of American History* 78, 4 (March 1992): 1374–75. Cronon thanks Jim O'Brien for this insight, as I do for so many other interventions in my own thinking and writing.

29. David Thelen, "The Practice of History," *Journal of American History* 81, 3 (Spring, 1989): 942–43.

30. Walter Benjamin, "The Story Teller," in *Illuminations,* Hannah Arendt, ed. (New York: Schocken Books, 1969), 86–87.

31. The following editorials and reviews written for the *Boston Globe* applied movement history to contemporary political concerns: "Where's Labor's Solidarity?" (23 November 1981); "King, Flynn and Populism" (28 October 1983); "Local 201 Shows Labor the Comeback Trail" (11 March 1986); "Labor Day: The Past Resurfaces" (6 September 1987), "For Jackson, Populism Is a Class A̶c̶t̶" (2 April 1988); "C̶o̶r̶p̶o̶r̶a̶t̶e̶ C̶u̶l̶t̶u̶r̶e̶'s̶ F̶a̶i̶l̶u̶r̶e̶ i̶n̶ D̶e̶a̶l̶i̶n̶g̶ w̶i̶t̶h̶ C̶o̶a̶l̶ M̶i̶n̶e̶r̶s̶" (27 June 1988); "Conflict and Consensus in America" (12 August 1990); "A Giant of American Labor" (14 July 1991); "The Life and Legacy of Jimmy Hoffa" (8 September 1991); "A Multicultural History" (10 May 1992); "A Vision of Parity Brutally Extinguished" (5 July 1992); "Sacco, Vanzetti and Labor" (1 September 1997); and "Uncommon History" (5 October 1997). For a similar effort to focus on workers' rights for the bicentennial of the Constitution, see "The Fruits of Their Labor," from "The Constitution Alive!" *Philadelphia Inquirer* (29 September 1987): 30.

32. Thomas Geoghegan, *Which Side Are You On? Trying to Be for Labor When It's Flat on Its Back* (New York: Farrar, Strauss & Giroux, 1991).

33. Leon Fink, "The New Labor History and the Powers of Historical Pessimism," *Journal of American History* 96, 2 (April 1991): 418–20.

34. Howard Zinn, *The Politics of History* (Boston: Beacon Press, 1970), 47, 51. Staughton Lynd, for example, has continued to fulfill these responsibilities in his studies of the labor movement, explaining why an "alternative unionism" based on rank-and-file activism was displaced by less democratic, more bureaucratic union institutions. Staughton Lynd, Introduction to *"We Are All Leaders": The Alternative Unionism of the Early 1930s,* Staughton Lynd, ed. (Urbana: University of Illinois Press, 1996), 1–18.

35. Richard Flacks, *Making History: The American Left and the American Mind* (New York: Columbia University Press, 1988), 244.

36. Barbara Kingsolver, *Holding the Line: Women and the Great Arizona Mine Strike of 1983* (Ithaca: ILR Press, 1989).

37. John Berger, "From 'Who Governs' to 'How to survive,'" *New Statesman* 11 (March 1988): 28–29.

38. Roy Rosenzweig and David Thelen, *The Presence of the Past: Popular Uses of History in American Life* (New York: Columbia University Press, 1998), 132, 137, 160–61.

39. See Henry Hampton, "Preface: Toward a More Perfect Union," in *Voices of Freedom: An Oral History of the Civil Rights Movement from the 1950s through the 1980s,* Henry Hampton and Steve Fayer, eds. (New York: Bantam, 1990); and Vincent Harding, *Hope and History: Why We Must Share the Story of the Movement* (Maryknoll, N.Y.: Orbis Books, 1990).

40. Berger, "From 'Who Governs' to 'How to Survive,'" 28–29. Also see Francis Fukuyama, *The End of History and the Last Man* (New York: Avon 1992). For his intelligent reading of Berger and Fukuyama I am indebted to Harvey Kaye, *The Education of Desire and the Writing of Marxist History* (New York: Routledge and Kegan Paul, 1992), 160–71.

41. Rosenzweig and Thelen, *The Presence of the Past,* 160–61.

42. On democratic experiments in insurgent movements, see Lawrence Goodwyn, *Democratic Promise: The Populist Moment in America* (New York: Oxford University Press, 1976), 542. For an application of Goodwyn's notion of democratic movement culture to the late nineteenth-century labor movement, see *Bruce Laurie, From Artisan to Worker: Labor in Nineteenth Century America* (New York: Hill & Wang 1989). And for a important contemporary exploration of defensive labor struggles, see Rick Fantasia, *Cultures of Solidarity: Consciousness, Action, and Contemporary American Workers* (Berkeley: University of California Press, 1988).

43. Francis Fukuyama, "The End of History?" *The National Interest* 16 (Summer 1989): 3–4. The best sustained critique of late twentieth-century capitalism and its erosion of democracy can be found in the powerful works of William B. Greider, *Who Will Tell the People? The Betrayel of American Democracy* (New York: Simon & Schuster 1992); *Secrets of the Temple: How the Federal Reserve Runs the Country* (New York: Simon & Schuster, 1987); and *One World, Ready or Not: The Manic Logic of Global Capitalism* (New York: Simon & Schuster, 1997). For a more hopeful reading in a similar populist vein, see Harry C. Boyte, *Commonwealth a Return to Citizen Politics*

(New York: The Free Press, 1989) based on a sharp reading of movement history to which the author has contributed important new chapters. See his *Backyard Revolution: Understanding the New Citizen Movement* (Philadelphia: Temple University Press, 1980). For a more recent discussion on an international scale, see the work of movement historians Jeremy Brecher and Tim Costello, *Global Village or Global Pillage? Economic Reconstruction from the Bottom Up* (Boston: South End Press, 1994).

44. Editorial, *History Workshop Journal* 1 (1976), 1 and Michael Frisch, *A Shared Authority: Essays on Craft and Meaning of Oral History and Public History* (Albany: State University of New York Press, 1990).

45. Freire, quoted in *We Make the Road by Walking: Conversations on Education and Social Change, Myles Horton and Paulo Freire,* Brenda Bell, John Gaventa, and John Peters, eds. (Philadelphia: Temple University Press, 1990), 215–18.

46. See the introduction to the Leon Fink's challenging book *Progressive Intellectuals and the Dilemmas of Democratic Commitment* (Cambridge: Harvard University Press, 1998) and Russell Jacoby, *The Last Intellectuals: American Culture in the Age of Academe* (New York: Basic Books, 1987).

47. John Keane, *Democracy and Civil Society* (London: Verso, 1988), 33.

48. The reference is to lectures given at the Boston Public Library, which later published them in a book coauthored with Hugh Carter Donahue and titled *Boston's Workers: A Labor History* (Boston: Boston Public Library and the National Endowment for the Humanities, 1979).

49. The Labor History Theme Study was completed in 1995 for the National Park Service by James Grossman and Robin Bachin of the Newberry Library in Chicago. It includes my introduction, "Marking Labor History on the National Landscape.

50. William Gamson, "Social Psychology to Collective Action," in *Frontiers of Social Movement Theory,* Aldon D. Morris and Carol M. Mueller, eds. (New Haven: Yale University Press, 1992), 53–76; Andres Torres, "Political Radicalism in the Diaspora—The Puerto Rican Experience," in *The Puerto Rican Movement,* Andres Torres and Jose E. Velazquez, eds. (Philadelphia: Temple University Press, 1989), 16. For a helpful review of old and new social movement theory, see Robert Fischer, "Grass-Roots Organizing Worldwide," in *Mobilizing the Community,* Robert Fischer and Joseph Kling, eds. (London: SAGE Publications, 1993), 3–27.

51. For example, a leading sociologist of the civil rights movement, Aldon D. Morris, explains how for poor blacks "class consciousness is correlated with racial awareness" in his essay "Political Consciousness and Collective Action," ibid., 366. Many relevant historical monographs might be cited, but a few of the most revealing are Joe William Trotter Jr., *Coal, Class and Color: Blacks in Southern West Virginia* (Urbana: University of Illinois Press, 1990) and Earl Lewis, *In Their Own Interests: Race, Class and Power in in Twentieth Century Norfolk, Virginia* (Berkeley: University of California Press, 1993), which examine "racialized" forms of class consciousness. On women's consciousness in local class struggles, see the important books by Elizabeth Faue, *Community of Suffering and Struggle: Women, Men and the Labor Movement in Minneapolis, 1915–1945* (Chapel Hill: University of North Carolina Press, 1991) and Dana Frank, *Purchasing Power: Consumer Organizing, Gender, and the Seattle Labor Movement, 1919–1929* (Cambridge: Cambridge University Press, 1994).

52. Kim Scipes, "Social Movement Unionism: Developing the Conceptualization," unpublished paper. Also see Kim Moody, "Towards an International Social Movement Unionism, *New Left Review* 225 (1997): 52–72.

53. Stephen Lerner, "Taking the Offensive, Turning the Tide," in *A New Labor Movement for a New Century,* Gregory Mantsios, ed. (New York: Monthly Review Press, 1998), 76.

1. Discovering Movement History with the "Radical Americans"

1. Hoover, quoted in *Time* 1 August 1969, p. 65, which also quoted hostile labor union leaders.

2. For a sharp interpretation of movement politics in 1969, see James Miller, *Democracy in the Streets: From Port Huron to the Siege of Chicago* (New York: Simon and Schuster, 1987).

3. Jonathan M. Wiener, "Radical Historians and the Crisis in American History," *Journal of American History* 76, 2 (September 1989): 399–434.

4. Staugton Lynd, "Intellectuals, the University, and the Movement," speech to the founding convention of the New University Conference (May 1968), pamphlet in author's possession.

5. Grady McWhiney, "Louisiana Socialists in the Early Twentieth Century: A Study of Rustic Radicalism," *Journal of Southern History* 20 (1954): 315–36.

6. Many quoted in Alan Draper, *Conflict of Interests: Organized Labor and the Civil Rights Movement in the South, 1954–1968* (Ithaca: ILR Press, 1994), 4–5 which also describes the AFL-CIO president's opposition to the civil rights March on Washington in 1963.

7. Wallace Stegner, *Angle of Repose* (New York: Doubleday, 1971), 153.

8. Wiener, "Radical Historians," 399–434. Lemisch's critique of establishment historians was later published as *On Active Service: Politics and Ideology in the American Historical Profession* (Toronto: New Hogtown Press, 1975).

9. Wiener, "Radical Historians," 422.

10. Peter Novick, *That Noble Dream: The "Objectivity Question" and the American Historical Profession* (Cambridge: Cambridge University Press, 1988), 416–17. Noam Chomsky, "Objectivity and Liberal Scholarship," in *American Power and the New Mandarins* (New York: Pantheon, 1969), 23–138.

11. Introduction to a "Special Issue on Radical Historiography," *Radical America* 4 (November 1970): 2, 4.

12. Ibid.

13. Francine du Plessix Gray, "The Panthers at Yale," *New York Review of Books* (4 June 1970): 35.

14. Maurice Isserman, "Four Dead in Ohio, Twenty-five Years Later," *Chronicle of Higher Education* 61, 34 (5 May 1995): B1–2.

15. *New Haven Register* (2, 3 May 1970).

16. Gray, "The Panthers at Yale," 35.

17. "May Day, New Haven," an information newspaper published by View from the Bottom, Yale Strike News, and the Committee to Defend the Panthers (1 May 1970): 10; "Canvassing Instructions" by the "Steering Committee" of the student strike, mimeographed copies in author's possession; Jim Green, "Research for Control: Yale's Social Science Center," unpublished text of speech, in author's possession; *New Haven Journal Courier* (27 April 1970); *Yale Daily News* 28 April, 11 May 1970.

18. Jim Green, "Intellectuals and Activism: The Dilemma of Radical Historians," *The Activist: A Student Journal of Politics and Opinion* 2, 3 (1971): 3–4, 28.

19. *Liberation* (February 1970): 34.

20. Eugene D. Genovese, "On Being a Socialist and a Historian," in *In Red and Black: Marxian Explorations in Southern and Afro-American History* (New York: Pantheon, 1971), 7.

21. Melvyn Dubofsky, *We Shall Be All: A History of the Industrial Workers of the World* (Chicago: Quadrangle, 1967), xiii.

22. Herbert Gutman, Introduction to *Working Lives: The 'Southern Exposure' History of Labor in the South* (New York: Pantheon 1980), xi–xvii.

23. Paul Buhle letter to the author, Madison, 12 April 1971; Paul Buhle, "*Radical America* and Me," in *History and the New Left: Madison and the New Left, 1950–1970*, Paul Buhle, ed. (Philadelphia: Temple University Press, 1990), 216–32. Quote on p. 222.

24. Paul Berman, "The Spirit of '67: Radical Americanism and How It Grew," *Village Voice Literary Supplement* 19 (September 1983): 17.

25. "*Radical America* Komix," *Radical America* (cited hereinafter as *RA*) 3, 1 (1969), and ibid., 3–4.

26. Ronald Aronson, "Dear Herbert," *RA* 3, 3 (April 1970): 16–18.

27. Quotes from Jonathan M. Wiener, "Radical Historians and the Crisis in American History, 1959–1980," *Journal of American History* 76, 2 (September 1989): 424, and David Montgomery,

"What's Happening to the American Worker," *Radical America* pamphlet (Madison: Radical America, 1970), 1.

28. Paul Buhle, on Montgomery, in James O'Brien et al., "New Left Historians of the 1960s," *Radical America* 4, 8–9 (November 1970): 90–91. Interview with David Montgomery, in Henry D. Abelove et al., *Visions of History* (New York: Pantheon, 1984), 177.

29. Buhle, introduction to *History and the New Left,* 3–4.

30. C. L. R. James et al., *Facing Reality* (Detroit: Correspondence Publishing, 1958), 93–94.

31. Paul Berman "*Facing Reality,*" in Paul Buhle, ed. "C. L. R. James: His Life and Work," *Urgent Tasks* 12 (1981): 105–07.

32. Berman, "The Spirit of '67," 13. Also see Paul Buhle's important recollections of James and his influence, in Buhle, "*Radical America* and Me," in *History and the New Left,* 227–28.

33. George Rawick, "Working-Class Self-Activity," *RA* 3, 2 (1969): 23–31, reprinted in *Workers' Struggles, Past & Present: A 'Radical America' Reader,* James Green, ed. (Philadelphia: Temple University Press, 1983).

34. John Evansohn, Laura Foner, Mark Naison, Ruth Meyerowitz, and Will Brumbach, "Literature on the American Working Class," and Paul Faler, "Working-Class Historiography," *RA* 3, 2 (1969): 32–68.

35. See James Weinstein, "Gompers and the New Liberalism, 1909–1919," and Ronald Radosh, "The Corporate Ideology of American Labor Leaders from Gompers to Hillman," in *For a New America: Essays in History and Politics from 'Studies on the Left', 1959–1967,* David Eakins and James Weinstein, eds. (New York: Vintage, 1970), 101–14, 125–51.

36. "New Radical Historians in the Sixties: A Survey," *RA* 4 (November 1970): 104–06.

37. Buhle, *History and the New Left,* 30, 226.

38. Paul Buhle, introduction to "*Radical America:* A Fifteen Year Anthology," *RA* 16 (May 1982): 2.

39. Mari Jo Buhle, Ann D. Gordon, and Nancy Schrom, "Women in American Society: A Historical Contribution," *RA* 5 (July–August 1971): 3, and final quote from Paul Buhle, "Introduction to Fifteen Years of *Radical America,*" 5.

40. Harold M. Baron, "The Demand for Black Labor: Notes on the Political Economy of Racism," reprinted in Green, *Workers' Struggles,* quote on p. 56.

41. Buhle, Gordon, and Schrom, "Women in American Society," 3.

42. Wiener, "Radical Historians," 425.

43. Berman, "The Spirit of '67," 18.

44. E. P. Thompson interview in Henry D. Abelove et al., ed. *Visions of History* (New York: Pantheon Books, 1984) 22–23.

45. Thompson recalls his working-class students in ibid., 1.

46. Marcus Rediker, quoted in Harvey J. Kaye, "E. P. Thompson, the British Marxist Historical Tradition and the Contemporary Crisis," E. P. Thompson, *Critical Debates,* Harvey J. Kaye and Keith McClelland, eds. (Philadelphia: Temple University Press, 1990), 264.

47. E. P. Thompson, "The Politics of Theory," in *People's History and Socialist Theory,* Raphael Samuel, ed. (London: Routledge and Kegan Paul, 1981), 406, and *The Poverty of Theory and Other Essays* (New York: Monthly Review Press, 1978), 42–43, 47.

48. Paul Berman, "The Spirit of '67," 17.

49. Quotes from Berman, "The Spirit of '67," p. 13, and Jacquelyn Dowd Hall, "In the Beginning: A Personal View of *Southern Exposure*'s First Ten Years from the People Who Made It Happen," *Southern Exposure* 11, 3 (1983): 7.

50. Linda Gordon (1981), in Abelove, *Visions of History,* 86–87.

51. Paul Faler, Tom Dublin, and Jim O'Brien, *The New England Working Class: A Bibliographical History* (Boston: New England Free Press, 1972), and Jim O'Brien, Jim Green, Paul Faler, John Battye, David Frank, Greg Kealey, and Ian McKay, *A Guide to Working Class History* (Somerville and Toronto: New England Free Press and New Hogtown Press, 1974).

52. O'Brien's beaver history appeared in *Free Spirits: Annals of the Insurgent Imagination,* Paul Buhle et al., eds. (San Francisco: City Lights Books, 1982), 39–48.

53. Nick Thorkelson and Jim O'Brien, "An Underhanded History of the USA," *RA* 7, 3 (1973),

and "A Marxist Analysis of Baseball," ibid., 11, 5 (1978). Both reprinted by the New England Free Press.

54. James Green, "Working-Class Militancy in the Great Depression," *RA* 6, 6 (November–December 1972).

55. Staughton Lynd, "The Possibility of Radicalism in the Early 1930s: The Case of Steel," ibid., reprinted in Green, *Workers' Struggles*, 190–208.

56. Theodore Rosengarten and Dale Rosen, "Shootout at Reeltown," *RA* 6, 6 (November–December 1972).

57. Theodore Rosengarten, *All God's Dangers: The Life of Nate Shaw* (New York: Alfred Knopf, 1974), xiv–xv.

58. See, for example, the autobiographies of labor movement militants including Len DeCaux, *Labor Radical from the Wobblies to the CIO: A Personal History* (Boston: Beacon Press, 1970); Wyndam Mortimer, *Organize! My Life as a Union Man* (Boston: Beacon Press, 1971); Farrell Dobbs, *Teamster Rebellion* (New York: Monad Press, 1972); Al Richmond, *A Long View from the Left: Memoirs of an American Revolutionary* (Boston: Houghton Mifflin, 1973); James J. Matles and James Higgins, *Them and Us: Struggles of a Rank and File Union* (Englewood Cliffs, N.J.: Prentice Hall, 1974); Frank Marquart, *An Auto Worker's Journal: The UAW from Crusade to One Party Union* (College Park: Pennsylvania State University Press, 1975); H. L. Mitchell, *Mean Things Happening: The Life and Times of H. L. Mitchell Co-founder of the Southern Tenant Farmers Union* (Montclair, N.J.: Allenheld, Osmun, 1979); and Nell Irvin Painter, *The Narrative of Hosea Hudson: His Life As a Negro Communist in the Deep South* (Cambridge: Harvard University Press, 1979), from which a segment was excerpted for *Radical America*.

Mario T. Garcia offers insights into the ethnic "oppositional narrative" in his introduction to *Memories of Chicano History: The Life and Narrative of Bert Corona* (Berkeley: University of California Press, 1994).

59. E. J. Hobsbawm, "Ideology and Labor History," *Journal of Social History* 7, 4 (Summer 1974): 371–81.

60. James Green, "Labor Militancy and Union Democracy" (a review of Alice and Staughton Lynd, eds., *Rank and File: Personal Histories of Working Class Organizers*), *The Nation* (6 September 1975), 183–84.

61. David Montgomery, "The New Unionism and the Transformation of Workers' Consciousness in America, 1909–1922," and James Green, "Comments on the Montgomery paper" *Journal of Social History* 7, 4 (summer 1974): 509–35.

62. Jeremy Brecher, *Strike! A True History of Mass Insurgence in America from 1877 to the Present* (San Francisco: Straight Arrow Books, 1972), and for the *RA* symposium on the book, see David Montgomery, "Spontaneity and Organization: Some Comments," *Radical America* 7, 6 (1973); 70–77, and Brecher's response, in "Who Advocates Spontaneity?" ibid., 91–92.

63. Mike Davis, "The Stop Watch and the Wooden Shoe: Scientific Management and the Industrial Workers of the World"; Dorothy Fennell, "Beneath the Surface: The Life of a Factory," in Green, *Workers' Struggles*, 83–116 and 293–311. Also see Susan Porter Benson, "The Clerking Sisterhood: Rationalization and Work Culture of Saleswomen in American Department Stores, 1890–1960," in Green, *Workers' Struggles*.

64. Casey Blake, "Where Are All the Young Left Historians?" *Radical History Review* 28–30 (1984): 117.

65. Noel Ignatin (now Ignatiev), "Black Workers and White Workers," *RA* 8, 4 (1974): 41–60.

66. The racist attacks on the Debnam family and the response of the defense group Racial Unity Now are described in J. Anthony Lukas (*Common Ground: A Turbulent Decade in the Lives of Three American Families* [New York: Vintage 1986], 513–24), who through the words of another supporter of the Debnam family accused RUN of being "radical missionaries from Cambridge" who sought "to make race the central issue in the city." I did not participate in RUN meetings and do not recall its leaders' ideological agenda, but race was the central issue in Boston then and it did not take a group of radicals to make it so.

67. Liberal critics of busing, like Harvard psychologist Robert Coles, are cited in ibid., 506.

68. Jim Green and Allen Hunter, "Racism and Busing in Boston" *RA* 8, 6 (1974): 3–13. Re-

printed as a pamphlet by the New England Free Press, and in William Tabb and Larry Sawyers, eds., *Marxism and the Metropolis* (New York: Oxford University Press, 1978), 271–96.

69. Green and Hunter, "Racism and Busing in Boston," 296.

70. Quote from Linda Gordon, interview in Abelove, *Visions of History,* 87.

71. See Green, introduction to *Workers Struggles,* 11–12. The World War II wildcat strike wave became a key focus in a special issue on labor politics in the 1940s. See James Green, "Fighting on Two Fronts: Working Class Militancy in the 1940s," *RA* 9, 4–5 (1975): 5–47.

72. Mary Bularzik, "Sexual Harassment at the Workplace: Historical Notes," *RA* 12, 4 (1978), reprinted in Green, *Workers' Struggles,* 117–36.

73. Editors' introduction to a special issue on "Women's Labor," *RA* 7, 4–5 (1973): 7.

74. Green, *Workers' Struggles,* 10–11.

75. Green, "Fighting on Two Fronts," and Ed Jennings, "Wildcat! The Wartime Strike Wave in Auto," in "Labor in the 1940's," *RA* 9, 4–5 (1975), 7–48, 77–105.

76. Stan Weir, "American Labor on the Defensive: A 1940's Odyssey," in ibid., 178–80.

77. Nelson Lichtenstein, "Defending the No Strike Pledge: CIO Politics during World War II," and Ronald Schatz, "The End of Corporate Liberalism: Class Struggle in the Electrical Manufacturing Industry," in ibid., 49–76, 187–205.

78. For criticisms of *RA's* treatment of wartime labor militancy, see Joshua Freeman, "Delivering the Goods: Industrial Unionism during World War II," *Labor History* 19, 4 (1978), 570–93.

79. Mary Bularzik, "Sexual Harassment at the Workplace," and Susan Porter Benson, "The Clerking Sisterhood: Rationalization and the Work Culture of Saleswomen in American Department Stores," in Green, *Workers' Struggles,* 101–36.

80. John Lippert, "Shop Floor Politics at Fleetwood," in Green, *Workers' Struggles,* 344–61, and Frank Kashner, "A Rank-and-File Strike at G.E.," in *RA* 12, 6 (1978): 43–60.

81. James Green, "Holding the Line: Miners' Militancy and the 1978 Coal Strike," originally appeared in *RA* in the spring of 1978 and is reprinted in Green *Workers' Struggles,* 321–43.

82. Stan Weir, "The Conflict in American Unions and the Resistance to Alternative Ideas from the Rank and File," in ibid., 254. Weir's article first appeared in 1972.

83. See Linda Gordon and Allen Hunter, "Sex, Family and the New Right: Anti-Feminism As a Political Force," *Radical America* 12, 1 (1977–78): 9–26, and "Feminism, Leninism and the U.S.," ibid., 13, 5 (1979): 35.

84. Gordon interview in Abelove, *Visions of History,* 88. For a discussion of the extremely hostile reviews of Gordon's 1976 book, *A Woman's Body, A Woman's Right,* see Wiener, "Radical Historians," 426–27.

85. Montgomery, "Spontaneity and Organization," 77.

86. *The World of the Worker* was first published by Hill and Wang, a division of Farrar, Straus and Giroux, in 1980, as part of the American Century Series edited by Eric Foner. The book was reprinted thirteen times and sold roughly 25,000 copies before it was taken out of print in 1995. A new paperback edition of the original text was published by the University of Illinois Press in 1998. For criticisms of the book's interpretation and its style, see Robert Zieger, "James Green's World," *Reviews in American History* (December 1981): 525 and Paul L. Berman, "The World of the Radical Historian," *Village Voice* (18–24 March 1981): 38–39.

2. "Bringing the Boundaries of History Closer to People's Lives"

1. E. J. Hobsbawm, *Primitive Rebels: Studies in Archaic Forms of Social Movement in the Nineteenth and Twentieth Centuries* (New York: W. W. Norton, 1965).

2. For Hobsbawm's criticisms, see his 1974 essay "Ideology and Labour History," reprinted in *Workers: Worlds of Labor* (New York: Pantheon, 1984), 9. Lynd's 1972 article, "The Possibility of Radicalism in the Early 1930s: The Case of Steel," was reprinted in *Workers' Struggles, Past and Present: A 'Radical America' Reader,* James Green, ed. (Philadelphia: Temple University Press, 1983), 190–208. The paper I presented at Birkbeck was translated into French and published as "L'historie de mouvement ouvrier et la gauche americaine," *Le Mouvement social* 102 (1978): 9–40.

3. Jim Green, "Intellectuals and Activism: The Dilemma of Radical Historians," *The Activist* 2, 3 (1971): 3–4.

4. Stuart Hall, "Raphael Samuel: 1934–96," *New Left Review* 221 (January/February, 1997): 120–21.

5. Raphael Samuel, "History Workshop, 1966–1980," in *People's History and Socialist Theory,* Raphael Samuel, ed. (London: Routledge and Kegan Paul, 1981), 410, 412.

6. Hall, Raphael Samuel, 124.

7. E. M. H., Report on East Anglian History Workshop, *History Workshop Journal* 3 (Spring 1977): 204.

8. Report on East London History Workshop, ibid., 4 (Autumn, 1977): 215.

9. Hall, "Raphael Samuel," 124.

10. Ronald J. Grele, "Whose Public? Whose History? What Is the Goal of a Public Historian?" *The Public Historian* 3 (Winter 1981): 46–48.

11. Paul Faler, "Lynn in History," *Radical America* 13, 4 (1979): 44–45.

12. Vincent Ferrini, "The City" in *Selected Poems* (Storrs: University of Connecticut Library, 1976), 1, with a biographical sketch by George F. Butterick.

13. William Carlos Williams, *Against the American Grain* (New York: Alfred Knopf, 1925), 189.

14. Faler, "Lynn in History," 45.

15. Alan Dawley, *Class and Community: The Industrial Revolution in Lynn* (Cambridge: Harvard University Press, 1976); Paul Faler, *Mechanics and Manufacturers in the Early Industrial Revolution: Lynn, Massachusetts, 1780–1860* (Albany: State University of New York Press, 1981); John T. Cumbler, *Working Class Community in America: Work, Leisure and Struggle in Two Industrial Communities, 1880–1930* (Westport, Conn.: Greenwood Press, 1979); and Mary H. Blewett, *Men, Women, and Work: Class, Gender, and Protest in the New England Shoe Industry, 1780–1910* (Urbana: University of Illinois Press, 1988).

16. For a fuller report, see Marty Blatt, Jim Green, and Susan Reverby, "The First Massachusetts History Workshop," *Radical America* 14 (January/February 1980): 67–73.

17. Editorial, *History Workshop Journal,* 1 (1976): 1.

18. Interview with Ralph Fasanella (10 January 1977). For the artist's personal and professional history, see Patrick Watson, *Fasanella's City: The Paintings of Ralph Fasanella with the Story of His Life and Art* (New York: Alfred A. Knopf, 1973).

19. Tom Herriman, "Paintings of Workers by a Working Painter," *Labor Unity* 66, (April 1980): 12–13.

20. Paul Cowan, "Whose America Is This?" *Village Voice* (2 April 1979).

21. Herbert Gutman, "Historical Consciousness in Contemporary America," in Herbert G. Gutman, *Power and Culture: Essays on the American Working Class* (New York: Pantheon, 1987), 400.

22. Michael Knight, "Lawrence, Mass., Reliving 1912 Strike," *New York Times* (26 April 1980).

23. Jim Green, "The Second Massachusetts History Workshop," *History Workshop Journal* 11 (Spring 1981): 188–90.

24. For a version, in Italian, of what Rocco said that day, see Peppino Ortoleva, "Una voce dal coro: Angelo Rocco e lo sciopero di Lawrence del 1912," *Estratto da Movimento Operaio e Socialista,* 1–2 (Gennaio–Giugno 1981): 5–27. For the edited version of Rocco's story collected by Studs Terkel, see his *American Dreams, Lost and Found* (New York: Pantheon, 1980), 96–101.

25. See Ardis Cameron, "Bread and Roses Revisited: Women's Culture and Working-Class Activism in the Lawrence Strike of 1912," in *Women, Work and Protest: A Century of Women's Labor History,* Ruth Milkman, ed. (Boston: Routledge & Kegan Paul, 1985), 42–61.

26. *Life and Times in Immigrant City: Memories of a Textile City: A Booklet Commemorating the Second Massachusetts History Workshop,* October 12, 1980, edited by Martha Coons (Boston: Red Sun Press, 1980).

27. Mary H. Blewett, *The Last Generation: Work and Life in the Textile Mills of Lowell, Massachusetts, 1910–1960* (Amherst: University of Massachusetts Press, 1990).

28. Tom Leary to History Workshop (25 October 1980), in author's possession.

29. Michael Frisch's 1982 essay, "Quality in History Programs: From Celebration to Exploration of Values," is reprinted in his collection *A Shared Authority: Essays on the Craft and Meaning of Oral and Public History* (Albany: State University of New York Press, 1990), 189–90.

30. Katie Neff, "Former Mill Workers Tell of Past in Living History Workshop," *Lawrence Eagle Tribune* (12 October 1980).

31. Bob Hohler, "Memories of 'Bread and Roses' Spur 1912 Striker to Seek Others," *Boston Globe* (8 September 1987).

32. William Cahn, *Lawrence, 1912: The Bread and Roses Strike* (New York: Pilgrim Press, 1980).

33. Edward Thompson, "The Politics of Theory," and Stuart Hall, "In Defence of Theory," in *People's History and Socialist Theory,* 396–408, 382–84.

34. Lawrence Goodwyn, "The Cooperative Commonwealth and Other Abstractions," *Marxist Perspectives* 10 (Summer 1980): 1–44, and James Green, "Populism, Socialism and the Promise of Democracy," *Radical History Review* 24 (Fall 1980): 7–40.

35. For a written version of these remarks, see Raphael Samuel, "People's History" in ibid., xxx–xxxi.

36. For another rendering of these points, see James Green, "People's History and Socialist Theory: A Review Essay," *Radical History Review* 28–30 (1984): 169–86.

37. Ken Worpole, "The Ghostly Pavement: The Political Implications of Local Working-Class History," in *People's History and Socialist Theory,* 24–31. Gramsci quoted on p. 22.

38. William Serrin, "Workers and Historians Share Views," *New York Times* (16 August 1982).

39. Susan Reverby, "From Aide to Organizer: The Oral History of Lillian Roberts," in *Women of America: A History,* Carol Berkin and Mary Beth Norton, eds. (Boston: Houghton Mifflin, 1979), 290–309.

40. See Preface to Jacquelyn Dowd Hall et al., *Like a Family: The Making of a Southern Cotton Mill World* (Chapel Hill: University of North Carolina Press, 1987).

41. Mark Erlich, *With These Hands: The Story of Carpenters in Massachusetts* (Philadelphia: Temple University Press, 1986).

42. Introduction to *Guide to the Oral History of the American Left,* Jonathan Bloom and Paul Buhle, eds. (New York: New York University Libraries and Tamiment Institute, 1984), 1.

43. See Hall, *Like a Family,* xvii, for reference to the textile workers' own interpretation of mill village paternalism and familalism.

44. Jeremy Brecher, "A Report on Doing History from Below: The Brass Workers History Project," in *Presenting the Past: Essays on History and the Public,* Susan Porter Benson, Stephen Brier, and Roy Rosenzweig, eds. (Philadelphia: Temple University Press, 1986), 267–77.

45. "The Brass Workers' Project: A Talk with Jeremy Brecher," interview by Dan Letwin in *Radical Historians' Newsletter* 40 (May 1982): 3.

46. "We Are What We Do," *Boston Globe* (30 March 1980), 18.

47. For a powerful expression, see Jean Tepperman, *Not Servants, Not Machines: Office Workers Speak Out* (Boston: Beacon Press, 1976).

48. For essays on clerical workers and informal work groups published in *Radical America* by Roz Feldberg, Susan Porter Benson, Stan Weir, and Dorothy Fennell, see Green, *Workers' Struggles,* 101–16, 151–67, 251–68, and 293–311; Jeremy Brecher, and the Work Relations Group, "Uncovering the Hidden History of the American Workplace," *Review of Radical Political Economics* 10 (Winter 1978): 1–23; and Jacquelyn Dowd Hall, "An Oral History of Industrialization: Learning by Listening," *Institute for Research in Social Science Newsletter* 66 (April 1981): 5–9.

49. The 1988 meetings of the Oral History Association in Baltimore offered a fascinating group of reports on projects about oral history and community activism, especially in communities of color. The most striking report on these themes came from Lani Fanjek, an activist in the Day of Remembrance Committee for Japanese-American Redress, who described the way in which oral history helped break a "wall of silence" about the World War II internments and how a "community mobilization of memory" helped create a powerful movement for human and civil rights.

50. For a brilliant discussion of the collaborative writing and thinking involved in the Southern Oral History Project, as well as a consideration of the importance of feminist discourse and the emphasis on the dialogue of voices in literary theory, see Jacquelyn D. Hall and Della Pollack,

"The Making and Remaking of a Cotton Mill World," in, *Rewriting American Literary History*, Gunter H. Lenz and Hartmut Keil, eds. (Frankfurt and New York: Campus Publishers, 1990).

51. On *The Mill Hunk Herald*, see Larry Evans, "Blue Collar Scholar: A Former Steel Worker Hits the Books," *The Progressive* (April 1989), 24–25. Also see "Working Class Writing," *UAW Solidarity* (16–31 December 1981). On "Dig Where You Stand," in Sweden, see Steve Brier, "People's History Around the World: Sweden," *Radical History Review* 25 (October 1981), 173– 76. The quote from Stan Weir appeared on all the Singlejack booklets he and Bob Miles published in San Pedro.

52. Gerald Sider, "Cleansing History: Lawrence, Massachusetts, the Strike for Four Loaves of Bread and No Roses, and the Anthropology of Working-Class Consciousness," *Radical History Review* 65 (1996): 48–73, with comments by Ardis Cameron, 92–93.

53. "Labor History and Public History," a special issue edited by Brian Greenberg of *The Public Historian* 11, 4 (Fall 1989).

54. See Liz McMillen, "New Professionalism and Surging Interest Boost the Academic Credibility of 'Public Historians'," *Chronicle of Higher Education* (20 May 1987): 13, and Grele, "Whose History? Whose Public?" 48.

55. Susan Porter Benson, Steve Brier, and Roy Rosenzweing, introduction to *Presenting the Past: Essays on History and the Public* (Philadelphia: Temple University Press, 1986), xxii–xxiv.

56. The connection between movement building and people's history is discussed more fully in James Green, "Engaging in People's History: The Massachusetts History Workshop," in ibid., 360, 341–42.

3. Learning to Teach Movement History to Workers

1. On Charles Beard's role in founding Ruskin College, see Richard Hofstadter, *The Progressive Historians: Turner, Beard, Parrington* (New York: Alfred A. Knopf, 1968), 174–77. On Mary Ritter Beard, see Bonnie G. Smith, "Seeing Mary Beard," *Feminist Studies* 10 (Fall 1984): 399–416, and on the course she taught to women workers, see Nancy Schrom Dye, "Creating a Feminist Alliance: Sisterhood and Class Conflict in the New York Women's Trade Union League, 1903– 1914," in Milton Cantor and Bruce Laurie, eds., *Class, Sex and the Woman Worker* (Westport, Conn.: Greenwood Press, 1977), 232. For more on Mary Beard, whose "dream" it was "to develop young women to help in the awakening of their class," see Nancy Cott, ed., *A Woman Making History: Mary Ritter Beard through Her Letters* (New Haven: Yale University Press, 1991). On R. H. Tawney, the "greatest figure" in British workers education, see Ross Terrill, *R. H. Tawney and His Times: Socialism As Fellowship* (Cambridge: Harvard University Press, 1973), 36–47. On A. J. Muste at Brookwood, see Nat Hentoff, *Peace Agitator: The Story of A. J. Muste* (New York: Macmillan, 1963), 56–72; and on Horton, see Myles Horton with Judith Kohl and Herbert Kohl, *The Long Haul: An Autobiography* (New York: Doubleday, 1990). On Highlander, see Frank Adams, *Unearthing Seeds of Fire: The Idea of Highlander* (Charlotte: John F. Blair, 1975), and John M. Glenn, *Highlander: No Ordinary School, 1932–1962* (Lexington: University of Kentucky Press, 1988). Information on these two schools as well as the story of Commonwealth College in Arkansas can be found in Richard J. Altenbaugh, *Education for Struggle: The American Labor Colleges of the 1920s and 1930s* (Philadelphia: Temple University Press, 1990).

2. Myles Horton, interview with Mary Frederickson, "The Spark That Ignites," *Southern Exposure*, 4, 1–2 (1976): 154.

3. See Leon Fink, "'Intellectuals' versus 'Workers': Academic Requirements and the Creation of Labor History," *American Historical Review* 96, 2 (1991): 410.

4. Merle Curti, "Intellectuals and Other People," *American Historical Review* 60, 1 (October 1954): 272, 275, 280.

5. For a historical treatment of these tensions, and how they were exacerbated, see Joshua Freeman, "Hardhats: Construction Workers, Manliness and the 1970 Pro-War Demonstrations," *Journal of Social History* 26, 4 (1993): 725–44.

6. *1968: A Student Generation in Revolt—An International Oral History*, Ronald Fraser, ed. (New York: Pantheon, 1988), 367. Fraser's interviews showed that roughly twice as many sixty-eighters

in the United States engaged in labor and social work twenty years later than their cohorts in Europe.

7. See James Green, "Introduction," and "Holding the Line: Miners' Militancy and the 1978 Strike," as well as John Lippert, "Shop Floor Politics at Fleetwood," in *Workers' Struggles, Past and Present: A 'Radical America' Reader,* James Green, ed. (Philadelphia: Temple University Press, 1983).

8. James R. Green and Hugh Carter Donahue, *Boston's Workers, A Labor History* (Boston: Boston Public Library, 1979).

9. Richard M. Freeland, *Academia's Golden Age: Universities in Massachusetts, 1945–1970* (New York: Oxford University Press, 1993), 333.

10. John Strange, "The Experience of the College of Public and Community Service," *Liberal Education* 63, 2 (1977): 25–30.

11. Herrick Chapman, "Emancipating the Liberal Arts: The Integration of Liberal and Career Education," unpublished paper by the first CPCS dean of academic affairs, 1975. Copy in author's possession.

12. Russell Edgerton, quoted in Thomas Ewens, "Analyzing the Impact of Competence-Based Approached on Liberal Education," in *On Competence: An Analysis of a Reform Movement in Higher Education* (Syracuse: Syracuse University Press, 1978), 174.

13. For the use of competency-based education in various settings, see *On Competence: An Analysis of a Reform Movement in Higher Education,* Gerald Grant, ed. (Syracuse, 1978).

14. The curriculum used by the Labor Studies Program at the University of Massachusetts-Boston is described in Ann Withorn and Loretta Cedrone, "Assessing Ourselves: The Experience of the College of Public and Community Service," in *Defining and Measuring Competence,* Paul S. Pottinger et al., eds. (San Francisco: Jossey Bass, 1979), 65–84.

15. Michael Merrill, "Selling Socialism Door to Door," *Radical History Review* 18 (Fall 1978): 113–15.

16. Freire, quoted in *We Make the Road by Walking: Conversations on Education and Social Change with Myles Horton and Paulo Freire,* Brenda Bell, John Gaventa, and John Peters, eds. (Philadelphia: Temple University Press, 1990), 218. Also see Paulo Freire, *Education for Critical Consciousness* (New York: The Seabury Press, 1973), 16.

17. Ronald Filippelli, "The Uses of History in the Education of Workers," *Labor Studies Journal* 5 (Spring 1980): 3–7. Also see Ralph Samuel, "History Workshop Methods," *History Workshop Journal* 9 (Spring 1980): 162–65; James Green, "Worker Education and Labor History," *History Workshop Journal* 14 (Autumn 1982): 168–70.

18. Herbert G. Gutman, "Historical Consciousness in Contemporary America," in *Power and Culture: Essays on the American Working Class,* Ira Berlin, ed. (New York, 1987), 400–01.

19. Horton, quoted in Maurice Isserman, "Experiences in Democracy," *The Nation* (12 November 1990): 569–70.

20. John Dewey, *Education and Experience* (New York: Collier, 1963), 25.

21. Judith L. Catlett and Higdon Roberts Jr., "Looking Back: Meany Center Students Evaluate the College Degree Program," *Labor Studies Journal* 15 (Fall 1990): 10.

22. Horton, quoted in Frederickson interview, "The Spark that Ignites," 153.

23. James Green, "Universities Should Assist Labor Unions in Empowering a New Generation of Workers," *Chronicle of Higher Education* (27 June 1990): B2. For an earlier discussion of an attempt at Wayne State University to make a labor studies degree program accessible to working adults, see Hal Stack and Oscar Paskal, "The University and Weekend College: Beyond Access," in *Building New Alliances: Labor Unions and Higher Education in New Directions for Experiential Learning,* Hal Stack and Carol M. Hutton, eds. (San Francisco: Jossey Bass, 1980), 17–28.

24. For a history of the University of Massachusetts-Boston Labor Studies Program, see "Celebrating Ten Years of Workers Education, 1979–1989," a pamphlet available from Labor Studies Program, CPCS, University of Massachusetts-Boston, Boston, MA 02125. Quote from Michael D. Parsons, "Labor Studies in Decline," *Labor Studies Journal* 15 (Spring 1990): 66–81.

25. James Green, "Where's Labor's Solidarity?" *Boston Globe* (5 October 1981) later reprinted in *Labor Notes* (23 November 1981): 14. A classic and influential statement is by Karl Klare, "The

Judicial Deradicalization of the Wagner Act and the Origins of Modern Legal Consciousness," in *Marxism and the Law,* Piers Beirne and Richard Quinney, eds. (New York: John Wiley and Sons, 1981), 138–68. Karl offered me significant aid in shaping the PATCO editorial.

26. Green and Donahue, *Boston's Workers,* chapter 7.

27. Danny Williams, "The Crisis in Organized Labor," *Boston Sunday Globe Magazine* (6 September 1981): 25–26.

28. James Green, "Local 201 Shows Labor the Comeback Trail," *Boston Globe* (11 March 1986): 48.

29. James Green, "Not by Bread Alone," *Socialist Review* 90 (1986): 111–16.

30. Herbert Gutman, "Industrial Invasion of the Village Green," *Trans-Action* 3 (1966): 19–24, and "The Workers' Search for Power: Labor in the Gilded Age," in *Power and Culture,* 70–92.

31. James Green, "Labor Day: The Past Resurfaces," *Boston Globe* (6 September 1987).

32. James Green, "For Jackson, Populism Is a Class Act," *Boston Globe* (3 April 1988).

33. James Green, "Save the Prevailing Wage Law," *MTA Today* (30 August 1988): 3, 26.

34. Mark Erlich, *Labor at the Ballot Box: The Massachusetts Prevailing Wage Campaign of 1988* (Philadelphia: Temple University Press, 1990).

35. Quote from Susan Stone Wong, "From Soul to Strawberries: The International Ladies Garment Workers Union and Workers Education, 1914–1950," in Joyce L. Kornbluh and Mary Frederickson, eds., *Sisterhood and Solidarity: Workers Education and Women, 1914–1984* (Philadelphia: Temple University Press, 1984), 54.

36. For a discussion of educational programs, like Highlander Folk School and other resources for social change, which served as "movement half-way houses" for the southern black freedom struggle, see Aldon D. Morris, *The Origins of the Civil Rights Movement: Black Communities Organizing for Change* (New York: The Free Press, 1984), 139–73. For a discussion of the free spaces needed for radical movement building, see Sara M. Evans and Harry C. Boyte, "Schools for Action: Radical Uses of Social Space," *Democracy* 2, 4 (Fall 1982): 55–65.

37. Clyde W. Barrow, "Counter-Movement Within the Labor Movement: Workers' Education and the American Federation of Labor, 1900–1937," *The Social Science Journal* 27, 4 (1990): 395–417.

38. Labor/Higher Education Council, "Building Labor Campus Alliances," Proceedings of the National Meeting, 1989; John Joyce, "Address on Labor and Higher Education," to American Council on Education, San Francisco (12 December 1987), 3, 5–7.

39. See Robin Miller Jacoby, "The Women's Trade Union League Training School for Women Organizers, 1916–1926," in Joyce L. Kornbluh and Mary Frederickson, eds., *Sisterhood and Solidarity: Workers Education and Women, 1914–1984* (Philadelphia: Temple University Press, 1984), 5–42. Cohn, quoted in Susan Stone Wong, "From Soul to Strawberries: The International Ladies Garment Workers; Union and Workers Education, 1914–1950," in ibid., 46.

40. Cheryl Gooding and Pat Reeve, "Coalition Building for Community-Based Labor Education," *Policy Studies Journal* 18, 2 (Winter 1989–90): 452–60. Besides bringing the women's movement into the labor movement in an effective way, WILD took on a life of its own, taking on the challenge of multicultural education for union women.

41. Both speeches were published in "Ireland Today," a special issue of *forward motion* 7, 2 (March–April 1988), quote from Nell on p. 32.

42. Patricia Reeve, " 'If This Were Steel, I'd Know What to Do with It'—Making Historians' Discourse on Race and Gender Meaningful to Union Members," paper presented at the Organization of American Historians Meetings, Washington, D.C. (30 March 1995).

43. Peter Sexias, "The Community of Inquiry As a Basis for Knowledge and Learning: The Case of History," *American Educational Research Journal* 30, 2 (Summer 1993): 307.

44. Paulo Freire, *Pedagogy of the Oppressed* (New York: Seabury Press, 1970), 66–67.

45. See Leon Fink, "The New Labor History and the Powers of Historical Pessimism," *Journal of American History* 75, 1 (June 1988): 115–36.

46. See James Green, "Why Did the Labor Movement Grow? Two Labor History Workshops Presented to the United Mine Workers of America," unpublished curriculum available from author, presented in Beckley, W. V. (1988), and Washington, D.C. (1989)," and "A Problem-

Posing Approach to Teaching Labor History," paper presented to the University and College Labor Education Association, George Meany Center, Washington, D.C. (1990).

47. John Russo, "The Crisis in the Serving Model and Alternative Labor Education Approaches," address delivered at the University and College Labor Education Association Meeting, George Meany Center, Silver Springs, Md. (1990), 5–7.

48. For an instructive discussion of how public school history teachers can bridge the gap between "the scholarly community that produces knowledge and the classroom community that produces learning," see Sexias, "The Community of Inquiry As a Basis for Knowledge and Learning," 305–24.

49. Alan Dawley, "Keeping Time in Twentieth-Century America," unpublished paper presented to the Organization of American Historians, Atlanta (April 1994), 3–4.

4. Commemorating Moments of Solidarity in Massachusetts Labor History

1. William Serrin, "Workers and Historians Share Views," *New York Times* (16 August 1982).

2. Gutman's OAH address was reprinted in, "Historical Consciousness in Contemporary America," Herbert G. Gutman, *Power and Culture: Essays on the American Working Class* (New York, 1987), 400–01.

3. Ibid., 400, 408. And see Theodore Rosengarten, *All God's Dangers: The Life of Nate Shaw* (New York: Knopf, 1974).

4. See Ira Berlin, "Herbert G. Gutman and the American Working Class," Introduction to Gutman, *Power & Culture*, 64–65.

5. Michael Frisch, "Sixty Characters in Search of Authority: The Northern Illinois University NEH Conference on the Future of Labor History," *International Labor and Working Class History* 27 (Spring 1985): 102.

6. Leon Fink, "The New Labor History and the Powers of Historical Pessimism," *Journal of American History* 71, 1 (1988): 136.

7. Leon Fink, "'Intellectuals' versus 'Workers': Academic Requirements and the Creation of Labor History," *American Historical Review* 96 2 (April 1991), 418–20. Fink explores the dilemma facing contemporary labor historians who are isolated from the labor movement, just like other intellectuals who inhabit "ivory towers." He focuses on the inability of historians in our time to assume "a self-conscious group responsibility" for engaging the world they tried to interpret. But he does appreciate the efforts of individual historians, including those employed in worker-education programs, to play active roles that are "at once intellectually and politically meaningful." Ibid., 420 and notes 91 and 92 on p. 420.

8. Steve Brier, "Sweden: Dig Where You Stand," in "People's History around the World" in *Radical History Review* 25 (October 1981): 174–77.

9. Raphael Samuel, "People's History," in *People's History and Socialist Theory,* Raphael Samuel, ed. (London: Routledge & Kegan Paul, 1981), xxvii.

10. See David A. Gerber, "Local and Community History: Some Cautionary Remarks on an Idea Whose Time Has Returned," *History Teacher* 45 (Winter 1980): 15–16, and quotes from Linda Shopes, "The Baltimore Neighborhood History Project: Oral History and Community Involvement," *Radical History Review* 25 (October 1981): 27–46, reprinted in *Presenting the Past: Essays on History and the Public,* Steve Brier, Susan Porter Benson, and Roy Rosenzweig, eds. (Philadelphia: Temple University Press, 1986), 256–57.

11. Michael Frisch's 1982 essay, "Quality in Oral History Programs: From Celebration to Exploration of Values," is reprinted in his collection, *A Shared Authority: Essays on the Craft and Meaning of Oral and Public History* (Albany: SUNY Press, 1990), 190.

12. Roslyn L. Feldberg, "'Union Fever': Organizing Among Clerical Workers, 1900–1930," appeared in *Radical America* in 1980 and was reprinted in Green, *Workers' Struggles,* 151–67.

13. Meredith Tax, *The Rising of the Women* (New York: Monthly Review Press, 1980), and *Rivington Street* (New York: William Morrow, 1982).

14. Meredith Tax, "Speech at the Celebration Commemorating the Eightieth Anniversary of the

Founding of the Women's Trade Union League, Fanueil Hall, Boston, March 4, 1983," copy in the author's possession.

15. Michael Kazin and Steven J. Ross, "America's Labor Day: The Dilemma of a Workers' Celebration," *Journal of American History* 78, 4 (March 1992): 1294–323.

16. Donahue and I published our account of the 1 May 1886 strike for the eight-hour day in our *Boston's Workers: A Labor History* (Boston: Boston Public Library 1977) and drew on a seminar paper by Lazerow later published as "The Working Man's Hour: The 1886 Labor Uprising in Boston," *Labor History* 21, 2 (Spring 1980): 200–21.

17. Eric Hobsbawm, "Mass-Producing Traditions: Europe, 1870–1914," in Eric Hobsbawm and Terence Ranger, eds., *The Invention of Tradition* (Cambridge: Cambridge University Press, 1983), 283–86.

18. Robert W. Wiebe, *Self-Rule: A Cultural History of American Democracy* (Chicago, 1995), 136–37.

19. David Glassberg, "History and the Public: Legacies of the Progressive Era," *Journal of American History* 73, 4 (March 1987): 960–61.

20. David Glassberg, *American Historical Pageantry: The Uses of Tradition in the Early Twentieth Century* (Chapel Hill: University of North Carolina Press, 1990), 40.

21. See Philip S. Foner, *May Day: A Short History of the International Workers Holiday, 1886–1986* (New York: International Publishers, 1986), 43–44.

22. David Montgomery, *Beyond Equality: Labor and the Radical Republicans, 1862–1972* (New York: Alfred Knopf, 1967), 259–60, and James R. Green and Hugh Carter Donahue, *Boston's Workers: A Labor History* (Boston: Boston Public Library, 1979), chapter 2.

23. See B. K. Hunnicutt, "The End of Shorter Hours," *Labor History* 25 (Summer 1984): 373–404.

24. James Green, "Not by Bread Alone," *Socialist Review* 90 (1986): 111–16.

25. Steven Golin, "The Paterson Pageant: Success or Failure?" *socialist review* 70 (May–June 1983), 145–78.

26. Jim Green, "Centennial Events Celebrating the May Days of 1986," Reports and Letters, *History Workshop Journal* 23 (Autumn 1987): 211–12.

27. Mark Erlich, *With These Hands: The Story of Carpenters in Massachusetts* (Philadelphia: Temple University Press, 1986).

28. Jim Bollen and Steve Miller, *The Colonial Strike* (Boston: Boston Community School, 1974).

29. For other interracial stories from the Packinghouse Workers' history, see Roger Horowitz, *"Negro and White Unite and Fight": A Social History of Industrial Unionism in Meat Packing, 1930–1990* (Urbana: University of Illinois Press, 1997).

30. On the politics of oral history and the dynamics of the human relations involved, see the inspiring and thought-provoking essays by Portelli, *The Battle of Vale di Guilia*, especially "There's Gonna Always Be a Line: History Telling As a Multi-Vocal Art," in ibid., 38–39.

31. Jim Bollen and Jim Green, "'The Long Strike': The Practice of Solidarity among Boston's Packinghouse Workers," in *Labor in Massachusetts: Selected Essays*, Kenneth Fones-Wolf and Martin Kaufman, eds. (Westfield: Institute for Massachusetts Studies, 1990), 233–57.

32. Tom Juravich, William H. Hartford, and James R. Green, *Commonwealth of Toil: Chapters from the History of Massachusetts Workers and Their Unions* (Amherst: University of Massachusetts Press, 1996).

33. See James Green, "Why Teach Labor History?," *OAH Magazine for Teachers of History* (April 1997).

34. Review of *Commonwealth of Toil* by Robert Macieski, *Journal of American History* 83, (December 1997): 1083.

35. James R. Green and Robert C. Hayden, "A. Philip Randolph and Boston's African-American Railroad Worker," *The Trotter Review* (of the William Monroe Trotter Institute, University of Massachusetts, Boston), 6, 2 (1992): 20–24.

36. See Howard Green, "A Critique of the Professional Public History Movement," *Radical History Review* 25 (October 1981): 164–71.

37. Peter M. Crow to National Park Service (12 December 1995), copy to Senator Diane Feinstein. For a careful and helpful criticism of the debate approach in the slide show, see Gregg D. Kimball, "Rise and Decline: the Legacy of Lowell," *The Public Historian* 16, 2 (Spring 1994): 132–36.

38. Marc Vagos, Boott Mills District Ranger, to Marty Blatt, Memo on Boott Cotton Mills Museum Visitor Comments (25 April 1994), copy in author's possession.

39. Russell Jacoby, *The Last Intellectuals: American Culture in the Age of Academe* (New York: Basic Books, 1987), 164.

40. Pierre Nora, "Between Memory and History: Les Lieux de Memoire," *Representations* 26 (Spring 1989): 8.

41. David Thelen, "The Practice of American History," *Journal of American History* 81, 3 (December 1994): 943.

42. Nora, "Between Memory and History," 15.

43. Patrick H. Hutton, *History As an Art of Memory* (Hanover: University of New Hampshire Press, 1993), xxiv–xxv, 5–6, 120.

44. David Lowenthal, *The Past is a Foreign Country* (Cambridge: Cambridge University Press, 1985); Frank Hearn, "Remembrance and Critique: The Uses of the Past for Discrediting the Present and Anticipating the Future," *Politics and Society* 5 (1975): 201–28.

45. Robert N. Bellah, *Habits of the Heart: Individualism and Commitment in American Life* (Berkeley: University of California Press, 1985), 153.

5. Remembering Haymarket

1. Michael Kammen, *Mystic Chords of Memory: The Transformation of Tradition in American Culture* (New York, 1991), 517. Lincoln is quoted on the frontispiece.

2. The National Historic Landmarks Program, "Criteria of National Significance," unpublished document (Washington, D.C.: National Park Service, History Division, 1992).

3. James Green, "Marking Labor History on the National Landscape," introduction to the Labor History Theme Study for the Historic Landmarks Program, National Park Service, unpublished report (Chicago: Newberry Library, 1995).

4. John Bodnar, *Remaking America: Public Memory and Patriotism in the Twentieth Century* (Princeton, 1992), 14.

5. Pierre Nora, "Between Memory and History: Les Lieux de Memoire," *Representations* 26 (Spring 1989): 8. The French sites of memory in Nora's seven-volume survey range from libraries, dictionaries, and museums, to commemorations and celebrations, from the Arche de Triomphe to the Wall of the Federes, where the last defenders of the Paris Commune were massacred in 1871, a site that resembles Haymarket Square and Waldheim Cemetery. See Madeleine Reberioux, "Le Mur des Federes," in Pierre Nora, ed., *Les Lieux de Memoire*, vol. 1 (Paris: Gallimard, 1986), 619–49. For a discussion of Nora's work, recently translated into English, see Adam Shatz, "How Nations Think," *Lingua Franca* (February 1997): 21–22.

6. Raphael Samuel, *Theatres of Memory* (London: Verso, 1994).

7. Bruce Nelson, *Beyond the Martyrs: A Social History of Chicago's Anarchists, 1870–1900* (New Brunswick: Rutgers University Press, 1988), 79–126.

8. Ibid., 21.

9. Paul Avrich, *The Haymarket Tragedy* (Princeton: Princeton University Press, 1984), 163–69, and quote on p. 73.

10. Ibid. Even the reformist leaders of the Knights and the syndicalist leaders of the Trades feared that the ideals of the republic had been arrogantly subverted by the capitalists who had now taken control of the state from the people. For a fascinating study of worker ideas about the state, see David Montgomery, *Citizen Worker: The Experience of Workers in the United States with Democracy and the Free Market during the Nineteenth Century* (Cambridge: Cambridge University Press, 1993).

11. Bruce C. Nelson, "'We Can't Get Them to Do Aggressive Work': Chicago's Anarchists and the Eight-Hour Movement," *International Labor and Working-Class History* 29 (Spring 1986): 1–13; Dave Roediger, "Albert R. Parsons: Anarchist as Trade Unionist," Bruce Nelson, "Dancing and Picnicking Anarchists?" and Alan Dawley, "The International Working People's Association," in *Haymarket Scrapbook*, Dave Roediger and Franklin Rosemont, ed. (Chicago: Charles H. Kerr, 1986), 31–35, 76–78, 84–86.

12. David R. Roediger and Philip S. Foner, *Our Own Time: A History of American Labor and the Working Day* (London: Verso, 1989), p. 138.

13. Ibid., and Nelson, *Beyond the Martyrs*, 9–51.

14. The narrative is based on the excellent account by Avrich, *The Haymarket Tragedy*, quote on p. 223.

15. Carl Smith, *Urban Disorder and the Shape of Belief: The Great Chicago Fire, The Haymarket Bomb and the Model Town of Pullman* (Chicago: University of Chicago Press, 1995), part 2.

16. John Higham, *Strangers in the Land: Patterns of American Nativism, 1860–1925* rev. ed. (New York: Atheneum, 1971), 55.

17. Kermit L. Wall, William M. Wiecek, and Paul Finkleman, *American Legal History: Cases and Materials* (New York: Oxford University Press, 1966), 358–59.

18. Avrich, *The Haymarket Tragedy*, 354.

19. Joseph R. Buchanan, *The Story of a Labor Agitator* (1903, reprint, Westport, Conn.: Greenwood Press, 1970), 313.

20. Samuel Gompers, *Seventy Years of Life and Labor* (New York: E. P. Dutton, 1925), 238–39.

21. Quoted in Avrich, *The Haymarket Tragedy*, 436.

22. Gompers, *Seventy Years of Life and Labor*, 239.

23. Smith, *Urban Disorder*, 142–43, 137.

24. Ibid., 168. Quote from words of Rev. H. W. Thomas. The suicide of Louis Lingg created a remarkable impression as well. Those who declared Lingg a maniac, like John Brown, only contributed to his mystique in the minds of those like Emma Goldman to whom he was the "sublime hero of the eight." Franklin Rosemont, "The Most Dangerous Anarchist of All': The Legend and Legacy of Louis Lingg," in Roediger and Rosemont, *Haymarket Scrapbook*, 51–56.

25. Franklin Rosemont, "A Bomb-Throwing, Long-Haired Wild-Eyed Fiend: The Image of the Anarchist in Popular Culture," in Roediger and Rosemont, and Theodore Watts, "Year of the Hangman's Noose," ibid., 203–05, 127.

26. Buchanan, *The Story of a Labor Agitator*, 336–39.

27. See Peter Linebaugh, *The London Hanged: Crime and Civil Society in the Eighteenth Century* (London: Allen Lane, 1991), xx, and 114 on the "pedagogy of the gallows" in Britain. See Louis P. Mazur, *Rites of Execution: Capital Punishment and the Transformation of American Culture, 1776–1865* (New York: Oxford University Press, 1989) on the use of public hanging to preserve order in the United States.

28. Watts, "The Year of the Hangman's Noose," in Roediger and Rosemont, *Haymarket Scrapbook*, 127.

29. J. Anthony Lukas, *Big Trouble: A Murder in a Small Western Town Sets Off a Struggle for the Soul of America* (New York: Simon and Schuster, 1997), 188, and Wayne Broehl Jr., *The Molly Maguires* (Cambridge: Harvard University Press, 1964), 362.

30. Kevin Kenney, *Making Sense of the Molly Maguires* (New York: Oxford University Press, 1998), 283–84.

31. I am indebted to Professor Thomas Brown for this suggestion.

32. Broehl, *The Molly Maguires*, 344–45, 350.

33. Quoted in Avrich, *The Haymarket Tragedy*, 436.

34. Roediger and Rosemont, *Haymarket Scrapbook*, 172.

35. Nora, "Between Memory and History," 22.

36. William J. Adelman, *Haymarket Revisited: A Tour Guide of Labor History Sites and Ethnic Neighborhoods Connected with the Haymarket Affair*, 2d ed. (Chicago: Illinois Labor History Society, 1986), 35–37.

37. Ibid., 39.

38. Robert W. Wiebe, *Self-Rule: A Cultural History of American Democracy* (Chicago: University of Chicago Press, 1995), 136–37.

39. David Glassberg, "History and the Public: Legacies of the Progressive Era," *Journal of American History* 73, 4 (March 1987): 960–61.

40. Eric Hobsbawm, "Man and Woman in Socialist Iconography," *History Workshop Journal* 6 (1978): 123–24, 127.

41. Nora, "Between Memory and History," 19.

42. Adelman, *Haymarket Revisited,* 105, and Avrich, *The Haymarket Tragedy,* 415–22.

43. Ibid., 413–14.

44. Nora, "Between Memory and History," 12.

45. On the redemptive power of storytelling in peasant life, see John Berger, *About Looking* (New York: Pantheon, 1980), 54–55.

46. Emma Goldman, *Living My Life* (New York: Alfred A. Knopf, 1931), 9–10, 508.

47. Abraham Bisno, *Union Pioneer* (Madison: University of Wisconsin Press, 1967), 90.

48. Adelman, *Haymarket Revisited,* 107.

49. Blaine McKinley, "'A Religion of a New Time': Anarchist Memorials to the Haymarket Martyrs, 1888–1917," *Labor History* 28 (Summer 1987): 386–400.

50. Review by General M. M. Trumbul, quoted in Roediger and Rosemont, *Haymarket Scrapbook,* 29.

51. Carolyn Ashbaugh, *Lucy Parsons, American Revolutionary* (Chicago: Charles H. Kerr, 1976), 170–76, 206. Quote from p. 227.

52. Nelson, *Beyond the Martyrs,* 239, 236.

53. Quoted in Avrich, *The Haymarket Tragedy,* 435, 434.

54. On the influence of anarchism and the Chicago idea of direct action unionism on the IWW, see Sal Salerno, "The Impact of Haymarket on the Founding of the IWW," in David Roediger and Franklin Rosemont, eds., *Haymarket Scrapbook* (Chicago: Charles H. Kerr, 1986), 189–92.

55. Hubert Perrier and Michel Cordillot, "The Origins of May Day: The American Connection," *In the Shadow of the Statue of Liberty: Immigrants, Workers, and Citizens in the American Republic, 1880–1920,* Marianne Debouzy, ed. (Urbana: University of Illinois Press, 1992), 157–80, and Rudolph Vecoli, "The American Republic Viewed by the Italian Left," in ibid., 24–25.

56. Vecoli, "The American Republic Viewed by the Italian Left," in *In the Shadow of the Statue of Liberty,* 24–25; Robert D'Attilio, "Primo Maggio: Haymarket as Seen by Italian Anarchists in America," in Roediger and Rosemont, *Haymarket Scrapbook,* 230; and on Galleani, see Paul Avrich, *Sacco and Vanzetti: The Anarchist Background* (Princeton: Princeton University Press, 1991), 45–47.

57. For a study of working class memory as construction, see Michelle Perrot, "The First of May 1890 in France: The Birth of a Working-Class Ritual," in P. Thane et al., eds., *The Powers of History: Essays for E. J. Hobsbawm* (Cambridge: Cambridge University Press, 1984), 143–44.

58. *New York Times* (1, 2 May 1929 and 2 May 1936).

59. The author thanks John Womack for this insight. Also see John M. Hart, *Anarchism and the Mexican Working Class, 1860–1931* (Austin: University of Texas Press, 1978), on the dominant influence of anarchists on the urban labor movement.

60. Avrich, *The Haymarket Tragedy,* 435.

61. Ibid., 435–36.

62. Reuben Martinez, "Mexico's Search for Itself," *The Nation* (28 April 1997): 22.

63. Lukas, *Big Trouble,* 470–95.

64. Eugene Debs, "Arouse Ye Slaves," *Appeal to Reason* (10 March 1906).

65. Ashbaugh, *Lucy Parsons,* 206, 228–29.

66. William E. Forbath, *Law and the Shaping of the American Labor Movement* (Cambridge: Harvard University Press, 1991), 16. Forbath argues that the antistatist posture of the AFL was reactionary and led to the minimalist approach of "pure and simple unionism" rather than to a return to the Chicago idea.

67. Franklin Rosemont, "In November, We Remember: The IWW and the Commemoration of Haymarket," in Roediger and Rosemont, *Haymarket Scrapbook,* 193.

68. Philip S. Foner, *May Day: A Short History of the International Workers Holiday, 1886–1986* (New York: International Publishers, 1986), 76–79, 87–90. On the attacks in the two cities, see Bodnar, *Remaking America,* 97, and Frances Russell, *A City in Terror: 1919, The Boston Police Strike* (New York: Viking, 1975), 21.

69. Silly attempts were also made to replace the radical holiday by restoring the old Anglo-Saxon celebration of spring. Alan Dawley, *Struggles for Justice: Social Responsibility and the Liberal State* (Cambridge: Harvard University Press, 1991), 309. On Memorial Day after World War I, see Bodnar, *Remaking America.*

70. Bodnar, *Remaking America,* 83, 85–88.

71. Alessandro Portelli, "The Massacre of Civitella Val di Chiana," in *The Battle of Valle di Giulia: Oral History and the Art of Dialogue* (Madison: University of Wisconsin Press, 1997), 157.

72. Rhodes and Ellis Paxson Oberholtzer, quoted in Henry David, *The Haymarket Affair* (New York: Farrar & Rinehart, 1936), 446. Another popular interpretation, Charles and Mary Beard's popular progressive text *The Making of American Civilization* (New York: Macmillan, 1927), ignored Haymarket.

73. David, *The Haymarket Affair,* 446–47, 5. In the same year Samuel Yellen published an account of Haymarket in his well-written popular book entitled *American Labor Struggles, 1877–1934* (New York, 1936) in which he thanked David for his advice.

74. Alfred F. Young to the author, Oak Park, Ill. (27 September 1998).

75. Sam Dolgoff, "Recollections of Lucy Parsons and the Fiftieth Anniversary of November 11," in Roediger and Rosemont, *Haymarket Scrapbook,* 246.

76. Barbara Warne Newell, *Chicago and the Labor Movement: Metropolitan Unionism in the 1930s* (Urbana: University of Illinois Press, 1961), 252–53, and Lisabeth Cohen, *Making a New Deal: Industrial Workers in Chicago, 1919–1939* (Cambridge: Cambridge University Press, 1990), 303.

77. Anthony Bimba, *The History of the American Working Class,* 3d ed. (New York: International Publishers, 1927), 312, 184–85. Communist historian Anthony Bimba acknowledged the Haymarket martyrs' anarchism but distinguished it from the European version, which involved action, including assassination, by "small, isolated groups." The Chicago anarchists believed in "mass proletarian action," advocated union organizing, and favored arming workers "as a class not as individuals." There is validity in Bimba's distinction. In his recent study of the Chicago labor movement, Bruce C. Nelson explains that the Haymarket martyrs and their comrades defied those who accused them of being anarchists by adopting that name for themselves. However, these so-called anarchists originally called themselves social revolutionaries and followed the ideas of Marx rather than of anarchists like Kropotkin and Bakunin. Nelson, *Beyond the Martyrs,* 153–73.

78. Ibid., 188, Adelman, *Haymarket Revisited,* 119–30, and Asbaugh, *The Life of Lucy Parsons,* 226.

79. Roediger and Rosemont, *Haymarket Scrapbook,* and Nora, "Between History and Memory," 11–12.

80. Rexroth's poem is reprinted in *Haymarket Scrapbook,* 227.

81. For a review of this period, see James R. Green, *The World of the Worker: Labor in Twentieth-Century America* (New York: Hill and Wang, 1980), 133–209. For a brilliant examination of this process in one city, see Gary Gerstle, *Working-Class Americanism: The Politics of Labor in a Textile City, 1914–1960* (Cambridge: Cambridge University Press, 1989).

82. Marianne Debouzy, "In Search of Working-Class Memory: Some Questions and a Tentative Assessment," *History and Anthropology* 2 (1986): 276.

83. Roediger and Rosemont, *Haymarket Scrapbook,* 62.

84. Bruno Cartosio, "Memoria Privata e Memoria Pubblica Nella Storiografia del Movimento Operaio," *Studi Storici* 38, 4 (1997): 897–910.

85. Adelman, *Haymarket Revisited,* 38–40.

86. Ibid., and Roediger and Rosemont, *Haymarket Scrapbook,* 239.

87. Avrich, *The Haymarket Tragedy,* xiv.

88. Nora, "Between Memory and History," 10.

89. Oz Frankel, "Whatever Happened to 'Red Emma'? Emma Goldman, from Alien Rebel to American Icon," *Journal of American History* 83, 3 (December 1996): 903–42, quotes on pp. 931, 939.

90. "The Haymarket," special issue of *International Labor and Working Class History* 29 (Spring 1986); *Haymarket Scrapbook;* and Bruce C. Nelson, "Anarchism: The Movement beyond the Martyrs," *Chicago History* 15 (Summer 1986): 4–19. Nelson's book-length social history, *Beyond the Martyrs,* appeared two years later.

93. Studs Terkel's book *Division Street America* (New York: Pantheon 1967) was a collection of interviews with colorful Chicagoans. His next book, *Hard Times: An Oral History of the Great Depression* (New York: Pantheon, 1970) also included many oral histories recorded in Chicago.

92. Ibid., and Roediger and Rosemont, *Haymarket Scrapbook,* 239.

93. Telephone interview with Les Orear (28 February 1999).

94. Quotes from Smith, *Urban Disorder,* 277.

95. National Historic Landmark Nomination for Haymarket Martyrs Monument, 1996, photocopy in author's possession.

96. Robin F. Bachin, "Structuring Memory—the Haymarket Martyrs Monument," *Cultural Resources Management* 21, 11 (1998): 45–46.

97. Quotes from Smith, *Urban Disorder,* 277.

98. Quotes from Jeff Huebner, "Haymarket Revisited," *Reader: Chicago's Free Weekly* (10 December 1993): 20.

99. Berger, *About Looking,* 54–55.

6. Releasing Silenced Voices and Uncovering Forgotten Places in the American South

1. Eudora Welty, quoted in Carl Degler, *Place Over Time: The Continuity of Southern Distinctiveness* (Baton Rouge: Louisiana State University Press, 1978), 15.

2. C. Vann Woodward, "The Search for Southern Identity," in *The Burden of Southern History* (New York: Vintage, 1960), 3–25.

3. See David Roediger, "Covington Hall: The Poetry and Politics of Southern Nationalism and Labour Radicalism," *History Workshop Journal* 19 (Spring 1985): 162–67.

4. Jacquelyn Dowd Hall, "'You Must Remember This': Autobiography as Social Critique," *Journal of American History* 85, 2 (September 1998): 458–62. Also see her essay "Open Secrets: Memory, Imagination and the Refashioning of Southern Identity," *American Quarterly* 50, 1 (March 1988): 109–24.

5. Quoted from Eudora Welty, in Richard Gray, *Writing South: Ideas of an American Region* (Cambridge: Cambridge University Press, 1994), 172. For references to Margaret Walker's sense of the South as a place shared by blacks and whites, see Jerry W. Ward Jr., "A Writer for Her People: An Interview with Dr. Margaret Walker," *Mississippi Quarterly* 41 (Fall 1988): 515–27.

6. Hazel Carby, "The Politics of Fiction, Anthropology, and the Folk: Zora Neale Hurston," in *History and Memory in African American Culture,* Geneviève Fabre and Robert O'Meally, eds. (New York: Oxford University Press, 1994), 28–45.

7. David Goldfield, "A Sense of Place: Jews, Blacks, and White Gentiles in the American South," *Southern Cultures* 3, 4 (Spring 1977): p. 58.

8. Joel Williamson, *William Faulkner and Southern History* (New York: Oxford University Press, 1995), 404.

9. Ibid., 402–03.

10. Quotes from Richard Gray, *Writing South,* 172, 180.

11. Pierre Nora, "Between Memory and History: *Les Lieux de Mèmoire,*" in Fabre and O'Meally, *History and Memory in African American Culture,* 284–300.

12. Charles Reagan Wilson, "Stone Mountain," in *Encyclopedia of Southern Culture,* Charles Reagan Wilson and William Ferris, eds. (Chapel Hill: University of North Carolina Press 1989), 703.

13. Nora, "Between Memory and History," in Fabre and O'Meally, *History and Memory in African American Culture*, 284–85, 289.

14. Stephen Davis, "Empty Eyes, Marble Hand: The Confederate Monument and the South," *Journal of Popular Culture* 16 (Winter 1982): 2–21.

15. See Gaines M. Foster, *Ghosts of the Confederacy: Defeat, the Lost Cause, and the Emergence of the New South, 1865–1913* (New York: Oxford University Press, 1987).

16. William Faulkner, *The Sound and the Fury* (1929; reprint, New York: Modern Library), 1964), 12, and Nora, "Between History and Memory," in Fabre and O'Meally, *History and Memory in African American History*, 289.

17. V. S. Naipaul, *A Turn in the South* (New York: Vintage, 1990), 100.

18. The following account is based on Lawrence Powell, "A Concrete Symbol," *Southern Exposure* (Spring 1990): 40–43.

19. Quoted in the frontispiece of John Edgerton, *Let Us Speak Now against the Day: The Generation before the Civil Rights Movement in the South* (New York: Alfred A. Knopf, 1994).

20. James Green, "Marking Labor History on the National Landscape," introduction to the labor history theme study for the National Park Service by the Newberry Library (1995).

21. E. P. Thompson, *The Making of the English Working Class* (New York: Pantheon, 1963), 156.

22. Criteria for nominations, National Historic Landmarks Program, undated, photocopy, 1, 6–7.

23. On the great Southwest strike, see Ruth Allen, *The Great Southwest Strike* (Austin: University of Texas Press, 1942), and for a photo of Martin Irons's grave, see Ruth A. Allen, *Chapters from the History of Organized Labor in Texas* (Austin: University of Texas Press, 1941).

24. Lawrence C. Goodwyn, "Populist Dreams and Negro Rights: East Texas as a Case Study," *American Historical Review* 76 (December 1971): 1435–56, and Manning Marable, "Black History and the Vision of Democracy," in *The New Populism: The Politics of Empowerment*, Harry C. Boyte and Frank Reissman, eds. (Philadelphia: Temple University Press, 1986), 199–204.

25. Sayles and Matewan mayor Johnny Fullen, quoted in Martha Bryson Hodel, "Matewan's Struggle Isn't Over," *Charleston Gazette* (10 January 1993).

26. The dedication of Hatfield's new gravestone by UMWA vice president Cecil Roberts is seen in the video *Out of Darkness* produced by Barbara Kopple and Cabin Creek Films for the United Mine Workers of America. Sayles describes his film in *Thinking in Pictures: The Making of the Movie Matewan* (Boston: Houghton Mifflin, 1987).

27. Alessando Portelli, "Form and Meaning of Historical Representation: The Battle of Evarts and the Battle of Crummies (Kentucky: 1931, 1941)," in Alessandro Portelli, *The Battle of Valle Giulia: Oral History and the Art of Dialogue* (Madison: University of Wisconsin Press, 1997), 104–05.

28. Criteria for nominations, Historical Landmarks Program, 6–7.

29. Richard A. Couto, "The Memory of Miners and the Conscience of Capital: Coal Miners Strikes As Free Spaces," in *Fighting Back in Appalachia: Traditions of Resistance and Change*, Stephen L. Fischer, ed. (Philadelphia: Temple University Press, 1992), 185–87.

30. Harry Boyte and Sara Evans, *Free Spaces: The Sources of Democratic Change in America* (New York: Harper & Row, 1986), 17.

31. Couto, "The Memory of Miners," in Fischer, *Fighting Back in Appalachia*, 187, and Alessandro Portelli, "No Neutrals There: The Cultural Class Struggle in the Harlan Miners' Strike of 1931–32," in Allesandro Portelli, *The Death of Luigi Trastulli and Other Stories* (Albany: State University of New York Press, 1991), 225.

32. Cecil Roberts's testimony before the U.S. House Committee on Mining and Natural Resources (21 February 1991). Typed copy in author's possession.

33. Ibid., and see David Corbin, *Life, Work, and Rebellion in the Coal Fields: The Southern West Virginia Miners, 1880–1922* (Urbana: University of Illinois Press, 1981).

34. Roberts's testimony.

35. For a fascinating study on the marking of military battlefields, and the conflicts aroused in doing so, see Edward T. Linenthal, *Sacred Ground: Americans and Their Battlefields* (Urbana: University of Illinois Press, 1993).

36. Thomas Schlereth, "Causing Conflict, Doing Violence," in *Cultural History and Material Culture: Everyday Life, Landscapes, and Museums* (Charlottesville: University of Virginia, 1992), 369.

37. Denise Giardina, *Storming Heaven: A Novel* (New York: Ivy Books, 1987). The author acknowledges several historians of the West Virginia resistance movement.

38. Hans Bungert, "Southern Identity in Contemporary Southern Literature," in *The United States South: Regionalism and Identity,* Valeria Gennaro Lerda and Tjebbe Westendorp, eds. (Rome: Bulzoni, 1991), 18–19.

39. Morrison, quoted in Catherine Clinton, " 'With a Whip in His Hand': Rape, Memory, and African American Women," in Fabre and O'Meally, *History and Memory in African American Culture,* 211. I am indebted to the author for the words I quote from her written response to Morrison.

40. Melvin Dixon, "The Black Writer's Use of Memory," in Fabre and O'Meally, *History and Memory in African American Culture,* 22. On black historical memory, see David W. Blight, "W.E.B. Du Bois and the Struggle for American Historical Memory," in ibid., 45–71. Also see Nora's reference to Jews, as "one of those 'peoples of memory' who traditionally had little use for historians." Nora, "Between Memory and History," ibid., 285.

41. Robert G. O'Meally, "On Burke and the Vernacular: Ralph Ellison's Boomerang of History," in ibid., 246–47, which also includes quotes from Ellison.

42. Jane Dailey, "Deference and Violence in the Post-Bellum Urban South: Manners and Massacres in Danville, Virginia," *Journal of Southern History* 63, 3 (August 1997): 563–75.

43. On the destruction of Rosewood, Florida, and the recent film about it, see E. W. Shipp, "Taking Control of Old Demons by Forcing Them into the Light," *New York Times* (16 March 1997): 13, 26.

44. See Scott Ellsworth, *Death in a Promised Land: The Tulsa Race Riot of 1921* (Baton Rouge: Louisiana State University Press, 1982). Ellison quoted in O'Meally, "On Burke and the Vernacular," in Fabre and O'Meally, *History and Memory in African American Culture,* 247–48.

45. Goodwyn, "Populist Dreams and Negro Rights," 1437–46.

46. Ibid., 1451.

47. Dixon, "The Black Writer's Use of Memory," in Fabre and O'Meally, *History and Memory in African American Culture,* 22.

48. Ellsworth, *Death in A Promised Land,* 105–06.

49. Karen Fields, "What One Cannot Remember Mistakenly," in Fabre and O'Meally, *History and Memory in African American Culture,* 160, and Mamie Garvin Fields and Karen Fields, *Lemon Swamp and Other Places: A Carolina Memoir* (New York: The Free Press 1983), xxiii.

50. Theodore Rosengarten, *All God's Dangers: The Life of Nate Shaw* (New York: Alfred A. Knopf, 1974), 547–48.

51. Theodore Rosengarten, "Stepping over Cockleburs: Conversations with Ned Cobb," in *Telling Lives: The Biographer's Art,* Marc Pachter, ed. (Washington: New Republic Books, 1979), 122–23.

52. Jimmie Lewis Franklin, "Black Southerners, Shared Experience, and Place: A Reflection," *Journal of Southern History* 60 (February 1994): 15. Hartman Turnbow is interviewed in Howell Raines, *My Soul is Rested: Movement Days in the Deep South Remembered* (New York: Penguin, 1983), 19–20.

53. Quotes from Portelli, introduction to *The Death of Luigi Trastulli,* vii–ix, viii. For his subtle use of oral history to interpret white workers' resistance to those who controlled the South and to show how paternalism affected their memory, see "Patterns of Paternalism," in ibid., 195–240.

54. Jacquelyn Dowd Hall, "Disorderly Women: Gender and Labor Militancy in the Appalachian South," *Journal of American History* 73 (September 1986).

55. Jacquelyn Dowd Hall, "Partial Truths," *Signs* 14, 4 (Summer 1989): 905–08, and "O. Delight Smith's Progressive Era: Labor, Feminism and Reform in the Urban South," in Nancy Hewitt and Suzanne Lebsock, eds., *Visible Women: New Essays on American Activism,* Nancy Hewitt and Suzanne Lebsock, eds. (Urbana: University of Illinois Press, 1993), 166–98.

56. Jacquelyn Dowd Hall et al., *Like a Family: The Making of a Southern Cotton Mill World* (Chapel Hill: University of North Carolina Press, 1987).

57. Hall, *Like a Family,* 353. For an excellent study of why the strike surprised so many people and why it has been a mystery to historians, see Janet Irons, "The Challenge of National Coordination: Southern Textile Workers and the General Strike of 1934," in *We Are All Leaders: The Alternative Unionism of the Early 1930s,* Staughton Lynd, ed. (Urbana: University of Illinois Press, 1996), 72–101.

58. Jim DuPlessis "Massacre at Honea Path," *Southern Exposure* (Fall 1989): 60–63.

59. Hall, *Like a Family,* xv.

60. For another conspiracy of silence—this about the lynching of Wesley Everest, a member of the IWW, in Centralia, Washington, see Robert R. Weyeneth, "History, He Wrote: Murder, Politics, and the Challenges of Public History in a Community with a Secret," *The Public Historian* 16, 2 (1994): 51–73.

61. Judith Helfand, "Sewing History," *Southern Exposure* 22 (Spring 1994): 42–45. Quote on p. 42.

62. Kathy Lamb, remarks before a public screening of *The Uprising of '34,* Greenville, South Carolina (21 October 1994). Thanks to Judith Helfand for sharing a copy of this manuscript.

63. Nora, "Between Memory and History," in Fabre and O'Meally, *Memory and History in African American Culture,* 291.

64. Catherine Howett, "Interpreting a Painful Past: Birmingham's Kelly Ingram Park," *Cultural Resources Management* 7 (1994): 38–40.

65. Michael Honey, "Doing Public History at the National Civil Rights Museum," *The Public Historian* 17 (Winter 1975): 72, and quote from p. 73.

66. Robert R. Weyeneth, "Historic Preservation and the Civil Rights Movement," *Cultural Resources Management* 2 (1996): 26–28.

67. Gregg D. Kimball and Marie Tyler-McGraw, "Integrating the Interpretation of a Southern City: An Exhibition Case Study," *The Public Historian* 12 (Spring 1990): 41.

68. See Carol Stack, *Call to Home: African Americans Reclaim the Rural South* (New York: Basic Books, 1996).

69. Franklin, "Black Southerners," 18, and Nell Irvin Painter, " 'The South' and 'the Negro': The Rhetoric of Race Relations and Real Life," in Paul D. Escott and David R. Goldfield, eds., *The South for New Southerners* (Chapel Hill: University of North Carolina Press, 1991), 42–66.

70. Eula Grant quoted in Stack, *Call to Home,* 199.

71. Rosengarten, *All God's Dangers,* 35, 489.

72. Rick Halpern, "Organized Labour, Black Workers and the Twentieth-Century South: The Emerging Revision," *Social History* 19, 3 (October 1994): quote on p. 364.

73. Ibid., 373, 380, 382.

74. For an account of Sol Dacus's struggle to survive as an organizer, see Stephen H. Norwood, "Bogalusa Burning: The War against Biracial Unionism in the Deep South, 1919," *Journal of Southern History* 63, 3 (1997): 591–628. References to victims can be found in Goodwyn, "Populist Dreams and Negro Rights," 1437–46; James R. Green, *Grass-Roots Socialism: Radical Movements in the Southwest, 1894–1943* (Baton Rouge: Louisiana State University Press, 1978), 300; Donald H. Grubbs, *Cry from the Cotton: The Southern Tenant Farmers Union and the New Deal* (Chapel Hill: University of North Carolina Press, 1971), 109–10.

7. Seeing the Past with "Movement Eyes"

1. See Ronald Radosh, "The Corporate Ideology of American Labor Leaders from Gompers to Hillman," in *Towards a New America,* David Eakins and James Weinstein, eds. (New York: Vintage, 1970), 125–52.

2. "The Making of *Harlan County, U.S.A.:* An Interview with Barbara Kopple" by Gail Pellet, *Radical America* 11, 2 (1977): 35–36.

3. Lyn Garafola, "Hollywood and the Myth of the Working Class," *Radical America* 14, 1 (1980): 7, 15.

4. For a review of two of these films, *Northern Lights* and *The Wobblies,* see John Demeter, "Independent Film and Working-Class History," *Radical America* 14, 1 (1980): 29–50.

5. Quotes from introduction to *Eyes on the Prize,* part I, episode 1. Produced by Blackside, Inc., Boston, Mass. (1986). Executive producer, Henry Hampton; series writer, Steve Fayer.

6. Hampton interview on National Public Radio, 21 January 1995.

7. Quotes from "No Easy Walk," from *Eyes on the Prize,* part I, episode 4. Produced by Blackside, Inc., Boston, Mass. (1986). Executive producer, Henry Hampton; series wrtier, Steve Fayer.

8. This is a point Hampton clarified in the radio interview, Martin Luther King Day 1995.

9. Judy Richardson, quoted in *Telling the Story: The Media, the Public and American History,* Sean B. Dolan, ed. (Boston: The New England Foundation for the Humanities, 1994), 39–40.

10. Norman Boucher, "The Vision of Henry Hampton: Eyes on the Prize I and II," *The World: Journal of the Unitarian Universalist Association* 4, 1 (January–February, 1990): 8–11. Quote from p. 46.

11. Ibid., 48.

12. Vincent Harding, *Hope and History: Why We Must Share the Story of the Movement* (Maryknoll, N.Y.: Orbis Books, 1990), 11.

13. John Bracey, review of *Eyes on the Prize II, Radical History Review* 50 (Spring 1991): 184–85.

14. Ibid., 157.

15. Report by the Committee for Cultural Studies, City University of New York, quoted in Bruce McCabe, "Study Chides PBS for Elitist Programs," *Boston Globe* (30 June 1990).

16. See review of *Glory Days* by Daniel Walkowitz, in "Labor History and Public History," a special issue of *The Public Historian* 11, 4 (Fall 1989): 156–58.

17. For an informed criticism of the film by a movement historian deeply involved in the P9 struggle, see Peter Rachleff, *Hard Pressed in the Heartland: The Hormel Strike and the Future of the Labor Movement* (Boston: South End Press, 1993), 4–5, 91.

18. Wil Haygood, "Hampton: Back from Hard Times," *Boston Globe* (29 October 1993): 58.

19. Alan Brinkley, *Voices of Protest: Huey Long, Father Coughlin and the Great Depression* (New York: Alfred A. Knopf, 1982).

20. Vincent Harding, interviewed in Henry D. Abelove et al., eds. *Visions of History* (New York: Pantheon, 1984), 219–44.

21. Harding, *Hope and History,* 7, 9–10.

22. James Green, "The Siege of the Rouge: Industrial Unionism Confronts Fordism," unpublished film treatment for Blackside, Inc. (1 March 1991).

23. Terry Kay Rockefeller, quoted in *Stories from Blackside Alums,* in program of Boston Film/Video Foundation Vision Award (1995).

24. Timothy J. McNulty, "Keeper of National Scrapbook," *Chicago Tribune* (26 October 1993).

25. Judith Vecchione, remarks at "A Tribute to Henry Hampton," John F. Kennedy Library, 18 April 1998. Hampton quoted in "Preface: Toward a More Perfect Union" in *Voices of Freedom: An Oral History of the Civil Rights Movement from the 1950s through the 1980s,* Henry Hampton and Steve Fayer, eds. (New York: Bantam Books, 1990), xii.

26. Richard Bernstein, "Doubts Mar PBS Film on Black Army Unit," *New York Times* (1 March 1993): B1 and B3, Joseph B. Treaster, "Film Halted on Blacks Freeing Jews," ibid. (12 February 1993): B3, and "WNET Inquiry Finds No Proof Black Unit Freed Two Nazi Camps," ibid. (8 September 1993): B1.

27. Jon Else to Terry Rockefeller, producers, associate producers, "Standards and Practices for The Great Depression, Draft" (21 September 1991), 1. Typed copy in author's possession.

28. Steve Fayer, Memorandum to *Eyes on the Prize* production teams (18 May 1988), 1, and "Eyes-Style Rules," (27 February 1990), photo copies in author's possession.

29. Jacquelyn Dowd Hall et al., *Like a Family: The Making of a Southern Cotton Mill World* (Chapel Hill: University of North Carolina Press, 1987), xv.

30. On the Chicago stockyards story, see Lizabeth Cohen, *Making a New Deal: Industrial Workers in Chicago, 1919–1939* (Cambridge: Cambridge University Press, 1990), photo on p. 323. An interview with Victoria Kramer, who is called Stella Nowicki, appeared in *Rank and File: Personal Histories by Working-Class Organizers,* Alice and Staughton Lynd, eds. (Boston: Beacon Press, 1972), 67–88, in which she speaks about her work in the CP.

31. When the film segment was nearly completed, I wrote a historical essay based on our script.

See James Green, "Democracy Comes to 'Little Siberia': Steel Workers Organize in Aliquippa, Pennsylvania, 1933–1937," *Labor's Heritage* 5, 2 (1993). 4–24

32. John Sayles, *Thinking in Pictures: The Making of the Movie* Matewan (Boston: Houghton Mifflin, 1987), 130.

33. See Hayden White, *Metahistory: The Historical Imagination in Nineteenth-Century Europe* (Indianapolis: Indiana University Press, 1973).

34. Alan Dawley, "Keeping Time in Twentieth-Century America," a paper presented to the Organization of American Historians, Atlanta (April 1994), 4. Thanks to Alan Dawley for permission to quote from his remarks.

35. David Carr, *Time, Narrative and History* (Bloomington: Indiana University Press, 1986), 12, 16–17, 61.

36. Elsa Rassbach's remarks are reproduced along with those of many other historians and filmmakers who attended a 1993 conference in Boston on historical filmmaking, in Dolan, ed. *Telling the Story,* 29. For an excellent review of the conference and the political debates it generated, see Daniel Walkowitz, "Telling the Story," *Perspectives: American Historical Association Newsletter* 31, 7 (October 1993): 1, 6–9.

37. Geoffrey C. Ward, "The Life and Times," *American Heritage* (November 1993): 16.

38. Timothy J. McNulty, "Keeper of a National Scrapbook," *Chicago Tribune* (26 October 1993).

39. James Green, "Making 'The Great Depression' for Public Television: Notes on the Collaboration of Historians and Film Makers," *Perspectives: Newsletter of the American Historical Association,* 32, 7 (1995), 3–5.

40. Ed Seigel, "Hampton Makes History Again," *Boston Globe* (24 October 1993).

41. Lewis Cole, Review of "The Great Depression," *Nation* (29 November 1993), 669.

42. Jonathan Storm, "PBS Plumbs the Depths of the Great Depression," *Philadelphia Inquirer* (24 October 1993), 25.

43. Richard Zoglin, "Democracy's Toughest Test," *Time* (25 October 1993): 80.

44. Robert A. Rosenstone, "History in Images/History in Words," in *Visions of the Past: The Challenge of Film to Our Idea of History* (Cambridge: Harvard University Press, 1995), 30–31.

45. Introduction to *The Great Depression,* written by Jon Else, episode I, "A Job at Ford's," produced by Blackside, Inc., Boston, Mass. (1993). Executive producer Henry Hampton; series producer, Terry Kay Rockefeller.

46. Cole, review of *The Great Depression,* 669.

47. Ibid., 670–71.

48. Ibid., 670–71.

49. For reflections on the process of "thinning out" required in filmic story telling, see Rosenstone, "History in Images," 34. This need to keep the story moving forward means leaving some episodes out. The process doesn't necessarily make for bad history if the story stays within the bounds of historical accuracy. In fact, these tough decisions can improve the quality of history telling. For example, the story our series told of protest in Harlem in 1935 is incomplete. It leaves out important Communist and black nationalist figures, but it is not an inaccurate portrayal of the boycott campaign which the Party at first opposed. See Mark Naison, *Communists in Harlem during the Depression* (Urbana: University of Illinois Press, 1983), 50–51.

50. Rosenstone quoted in Dolan, *Telling the Story,* 40.

51. Richard Flacks, *Making History: The American Left and the American Mind* (New York: Columbia University Press, 1988), 247.

52. Michael J. Sandel, *Democracy's Discontent: America in Search of a Public Philosophy* (Cambridge: Harvard University Press, 1996), 350.

53. Arthur M. Schlesinger Jr., *The Disuniting of America: Reflections on a Multicultural America* (New York: W.W. Norton, 1992), 16–17.

54. Ibid., 17.

55. Ralph Ellison, *Going into the Territory* (New York: Vintage, 1986), 124.

56. Hampton quoted in Andy Meisler, "Survivors of the Ordeal," *San Francisco Chronicle* (24 October 1993).

57. For a helpful discussion of filmmaking not intended for education or consumption but for

thoughtful reflection, see Michael Frisch, "The Memory of History," in *A Shared Authority: Essays on the Craft and Meaning of Oral and Public History* (Albany: State University of New York Press, 1990), 23–24. Also see Alessandro Portelli, "Oral History as Genre," in *The Battle of Valle Giulia: Oral History and the Art of Dialogue* (Madison: University of Wisconsin Press, 1997), 14–15.

58. Rosenstone, "History in Images," 34, and Green, "Making The Great Depression for Public Television," 3–5. An explicit effort to apply Blackside's dramatic structure in a traditional historical account can be found in Green, "Democracy Comes to 'Little Siberia.'"

59. Rosenstone, Introduction to *Visions of History,* 24, and "History in Images, 24, 42–43.

8. Why Movement History Matters

1. For good histories, see Byron Rushing, "Black Schools in White Boston," and Henry Allen, "Segregation and Desegregation in Boston Schools" in *From Common School to Magnet School: Selected Essays in the History of Boston Schools,* James Fraser et al., eds. (Boston: Boston Public Library, 1979).

2. The Garrity decision can be found in *The Boston School Decision* (Boston: Paperback Booksmith, 1974).

3. Alan Lupo, *Liberty's Chosen Home: The Politics of Violence in Boston* (Boston: Beacon Press, 1977), 334, 265.

4. Ibid., 350.

5. Ronald Formisano, *Boston against Busing: Race, Class and Ethnicity in the 1960's and 1970's* (Chapel Hill: University of North Carolina Press, 1991).

6. J. Anthony Lukas, *Common Ground: A Turbulent Decade in the Lives of Three Families* (New York: Alfred A. Knopf, 1985).

7. J. Anthony Lukas, "A Touch of Class," *Boston Observer* 4, 2 (June 1985): 9.

8. Quotes from reviews in *Los Angeles Times* and *Time* magazine, front matter of paperback edition of J. Anthony Lukas, *Common Ground* (New York: Vintage, 1986).

9. Lukas, *Common Ground,* 27.

10. Brian Powers, "Schooling in America," *Socialist Review* (November–December 1986): 123.

11. Thomas Byrne Edsall, *The New Politics of Inequality* (New York: Norton, 1988), 50.

12. Lukas, "A Touch of Class," 9, and J. Anthony Lukas, "Garrity As Scapegoat," *Boston Globe* (18 September 1985).

13. Batson, quoted in Ian Menzies, "A Dissenting Opinion on 'Common Ground,'" *Boston Globe* (23 March 1986): A24.

14. Mel King, *Chain of Change: Struggles for Black Community Development* (Boston: South End Press, 1981).

15. Lukas, "A Touch of Class," 9–10.

16. Lukas, *Common Ground,* 304.

17. John Mollenkopf, *The Contested City* (Princeton: Princeton University Press, 1983), 150–59.

18. James Green, ed., *The South End: A Neighborhood History* (Boston: Boston 200 Corporation, 1976).

19. Ibid., and James Green, "Learning the South End's Ethnic Tradition," *Boston Phoenix* (24 June 1975), 21.

20. Mel King, *Chain of Change,* 10–13.

21. See Jim Green and Allen Hunter, "Racism and Busing in Boston," in *Marxism and the Metropolis,* William K. Tabb and Larry Sawers, eds. (New York: Oxford University Press, 1978), 271–96.

22. King, *Chain of Change,* 32–34.

23. Peter Schrag, *Village School Downtown: Boston Schools, Boston Politics* (Boston: Beacon Press, 1967), 13, 18–20.

24. King, *Chain of Change,* pp. 34–36, 85–94.

25. Ibid.

26. James Jennings, "Urban Machinism and the Black Voter: The Kevin White Years," in *From*

Access to Power: Black Politics in Boston, James Jennings and Mel King, eds. (Cambridge: Schenkman, 1986), 70.

27. Ibid. passim.

28. Ibid., 23–24, and James Jennings, "Boston Machinism and Black Politics in Boston," unpublished manuscript in author's possession.

29. Stephan Thernstrom, *The Other Bostonians: Poverty and Progress in the American Metropolis, 1880–1970* (Cambridge: Harvard University Press, 1973).

30. King, *Chain of Change,* 95–127, 201–02.

31. Jennings, "Urban Machinism," 62–64.

32. King, *Chain of Change,* 155–58.

33. Ibid., 163–64.

34. Ruth Batson, quoted in Henry Hampton and Steve Fayer, *Voices of Freedom: An Oral History of the Civil Rights Movement from the 1950s through the 1960s* (New York: Bantam Books, 1990), 618–19.

35. Lukas, *Common Ground,* 554.

36. Lupo, *Liberty's Chosen Home,* 320.

37. King, *Chain of Change,* 219.

38. For a discussion of the seemingly obvious possibility that "a desegregation order can also work as a catalyst for other school reforms if the school system takes the opportunity," see Jennifer Hochschild, *The New American Dilemma: Liberal Democracy and School Desegregation* (New Haven: Yale University Press, 1984), 80–81.

39. James Jennings, "A New Kind of Black Politics," *In These Times* (5 October 1983): 15.

40. Interview with Marie Kennedy (7 March 1999).

41. David Nyhan, "Populism Was the Big Victor in This Election," *Boston Globe* (13 October 1983): 19, 30.

42. *Time* magazine (10 October 1983): 10.

43. Green, "Learning from the South End's Ethnic Tradition."

44. Jill Nelson-Ricks, "Rainbow Politics: Mel King's Boston Dream," *Village Voice* (25 October 1983): 22–24.

45. *Boston Globe* (16 October 1983): A25, 149.

46. Howard Husock, "Getting Their Fair Share," *Boston Globe Magazine* (14 June 1981): 10, 28, 33.

47. Ibid.

48. See James Green, "King, Flynn, and Populism," *Boston Globe* (28 October 1983).

49. James Green, "Populism, Socialism, and the Promise of Democracy," *Radical History Review* 24 (Fall 1980), 7–40, and "Culture, Politics, and Workers Response to Industrialization," *Radical America* 16 (Winter 1982) 110–28.

50. James Green, "King, Flynn, and Populism," *Boston Globe* (28 October 1983): 19. In response to my editorial, two of Flynn's leftist supporters argued that their candidate showed a "greater willingness to reach out" than did King, and that this former defender of school segregation was better able to heal the "city's social, economic, and racial wounds." Peter Drier and Kevin Sidel, "Building a Governing Coalition," *Boston Globe* (5 November 1983): 15.

51. For a discussion of fair shares and equal shares thinking, see William Ryan, *Equality* (New York: Pantheon, 1982).

52. For a fuller discussion of the new populism King articulated, see the article by three activist intellectuals who supported his movement: Marie Kennedy and Chris Tilly with Mauricio Gaston, "Transformative Populism and the Development of a Community of Color," in Joseph M. Kling and Prudence Posner, eds., *Dilemmas of Activism: Class, Community and the Politics of Local Mobilization* (Philadelphia: Temple University Press, 1990), 302–24.

53. *Boston Globe* (16 November 1983): 1, and King, *Chain of Change,* 31.

54. Robert Coles, "A Working People's Politics: Boston's Mayor Flynn," in Harry C. Boyte and Frank Reisman, *The New Populism: The Politics of Empowerment* (Philadelphia: Temple University Press, 1986), 198–206.

55. *South Boston Tribune,* quoted in Lupo, *Liberty's Chosen Home,* 345.

56. Marie Kennedy and Chris Tilly, "The Mandela Campaign," *Radical America* 20, 5 (1987): 23–26.

57. Lupo, *Liberty's Chosen Home,* 346.

58. Lukas criticized the Garrity order for creating white flight and furthering "racial imbalance in the schools," leaving the public schools "poverty stricken." Lukas, "Garrity as Scapegoat," *Boston Globe* (18 September 1985).

59. Thomas Atkins, review of *Common Ground* in *Social Policy* (Winter 1986): 61–62.

60. Mel King's remarks at a conference on the New Boston at Boston College, (5 October 1984). Thanks to Judy Smith and Sharlene Voogd Cochrane for a videotape of this speech.

61. Doris Brown was one of the African American students to enter first grade the year desegregation began. When she entered Hyde Park School eight years later, she said everyone expected violence because of the riots that had broken out during the busing in 1974. "But when I got here, it had all changed," she said. "There was a whole different set of kids here. We had all grown up together in elementary and secondary school. Why all of a sudden would we start fighting?" She worried about white flight out of the public schools, but pointed out, "If the schools had remained separate, I wouldn't have had a chance to meet a lot of different kinds of people." Doris Brown, quoted in "Twelve Years Under Desegregation," *Boston Globe* (27 April 1986): 1.

62. Beth Daley, "Schools Have Gone Downhill since Busing, Right? Wrong," *Boston Globe* (21 February 1999): E1–2.

63. Charles V. Wylie, "Backtracking on City's Schools," *Boston Globe* (18 January 1999): A13.

64. Lawrence Goodwyn, *The Populist Moment: A Short History of the Agrarian Revolt in America* (New York: Oxford University Press, 1978), 295.

65. Janice Fine, "Rainbow Coalitions: An Interview with Mel King," in *Building Bridges: The Emerging Grassroots Coalition of Community and Labor,* Jeremy Brecher and Tim Costello, eds. (New York: Monthly Review Press, 1990), 147.

66. The characterization of Dukakis is from Steve Fraser and Gary Gerstler, epilogue to *The Rise and Fall of the New Deal Order, 1930–1980* (Princeton: Princeton University Press, 1989), 295.

67. Ibid.

68. James Green, "For Jackson, Populism Is a Class Act," *Boston Globe* (3 April 1988), 63, 65.

69. King, *Chain of Change,* 260.

70. Ibid.

9. Planting the Seeds of Resurgence

1. Denise Giardina, "Strike Zone: The 'Appalachian Intifada' Rages," *Village Voice* (29 August 1989): 31–36.

2. Jim Green, "Camp Solidarity," *New England Labor News and Commentary* (November 1989), 1, 6–7.

3. Ibid.

4. "Today the Mine Workers—Tomorrow, the AFL-CIO," *Business Week* (15 February 1988): 65–66.

5. Richard Couto, "The Memory of Miners and the Conscience of Capital: Coal Miners' Strikes as Free Space," in *Fighting Back in Appalachia: Tradition, Resistance and Change,* Stephen L. Fischer, ed. (Philadelphia: Temple University Press, 1993), 178–79, 173.

6. Couto, "The Memory of Miners," 178–79.

7. United Mine Workers of America, "The United Mine Workers Strike against the Pittston Coal Company," background briefing paper, unpublished manuscript in author's possession.

8. Ibid., and *Betraying the Trust: The Pittston Company's Drive to Break Appalachia's Coalfield Communities* (Washington: United Mine Workers of America, 1989); Martha Hodel, "The Pittston Company," *Charleston Gazette* (29 August 1989); and Moe Seager, "One Day Longer than Pittston," *Z Magazine* (October 1989): 14.

9. "The United Mine Workers Strike against Pittston," 3; and *Betraying the Trust,* 1–4.

10. James Green, "Corporate Culture's Failure in Dealing with Coal Miners," *Boston Globe* (27 June 1989).

11. See Peter Rachleff, *Hard-Pressed in the Heartland: The Hormel Strike and the Future of the American Labor Movement* (Boston: South End Press, 1993).

12. Dwayne Yancey, "Thunder in the Coal Fields: The UMW's Strike against Pittston," a special report of the *Roanoke Times and World News* (29 April 1990): 2.

13. Author's interview with Richard Trumka, Nemacolin, Pa., July 12, 1990. "Today, The Mine Workers," 66.

14. See Kim Moody, *An Injury to All: The Decline of American Unionism* (London: Verso 1988); and on the International Paper and Hormel strikes, see Jane Slaughter, "Corporate Campaigns: Labor Enlists Community Support," and Peter Rachleff, "Supporting the Hormel Strikers," in *Building Bridges: The Emerging Grassroots Coalition of Community and Labor,* Jeremy Brecher and Tim Costello, eds. (New York: Monthly Review Press, 1990), 47–69.

15. David Moberg, "Envisioning a New Day for the Labor Movement," *In These Times* (30 August–5 September 1989).

16. Yancey, "Thunder in the Coal Fields," 2–3.

17. Interview with Ron Baker by the author (17 July 1993).

18. Yancey, "Thunder in the Coal Fields," 3.

19. Ibid., 3.

20. Ibid., 3.

21. Marat Moore, "Ten Months That Shook the Coal Fields," unpublished manuscript in author's possession.

22. Roberts, quoted in "Out of Darkness: The Mine Workers' Story," video produced by Barbara Kopple, directed by Bill Davis (New York: Cabin Creek Films, 1990).

23. Moore, "Ten Months That Shook the Coal Fields," 13; Yancey, "Thunder in the Coal Fields," 4; and Nicolaus Mills, "Solidarity in Virginia: The Mine Workers Remake History, *Dissent* (Spring 1990): 238.

24. Yancey, "Thunder in the Coal Fields," 4; also see Bill McKelway, "Defiant Miners Clog Roads," *Richmond Times Dispatch* (7 July 1989).

25. Yancey, "Thunder in the Coal Fields," 4; and Moore, "Ten Months That Shook the Coal Fields," 10.

26. Yancey, "Thunder in the Coal Fields," 4.

27. Ibid., 4–5; and John Clarks, "Students Protest for UMWA," *The Cumberland Times* (26 April 1989); and Moore, "Ten Months That Shook the Coal Fields."

28. Yancey, "Thunder in the Coal Fields," 5.

29. Ibid., 5.

30. "Jackson Makes Pledge to Miners," *Richmond Times-Dispatch* (1 May 1989); and "The Message Comes to the Mountains," *Herald-Courier,* Bristol, Va. (1 May 1989); and Greg Edwards, "Jackson to Miners: Don't Go Back," *Roanoke, Virginia Times and World News* (1 May 1989); and Tracy Wimmer, "Miners Lifted by Jackson Magic," ibid. (1 May 1989).

31. Dana Priest, "Jesse Jackson Joins Forces with Striking Miners in Va.," *Washington Post* (1 May 1989); and Wayne Barber, "Westmoreland Workers Will Remain Off Jobs," *Bristol Herald Courier* (1 May 1989).

32. Yancey, "Thunder in the Coal Fields," 7.

33. *Betraying the Trust,* 3.

34. Yancey, "Thunder in the Coal Fields," 7.

35. Couto, "The Memory of the Mines," 179–80.

36. Yancey, "Thunder in the Coal Fields," 8–9. Author's interview with Marat Moore, Washington, D.C. (15 December 1993). For a discussion of other recent strike communities, see Rick Fantasia, *Cultures of Solidarity: Consciousness, Action and Contemporary American Workers* (Berkeley: University of California Press, 1988).

37. Yancey, "Thunder in the Coal Fields," 8.

38. "Wildcat Strikes Break Out in West Virginia," *Bristol Herald Courier* (13 June 1989).

39. "Miners Defiant," *USA Today* (14 June 1989), and "Wildcat Coal Strike Continues Despite Order," *New York Times* (15 June 1989).

40. Martha Hodel, "Wildcat Walkout: Trumka Not Doing Enough to Get Miners Back, Companies Say," *Charleston Sunday Gazette Mail* (9 July 1989).

41. Yancey, "Thunder in the Coal Fields," 8.

42. Ibid., 2, 3.

43. James Buchan, "A Marriage of Coal and Violence," *Financial Times* (10 July 1989); and Wayne Barber, "Explosion Rocks Pittston Building," *Bristol Herald Couriers/Virginia-Tennesseean* (6 July 1989).

44. Jules Loh, "UMW Now Negotiates from Position of Civility," *Alleghany Journal* (23 July 1989).

45. Yancey, "Thunder in the Coal Fields," 9.

46. Richard Trumka, speech at Harvard Trade Union Program (4 March 1990), and quoted in *Roanoke Times* (7 June 1989); and Richard Phalon, "Mis-Calculated Risk?" *Forbes* 142 (12 June 1989); Yancey, "Thunder in the Coal Fields," 9; and "Producers Fear Lengthy Strike, Loss of Sales," *The Journal of Commerce* (7 June 1989).

47. For an excellent account of the miners' march, see David Alan Corbin, *Life, Work, and Rebellion in the Southern West Virginia Coal Fields: The Southern West Virginia Miners, 1880–1920* (Urbana: University of Illinois Press, 1981), 195–252.

48. Author's interview with Cecil Roberts (22 April 1990) on the road from Norton, Virginia, to Welch, West Virginia; and in Washington, D.C. (15 December 1993).

49. Yancey, "Thunder in the Coal Fields," 9; and Wayne Barber, "UMW Official Calls for Law That at Least Levels 'Playing Field,'" *Bristol Herald Courier* (18 June 1989).

50. David Reed, "UMW: Pittston Strike Is More than Labor Dispute," (AP) *Williamson Daily* (29 June 1989); and Yancey, "Thunder in the Coal Fields," 10–11.

51. Martha J. Hall, "NLRB Ruling May Protect Union Jobs," *Kingsport Times-News* (5 July 1989); and Deborah Rouse, "Striking UMWA Miners Hear Encouraging Words from Cesar Chavez of United Farm Workers," *The Coalfield Progress* (6 July 1989).

52. Jonathan Gill, "Union Leaders Stress Merits of Nonviolence," *Williamson Daily* (30 June 1989); and "U.M.W. Fines Again in Virginia Coal Fight," *The New York Times* (6 July 1989); and Bill McKelway, "Extra Police Sent to Coalfields As Acts Spread to West Virginia," *Richmond Times Dispatch* (10 July 1989).

53. Mike Wright, "Forty-nine Strike Related Cases Dismissed by Greenwalt," *The Dickenson Star* (13 July 1989); and "Union Set for Memorial Period, President 'Willing' to Go to Jail," *Bristol Herald Courier/Virginia-Tennesseean* (10 July 1989); and Harry E. Stapleton, "It Was Old Men That Made This Union," *New York Times* (9 July 1989).

54. Jeff Moore, "Nun Arrested; Community Angered," *Coalfield Progress* (13 July 1989); and "U.S. Marshals Halt Strikers' Convoys," *Bluefield Daily Telegraph* (7 July 1989).

55. "Baliles' Appearance Postponed," *Bristol Herald Courier* (7 July 1989); and Jeff Moore, "Export Clients Told Shipments Can't Be Filled," *The Coalfield Progress* (11 July 1989); also see, Letter from Baliles, "Baliles Calls for New Bargaining," *Bristol Herald Courier/Virginia-Tennesseean* (11 July 1989); "Coal Miners' Strike Reaches Critical Point," *Journal of Commerce* (1 July 1989).

56. Dana Priest, "Striking Coal Miners Fear End of Union, Way of Life in Va.," *Washington Post* (6 July 1989); David Reed, "UMW: Pittston Strike Is More than Labor Dispute," *Williamson Daily* (29 June 1989); and David Moberg, "Envisioning a New Day for the Labor Movement," *In These Times* (30 August 1989).

57. Yancey, "Thunder in the Coal Fields," 9; and Jenny Burman, "Daughters of Mother Jones," *Z Magazine* (November 1989); and Fred Brown, "Striking Miners Gather to Relax at Camp Solidarity, *The Knoxville News-Sentinel* (22 July 1989); and Gene Carroll, "Camp Solidarity: The Heart of the Pittston Strike," *United Mine Workers' Journal* 100, 10 (November 1989): 15–17.

58. Quotations from Yancey, "Thunder in the Coal Fields," 9; Burman, "Daughters of Mother Jones"; and Moore, "Ten Months That Shook the Coal Fields."

59. Ibid.

60. Moore, "Ten Months That Shook the Coal Fields," 13–14.

61. Barbara Kingsolver, *Holding the Line: Women in the Great Arizona Mine Strike of 1983* (Ithaca: Cornell University Press, 1989), 140.

62. Ibid., 182.

63. Yancey, "Thunder in the Coal Fields," and James Green, "Camp Solidarity: The United Mine Workers, The Pittston Strike, and the New People's Movement," in Brecher and Costello, eds., *Building Bridges*, 15–24.

64. Greg Edwards, "UMW Chief Faults Labor Law," *Roanoke Times & World News* (9 July 1989).

65. John F. Harris, "Trade Unions Pledge Support to Striking Miners," *Washington Post* (9 July 1989); and "World-Wide Support for Miners," *Free Labour World* 13 (31 August 1989); and "Foreign Miners Chief Supports UMW," *Washington Times* (23 August 1989).

66. "Labor Ruling Finds Coal Company Guilty in Strike," *New York Times* (12 July 1989); also see, Phil Primack, "UMW Chief to Drum Up Hub Support," *Boston Herald* (12 July 1989).

67. Bill McKelway, "Pittston Mum on Plea for New Talks," *Richmond Times-Dispatch* (12 July 1989); "Report on the Strike at the Pittston Coal Company," prepared by the Majority Staff Subcommittee on Labor-Management Relations (31 August 1989), 22.

68. Michael Freitag, "The Battle Over Medical Costs," *New York Times* (17 August 1989); also see "Health Care, Pensions Key Issues in Strike Against Pittston Group," *Washington Post* (6 July 1989).

69. Wayne Barber, "More Than $4 Million in UMW Fines Imposed," *Bristol Herald Courier-Bristol Virginian/Tennesseean* (28 July 1989).

70. "UMW Official Pleads Innocent in Virginia," *Charleston Gazette* (4 August 1989); and "Efficiency Panel Proposed by UMW," *Richmond Times Dispatch* (9 August 1989); and "UMW Makes New Proposal to Pittston in Coal Strike," *The Washington Post* (9 August 1989); and "UMW Officials: 'Is a national strike in the offing?'" *Coal Outlook* (7 August 1989).

71. "UMW Vice President Arrested," *Kingsport Times-News* (26 July 1989); and "Mine Worker Officers, Others Are Arrested," *The Wall Street Journal* (26 July 1989); and Yancey, "Thunder in the Coal Fields"; and Tim Sansbury, "Pittston Coal, Miners' Union to Resume Talks Today," *The Journal of Commerce* (1 August 1989); and "UMW Vice President Dares Federal Judge to Jail Him," *Charleston Gazette* (9 August 1989).

72. *Labor in America, 'We Won't Go Back': The UMWA/Pittston Strike, 1989–90* (Clinchco, Va.: The Dickenson Star, 1990), 69, 98.

73. Ibid., 69; and Report to Subcommittee, 17; and Wright, "Trumka's 'Call to Conscience' Answered."

74. "The Strike at Pittston," *Trade Union Advisor* 2, 15 (25 July 1989); and Ken Jenkins Jr., "Coal Miners' Discontent Gets Political," *The Washington Post* (6 August 1989); and "Sheriff Blasts Coalfield Troopers," *Roanoke Times and World News* (24 September 1989).

75. Yancey, "Thunder in the Coal Fields," 4, 17–20.

76. Charles Isenhart, "A Coal Strike Comes to Affluent Greenwhich, Conn.," *National Catholic Register* (August 1989); and Yancey, "Thunder in the Coal Fields," 10; and "A Letter to Paul Douglas, Chairman the Pittston Company," by Religious Leaders of Fairfield County, Leaflet, N.D., in author's possession.

77. Yancey, "Thunder in the Coal Fields," 10.

78. Paul Cannon, "Miners Reach Out for Our Help," *New England Labor News and Commentary* (July/August 1989).

79. Joe Sciacca, "Council Votes to Close Its Shawmut Accounts," *The Boston Herald* (27 July 1989); and "Flynn Remarks Anger Mass. Cops," *Boston Herald* (22 July 1989); and, "Flynn Visits Miners," ibid. (21 July 1989); and "Boston Council Cites Pittston-Bank Link," *Journal of Commerce* (28 July 1993); and "AFL-CIO Threatens to Sever Ties with CNB," *Greenwich Times* (23 August 1989); and Yancey, "Thunder in the Coal Fields," 10.

80. Mike Wright, "Trumka's 'Call To Conscience' Answered," *The Dickenson Star* (31 August 1989); Yancey, "Thunder in the Coal Fields," 10–11; and Frank Swoboda, "Organized Labor Toughens Its Stance," *Washington Post* (3 September 1989); and "Labor Leaders Arrested at Rally Held to Support Striking Union," *New York Times* (25 August 1989); and Dana Priest, "Labor Leaders Arrested in Va.," *Washington Post* (24 August 1989), and author's interviews with Trumka (19 January 1990) and Roberts (22 April 1990).

81. For critical news coverage of Pittston, see Martha Hodel, "The Pittston Co.," Alexander Cockburn, "Their Miners and Ours," *The Nation* (21, 28 August 1989); and "Corrupt Firm," *Charleston Gazette* (18 August 1989); and Wayne Barber, "Religious Leaders Rally behind UMW," *Bristol Herald Courier* (10 September 1989); and Stephen Coats, "Churches Respond to the Pittston Strike," *Christianity and Crisis* (25 September 1989). Quotes from Carol Schoettler "After Five Months, Striking Miners Remain United," *Baltimore Sun* (5 September 1989), and Bob Baker, "Coal Strike a Fight Union Has to, but May Not, Win," *Los Angeles Times* (23 August 1989).

82. Jim Sessions and Fran Ansley, "Singing Across Dark Spaces: The Union/Community Takeover of Pittston Moss 3 Plant," in Stephen L. Fischer, *Fighting Back in Appalachia,* 199–222; and Yancey, "Thunder in the Coal Fields," 10–11; and "Striking Coal Miners Hold Pittston Processing Plant," *Washington Post* (19 September 1989).

83. Yancey, "Thunder in the Coal Fields," 11–13; Dana Priest, "Miners Heed Court Order, End Va. Plant Takeover," *Washington Post* (21 September 1989); and Priest, "Striking Miners Settle in at Va. Processing Plant," *Washington Post* (20 September 1989); and Paul Kwik, "Pittston Power," *The Nation* (16 October 1989).

84. Author's interview with Trumka (19 January 1989).

85. Dana Priest, "Senate Bill May Settle Big Issue in Coal Strike," *Washington Post* (3 October 1989); and "Coal Accord?" *Charleston Gazette* (5 October 1989); and Pamela Porter, "Panel OKs Plan to Salvage Miners' Fund," *Bluefield Daily* (10 October 1989); and Joel Chernoff, "Miners Fighting for Health Plans," *Pensions and Investment Age* (30 October 1989).

86. "Secretary Dole to Visit Site of Pittston Strike," *Daily Labor Report* (13 October 1989); and "ICFTU Tour Appalled at Pittston, U.S. Law," *AFL-CIO News* (14 October 1989); and William Keesler, "Foreign Unions Pressure Firms to Cut Purchases from Pittston," *Louisville Courier Journal* (13 October 1989).

87. Yancey, "Thunder in the Coal Fields," 14; and "Dole Leads Coal Strike Summit," *Washington Post* (15 October 1989); and "Ex-Labor Secretary Usery to Mediate Va. Coal Strike," ibid. (25 October 1989).

88. Joe Battenfeld, "Mine Workers Applaud As Shawmut Exec Resigns," *Boston Herald* (20 October 1989): 10; and Doug Bailey and Bruce Butterfield, "Shawmut Boycott Off As Craig Quits," *Boston Globe* (20 October 1993).

89. "Pittston Net Plunged 79% in 3rd Quarter, Coal Strike is Cited," *Wall Street Journal* (23 October 1989); and "Pittston Income Falls 79%," *Greenwich Time* (21 October 1989); and "Judge Says Pittston Co. Violated Securities Rules," *New York Times* (30 November 1989).

90. Yancey, "Thunder in the Coal Fields," 14.

91. *Labor in America: "We Won't Go Back,"* 90.

92. Dana Priest, "Va. Coal Miner Strikes Gold in Politics," *Washington Post* (20 November 1989); and Yancey, "Thunder in the Coal Fields," 15.

93. "Pittston Company Misread Strike," UPI, *Charleston Gazette* (21 November 1989); and Dana Priest, "Big Machines, Ready Replacements and the Strike's Bottom Line," *Washington Post* (26 November 1989).

94. Yancey, "Thunder in the Coal Fields," 15.

95. Ibid.; *Camo Call,* Dec. 8, Dec. 29, 1989; and "Union 'Santas' Aid Striking Miners," *Bridgeport Post-Telegram* (Bridgeport, Conn.,) (10 December 1989).

96. Yancey, "Thunder in the Coal Fields," 15; and "A Healthy Settlement for Mine Workers," *U.S. News & World Report* (15 January 1990).

97. Ibid., 16; Peter Kilborn, "Pittston and Miners in Accord to Resolve Bitter Coal Strike," *New York Times* (2 January 1990); and Dana Priest, "Light at the End of the Tunnel," *Washington Post* (26 February 1990).

98. Dana Priest, "Striking Miners Vote on New Contract," *Washington Post* (19 February 1990); "Labor in America: 'We Won't Go Back,'" 98, 99; David Reed, "Pittston Miners OK Contract," *Greenwich Time* (21 February 1990); Dana Priest, "Contract Approved by Miners," *Washington Post* (21 February 1999); Lionel Barber, "Miners' Settlement May Herald New Era," *Financial Times* (3 January 1990); Greg Tarpinian, "Pittston: Rebirth of the Unions?" *Wall Street Journal*

(20 November 1989); and Jane Slaughter, "Is the Labor Movement Reaching a Turning Point?" *Labor Notes* (January 1990).

99. Author's interview with Trumka 19 January 1994; and Richard L. Trumka, "On Becoming a Movement," *Dissent* (Winter 1992): 57–60.

100. See Fantasia, *Cultures of Solidarity*, 218–25, 242.

10. On Becoming a Movement Again

1. Richard L. Trumka, "On Becoming a Movement," *Dissent* 39, 1 (Winter 1992): 57–60.

2. Ibid.

3. On the return to historical practices in AFL construction union organizing, see Janice Fine, "Moving Innovation from the Margins to the Center," in *A New Labor Movement for a New Century,* Gregory Mantsios, ed. (New York: Monthly Review, 1998), 119–46.

4. Elizabeth Faue, "'Amnesiacs in a Ward on Fire': Gender and the Crisis of Labor Viewed from the 1930s," unpublished paper presented at the proceedings of the Industrial Relations Research Association (3 January 1994). Also see Elizabeth Faue, *Community of Suffering and Struggle: Women, Men and the Labor Movement in Minneapolis, 1915–1945* (Chapel Hill: University of North Carolina Press, 1991); Jeremy Brecher and Tim Costello, "American Labor: The Promise of Decline," in *Building Bridges,* 198–207; Staughton Lynd, Introduction to *We Are All Leaders: The Alternative Unionism of the 1930s* (Urbana: University of Illinois Press, 1996).

5. Bruce Nissen, "Utilizing the Membership to Organize the Unorganized," in *Organizing to Win: New Research on Union Organizing,* Kate Bronfenbrenner et al., eds. (Ithaca: Cornell University Press, 1998), 134; and 141.

6. David Moberg, "Hard Organizing in Sunbelt City," *The Progressive* (August 1983): 34–36.

7. Steve Early and Larry Cohen, "Jobs with Justice: Mobilizing Labor-Community Coalitions," *WorkingUSA* (November/December 1997): 49–53.

8. See Richard Bensinger, "When We Try More, We Win More: Organizing the New Workforce," in *Not Your Father's Union Movement: Inside the AFL-CIO,* Jo Ann Mort, ed. (London: Verso, 1998), 27–41.

9. See Harry Braverman, *Labor and Monopoly Capital: The Degradation of Work in the Twentieth Century* (New York: Monthly Review Press, 1974), 379, 277. This service sector exploded from a total of 15.8 million in 1950 to 27.7 million in 1970 while the numbers of operatives, laborers, and craftspeople grew much more slowly to a total of 27.6 million. Braverman describes this process as the expansion of a universal market into realms of family and community with "new services and commodities" providing "substitutes for human relations in the form of market relations." As the care of humans for each other became even more institutionalized in market relations, service providers drew upon a pool of unskilled labor to create more low-wage, largely non-union jobs.

10. AFL-CIO Committee on the Evolution of Work, *The Future of Work* (Washington, D.C.: AFL-CIO, 1983), 11.

11. Bennett Harrison and Barry Bluestone, *The Great U-turn: Corporate Restructuring and the Polarizing of America* (New York: Basic Books, 1988), 127.

12. AFL-CIO Harris poll, cited in James Green and Chris Tilly, "Service Unionism: New Directions in Organizing," *Labor Law Journal,* 38, 8 (August 1987): 486–87.

13. William Serrin, "Labor As Usual: At the AFL-CIO the Mikes Are Covered," *Village Voice* (23 February 1988): 30. For examples of how labor history contradicts the conventional wisdom about organizing women, see Alice Kessler-Harris, "Organizing the Unorganizable," in *Class, Sex, and the Woman Worker,* Milton Cantor and Bruce Laurie, eds. (Westport: Greenwood Press, 1977), 144–65; and Ava Baron, "Gender and Labor History," in *Work Engendered: Toward a New History of American Labor,* Ava Baron, ed. (Ithaca: Cornell University Press, 1991), 11–12. For studies of how workers of color responded to union organizing, see Philip Foner, *Organized Labor and the Black Worker, 1619–1973* (New York: Praeger, 1974); Ronald Takaki, *From a Different Shore: A History of Asian Americans* (Boston: Little Brown, 1991); and Juan Gomez-Quinones, *Mexican-American Labor, 1790–1990* (Albuquerque: University of New Mexico Press, 1994).

14. Thomas Kochan, "How American Workers View American Unions," *Monthly Labor Review* 102 (April 1979): 21–31; and Arthur B. Shostak, *Robust Unionism: Innovations in the Labor Movement* (Ithaca: ILR Press, 1991), 86, 93.

15. The 1989 Associated Press poll of eleven thousand Americans, cited in Manning Marable, "Black Leadership and the Labor Movement," *Working USA* (September–October 1997): 46–48.

16. Green and Tilly, "Service Unionism: Directions for Organizing," 486–95.

17. Kate L. Bronfenbrenner, "Employer Behavior in Certification Elections and First Contract Campaigns," in *Restoring the Promise of American Labor Law,* Richard W. Hurd, Rudolph A. Oswald, and Ronald L. Seeber, eds. (Ithaca: ILR Press, 1994), 75–89.

18. Rick Hurd, "Bottom Up Organizing: HERE in New Haven and Boston," *Labor Research Review* 8 (Spring 1986): 6–11. Wilhelm, quoted in Toni Gilpin, Gary Isaac, Dan Letwin, and Jack McKivigan, *On Strike for Respect: The Yale Strike of 1984–85* (Chicago: Charles H. Kerr, 1988), 22.

19. Susan C. Eaton, "Union Leadership Development in the 1990s and Beyond: A Report with Recommendations," paper prepared for the Seminar on Industrial Relations, Sloan School, MIT (11 May 1992), 56–57. Rondeau quoted on p. 57.

20. Ibid., 59.

21. "Women's Ways of Organizing: A Conversation with AFSCME Organizers Kris Rondeau and Gladys McKenzie," *Labor Research Review* 18 (1991): 53.

22. "Union Victory: An Interview with Kristine Rondeau" by James Green, *Democratic Left* (September–October 1988): 4. And see the full account, by John Hoerr, *We Can't Eat Prestige: The Women Who Organized Harvard* (Philadelphia: Temple University Press, 1997).

23. Roger Waldinger, Chris Erickson, Ruth Milkman, Daniel J. B. Mitchell, Abel Valenzuela, Kent Wong, and Maurice Zeitlin, "Helots No More: A Case Study of the Justice for Janitors Campaign in Los Angeles," in Bronfenbrenner, *Organizing to Win,* 102–20.

24. M. J. Piore, "Unions: A Reorientation to Survive," in *Labor Economics and Industrial Relations,* Clark Kerr and Paul D. Stauohar, eds. (Cambridge: Harvard University Press, 1994), 512–41.

25. Waldinger et al., "Helots No More," 103–19.

26. For an excellent account of JfJ, see Paul Johnston, *Success While Others Fail: Social Movement Unionism and the Public Workplace* (Ithaca: ILR Press, 1994), 164–67.

27. Stephen Lerner, "Let's Get Moving," *Labor Research Review* 18 (1991): 1–15; and "Taking the Offensive, Turning the Tide," in *A New Labor Movement,* 76–77.

28. Frances Fox Piven and Richard A. Cloward, *Poor People's Movements: Why They Succeed, How They Fail* (New York: Pantheon, 1977). Piven and Cloward have recently criticized "resource mobilization" theorists who reduce the role of confrontation to a mere mobilizing tactic; see their "Normalizing Collective Protest," in *Frontiers in Social Movement Theory,* Aldon Morris and Carolyn McClurg Mueller, eds. (New Haven: Yale University Press, 1992), 312, 319.

29. Lerner, "Taking the Offensive," 73–75.

30. Thomas A. Kochan, Harry C. Katz, and Robert McKersie, *The Transformation of American Industrial Relations* (Ithaca: ILR Press, 1986); and Thomas Kochan and Kirsten Weaver, "American Unions and the Future of Worker Representation," in *The State of the Unions,* George Strauss, Daniel Gallagher, and Jack Piorito, eds. (Madison: University of Wisconsin Press, 1991), 378.

31. Johnston, *Success While Others Fail,* 170.

32. David Bacon, writing in the *LA Weekly* (28 February 1997): 12.

33. Waldinger et al., "Helots No More," 119–20.

34. Mike Davis, "Local 226 S. MGM Grand: Armageddon at the Emerald City," *The Nation* (11 July 1994): 48–49.

35. See Jose La Luz and Paul Finn, "Getting Serious about Inclusion," in *A New Labor Movement,* 177–79; and Rudolfo Acuna, *Anything but Mexican: Chicanos in Contemporary Los Angeles* (New York: Verso, 1996), 180–90.

36. Bill Fletcher Jr. and Richard W. Hurd, "Beyond the Organizing Model: The Transformation Process in Local Unions," in *Organizing to Win,* 38–53.

37. Ruth Needleman, "Building Relationships for the Long Haul: Unions and Community

Groups Working Together to Organize Low-Wage Workers," in *Organizing to Win*, 73–74. Also see Immanuel Ness, "Organizing Immigrant Communities: UNITE's Workers Center Strategy," in ibid., 87–101.

38. Ardis Cameron, *Radicals of the Worst Sort: Laboring Women in Lawrence, Massachusetts, 1860–1912* (Urbana: University of Illinois Press, 1993); and Faue, *Community of Suffering and Struggle*, 88–99.

39. Dan Cornfield, Holly McCammon, Darren McDaniel, and Dean Latham, "In the Community or in the Union? The Impact of Community Involvement on Nonunion Workers Attitudes about Unionizing," in *Organizing to Win*, 247–58, quotes pp. 255–56.

40. See the interview with Boston civil rights leader and coalition builder Mel King by Janice Fine, in *Building Bridges*, 144–50.

41. Fine, "Moving Innovation from the Margins to the Center," 129–31.

42. Brecher and Costello, "Labor-Community Coalitions and the Restructuring of Power," in *Building Bridges*, 330–44.

43. On the separation of industrial and communal identities, see Ira Katznelson, *City Trenches: Urban Politics and the Patterning of Class in the United States* (New York: Pantheon, 1981).

44. For examples of how the labor movement crossed the trenches of workplace and community in different periods and settings, see Alan Dawley, *Class and Community: The Industrial Revolution in Lynn* (Cambridge: Harvard University Press, 1976); Daniel Walkowitz, *Worker City, Company Town: Iron and Cotton Worker Protest in Troy and Cohoes, New York, 1855–1884* (Urbana: University of Illinois Press, 1978); Richard Jules Ostreicher, *Solidarity and Fragmentation: Working People and Class Consciousness in Detroit, 1875–1900* (Urbana: University of Illinois, 1986); Paul Krause, *The Battle for Homestead, 1880–1892: Politics, Culture, and Steel* (Pittsburgh: University of Pittsburgh Press, 1993); Dana Frank, *Purchasing Power: Consumer, Organizing, Gender and the Seattle Labor Movement, 1919–1929* (New York: Cambridge University Press, 1994); David Corbin, *Life, Work, and Rebellion in the Coal Fields: The Southern West Virginia Miners, 1880–1922* (Urbana: University of Illinois Press, 1981); Gary Gerstle, *Working Class Americanism: The Politics of Labor in a Textile City, 1914–1960* (Cambridge: Cambridge University Press, 1989); and Gunther Peck, "Mobilizing Community: Migrant Workers and the Politics of Labor Mobility in North American West, 1900–1920," in *Labor Histories: Class, Politics, and the Working Class Experience*, Eric Arnesen, Julie Greene, and Bruce Laurie eds. (Urbana: University of Illinois Press, 1998), 176, 193.

45. See David Firestone, "Victory for Union at Plant in the South is a Labor Milestone," *New York Times* (25 June 1999), A1, 20, and Sam Howe Verhovek, "The New Language of American Labor," *ibid.* (26 June 1999), A8.

46. See Staughton Lynd, *Solidarity Unionism* (Chicago: Charles H. Kerr, 1992) and "We Are All Leaders." For a good argument on the challenges posed by community unionism, see Andy Banks, "The Promise of Community Unionism," *Labor Research Review* 18 (1991), 18–20.

47. For an excellent overview of the changing construction industry and the role of unions, see Mark Erlich, "Who Will Build the Future?" *Labor Research Review* 12 (Fall 1988): 1–19.

48. Janet Lewis and Bill Mirand, "Creating an Organizing Culture in Today's Building and Construction Trades: A Case Study of IBEW Local 46," in *Organizing to Win*, 297–308.

49. Ibid., 299–302; and Erlich, "Who Will Build the Future?" 5–7.

50. "Bottom-Up Organizing in the Trades: An Interview with Mike Lucas," Jeffery Grebelsky, in *Labor Research Review* 12 (Fall 1988): 21–36; and Fine, "Moving Innovation from the Margins to the Center," in *A New Labor Movement*, 120–23.

51. Ibid., and Jeff Grebelsky, "Lighting the Spark," *Labor Studies Journal* 20 (Summer 1995): 4–21, plus interviews with COMET activists in unions of electricians, carpenters, and bricklayers.

52. Lewis and Mirand, "Creating an Organizing Culture," in *Organizing to Win*, 297–308.

53. Fine, "Moving Innovation from the Margins to the Center," in *A New Labor Movement*, 42–43. On the feeling of powerlessness in the face of global economic forces, see Jeremy Brecher and Tim Costello, *Global Village or Global Pillage: Economic Restructuring from the Bottom Up* (Boston: South End Press, 1994), 107.

54. Kate Bronfenbrenner and Tom Juravich, "Union Tactics Matter: The Impact of Union Tactics on Certification Elections, First Contracts and Membership Rates," Working Papers, Institute for the Study of Labor Organizations (1993), 6–8.

55. Kate Bronfenbrenner and Tom Juravich, "It Takes More than House Calls: Organizing to Win with a Comprehensive Union Building Strategy," in *Organizing to Win,* 33.

56. Bob Muhlenkamp, "Organizing Never Stops," *Labor Research Review* 17 (1991), 3–6.

57. Robert B. Reich, *Locked in the Cabinet* (New York: Alfred A. Knopf, 1997), 66, 137. Kirkland later challenged the veracity of Reich's account but not of the conversations quoted here. Lane Kirkland to Robert Reich, letter reprinted in *Working USA* 1, 2 (July–August 1997): 83.

58. Serrin, "Labor as Usual," 28–30.

59. Reich, *Locked in the Cabinet,* 107.

60. Sweeney, quoted in Gregory Mantsios, "A New Labor Movement for a New Century," in *A New Labor Movement,* 50, 52.

61. Ibid., 52.

62. In 1996 the Federation helped elect pro-union Democrats in several key Senate races and organized effectively against other candidates, like reactionary Republican congressmen who opposed increasing the minimum wage. After helping Bill Clinton win a second term in 1996 and contributing to the Republicans' stunning loss of seats in the Congress, the AFL-CIO turned around and handed the president a defeat one year later. Having incurred labor's wrath by supporting the North American Free Trade Agreement, House Democrats refused the president's attempt to renew NAFTA on a "fast track" so that it could not be amended by Congress. "Union opposition was the key factor" in causing most of the House Democrats to defect from Clinton, according to one commentator who believed organized labor was again becoming "the strongest voice in the Democratic Party." David Warsh, "Incompetence or Intransigence?" *The Boston Globe* (11 November 1997): D1. See presidential election commentary coverage in *The Nation,* (16 December 1996), 18–20 for a discussion of the AFL-CIO's new grassroots method. Also see Peter Rachleff, "Seeds of a Labor Insurgency," *The Nation* (24 February 1994): 7–9.

63. Dorothy Sue Cobble, "Reviving the Federation's Historic Role in Organizing," unpublished paper, Rutgers University Labor Center (March 1996), and Los Angeles Area Manufacturing Action Project, "Organizing the Future," typed presentation to AFL-CIO Ad Hoc Committee on the Role of the Federation in Organizing (20 July 1995). Manuscripts in the author's possession.

64. Steven Greenhouse, "Labor Uses an Old Idea to Recruit the Young," and "Students Looking for Careers in Social Change," *New York Times* (25 February 1996: 25, and 11 March 1996 (sec. B): 1, 4.

65. Steve Early, "Membership-Based Organizing," in *A New Labor Movement,* 83–85, and passim.

66. Fernando Gapasian and Howard Wial, "The Role of Central Labor Councils in Union Organizing in the 1990s," in *Organizing to Win,* 54–55.

67. On the Chicago Federation of Labor, see James R. Barrett, *Work and Community in the Jungle: Chicago's Packinghouse Workers, 1894–1922* (Urbana: University of Illinois Press, 1997), 194–202; and on the Labor Party and Fitzpatrick's mayoral campaign, see *Lizabeth Cohen, Making a New Deal: Industrial Workers in Chicago, 1919–1939* (Cambridge: Cambridge University Press, 1990), 49–50.

68. The phrase "abiding particularism" is from David Brody, "The American Worker in the Progressive Age," in *Workers in Industrial America: Essays on the Twentieth-Century Struggle* (New York, 1980), 23. On the mixed assemblies of the Knights as a means of promoting "broader social identity," see Bruce Laurie, *Artisans into Workers: Labor in Nineteenth-Century America* (New York: Hill & Wang, 1989), 149.

69. Gapasin and Wial, "The Role of Central Labor Councils," in *Organizing to Win,* 54, 61, 67.

70. Fine, "Moving Innovation from the Margins to the Center," in *A New Labor Movement,* 126–27.

71. Some say Bensinger was fired (he was offered another position in the AFL-CIO but refused) because his Washington-initiated organizing projects offended union affiliates who claimed exclusive jurisdiction and angered officials who were stung by his criticisms. Others say Bensinger

had poor diplomatic and managerial skills, needlessly antagonized union officials, and ignored public-sector organizing in favor of manufacturing.

72. Bill Fletcher Jr., address to Organizing for Keeps conference sponsored by the University and College Labor Education Association and the AFL-CIO, San Jose, Calif. (1 May 1998). Copy in author's possession. Also see "A Dialogue about Capitalism: The AFL-CIO's Bill Fletcher Speaks His Mind," *dollars and sense* (September/October 1998): 26–27.

73. Ibid.

74. Interview with Bill Fletcher (2 October 1998).

75. Marable, "Black Leadership and the Labor Movement," 48.

76. Susan C. Eaton, "Women Workers, Unions, and Industrial Sectors in North America," Working Paper for the International Labor Office (Geneva: ILO, 1992), 37; and on Massachusetts and training efforts of the Women's Institute for Leadership Development, see Dale Melcher et al., "Women's Participation in Local Union Leadership: The Massachusetts Experience," *Industrial and Labor Relations Review* 45, 2 (1992): 267–80, and Cheryl Gooding and Patricia Reeve, "Coalition Building for Community-Based Labor Education," *Policy Studies Journal* 18, 2 (1990): 452–60.

77. Eaton, "Women Workers," 45, 61. And on innovative union leadership strategies, specifically of the Harvard Union of Clerical and Technical Workers, see Susan C. Eaton, "Union Leadership Development in the 1990s," unpublished paper in author's possession, 60–65.

78. See Needleman, "Women Workers: Strategies for Inclusion and Rebuilding Unionism," and LaLuz and Finn, "Getting Serious about Inclusion," in *A New Labor Movement,* 147–70. Also see the special issue, "An Organizing Model of Unionism," *Labor Research Review* 17 (Spring 1991).

79. Jeremy Brecher and Tim Costello, "A 'New Labor Movement' in the Shell of the Old?" in *A New Labor Movement,* 27.

80. Martha Gruelle, "If Jimmy Hoffa's the Teamster Front-Runner, You Couldn't Tell It from Local Union Elections," *Labor Notes* (February 1998): 3.

81. Jim Larkin, "Teamsters: The Next Chapter," *The Nation* (4 January 1999): 17–20.

82. Jack Fiorito and Charles Greer, "Gender Differences in Union Membership, Preferences and Beliefs," *Journal of Labor Research* 7, 2 (Spring 1986): 145; and Marable, "Black Leadership," 46.

83. Robert A. Jordan, "Labor's Brightening Future Can Absorb Teamster Troubles," *Boston Globe* (23 November 1997): D4; and Mark Erlich, "Wanted: Workers with a Voice," ibid. (17 January 1995): 9.

84. In Massachusetts, 22,590 people entered the wage-earning ranks in 1993 and 1994 but these new jobs paid only $21,000 a year annually, and many of them were temporary. At the same time, Massachusetts lost 28,231 jobs, including many in manufacturing, with an average wage of $43,416. Robert A. Jordan, "A Job Is a Job, Right?" *Boston Globe* (27 September 1998): C4.

85. Robert Pear, "Americans Lacking Health Care Put at 16 Percent," *New York Times* (26 September 1998): 1.

86. Rohatyn, quoted by A. M. Rosenthal in "American Class Struggle," *New York Times* (21 March 1995).

87. Sweeney, quoted in Mantsios, "What Labor Stands For," in *A New Labor Movement,* 52. See Linda Chavez-Thompson, "Communities at Work: How New Alliances Are Restoring Our Right to Organize," *New Labor Forum* 3 (Fall–Winter 1998): 110–17.

Acknowledgments

Most historians are lucky to have one caring mentor and a few devoted colleagues who share the same interests. As these acknowledgements indicate, I was blessed with many mentors and even more cohorts who offered comradeship as well friendship. Being a movement historian has been a wonderfully collaborative experience.

Therefore, these acknowledgments offer thanks to many kinds of collaborators. They refer to researchers, readers, editors, and other writers who have been helpful in shaping the contents of this volume, not only this version, but earlier renditions of my work as well. Some parts of this book draw upon essays published earlier, but only one chapter has been reprinted without significant change: the account of the Pittston strike. All the other work represented in this volume has been rewritten, rearranged, and in some cases, revised for this book.

Besides thanking those who helped with this book, I also wish to express graditude to those who contributed to the collective efforts described here—the friends and comrades, the students and fellow teachers, the organizers and agitators, the union sisters and brothers, the mentors and the critics, the coworkers and coconspirators with whom I have worked for three decades in movement-building projects and in public reclamations of movement history.

I owe special thanks to two fellow historians who read the entire manuscript in its earliest stage, and in its current form and made many crucial editorial suggestions. My friend and colleague Bruce Laurie from the University of Massachusetts Amherst has offered generous support and comradely criticism drawing upon his own depth of experience as a movement historian and teacher union leader. My debt to Jim O'Brien is highlighted in chapter 1. His friendship and intellectual comradeship have remained rock solid for going on three decades. Jim has been the best editor a friend could have, honest and supportive at the same time. This book has benefited a great deal from his skillful, careful attention. He was particularly helpful in making suggestions about how to shape the prologue which was also improved as a result of the comments made by Leon Fink and Susan Levine.

An earlier, briefer version of chapter 1, "Discovering Movement History with 'The Radical Americans,'" was translated into Italian and appeared in *Acoma: Rivista Internationale di Studi Nordamericani* 12 (Estate/Autunno 1998). It also incorporates a few passages from an introduction to *Workers' Struggles, Past and Present: A 'Radical America' Reader* (Philadelphia: Temple University Press, 1983). Thanks to *miei cari amici italiani*—to Bruno Cartosio for soliciting this essay and to Nando Fasce for translating and editing it. I am grateful to all my *Radical America* comrades who helped me find my voice and my perspective. All of us who learned from producing *Radical America* owe a special debt to its founder Paul Buhle whose own reflections on our collective experience offer many insights. I am also indebted to David Montgomery for being so encouraging in the movement history work I undertook in the 1970s; to Marianne Debouzy for valuing my *RA* essays and asking me to write about radical labor history for the only journal devoted solely to movement history, *Le Mouvement Sociale;* to Eric Foner, who thought well enough of those efforts to invite me to write a book about workers in the series he edited for Hill & Wang and then offered me excellent editorial support; and to Michael Ames and Janet Francendese of the Temple University Press for supporting my effort to publish a reader of *Radical America* pieces on workers' struggles.

Chapter 2, "'Bringing the Boundaries of History Closer to People's Lives'" incorporates some parts of "Engaging in People's History: The Massachusetts History Workshop," in *Presenting the Past: Essays on History and the Public*, Stephen Brier, Susan Porter Benson, and Roy Rosenzweig, eds. (Philadelphia: Temple University Press, 1986). Thanks to the editors of that volume for asking me to write about the workshop, to Anna Davin and Raph Samuel for introducing me to the people's history movement in Britain, to all the activists who volunteered for Massachusetts History Workshop projects, to the Massachusetts Foundation for the Humanities and the AFL-CIO union affiliates who supported our work. I owe a special debt to Martin Henry Blatt who shared my passion for the workshop and who offered his talent and energy to our projects. Over the years his courage, his loyalty, and his intelligence have sustained my own belief in the work we do.

Chapter 3, "Learning to Teach Movement History to Workers" draws upon a few sections of "Making Access to Higher Education Meaningful for Unionized Workers: A Case Report," *Labor Studies Journal* 17, 2 (1992). Thanks to my friend and colleague of many years, Patricia Reeve, for sharing her sense of this history, much of which we made together, and for taking on the responsibility of moving our shared project into the future. Thanks also to Bill Fletcher, Cheryl Gooding, Sarah Bartlett, Brad Honoroff, Tess Ewing, and Terry McLarney, who helped us build and sustain the Labor Studies Program, to Bobby Haynes for putting up with us and then standing up for us when we needed him, to my fellow travelers and "labor ed" collaborators Elaine Bernard, Father Ed Boyle, Erica Bronstein, Enid Eckstein, Bill Fletcher, Patricia Greenfield, Tom Juravich, Linda Kaboolian, Mike Merrill, Ruth Needleman, John Russo, and Jose Soler, and to the hundreds of worker students and trade union activists who have taught me so much of what they know.

Chapter 4, "Commemorating Moments of Solidarity in Massachusetts Labor History" includes some material from "Workers, Unions, and the Politics of Public History," *The Public Historian* 11, 4 (1989) and draws upon an article coauthored with Jim Bollen under the title "The Long Strike: The Practice of Solidarity among Boston Packinghouse Workers," in Kenneth Fones-Wolf and Martin Kaufman, eds., *Labor in Massachusetts: Selected Essays* (Westfield: Institute for Massachusetts Studies, 1990). I am grateful to the historically conscious trade unionists who supported these celebrations and reunions: Nancy Mills, Mark Erlich, Tommy Evers, Bobby Banks, Shelton Coats, and Jim Bollen. I also wish to express my gratitude to Bob Hayden for asking me to partner with him in marking the history of Boston African American railroad workers in a public place. Finally, I owe a great debt to the late Herbert Gutman for inspiring my generation of social historians and for imagining a cultural world in which workers and historians could share their knowledge in public.

Chapter 5, "Remembering Haymarket: Chicago's Labor Martyrs and Their Legacy," was presented in 1996 at the conference "Les Lieux de Memoire des les Etats Unis" at the University of Savoy in Chambery, France. Thanks to Jean Kempf for inviting me to present this paper and to Pierre Nora, whose writings about places of memory stimulated my thinking so sharply. I am also indebted to the following readers who offered helpful suggestions for improving the study: David Blight, Paul Buhle, Marianne Debouzy, David Glassberg, David Linenthal, David Montgomery, Pablo Pozzi, David Thelen, Al Young, and Howard Zinn. Thanks also to Robin Bachin for her excellent scholarly effort in making a case for the Waldheim monument as a national landmark and to Les Orear and his colleagues at the Illinois Labor History Society for their achievements in the field of working-class commemoration.

Chapter 6, on places of memory in the South, was presented in 1998 as the Fulbright Lecture, for the Department of Modern and Contemporary History at the University of Genoa in Italy. Thanks to Professor Valeria Gennaro Lerda for inviting me to the University of Genoa to teach a course and to present a public lecture on southern places and southern voices. And thanks again to Nando Fasce for making me feel at home in Genoa where so much of this book was written and for giving me a thoughtful first reading of the prologue.

Chapter 6 also draws upon segments from "Marking Labor History on the National Landscape," the introductory essay to the Labor History Theme Study for the Historical Landmarks Program of the National Park Service conducted by the Newberry Library in 1995 and directed by James Grossman. I am also indebted to the remarkable militants from West Virginia in the United Mine Workers, especially the union's president Cecil Roberts, who have helped me understand their sense of history and tradition. Though they are mentioned in the footnotes, I wish to express more clearly my debt to certain people who have supported my efforts to understand the South: C. Vann Woodward, who taught society how to see the South in new ways and to hear its oppositional voices; to my fellow graduate students at Yale who came to study southern history with him, especially Bill McFeely, a fellow Yankee, who gave me a chance to teach students from black colleges in the South and to learn from them and from his own insightful work on southern blacks and northern whites; and, finally, to those whose work in southern oral history has revealed so much—especially an old friend, Ted Rosengarten; a new friend, Allesandro Portelli; and a special friend, Jacquelyn Dowd Hall, who shared many of her own ingenious insights into the South, her deep feelings about movement storytelling, and her hopes for collecting the memories of working people and releasing their voices to the public.

Chapter 7, "Seeing the Past with 'Movement Eyes,'" has not been published previously but it recapitulates a few points made in "Making 'The Great Depression' for Public Television: Notes on a Collaboration of Filmmakers and Historians," *Newsletter of the American Historical Association* (October 1994). Thanks to Terry Rockefeller, Series Producer of the Great Depression at Blackside, Inc., for taking me on staff at Blackside and for inviting me to help organize a summer school on the Great Depression and then allowing me to be engaged in filmmaking far more than any historian has a right to be; to Orlando Bagwell for inviting me to join in discussions about Blackside's mission; to Jon Else and Steve Fayer for sharing with me their thoughts about how to create drama and truth with pictures and with just a few well-chosen words of narrative; to Lyn Goldfarb, Susan Bellows, and Rick Tejada-Flores for engaging me in discussions about the films they were trying to make; and to the talented producer Dante James for asking me to "tell" him the CIO story clearly, and for letting me join him in the editing suite. I also appreciate the thoughtful readings of this chapter by Terry Rockefeller and Judy Richardson, who have lived much of Blackside's history. Finally, I owe an unpayable debt to the late Henry Hampton for inviting me to join his company for a while and for challenging me to tell movement stories in ways that would engage the public.

Chapter 8, "Why Movement History Matters," draws upon portions of "The Making of Mel King's Rainbow Coalition: Political Change in Boston, 1963–1983," *Radical America* 17, 1–2 (1984), and "Searching for Common Ground: An Essay Review of *Common Ground*," *Radical America* 20, 5 (1986). Thanks to the *RA* editors, especially Allen Hunter and John Demeter, for their support and encouragement, to Ruth Batson for inspiring me to write about her movement, and to comrades in Rainbow politics: to James Jennings, then the Dean of CPCS, and to all the faculty of the Socialist Collective, especially Charlotte Ryan and Marie Kennedy who, along with Jim Tramel, helped me think through the problems of race and class as seen by populists and socialists. Finally, I am indebted to Mel King for articulating his vision and for telling us a story of Boston filled with instruction and shot through with inspiration.

Chapter 9, "Planting the Seeds of Resurgence," is an edited version of "Tying the Knot of Solidarity: The Pittston Strike and Social Movement Unionism." It originally appeared in John H. M. Laslett, ed. *The United Mine Workers of America, 1890–1990: A Model of Industrial Solidarity?* (College Park: Pennsylvania State University Press, 1996). The new preface includes some material from "Camp Solidarity: The Pittston Strike, the United Mine Workers, and the New People's Movement," in Jeremy Brecher and Tim Costello, eds., *Building Bridges: The Emerging Grassroots Coalition of Community and Labor* (New York: Monthly Review Press, 1990). I am indebted to Richard Trumka and Cecil Roberts for sharing their experience during and after the strike and to their superb staff members: Gene Carroll, Ron Baker, Marat Moore, and Lanny Shortridge. Thanks also to Barbara Kopple who helped me see how the Pittston strike played as a dramatic story that could be told visually.

Chapter 10, "On Becoming a Movement Again," is based on public presentations made in 1998 for the IGMetall Workers School in Berlin, the Institute of Political Science at Mendes-France University in Grenoble, the Sorbonne (Paris XII), as well as for the Faculty of Political Science at the University of Bologna. Some of these thoughts appeared in "USA: Crisi e Rinacita del Movimento Sindacale," in the daily newspaper *Il Manifesto,* June 12, 1998. Thanks to Christopher Scherrer, Frank Heidenreich, Elizabeth Chamorand, Catherine Collomp, and Federico Romero for inviting me to speak and for making my visits with workers and students exciting and interesting, and thanks to the Fulbright commissions in France, Germany, and Italy for supporting my journeys. Thanks again to Bill Fletcher for reading the chapter and making suggestions.

Finally, I am grateful to the University of Massachusetts Press and its staff for supporting this project: to the director, Bruce Wilcox, for his encouragement and enthusiasm, and to my editor, Paul Wright, who has talked with me about this project for ever so long, renewing a conversation that began in 1977 when he gave me my first opportunity to present movement history in public at a lecture series he directed for the Boston Public Library. I am also very indebted to the Labor Resource Center and the College of Public and Community Service at UMass-Boston for the many forms of assistance I have received. The Dean of CPCS, Ismael Ramirez-Soto, has been consistently supportive. I have been fortunate to receive expert help in preparing this manuscript from three brilliant UMass-Boston students who have offered me excellent assistance with research and word processing: Alexander Lubin, Donna Finn, and Chico Colvard.

To my wife and *compañera*, Janet Lee Grogan, and to my son, Nicholas James Green, I offer my heartfelt thanks for letting me squeeze this project into our life as a family. Thanks for forgiving me when I seemed lost in the past, and thanks for giving me the peace of mind and the contentment of heart that makes writing a pleasure.

Index

JAMES GREEN, a native of Illinois, received his B.A. from Northwestern University and his Ph.D. in American History from Yale University, where he was awarded a Woodrow Wilson Fellowship and worked with C. Vann Woodward. He is the author of *Grass-Roots Socialism: Radical Movements in the Southwest, 1895–1943* (Louisiana State University Press, 1978) and *The World of the Worker: Labor in Twentieth-Century America* (Hill and Wang 1980; second edition, University of Illinois Press, 2000), and co-author of *Boston's Workers: A Labor History* (Boston Public Library, 1979) and *Commonwealth of Toil: Chapters from the History of Massachusetts Workers and Their Unions* (University of Massachusetts Press, 1996). Professor Green has been an editor of *Radical America* and was a founder of the Massachusetts History Workshop. He served as research coordinator for the public television series "The Great Depression" (Blackside Productions). He is a professor of history and labor studies in the College of Public and Community Service at the University of Massachusetts Boston, where he has taught since 1977. He founded and directed UMass-Boston's Labor Studies Program and Labor Resource Center, of which he is currently academic coordinator. He has held a lectureship at Warwick University in England and was a Fulbright lecturer at the University of Genoa in Italy during 1998. Jim Green lives in Somerville, Massachusetts, with his wife, Janet Grogan, and son, Nicholas.

303.48   Green, James R.,
Gre   1944-

          Taking history to
          heart.

DATE			